EFFECTIVE BUSINESS
PSYCHOLOGY

Second Edition

EFFECTIVE BUSINESS PSYCHOLOGY

ANDREW J. DuBRIN

Professor of Behavioral Sciences
College of Business
Rochester Institute of Technology
Rochester, New York

RESTON PUBLISHING COMPANY
A Prentice-Hall Company
Reston, Virginia

Library of Congress Cataloging in Publication Data

DuBrin, Andrew J.
    Effective business psychology.

    Includes bibliographies and indexes.
    1. Psychology, Industrial.   2. Interpersonal
relations.   3. Communication in management.   I. Title.
HF5548.8.D775   1985   650'.13   84-8398
ISBN 0-8359-1570-0

*Editorial/production supervision and
interior design by Norma M. Karlin*

Cartoons by Bruce Bolinger

© 1980, 1985 by
Reston Publishing Company, Inc.
A Prentice-Hall Company
Reston, Virginia 22090

10   9   8   7   6   5   4   3   2   1

PRINTED IN THE UNITED STATES OF AMERICA

To Drew

CONTENTS

Chapter 4   Understanding Yourself   79

PART TWO   DEALING WITH INDIVIDUALS   101

Chapter 5   Motivating Others and Yourself   103

Chapter 6   Goals and Human Behavior   131

Chapter 7   Solving Problems and Making Decisions   155

PART FOUR DEALING WITH SMALL GROUPS   299

PART FIVE REALIZING YOUR POTENTIAL   381

PREFACE

An increasing number of students enrolled in business courses are demanding a satisfactory return on the time and money that they invest in education and training. Faculty members and administrators, too, are demanding textbooks that are useful in the development of practical insights and specific skills—yet still academically respectable. Virtually all applied psychology or human relations books contend that they "bridge the gap between theory and practice." Still, most students have difficulty walking across that bridge.

Effective Business Psychology has been written to fill the need for a basic, career-oriented text with a variety of suggestions for personal improvement and effectiveness. Despite its emphasis on prescription, the book is based on empirical studies and established psychological concepts and theories. The research findings cited and the concepts mentioned are all illustrated with concrete, reality-based examples.

This text is designed to meet the curriculum needs of courses in business psychology, applied psychology, and human relations offered in various settings: postsecondary vocational and technical schools, business schools and institutes, two-year colleges, and the lower-division courses in four-year colleges.

A major theme of this book is its self-help, "how to succeed" orientation. The majority of topics within the text include suggestions for handling problems and situations frequently encountered at work. At numerous places in the text, students are given the opportunity to add to their self-knowledge and self-insight by completing questionnaires.

The underlying design of this book is to present an overview of major psychological concepts and techniques that are relevant to the individual worker in attaining both good performance and personal satisfaction. Concise summaries are presented of major concepts of basic psychology, including learning, perception, personality, and motivation. Similarly, the major classical theories of human behavior at work are summarized. Modern developments stemming from these classical theories (such as participative management, organizational behavior modification, and modified work schedules) are treated at greater length.

Current topics in the fields of business psychology and human relations, such as computer stress, burnout, sexual harassment, and networking for career advancement, are also included. The literature cited in this text includes scientific and professional journals, magazines such as *Success* and *Psychology Today*, and trade books about business and self-help topics.

How will this book help you? A person who carefully studies the information in this book and incorporates its suggestions into his or her way of doing things should derive the four benefits listed below. However, knowledge itself is not a guarantee of success. People vary so widely in learning ability, personality, and life circumstances that some people will be able to attain some objectives and not others. As a case in point, you might be so naturally effective at dealing with stress that the chapter on this topic is unnecessary from your viewpoint. Or you might be so shy at this stage in your life that you are presently unable to apply some of the confrontation techniques described for resolving conflict. Instead, you would benefit more from reading the information in the text about overcoming shyness.

The major benefits this book provides are the following:

1. Awareness of relevant information. Part of feeling comfortable and making a positive impression in any place of work is being familiar with relevant general knowledge about the world of work. By reading this book you will become conversant with many of the buzz words used on the job, such as autocratic manager, positive reinforcement (or stroking), networking, and dressing for success.

2. Development of skills in dealing with people. Anybody who aspires toward higher-level jobs needs to develop proficiency in such interpersonal skills as how to motivate people, how to criticize others in a constructive manner, and how to overcome communication barriers.

3. Coping with job problems. Almost everybody who holds a responsible job inevitably runs into human problems. Reading about these problems and prescriptions for coping with them could save you considerable inner turmoil. Among the job survival skills that you will learn about in the following chapters are managing job stress and dealing with conflict between yourself and your boss.

4. Capitalizing on opportunities. Many readers of this book will spend part of their working time taking advantage of opportunities rather than resolving daily problems. Every career-minded person needs a few breakthrough experiences in order to make his or her life more rewarding. Toward this end, we devote attention to the subjects of creative decision making and methods of career advancement.

ACKNOWLEDGMENTS

My primary thanks on this project are extended to the editorial, production, and marketing staffs at Reston Publishing Company. Among the key people who helped launch the second edition were Ted Buchholz, Norma Karlin, and Anne Sumner. I thank cartoonist Bruce Bolinger for the fine contribution he has made to increasing the attractiveness and appeal of the text. Thanks also to the large number of instructors who adopted the first edition of the book, thus creating a demand for a new edition. Many of the changes made in this new edition are based on the suggestions offered by our adopters.

Dozens of students and participants in workshops I have conducted deserve credit for their anecdotes, which have served as examples and cases used in this book. Hundreds of researchers and authors have contributed ideas to this book. Many of their contributions are recognized by formal references. However, it is almost impossible to give proper credit to everybody in a comprehensive text of this nature. My secretary, Nancy Johnson, put in a substantial amount of work on this project.

Finally a special note of thanks to Maria Jeremias, whose love, emotional support, and spark for life enhanced the enjoyable task of preparing this manuscript.

ANDREW J. DUBRIN

BUSINESS PSYCHOLOGY AND HUMAN BEHAVIOR

This section of the book defines the meaning of business psychology as it is used here. Since this is the first course in psychology for many readers, this part of the book also provides a concise overview of psychology in general. Chapter 1 includes summaries of the major fields within psychology, along with a description of the major schools of thought within psychology. Chapters 2 and 3 present many of the key concepts used in understanding human behavior, including learning, perception, personality, abilities, and motivation. In Chapter 4 we examine the self, primarily because self-understanding is essential if one wants to both understand and deal effectively with others.

FOUNDATIONS OF BUSINESS PSYCHOLOGY

LEARNING OBJECTIVES

After reading and studying this chapter and doing the exercises, you should be able to

1. Define the term business psychology and explain what it means.
2. Describe several of the major fields within psychology.
3. Describe several of the major schools of thought within psychology.
4. Explain how business psychology fits into the human relations movement.
5. Understand why it is helpful to study business psychology even if you have a high degree of common sense.

WHAT IS BUSINESS PSYCHOLOGY?

The study of psychology, as it applies to the workplace, can help you come to grips with the wide range of human problems encountered in any job. It can also help you prepare for your career. An understanding of the basic principles of business psychology can help explain why people act as they do in certain situations and suggest what you can sometimes do to change their behavior.

In the chapters that follow, there are no sure-fire answers to getting along with employers and co-workers or making worthwhile things happen.

However, there are specific guidelines that have proved to be true most of the time in the past. You can rely on these guidelines to help you in your relations with other people in the future. **Business psychology**, as the term is used in this book, refers to *the application of organized knowledge about human behavior to improve personal satisfaction and productivity on the job.* Business psychology can thus be used in any work setting, such as a company, government agency, community agency, hospital, or school.

Psychology is most accurately defined as *the systematic study of behavior and all the factors that influence behavior.*[1] Almost any human activity might thus be the subject of study by a psychologist. Yet, in practice, psychology deals more with the mind than with the body. The term *psychology* has gained wide acceptance as the field associated with the scientific study of people and animals. (In fact, a major component of modern psychology called *behaviorism* is based upon early studies of rats and pigeons.) It is important to recognize, however, that fields such as sociology, anthropology, political science, and economics are also concerned with the study of human behavior. Although these fields have useful insights to offer, the focus of this book is on the application of selected principles of psychology.

Before proceeding with the study of business psychology, it will provide useful background material to examine psychology from two perspectives. First, we will describe what psychologists do by examining several fields within psychology. Second, we will describe the major schools of thought within psychology.

WHAT PSYCHOLOGISTS DO

Psychology touches our lives in thousands of ways. Among the best known contributions of psychologists to society have been mental tests, encounter groups, and helping to make equipment suitable to the physical and mental characteristics of human beings. About 55,000 people are official members of the American and Canadian psychological associations. An even larger number of people are engaged in work that is closely related to the application of psychological knowledge to improve the lives of people. Among such specialists performing psychological work are human resource specialists, who conduct training programs on how to get along better with people; organization development specialists, who conduct programs for increasing the effectiveness of organizations; and guidance counselors, who advise students on how to cope with personal problems.

Here we will mention several of the more established specialty areas within modern psychology, along with two emerging ones.[2] Currently there are 42 specialty areas within psychology, reflecting the diverse job activities within psychology. One problem in dividing psychology into different specialties is that they show so much overlap. For instance, both industrial and clinical psychologists might conduct workshops to help employees work together more smoothly. Or both school and child psychologists might try to determine what is preventing a specific child from learning how to achieve average reading skill.

Clinical and Counseling Psychology

About 50 percent of psychologists are specialists within this field. Clinical and counseling psychologists work with individuals or small groups to help them overcome personal problems. Clinical psychologists also play an important part in diagnosing mental illness. Counseling psychologists tend to work with people who do not have severe emotional problems. Clinical psychologists tend to work with people who do have such problems. Yet, in practice, there is sometimes very little distinction between the work of these two groups of psychologists.

People outside the field of psychology often confuse the occupations of psychiatrists, psychoanalysts, and clinical psychologists. The term psychotherapist adds to the confusion. A psychotherapist can be any mental health professional who helps people with their emotional problems through conversation with them.

Psychiatry is a medical specialty. To call yourself a psychiatrist, you must have a medical degree. As a psychiatrist you can legally treat people with drugs, electroshock, or through conversation. Psychiatrists, however, rarely have a formal degree in psychology, the study of behavior.

Psychoanalysis is a specialized type of psychotherapy in which the patient may spend up to three or four years, several times a week, working on his or her personal problems. According to psychoanalysts, psychoanalysis is the only true way of remaking your personality. Many psychologists doubt that psychoanalysis can make such an exclusive claim.

Clinical psychologists have formal degrees in psychology, generally a doctor of philosophy (Ph.D.), and sometimes a doctor of education (Ed.D.), or doctor of professional psychology (Psy. D.). A graduate degree in clinical psychology, as in all fields of psychology, requires extensive study of research methods, statistics, and the scientific method. In most states and provinces, you need a certificate and a license to call yourself a psychologist. Clinical psychologists work in hospitals, in educational institutions, in group practice with psychiatrists, and in individual, private practice. A jokester once said that the difference between a psychiatrist and a clinical psychologist is "fifteen dollars an hour in favor of the psychiatrist."

To become certified as a psychoanalyst, you have to attend a specialized training program (given by a society of psychoanalysts) beyond your regular medical or psychological training. Although the vast majority of psychoanalysts are psychiatrists, a few are clinical psychologists or psychiatric social workers. An interesting fact is that one of the world's best known psychoanalysts, Rollo May, was a clinical psychologist.

Educational Psychology

About 10 percent of all professional psychologists work in the area of educational psychology. These people are involved in developing effective methods of teaching, test construction, and the use of educational technology such as videotapes and cassettes. As with most specialties within psychology, many people who are not psychologists are engaged in similar work activities.

A major contribution of educational psychology has been the teaching machine. These machines are used in **programmed learning,** a method of allowing you to learn information step by step at your own rate. A student must first answer questions asked by the machine at one step in order to proceed to the next step. Programmed learning is now computerized.

Child and Developmental Psychology

Developmental psychologists study the behavior and growth patterns of people from the prenatal period through maturity and old age. Child psychologists concentrate their efforts on the study of the person from birth up through age 11. Many clinical psychologists specialize in dealing with the behavior problems of children. Approximately 3 percent of psychologists place themselves in the developmental category.

In recent years the world has become intensely interested in the study of adult phases of human development. The work of developmental psychologists has led to widespread interest in the problems of the middle years, such as the mid-life crisis.

Experimental Psychology

Experimental psychologists can be considered the most "scientific" of all psychologists. Their laboratories often rival those of biologists and medical scientists. Experimental psychologists are usually employed by colleges, universities, and research laboratories. Many of the principles of human behavior to be discussed in this book (such as those associated with learning, thinking, and perception) were developed by experimental psychologists. An example of the work of an experimental psychologist would be a study demonstrating that, if you are irritated by something like a loud noise, your productivity is likely to suffer.[3]

Ergonomics (or Human Engineering)

Ergonomics, a combination of engineering and psychology, is closely associated with experimental psychology. Human engineering, as the field is also called, attempts to design machinery, equipment, and the work environment to fit human characteristics, both physical and mental. During the 1960s and 1970s, Ralph Nader and his followers gave a big impetus to ergonomics. Nader rose to fame on the basis of his campaign to make automobiles more suitable for use by human beings. He was particularly concerned about the safety aspects of automobiles. Today, however, automobile manufacturers frequently promote the comfort features of their autos that are based on ergonomic principles. A case in point is the promotional material for the Thunderbird Turbo Coupe, which includes an ergonomic analysis of the front seats. The advertisement talks about person–machine unity in these terms:

> Seats you sit in. Not on. Turbo Coupe's front seats reward the demanding driver. (1) Under the thigh support adjusts. (2) The side thigh support adjusts. (3) The seat back angle adjusts. (4) The lumbar support adjusts with (5) an infinitely adjustable pneumatic actuating pump. In addition, the (6) firm side supports help hold you in place. And unlike some other high performance seats, you don't have to be an accomplished acrobat to get in and out. Considering that a Turbo Coupe is capable of .81G in a turn, seats that support you laterally as well as up and down are essential.[4]

Have you ever driven, or been driven in, a recent T-bird? Did ergonomics accomplish its mission by providing you a safer and more comfortable seat?

Computer Systems and Ergonomics. Recent attention in ergonomics has been directed to the compatibility between computer systems and human capabilities. Some evidence has been gathered that video display terminals (VDTs) lead to both physical discomfort and cataracts or other serious eye damage. However, the matter is controversial. A two-year study by the National Research Council concluded, "We find no scientifically valid evidence that occupational use of VDTs is associated with increased incidence of eye diseases or abnormalities, including cataracts."[5]

Another important finding, however, was that many VDTs are poorly designed for worker comfort because they are inexpensive adaptations of components originally designed for casual television viewing from a distance, rather than for intense work at close range. Poorly designed computer systems, according to the study, can both annoy workers and lower productivity. In recognition of these and similar findings, several computer manufacturers have engaged the services of human engineering psychologists to improve the design of their systems. One improvement has been green-on-black screens that also minimize glare. Exhibit 1–1 summarizes the human engineering features one manufacturer has incorporated in its information-processing system.

Industrial and Organizational Psychology

Much of this book deals with the ideas and methods of industrial and organizational psychologists. Business psychology is a general term for the methods and ideas of industrial and organizational psychologists that are rel-

Exhibit 1-1

THE APPLICATION OF ERGONOMICS TO THE DESIGN
OF A COMPUTER SYSTEM

An advertisement for Rayethon Data Systems states, "We were there at the birth of modern word processing. So it should come as no surprise that when we designed the Rayethon information processor, we didn't forget that human beings come with backs, arms, fingers, necks, eyes and other assorted parts. And use them in different ways to do different jobs in the office.

"Instead of demanding that people adapt to our system, we designed our RDS-200 Series of information processors to adapt to people. That's ergonomics, Raytheon-style. Result: an information processor that's one of the most comfortable and easiest to use." The seven features of the information processor that conform to human engineering principles are as follows:

"The characters on our screen are bigger than most. And our non-glare green-on-black screen is easy on the eyes.

Most computer companies ask you to memorize multiple keystroke command codes. Rayethon gives you the one-stroke command keys—each labeled in plain English.

Our hydraulic chair adjusts with the flick of a lever to support your back and reduce strain and fatigue.

We sculpted our keys to conform to the contours of the fingers. A small point perhaps, but it makes a big difference after hours at the keyboard.

A command key calls up a special full-page mode that lets you see exactly how your work will look on the finished page.

A tilting leaf lets you angle the keyboard instead of straining your wrists.

Our display swivels and tilts so your neck doesn't have to. A little extra comfort can mean a lot of extra productivity."

SOURCE: An advertisement appearing in the *Wall Street Journal*, September 22, 1983. Reprinted with permission of Rayethon Data Systems, Norwood, Massachusetts.

evant to the individual who wants to succeed on the job. About 7 percent of psychologists place themselves in the industrial and organizational category.

Among the major activities of specialists in this field are the design of employee selection methods (such as tests and interviews) and methods for training and developing employees at all job levels. Industrial and organizational psychologists have developed a number of methods for improving teamwork and cooperation in organizations.

New Frontiers in Psychology

During the last decade, the demand for psychologists in colleges and universities tapered off from previous years. About one-half of psychologists practice their specialties within college and university settings. Instead of psychology weakening as a profession, psychologists are expanding the fields in which they are making a contribution.

Police Psychology. In some instances, psychologists have become involved in conducting environmental studies, moved into the courtroom as forensic (legal) psychologists, and worked with architects in the design of buildings. As an example of a "new frontier" activity, here is a portion of the job description of a police psychologist:[6]

> I work primarily with the staff and personnel of a large urban police department to provide counseling and therapy services, teaching, research, and management consultation in regard to crime situations. This is a salaried, full-time position paid by the city government.
>
> The police psychologist role is open-ended and includes many of the clinical and industrial psychologist's functions, plus many more. Testifying as an expert witness on pornography, eliciting a psychological profile of a rape—murderer, and using hypnosis with a witness to a homicide to enhance recall are all part of a day's work, in addition to routine assessment, therapy, and organization development.

Sport Psychology. Another relatively new enterprise for psychologists is that of trying to help athletes achieve peak performance on the field. Most of the psychologists who enter this field have some sports background themselves. A prime example is Julie Anthony, a former professional tennis player who has worked as the team psychologist to the Philadelphia Flyers hockey team. Anthony's focus in her work is to provide "game enhancement" techniques to players who are already functioning well. She notes that sport psychology is not concerned primarily with the mental health problems of athletes.[7]

Anthony claims she won the support of players by persuading management to make some changes in factors that were affecting morale: the locker room arrangement, workout facilities, the schedule of warmups and practices. Much of her work, like that of most sport psychologists, involves relaxation and visual imagery techniques that are designed to build self-confidence, control, and concentration. She is also available to talk about personal problems. **Imagery techniques** deal with visualizing or imagining yourself to be doing something right, such as sinking a basketball or having a tennis serve land in precisely its intended spot.

SCHOOLS OF THOUGHT IN PSYCHOLOGY

To help explain the field of psychology, we have just described some of the major work activities of psychologists. An equally important way of understanding psychology is to review the major schools of thought, or theoretical positions, in psychology. It is these schools of thought that help influence which particular method a given psychologist will use to help solve a particular problem. For example, the cognitive school of psychology holds that people make rational decisions and are often driven by thoughts of self-fulfillment. An industrial psychologist who believes in the cognitive school would then recommend an employee motivation program that gives employees a chance to have a voice in making decisions about their own work.

Here we will describe briefly five schools of thought in psychology: structuralism, behaviorism, psychoanalysis, cognitive psychology, and humanistic psychology.[8] Business psychology today is influenced much more by behaviorism, cognitive psychology, and humanistic psychology than by the other two schools.

Structuralism and Functionalism

Many historians believe that modern psychology began in 1879 when Wilhelm Wundt established a laboratory in Leipzig, Germany, to study human consciousness. Wundt aimed to discover the structure of the mind by analyzing conscious experiences of the senses and by reducing it to its basic elements. His most important contention was that you could take some object in the physical world, present it to a trained subject, and have the subject describe the fundamental elements of his or her conscious experience. For example if you presented the subject a watermelon, she might say, "I see an elliptical shape, I see green and white, I feel a heavy weight." This method of looking into one's conscious experience is called **introspection.** By binding together the introspections of thousands of people, structuralists hoped to develop a science of conscious experience.

Although historically important, structuralism lost momentum as a useful method of understanding human behavior. William James, an American student of Wundt's, extended the narrow limits of structuralism to the study of many topics that are still of current interest, including learning, motivation, and emotions. James was also concerned with the struggle of people to reach their goals or become reconciled to failure. His school of thought became known as *functionalism* because he tried to understand the functioning of the mind. In time, James became America's premier psychologist and some of his work is still quoted today. William James' book, *The Principles of Psychology*, should not be overlooked by any serious student of human behavior.

Behaviorism

Structuralism and functionalism soon came under criticism because they focused too much on unscientific subjective experiences. In their place, John B. Watson offered the world a school of thought called *behaviorism*. He contended that mental life was something that cannot be seen or measured and thus cannot be studied scientifically. To Watson, and all subsequent behaviorists, the key to understanding human beings is to study their actual behavior, not their inner states.

Watson believed that everything we do is determined by our past experiences, and not by an ability to control our own destiny. In his thinking, all human behavior is a series of events in which a *stimulus* produces a *response*. According to behaviorists, almost any kind of stimulus could be made to produce any kind of response. Watson excited the imagination of millions of parents when he proclaimed, "I can take any dozen babies at birth and, by conditioning them in various ways, turn them into anything I wish— doctor, lawyer, beggar, or thief."[9] More will be said about conditioning in Chapter 2.

Modern Day Behaviorism. The next prominent leader of behaviorism was experimental psychologist B. F. Skinner, who has become one of the world's best known scientists. His work has lead to improved methods of learning and motivation in schools, psychiatric wards, prisons, and industry. Skinner's name is virtually synonymous with the terms positive reinforcement and behavior modification. When interviewed at age 79, Skinner remained convinced that his principles of 50 years are correct, despite the controversy they have caused.

Skinner holds that freedom is an illusion: the behavior of humans and lower forms of animals is shaped by environmental influences, not internal ones. He has championed the law of effect, which states that rewarded behavior tends to be repeated, while behavior that is ignored or punished tends not to be repeated. Feelings and other mental processes are simply the by-products of an endless cycle of pairings between stimuli and responses. Skinner believes strongly that "a scientific analysis doesn't have a place for the individual as the initiator of behavior."[10] (Chapter 5 describes several current applications of Skinner's ideas for motivating yourself and others.)

Psychoanalysis

Another major approach to understanding human behavior is psychoanalysis, founded by Sigmund Freud and his key associate, Carl Jung.[11] Psychoanalytic theory views men and women as constantly torn between internal unconscious forces and external social forces. People are born with powerful biological appetites and passions that demand constant satisfaction despite the needs of others or themselves. Thus an employee with an urge toward self-punishment may insult his boss even though it will anger the boss and possibly cost him his job. Our major job in life is to direct these irrational motives and emotions into socially acceptable behaviors. A key point of psychoanalytic theory is that we must learn to control our inborn desires and achieve their fulfillment in ways that are harmonious with others.

The best known part of Freudian theory deals with the structure of the human *personality* (an individual's characteristic way of behaving, feeling, and thinking). It consists of three major forces interacting with each other:

1. Id, unconscious instincts such as sex and aggression.
2. Ego, the conscious, rational self, or intellect.
3. Superego, the social rules and values of society that govern our behavior.

The ego, or conscious self, is under constant pressure to fight off the pleasure-seeking desires of the id. At the same time, the ego is pressured by the reality forces of the environment and the moral dictates of one's upbringing—the superego. The healthy personality has an ego that does an effective job of coping with the urges of the id and the restrictions of the superego. Thus the well-adjusted employee refrains from punching his boss, but at the same time is able to challenge authority in an acceptable way.

The psychoanalytic school has had a major impact on understanding human behavior, particularly in regard to analyzing mental health problems. Its impact, however, has shown a rapid decline in recent years. Very little of business psychology deals directly with psychoanalytic theory. There are times, however, when the concept of unconscious behavior can be helpful in resolving a work problem. One example is when people sometimes procrastinate because of an inner fear of success (see Chapter 17).

Cognitive Psychology

A growing movement in psychology is to explain the behavior of human beings in terms of their intellectual, rational selves. The term *cognitive* refers to the intellectual aspects of behavior. And a cognitive process is the means by which an individual becomes aware of objects and situations. It includes learning, reasoning, and problem solving. According to the cognitive school of thought, the mind processes information by producing new thoughts, making comparisons, and making decisions.[12] Cognitive psychology focuses on the way our perception of events influences our actions. Thus, if an employee perceives it to be true that hard work will lead to a bonus, he or she will put forth extra effort. More will be said about the cognitive school of thought in relation to perception and motivation (Chapter 2).

Humanistic Psychology

Humanistic psychology emphasizes the dignity and worth of people, along with their many other positive, but intangible or "soft" attributes. The formal movement of humanistic psychology began about 25 years ago. Its official role was defined in these terms:

> Humanistic psychology is primarily an orientation toward the whole psychology rather than a distinct area or school. It stands for the respect and worth of persons, respect for differences of approach, openmindedness as to acceptable methods, and interests in exploration of new aspects of human behavior. As a new force in contemporary psychology it is concerned with topics having little place in existing theories and systems. Among them are love, creativity, self, growth, basic need gratification, self-actualization, higher values, being, becoming, spontaneity, play, humor, affection, naturalness, warmth, ego-experience, peak experience, courage, and related concepts.[13]

Humanistic psychology has had a substantial impact on business psychology and human relations, both in terms of theories and techniques. Abraham Maslow, who developed the need hierarchy, was also a founder of humanistic psychology. Among the humanistic techniques to be described in this book are encounter groups, assertiveness training, and transactional analysis. In many ways, business psychology is a blend of behaviorism and humanistic psychology.

Closely related in philosophy to humanistic psychology is another major influence on business psychology, the human relations movement.

THE HUMAN RELATIONS MOVEMENT

The human relations movement was a concentrated effort by some managers and their advisors to become more sensitive to the needs of employees or to treat them in a more humanistic manner. In other words, employees were now to be treated as human beings rather than as machines in the productive process. As explained by management scholar Robert Kreitner, the human relations movement was supported by three different historic influences: the

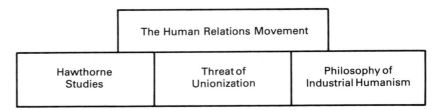

FIGURE 1-1
Influences supporting the human relations movement.

Hawthorne studies, the threat of unionization, and industrial humanism (see Figure 1-1).[14]

The Hawthorne Studies

The human relations school of management is generally said to have begun in 1927 with a group of studies conducted at the Hawthorne plant of an AT&T subsidiary. These studies were prompted by an experiment carried out by the company's engineers between 1924 and 1927. Following the tradition of scientific management, these engineers were applying research methods to investigate problems of employee productivity.

Two groups were studied to determine the effects of different levels of illumination on worker performance. As prescribed by the scientific method, one group received increased illumination, while the other did not. A preliminary finding was that when illumination was increased the level of performance also increased. Surprisingly to the engineers, productivity also increased when the level of illumination was decreased almost to moonlight levels. One interpretation made of these findings was that the workers involved in the experiment enjoyed being the center of attention. In other words, they reacted positively because management cared about them. Such a phenomenon taking place in any work or research setting is called the **Hawthorne effect.**[15]

As a result of these preliminary investigations, a team of researchers headed by Harvard professors Elton Mayo and Fritz J. Roethlisberger conducted a series of experiments extending over a six-year period. The conclusions they reached served as the foundations for later developments in the human relations approach to management. Business psychology has been equally influenced by these conclusions:

- Economic incentives are less important than generally believed in influencing workers to achieve high levels of output.
- Leadership practices and work-group pressures profoundly influence employee satisfaction and performance.

- Any factor influencing employee behavior is embedded in a social system. For example, to understand the impact of pay on performance, you have to understand the atmosphere that exists in the work group and how the leader approaches his or her job.

The Social Person Replaces the Economic Person. A major implication of the Hawthorne studies was that the old concept of an economic person motivated primarily by money had to be replaced by a more valid idea. The replacement concept was a social person, motivated by social needs, desiring rewarding on-the-job relationships, and more responsive to pressures from co-workers than from control by the boss.[16] Do you believe that workers are more concerned with social relationships than with money?

The Threat of Unionization

Labor union officials and their advocates contend that the benefits of unionization extend to many workers who themselves do not belong to unions. One example is that management in nonunion firms will often pay their employees union wages in order to offset the potential advantages of unionization. A similar set of circumstances contributed to the growth of the human relations movement. Labor unions began to grow rapidly in the United States during the late 1930s. Many employers feared that the presence of a labor union would have negative consequences for their companies. Consequently, management looked aggressively for ways to stem the tide of unionization.

As noted by Kreitner, early human relations thinking presented an interesting possibility: satisfied employees would be less inclined to join labor unions.[17] Company officials subsequently began to implement morale-boosting human relations techniques as a method of warding off unionization. Among such techniques were counseling programs to listen to employee problems, improved rest room and locker facilities, and a kinder approach to supervising employees. Many people question the ethics of using human relations techniques to prevent unionization, while others regard it as a smart business practice. What do you think?

The Philosophy of Industrial Humanism

Partly as a by-product of the Hawthorne studies, a new philosophy arose of human relations in the workplace. Elton Mayo was one of the two key figures in developing this philosophy of industrial humanism. He cautioned managers that emotional factors (such as a desire for recognition) were a more important contributor to productivity than were physical and logical factors. Mayo argued vigorously that work should lead to personal satisfaction for employees.

Mary Parker Follett was another key figure in advancing the cause of industrial humanism. Her experience as a management consultant led her to believe that the key to increased productivity was to motivate employees, rather than simply ordering better job performance. The keys to both productivity and democracy, according to Follett, were cooperation, a spirit of unity, and a coordination of effort.[18]

We have described the growth of the human relations movement because it is so closely associated with many aspects of business psychology. Since many aspects of human relations border on common sense, it is important to bring this issue to the surface.

BUSINESS PSYCHOLOGY AND COMMON SENSE

A student with several years of work experience commented after having attended the first few sessions of a class in business psychology, "Why should I study this field, it's just common sense? You can't learn how to deal with people by reading a book." The attitudes expressed by this student are shared by many other people who study business psychology or human relations. However logical such an opinion might sound, common sense is not a fully adequate substitute for formal knowledge about business psychology for several reasons.

Common Sense Is Uncommon

A small minority of people are truly effective in dealing with people or organizational forces. If common sense (meaning natural wisdom not requiring formal knowledge) were widely held, there would be fewer problem people on the job. The truth is that most organizations, even those that seem highly efficient to outsiders, are plagued with problems involving people. The five highest ranking executives from a motion picture company owned by a larger corporation resigned within a one-year period. If common sense were so widespread, might not top management at the parent company have prevented this chaotic situation?

Since few people have a high degree of common sense in matters dealing with people, a knowledge of business psychology (or a similar field such as human relations or organizational behavior) is necessary to improve on the chaos found in many business and not-for-profit organizations.

Common Sense Requires Experience

Alex, a full-time student and a part-time retail store clerk, said to his boss, Bev, "Maybe you can help me out Bev. I'm just so busy with work, I don't know where to begin. You want me to work more hours now that the holiday season is approaching. It's near the end of the term and I'm flooded with work studying for exams and writing papers. Besides all this, my girlfriend wants me to help her wallpaper her room. Do you have any advice that would help me out of my bind?"

Bev reflected for a few moments, and then commented: "Alex, why not make up a list of all the chores facing you in the next month? Label each chore A, B, or C. A means urgent; B means somewhat important; C means it can wait until the A and B items are well taken of." Alex responded somewhat reluctantly: "Doesn't sound too bad. I'll give your method a try."

One week later Alex reported back to Bev: "You're a miracle worker. I feel better already. Since I made up the list and assigned my priorities, I feel much more in control of my life."

Bev replied modestly, "I guess it's just a matter of common sense."

Bev is correct in her analysis that managing a heavy workload is a matter of common sense. But common sense of this nature requires lengthy experience, including a good deal of trial and error learning. It may also be common sense not to stay outside when the wind-chill factor is 45 degrees below zero. Yet many people have to get frostbitten before they develop a common sense about the wind-chill factor.

Alex might have learned to deal with the competing demands on his time if he had simply acquired a few more years of experience. A more efficient approach would have been to read a reliable source of information about improving his work habits *before* he felt so overwhelmed. Reading about business psychology (or any subject) is an economical way of gaining experience. If you study an applied subject, you will capitalize on the experience—and common sense—of others who have been there first. Before repairing the plumbing in your sink, why not read a plumbing manual?

Business Psychology Sharpens and Refines Common Sense

People with an adequate degree of common sense often benefit more from a study of business psychology than do people who do not yet possess a well-developed degree of common sense. People who already have some experience tend to derive the most from specialized knowledge in most fields. They tend to build upon strengths, which in general has a bigger payoff than overcoming weaknesses. A person with good common sense may already be making good use of his or her potential. With a few refinements, his or her ability to make good use of personal talents may multiply. One real estate broker is a case in point.

Alison was doing well in her work, achieving above average commissions for people in her office. But she wasn't content with slightly better than average performance in the highly competitive real estate field. Alison wanted to make better use of her potential and in the process make more money. She applied some information she read in a business psychology text about the value of goal setting in raising performance. Alison then set a series of tough but sensible goals for herself. In the past she had "winged it" or "played it by ear." Primarily as a result of goal setting, Alison increased her sales performance and her commissions by 15 percent. By using **realistic goal setting**, Alison's effectiveness multiplied.

BUSINESS PSYCHOLOGY DOESN'T ALWAYS WORK

A word of caution! Business psychology doesn't always work to your advantage right away. At times you may learn a new psychological technique, and later find out that it backfires in practice. Sometimes the technique you have learned may not be so valuable. At other times, you may have to develop skills in using that particular technique. Here is what happened in one awkward situation:

Tony attended a workshop on transactional analysis given in an adult education class. The purpose of the workshop was to provide techniques for establishing better relationships with people. One of the many techniques Tony learned about was "positive stroking." One aspect of giving positive strokes to people is to pay them a compliment for a job well done.

Tony thought he would try out some positive stroking with his boss (the manager of the supermarket where Tony worked). The next day he said to his boss, "Say, Mr. Galbo, I sure like that new soft drink display you put up in back of the store. I think it's a winner." Galbo replied angrily, "Stop trying to win points with me. That display is a bummer. We've sold a smaller amount of soft drinks since we set up the display. I made a bad decision."

Tony felt embarrassed because he had failed at his first attempt at giving positive strokes to another person.

SUMMARY OF KEY POINTS

☐ Business psychology is the application of organized knowledge about human behavior to improve personal satisfaction and productivity on the job. The general field of psychology is defined as the systematic study of behavior and all the factors that influence behavior. Among the many workers who practice business psychology, in addition to psychologists themselves, are human resource specialists and human relations trainers.

☐ Psychology has many different specialty areas, many of which overlap. The major specialties or subfields include (1) clinical and counseling psychology, (2) educational psychology, (3) child and developmental psychology, (4) experimental psychology, (5) ergonomics, and (6) industrial and organizational psychology. Two examples of new frontiers in psychology are police psychology and sport psychology.

☐ Another way of understanding psychology is to understand its major schools of thought or theoretical positions. Structuralism and functionalism are older schools that attempted to understand the workings of the mind. Behaviorism holds that behavior is shaped by its consequences (or the rewards and punishments we receive for our actions). Psychoanalysis views people as constantly torn between internal unconscious forces and external social forces. Cognitive psychology stresses the decision-making capabilities of people. Humanistic psychology focuses on the desirable qualities of people, such as love and creativity.

☐ The human relations movement was a concentrated effort to become more sensitive to the needs of employees, or to treat them in a more humanistic manner. The movement was supported by three different historic influences: the Hawthorne studies, the threat of unionization, and the philosophy of industrial humanism. One important conclusion reached by the Hawthorne studies was that showing concern for workers can increase their level of performance as much or more than improving physical working conditions.

☐ Business psychology is not simply common sense for several reasons: (1) Common sense is uncommon. (2) Common sense requires experience. (3) Business psychology sharpens and refines common sense.

☐ The application of business psychology does not inevitably help individuals and organizations, and in some instances may actually have negative consequences.

GUIDELINES FOR PERSONAL EFFECTIVENESS

1. Be careful about using common sense alone in solving problems you encounter at work. Most people do not have an abundance of common sense; common sense requires a long time to acquire; and common sense is often wrong.

2. One important supplement to common sense and intuition in dealing with people is to use knowledge provided by business psychology. Specifically, you are likely to increase your personal effectiveness if you learn to use many of the concepts and techniques presented in this text.

DISCUSSION QUESTIONS

1. Identify several work problems you have seen or heard about that you think could benefit from the application of business psychology.
2. Describe a problem you are currently facing that you think could be helped by the application of business psychology.
3. Give an example of a human engineering problem in a machine or piece of equipment used by the general public.
4. What do you think are one or two reasons that behaviorism is such a controversial school of thought?
5. What actions taken by a professor would lead you to believe that he or she is humanistic?
6. How much common sense do you have? How do you know?

A Business Psychology Problem
"WE CAN'T AFFORD TO CONDUCT RESEARCH"

After two years of job experience, you land a job in Montreal as an office supervisor in an insurance company. Your responsibilities are to supervise the work of a group of 15 raters. A rater sets the premium on applications for automobile insurance. After three months on the job it is apparent to you that there is high turnover on the job. You check into the records and find that the turnover rate is 47 percent. A particularly disconcerting fact is that Montreal is currently experiencing much less than a full-employment economy. The number of job applicants in the insurance field far outweighs the number of jobs available. Alarmed by this high turnover, you approach your boss with these thoughts:

"Jacques, I'm very worried about what I see happening here. Our turnover rate is about five times as high as that of other insurance rating departments. I think we should get to the bottom of this problem and discover why we are having such turnover problems. Maybe we should conduct a program of exit interviews. Or maybe we could design a survey to help us figure out what we are doing wrong." Jacques replies, "Enough of your theorizing. This is not a personnel laboratory. We are a busy place of work. I'll tell the personnel department to send us the right people for the job. We can't afford to conduct research."

1. What should you do next?
2. What do you think you might be able to do to convince Jacques that he is being shortsighted in his opinion about not wanting to conduct research?

3. Should you continue to work under these conditions? In other words, do you think it would be wise for you to join the ranks of those people who have quit the department?

REFERENCES

[1]Jerome Kagan and Ernest Haveman, *Psychology: An Introduction*, 4th ed. (New York: Harcourt Brace Jovanovich, 1980), p. 8.

[2]A good general reference here is Duane P. Schultz, *Psychology in Use: An Introduction to Applied Psychology* (New York: Macmillan, 1979).

[3]R. Douglas Allen, Michael A. Hitt, and Charles R. Greer, "Occupational Stress and Perceived Organizational Effectiveness: An Examination of Stress Level and Stress Type," *Personnel Psychology* (Summer 1982), pp. 359–370.

[4]Ford Motor Car advertisement appearing in many national publications including *Time*, Sept. 20, 1983.

[5]"VDTs No Threat to Users' Eyes, Says U.S. Study," Associated Press story appearing in Rochester *Democrat and Chronicle*, July 12, 1983, pp. 1A–2A.

[6]Paul J. Woods, ed., *Career Opportunities for Psychologists* (Washington, D.C.: American Psychological Association, 1976), p. 290.

[7]Kathleen Fisher, "Sport Psychology Comes of Age in the '80s," *APA Monitor* (Sept. 1982), pp. 1 and 8.

[8]A good general reference here is James F. Brennan, *History and Systems of Psychology* (Englewood Cliffs, N.J.: Prentice-Hall, 1982).

[9]Adaptation of a quotation in Kagan and Haveman, *Psychology*, p. 30.

[10]"Still Walking Faster and Longer," *Time*, Oct. 10, 1983, p. 42.

[11]The description of psychoanalysis is based on the synthesis in James O. Lugo and Gerald L. Hershey, *Living Psychology*, 3rd ed. (New York: Macmillan, 1981), pp. 28–30.

[12]A. Christine Parham, *Basic Psychology for the Work Life* (Cincinnati, Ohio: South-Western, 1983), p. 14.

[13]From the Articles of Association of the Association for Humanistic Psychology, quoted in Lugo and Hershey, *Living Psychology*, p. 25.

[14]Robert Kreitner, *Management*, 2nd ed. (Boston: Houghton Mifflin, 1983), p. 48.

[15]An original source of information about the Hawthorne studies is Elton Mayo, *The Human Problems of an Industrial Civilization* (New York: Viking Press), 1960. A useful summary and synthesis of these classic studies is Fred Luthans, *Organizational Behavior*, 3rd ed. (New York: McGraw-Hill, 1981), pp. 15–22.

[16]James A. F. Stoner, *Management*, 2nd ed. (Englewood Cliffs, N.J.: Prentice-Hall, 1982), p. 46.

[17]Kreitner, *Management*, p. 49.

[18]Kreitner, *Management*, p. 51.

SUGGESTED READING

BECK, ROBERT C. *Applying Psychology: Understanding People.* Englewood Cliffs, N.J.: Prentice-Hall, 1982.

HEBB, DONALD O. *"What Psychology Is About." American Psychologist* (Jan. 1974), pp. 71–79.

HOLAHAN, CHARLES J. *Environmental Psychology.* New York: Random House, 1982.

HUCHINGSON, R. DALE. *New Horizons for Human Factors in Design.* New York: McGraw-Hill, 1981.

MCCORMICK, ERNEST J., and DANIEL R. ILGEN. *Industrial Psychology*, 7th ed. Englewood Cliffs, N.J.: Prentice-Hall, 1980.

MCCORMICK, ERNEST J., and MARK S. SANDERS. *Human Factors in Engineering and Design*, 5th ed. New York: McGraw-Hill, 1982.

ROSCOE, STANLEY N. *Aviation Psychology.* Ames, Iowa: Iowa State University Press, 1980.

SCHULTZ, DUANE A. *History of Modern Psychology*, 2nd ed. New York: Academic Press, 1975.

SKINNER, B. F. *About Behaviorism.* New York: Knopf, 1974.

TAGESON, C. WILLIAM. *Humanistic Psychology: A Synthesis.* Homewood, Ill.: Dorsey Press, 1982.

GENERAL PRINCIPLES
OF HUMAN BEHAVIOR

LEARNING OBJECTIVES

After reading and studying this chapter and doing the exercises, you should be able to

1. Describe how perception influences job behavior.
2. Explain why our perceptions are often inaccurate.
3. Explain how people learn both simple skills and more complex activities.
4. Describe the need hierarchy and expectancy theories of motivation.
5. Illustrate several ways in which values and beliefs influence job behavior.

To understand and deal effectively with people in a job environment, you have to understand general principles about people that apply in a variety of situations. General principles help predict what will be the most probable behavior in a given situation. For instance, most people are conditioned to regard a flashing red light as a command to stop their forward movement completely or to proceed with extreme caution. When a flashing red light is placed over the entrance to an area within a factory, most people will sense that danger exists. Upon reading the sign under the flashing red light, "Protective gear must be worn in this area," most people will comply with the rule.

Despite the general success of conditioning people to learn the significance of a flashing red light, a few people will resist such conditioning. Some rebels who reject most authority will say to themselves, "I never pay attention to those kinds of things." A few other people will be so preoccupied with their own thoughts that they will have no particular response to the flashing red light.

In this chapter we emphasize general principles of four key aspects of behavior: perception, learning, motivation, and values and beliefs. In Chapter 3 we emphasize how individual differences influence behavior on the job. We have purposely used the term "emphasize," because the distinction between general principles and individual differences is not always so clearcut. For example, how individual differences influence behavior often follows a general pattern. We will return to this subject in Chapter 3.

PERCEPTION: THE SCIENCE OF FIRST IMPRESSIONS

The Nature of Perception

Most of us interpret what is going on in the world outside us as we see it—not as it really is.[1] You do not usually experience a mass of colors, you experience a color photograph. You do not experience a thousand different vibrations in the air, you hear a favorite record. When we answer a question, we answer in terms of our interpretation of what we hear.

An everyday happening, such as changes in air temperature, helps to illustrate the nature of human perception. Assume that you live in Vermont. A temperature of 52°F (11.1°C) would seem *warm* in January. The same temperature would seem *cold* in July. Our perception of temperature depends on many things going on inside our mind and body.

An old, standard psychology diagram is helpful in illustrating that "truth" depends on what we see as the "facts." Figure 2–1 was drawn by an anonymous artist to be intentionally ambiguous. Upon looking at this line drawing, many people will see an old woman with her chin tucked down, wearing a scarf around her head. Look at the drawing long enough, and you will see an attractive young woman glancing away from you. Another curiosity about human perception is that the figure and the background seem to switch back and forth (in such a drawing).

In summary, perception deals with the various ways in which people interpret things in the external world and how they act on the basis of these interpretations. Those aspects of perception most helpful to you on the job deal with two things: (1) how people interpret various cues and stimuli (things) in the environment, and (2) how they act as a consequence of these interpretations.

Perceptual Problems

You are most likely to encounter perceptual problems when the stimulus or cue to be perceived has an emotional meaning. Assume that Brian, an office supervisor, announces to the members of his department, "Look, folks, the new typewriter we ordered has arrived. We are using it to replace the oldest typewriter in the office. It has a five-year guarantee." Most people in the office will interpret this message at face value, and Brian will not experience a communications problem. (Communication and perception form a system. Our perception influences the messages that we receive and the messages that we send.) Most people will mutter to themselves, something to the effect, "Yes, that's a new typewriter for the office. We probably needed a new one."

Brian might have experienced problems in human perception if he had communicated this message to his employees: "Folks, I would like you to meet Brenda. She's an office temporary who is here to help us out this week." Announcing the presence of an office temporary would precipitate several

FIGURE 2–1
An old woman or a young woman? Look again.

different perceptions, depending on many motives, needs, and the knowledge of department employees. Among the possible interpretations are these:

"An office temporary? I wonder if this means the company is going to cut down the regular work force and use temporaries to help us through peak loads."

"This seems to be a sure sign that business has picked up. The front office would never authorize extra help unless business were booming. Things look good for getting a decent raise this year."

"I wonder if Brian has brought in a temporary worker to show us we had better get hustling or we could be replaced? I've heard a lot of these so-called temporaries usually wind up with a full-time job if they like the temporary assignment."

Characteristics of a Person That Influence Perception

As suggested by Brian's experiences, factors within people influence their perception of the external environment. Six factors influence perception in general, as well as in a job situation. One or more of these factors may influence perception at a given time, and some of these factors are generally more influential than others.[2] Perception is called a **cognitive process** since it relates to how we acquire knowledge.

Physiological and Anatomical Condition. A supervisor will have to speak loudly when giving direction to a hearing-impaired employee. Also, the supervisor must not use color-coded signals when dealing with a color-blind employee. A frail person might perceive lifting a 45-pound box to be a difficult task, while a physically strong person would perceive the task as pleasant exercise. Thus, basic body physiology and anatomy exert some influence on job perception and behavior.

Family Influences. A profound influence on the perception and behavior of most people is their family background, both present and past. A person reared in a family where parents have strong authority is likely to perceive a directive from a boss as a normal way of life. A person raised in a family where authority and power are shared with parents and children may have a more difficult time perceiving orders as legitimate. That particular employee may have a stronger need for freedom from supervision.

Cultural Influences. A person's cultural background is another major influence on his or her perception of stimuli in the job environment. A young man whose cultural values influence him to perceive work as a necessary evil or as punishment might have a negative attitude toward an extra assignment. Another young man whose cultural values influence him to perceive work as a privilege and a prime reason for living will take a different view of the stimulus of additional work. In contrast, he may express enthusiasm for the project, while his less work oriented counterpart may show passive resistance (drag his heels).

Motives, Needs, and Goals. A major determinant of people's perception is their motivation at the time with respect to the object or experience to be perceived (the stimulus or cue). A woman who believes that her family is deprived because they lack a color television will take an active interest in a suggestion system that offers cash awards. She may fantasize translating her suggestion idea into a cash award that is big enough to purchase a color television set. Another woman who is not currently interested in acquiring new possessions or who has a low need for recognition may barely notice the suggestion system box. An employee who is harboring guilt about having stolen office supplies may perceive a routine audit of department supplies as an investigation directed at him or her. Much more will be said about the influence of needs, motives, and goals on behavior later in this chapter and again in Chapter 5.

Past Experiences. How a man or woman perceives a stimulus today is heavily influenced by what happened when that stimulus was presented in the past. This basic perceptual fact is illustrated by the threadbare joke about the man who will never again volunteer for an assignment because of one experience. While in the army he volunteered for an assignment, only to wind up cleaning latrines. An older man may perceive a younger worker assigned to the department as a threat because in the past he was shown up by an energetic young worker. An employee who demands clarification on the smallest work rules, such as the limits to lunch hour, may be reacting to a past event: her last employer fired her for chronically returning late from lunch.

Personality Characteristics. How a person perceives an event is also influenced by his or her stable traits and characteristics, or personality. An optimistic, adventuresome individual might perceive a new boss as a welcome challenge, as another influential person to impress with his or her job competence. A pessimistic, cautious individual might perceive the same new boss as a threat, as another influential person who might think critically of his or her job performance. Similarly, an impulsive production inspector might perceive one defect in a sample as an indication that the department has a major quality problem. A more reflective or less impulsive production inspector might perceive the same defect as simply an indication that more sampling is necessary: something may or may not be wrong with the quality of goods produced in the department.

Devices That People Use to Deal with Sensory Information

Under ideal circumstances the employee perceives information as it is intended to be communicated or as it exists in reality. A junior accountant examining a set of figures will arrive, it is hoped, at a conclusion that will satisfy both his boss and generally accepted accounting principles. And the night maintenance worker who sees water on the floor will perceive it as a probable leak, not as simply the product of a careless person spilling a bucket of water. And a union steward offered a promotion to a supervisory position will perceive it as an act of good faith on the part of management, not as a plot to get him out of the union. In reality, people use a number of devices to help them simplify their perception of external events.[3]

Denial. If the sensory information is particularly painful to us, we often deny to ourselves and others that the information even existed. A secretary was confronted with the fact that her use of the office copying machine to make copies of her shrimp creole recipe was against company regulations. She replied, "I never saw that regulation," even though she had typed the company policy manual just six months previous to the confrontation. Similarly, many people use denial when reading the message from the surgeon general printed on each pack of American-made cigarettes.

Stereotyping. A common method of simplifying the perceptual process is to evaluate an individual or thing on the basis of our perception of the group or class to which he, she, or it belongs. One production employee said he preferred not to accept a transfer to the quality-control department, giving as his reason, "I don't want to work for a nit picker." One supervisor told the purchasing department that they were making a mistake by purchasing components made in Korea. He gave as his reason, "All Korean-made products are junk merchandise."

Halo Effect. A tendency exists to color everything that we know about a person because of one recognizable favorable or unfavorable trait. When a company does not insist on the use of objective measures of performance, it is not uncommon for a supervisor to give a favorable performance rating to people who dress well or smile frequently. The fine appearance or warm smile of these people has created a halo around them. Employees often create a negative halo about a supervisor simply because he or she is gruff or stern in manner or speech.

Expectancy. If a person perceives or expects that another individual will behave in a particular way, that person often lives up to such an expectancy. A manager who perceives an employee as being competent will actually help that person become competent by giving him or her subtle signs of encouragement. Unfortunately, if you expect somebody to fail, they will often live down to your expectation. How a supervisor's prophecy about an employee can become self-fulfilling will be discussed again in Chapter 5.

Projection. Another shortcut in the perceptual process is to project our own bad faults onto others instead of making an objective appraisal of the situation. A manager might listen to a supervisor's request for one additional clerk because of what the supervisor perceives as a heavy workload within her department. The manager might mutter, "Who does she think she is, trying to build an empire for herself?" In reality, the manager might be the empire builder and is projecting this undesirable characteristic onto her supervisor.

Selective Perception. A person uses this mechanism when he or she draws an unjustified conclusion from an unclear situation. Upon his return from a weekend of hunting, a tool and die maker might see his supervisor's car leaving his block. Once in the door, he confronts his wife with the *fact* that she and his boss are having an affair. Perhaps the tool and die maker in question is looking for an excuse to have a fight with his wife (or his boss). Since human behavior is always complex, it could also be concluded that he is thinking of having an affair himself!

Perceptual Defense. Once we hold a perception of something or somebody, we tend to cling to that perception by making things that we see, hear, smell, or touch consistent with that belief. All the previous perceptual shortcuts are involved in perceptual defense. Not only supervisors and individual performers engage in perceptual defense. The president of an American camera company insisted for a period of 10 years that the Japanese competitors were not a serious threat to his company's high-priced line of cameras. At this writing, that company has been out of business for 10 years, and the former president owns and operates a hardware store.

HOW PEOPLE LEARN

Much of human learning takes place on the job simply because people spend such a large proportion of their lives in a job setting. Learning is *a relatively permanent change in behavior based on practice or experience.* A person does not learn how to grow physically, hear sounds, or see light. These are innate, inborn patterns of behavior. But a person does learn how to wire a circuit board, program a computer, cut hair, fix flat tires, or balance a checkbook. Unless new learning takes place, almost no person would be able to perform his or her job in a satisfactory manner.

Here we will describe several different methods of learning, beginning with classical conditioning, the simplest type of learning. Then we will describe learning of an intermediate level of complexity, operant conditioning. Finally, we will describe the learning of complicated skills, called shaping and modeling. Complicated learning, particularly modeling, is called a cognitive process because it requires the learner to make a number of judgments and observations.

Classical Conditioning: Learning Simple Habits and Reflexes

In the late 1890s a Russian physiologist, Ivan Pavlov, conducted a long series of experiments about digestion. While studying a dog, he noticed that the dog salivated not only to the presence of food in the mouth, but at the sight of the food, the sound of the food trays, and even the footsteps of the experimenter. The principles of classical conditioning stemming from his experiments help us to understand the most elementary type of learning—how people acquire uncomplicated habits and reflexes.[4] Since most of work behavior involves more than reflexes and simple habits, classical conditioning itself is not of major consequence to the supervisor or individual worker. Yet its basic principles and concepts are included in more complicated forms of learning.

Classical conditioning works in this manner. Clyde, a physically normal individual, takes an entry-level, unskilled job in a factory. His first day on the job a bell rings in his department at 11:34 A.M. Suddenly, every other worker stops working and opens a lunch box or heads out to the company cafeteria. Clyde says to himself, "The bell must mean it's time for lunch."

By the third day on the job, Clyde develops stomach pangs and begins to salivate as soon as the bell rings. Prior to this job, Clyde was in the habit of eating lunch at 1 P.M. and did not begin to have stomach pangs until that time.

Looking at the essentials of classical conditioning, here is what happened to Clyde: since the food naturally and automatically elicits (brings forth) stomach pangs and salivation, it is referred to as the **unconditioned stimulus** (UCS). Salivating to the food in Clyde's lunch box or in the cafeteria occurs automatically, without any learning. It is therefore called the *unconditioned response* (UCR). The sound of the department bell was originally neutral with respect to the salivary or hunger pang response, since it did not naturally elicit the UCR. Conditioning has taken place when the previously neutral stimulus (the department bell in Clyde's case) acquires the capacity to bring forth hunger pangs and salivation. The previously neutral stimulus is now called the *conditioned stimulus* (CS), and the hunger pangs and salivation to the sound of the bell are known as *conditioned responses* (CR).

Two other conditioning concepts are also of major importance. If the department bell rings frequently when it is not time for lunch, Clyde's hunger pangs and salivation responses will gradually cease or **extinguish.** (An important exception is that time alone or the empty feeling in his stomach can also serve as a stimulus to Clyde.) As Clyde goes through life, he will learn not to salivate or experience hunger pangs to every bell that sounds like the one used in his department. At first he may **generalize** his learning by salivating to many different bells and experiencing hunger pangs in response to a variety of bells. After a while, Clyde will **discriminate** and only make such responses to the bell in his department (or any other bell that signals food time).

Classical conditioning helps to explain such elementary job behaviors as how people learn to avoid being conked on the head by cranes and low hanging pipes. It also explains how we learn to step to the side of an aisle when we hear the buzz of a forklift truck behind us. By classical conditioning, people also learn how to avoid being burned twice by a hot pipe or shocked twice by inserting a screwdriver into an electric outlet.

Operant Conditioning: Learning through the Consequences of Our Behavior

Operant conditioning is learning that takes place as a consequence of behavior. In other words, a person's actions are instrumental in determining whether or not learning takes place. A supervisor asked a darkroom technician how he learned to jiggle the trays of photochemicals while the prints were being processed. The technician replied, "I just tried it once and it seemed to help solve the problem of white spots appearing on the finished prints." In this case, the *operant* is the jiggling of the trays. The technician adopted jiggling as a standard practice because he received positive reinforcement for his initial effort—the troublesome white spots on the prints disappeared.

Operant conditioning is also referred to as **instrumental learning** because the behavior of the individual is instrumental in bringing forth the reward, absence of a reward, or punishment. Similarly, operant conditioning can be called **trial and error learning.** If you happen to do something right (such as making the right movement while water skiing) and it leads to a reward (such as a smooth turn), you will continue to practice that response.

Learning versus Motivation. Operant conditioning can also be referred to as learning through reinforcement theory, as implied in the discussion of behaviorism in Chapter 1. It is concerned with reinforcing or strengthening some behavior and at times weakening other behaviors. Reinforcement theory, including both positive reinforcement and punishment, applies equally well to the subjects of motivation and learning. Operant conditioning helps people learn new skills. Once the skill is learned, positive reinforcement is useful in getting the person to repeat that skill (or display motivated behavior).

Motivation and learning are separate but closely related processes. You cannot motivate people to perform a task that they do not know how to perform. Yet you can motivate a person to want to learn how to perform that task. Any manager whose job involves dealing with people is frequently faced with the problems of (1) helping subordinates to learn, and (2) motivating them to repeat the learned behaviors.

Operant Conditioning versus Classical Conditioning. Operant conditioning differs from classical conditioning in one major respect. In classical conditioning, we can specify the unconditioned stimulus (such as food or water) that brings forth the response (such as stomach contractions or salivation). Somehow the individual tries out a behavior or action. If it leads to a reward, that behavior tends to be repeated. Much human learning proceeds on this basis. Learning how to ride a bicycle, drive a car on ice, surf in the ocean, or order wine in a restaurant is largely attributable to operant conditioning. Through this process we acquire skills that we did not previously possess. Whenever a spontaneous behavior leads to **positive reinforcement**, it will tend to be repeated.

Negative Reinforcement. Spontaneous behavior will also tend to be repeated when it leads to a relief from an uncomfortable situation. This process of being rewarded by being relieved of discomfort is called **negative reinforcement.** A woman wearing cutoff jeans while riding a motorcycle might suddenly shriek in pain because the inside of her calves touched against an exposed part of the engine. She then wears full-length jeans (as undoubtedly recommended by the manufacturer of the motorcycle) and no longer gets burned. Negative reinforcement has taken place because something uncomfortable (the burning sensation) has been removed by means of a new behavior (wearing full-length jeans).

Note carefully that negative reinforcement is not the same thing as punishment. Negative reinforcement is pleasant, and therefore a reward. Punishment, by definition, is something unpleasant—unless the person involved likes to be punished. With masochists, however, the reward is to be punished!

Punishment. Being punished for your mistakes can be an important part of learning. Punishment can be regarded as the introduction of an unpleasant stimulus as a consequence of the learner having done something wrong (in the eyes of the person in control of the situation). Or the threat of punishment can be used instead of actually punishing people for the wrong response in a learning or motivational situation. Punishment aids the operant conditioning process because it weakens the particular response. You tend not to repeat a response because of its negative consequences. Yet some people continue to repeat behavior that leads to severe punishment, such as those individuals who receive a series of speeding tickets. One behavioristic explanation of this occurrence is that the thrill received from speeding is so rewarding that it overpowers the punishment of getting caught. (And one psychoanalytic explanation is that the speeder has a death wish!)

For punishment to facilitate operant conditioning, it must be of appropriate intensity. If the punishment is too mild, such as simply having to punch a delete key everytime you make an input error with a computer, it will have a small impact on learning. However, if you wipe out a file with an input error, such as turning off the computer before you stored your file, you probably will not repeat that mistake very often. If the punishment is too severe, you may withdraw from the situation and strike back with aggressive behavior of your own. For instance, if you flunked a computer utilization course simply because you wiped out one file by accident, you might knock the terminal off the desk and never voluntarily use a computer again.

The purpose of punishment is to **extinguish** or eliminate a response. The same result can often be accomplished by simply ignoring the undesirable behavior. As is well known to experienced teachers, one way to stop the class clown from acting up is for the teacher and classmates to ignore that person's antics.

How Often Should People Be Rewarded?. An important issue in operant conditioning (and in motivation) is how frequently to reward people when they make the correct response. So much experimentation has been conducted on this topic that some accurate guidelines are available. Two broad types of **schedules of reinforcement** are in use, continuous and intermittent.

Under a **continuous** schedule, behavior is reinforced each time it occurs, such as saying "good job" every time a bank teller comes out even at the end

S_1	R_1	S_2	R_2
Memo from supervisor informing sales repre- sentative to prepare inventory report	Prepares monthly report	Receives praise from superior	A sense of achievement and satisfaction
Conditioned stimulus	Conditioned operant response	Reward or reinforcing stimulus	Unconditioned response

FIGURE 2–2
Example of operant conditioning in practice.

of a day. Continuous schedules usually result in the fastest learning, but the desired behavior quickly diminishes when the reinforcement stops. Under an **intermittent** schedule, the learner receives a reward after some instances of engaging in the desired behavior, but not after each instance. Intermittent reinforcement is particularly effective in sustaining behavior, because the learner stays mentally alert and interested. At any point in time, the behavior might lead to the desired reward. Slot machines in gambling casinos operate on this principle.

In practice, learning through operant conditioning proceeds as a sequence of interrelated events, as illustrated in Figure 2–2.[5] A sales representative receives a memo from his supervisor to prepare a monthly report of customer inventories on the company's line of ski equipment. The memo is the conditioned stimulus. His conditioned operant response is to prepare the report. The operant response is referred to as conditioned because the sales representative did not spontaneously think of preparing the report. His boss generously praises the first report for its thoroughness and clarity. Such praise acts as a reward; the sales representative has received positive reinforcement. His unconditioned responses to this reward are feelings of achievement and self-satisfaction.

Modeling and Shaping: Learning Complicated Skills

When you acquire a complicated skill such as speaking in front of a group, photography, preparing a budget, or taking a store inventory, you learn much more than just a single stimulus–response relationship. You learn a large number of these relationships, and you also learn how to put them together in a cohesive, smooth-flowing pattern. Two important processes that help in learning complicated skills are modeling (or imitation) and shaping (learning through approximations until the total skill is learned). Modeling, in particular, is considered to represent cognitive learning because it is a complex intellectual activity. Shaping is often considered to be part of operant conditioning and therefore could be classified as noncognitive learning.

Modeling occurs when you learn a skill by observing another person perform that skill. Many apprentices learn part of their trade just by watching a journeyman practice his (or her) trade. Carefully observing professional athletes on television can improve your own game in that particular sport if you have the right physical equipment and motivation. Modeling or imitation often brings forth behaviors that people did not previously seem to have in their repertoire. A cogent example took place in a factory.

> A long-time foreman with a reputation for heavy-handed, authoritarian manner was transferred to a section run by a young, well-educated manager. The new manager treated the foreman with a great deal of respect and deference for his knowledge and experience. The foreman was initially uncomfortable in this new relationship because his previous managers, unlike his new manager, had almost never seriously sought his opinion on important matters relating to production operations. Now, the foreman is not only pleased that his opinions are valued and often put into effect, but he has begun to ask *his* subordinates, the line employees, for their views on a number of job-related matters. As the manager has done to him, the foreman also makes it a point to thank his employees for their ideas and lets them know when he implements their suggestions.[6]

Shaping involves the reinforcement of a series of small steps that build up to the final or desired behavior. It is another way in which complicated skills are learned. At each successful step of the way the learner receives some positive reinforcement. Unless the learner receives positive reinforcement at each step of the way, that person will probably not acquire the total skill. As the learner improves in his or her ability to perform the task, more skill is required to receive the reward. A young man might be shaped into an automobile mechanic through a series of small skills beginning with changing tires. He receives a series of rewards as he moves along the path from a garage helper to a mechanic who can diagnose an engine malfunction and repair the problem.

Among the forms of positive reinforcement he received along the way were approval for acquired skills, pay increments, and the feeling of pride as new minor skills were learned. The negative reinforcement he received was fewer bruised knuckles. When this series of small skills has been put together through a complicated pattern of response, the man has been converted from a fledgling garage assistant to a full-fledged mechanic. Shaping is a concept that applies to both learning and motivation. It will therefore be reintroduced in Chapter 5.

TWO KEY EXPLANATIONS OF MOTIVATION

Motivation, as it applies to the job, refers to why workers behave as they do and how much effort they will put into accomplishing things that the company thinks are worthwhile. Motivation is seen as a major factor in productivity (how much is produced in comparison to how many resources are consumed in the process). Therefore, the topic has always been of interest to managers and business psychologists. Here we will describe two key theories of human motivation: (1) the classical theory of Abraham Maslow, and (2) expectancy theory, a currently popular explanation of job motivation. In Chapter 5 we will describe several specific methods of motivating other people and yourself.

Maslow's Need Hierarchy

The most widely quoted systematic explanation of human motivation was developed by psychologist Abraham Maslow.[7] He reasoned that human beings have an internal need pushing them on toward self-actualization (meaning the same as self-realization or self-fulfillment) and personal superiority. However, before these higher-level needs are activated, certain lower-level needs must be satisfied. The need hierarchy is thus frequently referred to as the *need ladder*. According to the need hierarchy, a poor person thinks of finding a job as a way of obtaining the necessities of life. Once these are obtained, that person may think of achieving recognition and self-fulfillment on the job. When a person is generally satisfied at one level, he or she looks for satisfaction at a higher level. As Maslow describes it, a person is a "perpetually wanting animal." Very few people are totally satisfied with their lot in life, even the rich and famous.

Maslow arranged human needs into a five-rung ladder, as shown in Figure 2–3. Each rung refers to a group of needs, not one need for each rung. These groups of needs are described next in ascending order.

1. **Physiological needs** refer to bodily needs, such as the requirements for food, water, shelter, and sleep. In general, most jobs provide ample opportunity to satisfy physiological needs. Nevertheless, some people go to work hungry or in need of sleep. Until that person gets a satisfying meal or takes a nap, he or she will not be concerned about finding an outlet on the job for creative impulses.

2. **Safety needs** include actual physical safety, as well as a feeling of being safe from both physical and emotional injury. Many jobs frustrate a person's need for safety (policeman, policewoman, taxi cab driver). Therefore, many people would be motivated by the prospects of a safe

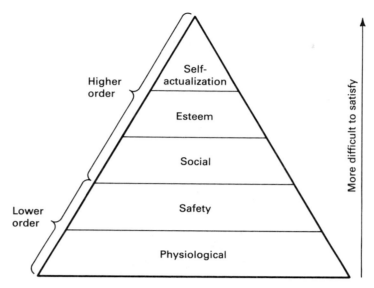

FIGURE 2–3
Maslow's need hierarchy.

environment. People who do very unsafe things for a living (such as racing-car drivers and tightrope walkers) find thrills and recognition more important than safety. Many people are exceptions to Maslow's need hierarchy.

3. **Social needs** are essentially love or belonging needs. Unlike the two previous levels of needs, they center on a person's interaction with other people. Many people have a strong urge to be part of a group and to be accepted by that group. Peer acceptance is important in school and on the job. Many people are unhappy with their job unless they have the opportunity to work in close contact with others.

4. **Esteem needs** represent an individual's demands to be seen by others—and to himself or herself—as a person of worth. Esteem needs are also called **ego** needs, pointing to the fact that people want to be seen as competent and capable. A job that is seen by yourself and others as being worthwhile provides a good opportunity to satisfy esteem needs.

5. **Self-actualizing needs** are the highest level of needs and include the needs for self-fulfillment and personal development. True self-actualization is an ideal to strive for, rather than something that automatically stems from occupying a challenging position. A self-actualized person is somebody who has become what he or she is capable of becoming. Few of us reach all our potential, even when we are so motivated. Not

every self-actualized person is a nationally or internationally prominent individual. A woman of average intelligence who attains an associate's degree and later becomes the owner–operator of an antique store might be self-actualized. Her potential and desire may both have been realized by self-employment as an antique dealer.

The Need Hierarchy in Perspective. Maslow's need hierarchy is a convenient way of classifying needs and has spurred thousands of people to take the subject of human motivation more seriously. Its primary value has been the fact that it highlights the importance of human needs in a work setting. A practical application of the need hierarchy is that, when a manager wants to motivate a subordinate, he or she must offer the individual a reward that will satisfy an important need.

Three frequent misinterpretations of the need hierarchy should be avoided. One is that people behave as they do because of their quest to satisfy one particular need. In reality, many different needs are dominant at any one time. For example, a drafting technician may satisfy a number of needs (including recognition, esteem, and self-satisfaction) by developing a design that works in practice.

A second misinterpretation is to view the need ladder as a rigid one-step-at-a-time procedure.[8] Each level of need does not have to be totally satisfied before a person can be motivated by a higher-level need. A third, and perhaps the most damaging, misinterpretation of the need hierarchy is that is represents all of human needs. To repeat, the ladder represents need categories. As such, they reflect only a sampling of human needs. Other important needs include power, recognition, achievement, accomplishment, competence, and the desire to submit to authority (deference).

The Expectancy Theory of Motivation

How much effort you expend to accomplish something depends on how much you expect to receive in return, according to **expectancy theory** (ET). Currently the most popular theory among business psychologists, ET assumes that people are rational decision makers. Based on mental calculations, they choose from among the alternatives facing them the one that appears to have the biggest personal payoff at the time. A specific example is that most people will choose an occupation they think will bring them the rewards they are seeking, providing they believe they can overcome the hurdles necessary to get into that occupation. Here we will examine several basic considerations about this cognitive explanation of the why of employee behavior.[9]

Basic Components. The expectancy model of motivation has three major components: effort-to-performance expectancy, performance-to-outcome expectancy, and valence (or value attached to something).

1. Effort–performance expectancy. An important question rational people ask themselves before putting forth effort to accomplish a particular task is, "If I put in all this work, will I really get the job done?" Each behavior is associated in the individual's mind with a certain expectancy (or subjective hunch) of the probability of success. Effort–performance ($E \rightarrow P$) expectancies thus influence whether or not you will even strive to earn a reward. Self-confident people have higher ($E \rightarrow P$) expectancies than do less self-confident people.

2. Performance–outcome expectancy. When people engage in a particular activity, they do so with the intention of achieving a desired result or outcome. If you didn't think that good performance would lead to a promised reward, you would probably not even strive to perform well. Performance–outcome ($P \rightarrow O$) expectancies are thus an important determinant of behavior. The stronger your subjective probability (hunch) that performance will lead to a desired outcome, the higher the probability that you will put forth effort (spring for it).

3. Valence. Each outcome has a value, worth, or attractiveness to a person called a **valence**. And there are substantial individual differences in the valence a given reward has for different people. At times the same object or situation may have a positive valence for one person and a negative valence for another person. One such situation is that of being assigned to a committee as a consequence of having performed well on an assignment. To quote an old saying, "One person's passion is another person's poison."

The valence you attach to a reward or outcome thus influences how willing you are to expend effort. It will contribute to your understanding of business psychology to recognize that a valence represents a person's perception, rather than the true quality of the reward or outcome. For example, some people are motivated to return bottles and cans to stores and recycling centers. Other people, who attach a smaller valence to small change (or to the idea of conservation), simply discard their "empties."

How You Calculate Motivation. According to expectancy theory, motivation is the product of both kinds of expectancy and valence. The relationship can be expressed by the following formula:

$$\text{Motivation} = (E \rightarrow P) \times (P \rightarrow O) \times \text{valence}$$

An example from career decision making will help explain how this process works. Roberto believes strongly that he will be able to complete a program of study in biomedical photography. He thus has a high ($E \rightarrow P$) expectancy, perhaps 0.90. He believes a little less strongly that a biomedical photography program will lead to a high-paying, interesting job. His ($P \rightarrow O$) expectancy is 0.85. Yet Roberto strongly values a potential career in biomedical photography. His valence on a scale from -1.0 to $+1.0$ is 0.95.

When these three factors are multiplied ($0.90 \times 0.85 \times 0.95 = 0.73$), it becomes apparent that Roberto's motivation to pursue biomedical photography will be strong.

The formula just presented helps explain in arithmetic terms why some people engage in activities such as playing a lottery or trying to become an astronaut or a professional athlete, although they recognize that the ($P \rightarrow O$) is quite low. The compensating factor is that they place an extraordinary valence on winning. One winning ticket may make you a millionaire, and becoming an astronaut or a professional athlete could provide you with enormous recognition. You would also have the potential for enormous income.

How Motivation and Ability Are Linked to Performance. Another important contribution of ET is that it helps explain how motivation and ability are linked to job performance. As depicted in Figure 2–4, to achieve performance (actual job results), both motivation and ability must be present.[10] If one is absent, no performance will be possible. It is important to recognize the contribution of ability in bringing about performance, because our culture tends to overdramatize the contribution of motivation to performance. Too many people uncritically accept the statement, "You can achieve anything you want if you try hard enough." In reality, a person also needs the proper education, ability, tools, and technology.

Motivation is often the key to attaining good results. Yet at other times, factors other than motivation come into play. For example, as a member of a work group you might want to be a high producer, but group pressures may keep you from producing much more work than the group standard.

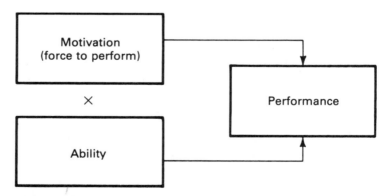

FIGURE 2–4
How motivation and ability influence performance.

HOW VALUES AND BELIEFS
INFLUENCE JOB BEHAVIOR

Another group of factors influencing how a person behaves on the job is that person's values and beliefs. A value refers to the importance a person attaches to something. If you believe that religion is one of the most important parts of your life, your religious values are strong. If you pay very little attention to conserving energy, energy conservation is a weak value of yours. Beliefs exert a similar influence on job behavior. If you believe that the company wants to take advantage of you, you might demand that an informal statement made by your manager be put into writing.

How Values Are Learned

A person is not born with a particular set of values. He or she learns them in the process of growing up. One important way we acquire values is through observing others, or using **models**. Quite often a person who places a high value on reading was reared around people who valued reading. Models can be parents, teachers, friends, brothers and sisters, and even public figures.

If we identify with a particular person, the probability is high that we will develop some of his or her major values. One young woman from a family of poor farmers moved to a large city and became a caseworker. Asked why she chose casework as an occupation, she explained:

> About once a year this kindly old woman would visit our farm to see how we were doing. She was sent by the county. My mother and father thought she was snooping into our business. Because of it, they almost hated her. I admired the kindness that she had for poor people like ourselves. I decided to do the same thing when I grew up.

Another major way in which values are learned is through the communication of attitudes. The attitudes that we hear expressed directly or indirectly help shape our values. Assume that using credit to purchase goods and services was talked about as an evil practice among your family and friends. You might therefore hold negative values about installment purchases.

Unstated, but implied, attitudes may also shape your values. If key people in your life showed no enthusiasm when you talked about spectator sports, you might not place such a high value on watching sports. If, on the other hand, your family and friends centered their lives around watching sports on television, you might develop similar values. (Or you might rebel against such a value because it interfered with other things that you might have wanted to do with your free time.)

Values Analysis: A Method
of Classifying Employee Values

A method of classifying values has been developed that is designed to provide employers with suggestions for dealing with employees. Called **value analysis**, the method classifies people into one of seven different value systems:

1. **Subsistence:** concerned primarily with survival or just staying out of trouble and getting by.
2. **Tribalistic:** superstitious, clannish, readily obeys strong authority figures.
3. **Absolutistic:** places high value on order, structure, discipline, and tradition.
4. **Egocentric:** concerned primarily with satisfying own needs, selfishly values own welfare much more than welfare of others.
5. **Achievist:** ambitious, competitive, valuing individual drive and intelligence.
6. **Sociocentric:** altruistic, socially concerned, values the welfare of the group over the ambitions of the individual.
7. **Individualistic:** tolerant, rational, values individual achievement but without hostility toward the group.[11]

Employers have experimented with values analysis in this way. The company calls in a psychological consultant who administers to employees a multiple-choice test that measures these seven values. The consultant then analyzes the test to classify employees by their predominant values. Suggestions are then given to management about handling employees according to their value systems. Suppose, for example, the company wanted to improve customer relations. Employees who placed in the *subsistence* category could be told that the firm cannot survive unless customers receive top treatment. Those with an *achievist* value system could be told that the way to get ahead in the company is to maintain excellent relationships with customers.

Note that value analysis is in the experimental stage and appears unlikely to become a widespread employment practice. Also, many people regard such a practice as both an invasion of privacy and an unfair manipulation of employees. Do you have an opinion on this issue?

Clarifying Your Values

The values that you develop early in life are directly related to the kind of person that you are now and will be and to the quality of the relationships that you form.[12] A recognition of this fact has led to hundreds of exercises

DIRECTIONS: Rank from 1 to 10 the importance of the following things to you as a person. The most important thing receives a rank of 1; the least important a rank of 10. Use the space next to "Other" if we have left out the most important thing in your life.

_____ Having my own place to live
_____ Having a child
_____ Having an interesting job and career
_____ Owning a car
_____ Having good health
_____ Being a religious person
_____ Being able to see and hear
_____ Loving and being loved by another person
_____ Making an above average income
_____ Other _____

1. Discuss and compare your ranking of these things with the person next to you.
2. Perhaps your class, assisted by your instructor, can arrive at a class average of each of these things or values. How does your ranking compare to the class ranking?

FIGURE 2–5
A method of examining your personal values.

designed to help people clarify and understand some of their own values. Almost all these value-clarification exercises ask you, in one way or another, to compare the relative importances that you attach to different things. One such exercise is presented in Figure 2–5.

Values Lead to Goals

Robert Fulmer notes that the worker's background, composed of job experiences, education, cultural influences, and personality, leads to the formation of values. "Through the lens of those values, the individual will perceive his or her needs."[13] Needs, in turn, lead to the setting of goals and career plans. As this process continues, the worker carves out a role for himself or herself that is consistent with those values.

Margot, an intelligent woman with an industrial engineering degree, had long been interested in occupying leadership positions. (She valued being dominant over other people.) She became the only woman in her high school graduating class to become an industrial engineer. Upon taking her first job in the industry, she told the employment interviewer that she wanted to become a high-ranking executive in the manufacturing field. She has geared her life toward accomplishing that goal.

Today, Margot is the highest-ranking woman in manufacturing (a second-level manager) in her company, a well-known manufacturer of office machines. Margot now says, "I won't rest until I become an officer of this company. I may be the highest-ranking woman in manufacturing, but I'm still too far down in the company to exert the influence I would like."

Conflict of Values

When the demands made by the organization or a superior clash with the basic values of the individual, that person suffers from **person–role conflict.**[14] He or she wants to obey orders, but does not want to perform an act that seems inconsistent with his or her values. A situation such as this might occur when an employee is asked to produce a product that he or she feels is unsafe or of no value to society. A saleswoman in a retail furniture store resigned, giving her boss this explanation:

> I'm leaving because I don't think we're doing right by our customers. We sell mostly to poor people who can't get credit elsewhere. The furniture we sell them is shoddy, overpriced merchandise. But that's only half the problem. We're really in the finance business but we don't admit it to our customers. If people paid cash or obtained bank financing for the furniture they bought from us, we would make no profits. Most of our profits come from interest paid by our customers. I'm very disturbed about what we're doing to people.

The Basic Beliefs We Hold about Others

Beliefs, similar to values, influence our actions on and off the job. One of the most influential set of assumptions about the nature of people, Theory X and Theory Y of Douglas McGregor, illustrates this point. If a supervisor accepts one of these extreme sets of beliefs (or stereotypes) about people, he or she will act differently toward them than if he or she believed the opposite stereotype. These famous assumptions are summarized as follows:[15]

Theory X assumptions

1. The average person dislikes work and therefore will avoid it if he or she can.
2. Because of this dislike of work, most people must be coerced, controlled, directed, or threatened with punishment to get them to put forth enough effort to achieve organizational goals.
3. The average employee prefers to be directed, wishes to shirk responsibility, has relatively little ambition, and highly values job security.

Theory Y assumptions

1. The expenditure of physical and mental effort in work is as natural as play or rest.
2. External control and the threat of punishment are not the only means for bringing about effort toward reaching company objectives. Employees will exercise self-direction and self-control in the service of objectives to which they attach high valence.
3. Commitment to objectives is related to the rewards associated with their achievement.
4. The average person learns, under proper conditions, not only to accept but to seek responsibility.
5. Many employees have the capacity to exercise a high degree of imagination, ingenuity, and creativity in the solution of organizational problems.
6. Under the present conditions of industrial life, the intellectual potentialities of the average person are only partially utilized.

How Do These Assumptions Influence a Manager's Actions?. It is easy to visualize that a Theory X manager would treat employees quite differently than would a Theory Y manager. Here is an example of the difference:

Should a marketing manager harbor Theory X assumptions about sales representatives, he or she might attempt to motivate them with the following set of management practices and behavior:

> We have established sales quotas for each of you. Each year that your quota is reached, the company will pay for a five-day trip for you and your spouse. This will be in addition to your normal vacation. If you meet your quota for five consecutive years, you are almost guaranteed a permanent position with our company. Sales representatives who are unable to meet their quotas for three consecutive quarters will probably not be invited back for a fourth quarter.

In contrast, should a marketing manager harbor Theory Y assumptions about sales representatives, he or she might attempt to lead them in the following manner:

> You and your sales managers will get together on establishing sales quotas for each year. If you achieve your quotas, you will receive extra money. High performance in sales is one important factor in being considered for a management assignment. Another important part of your job besides selling is to keep our product-planning group informed about changes in consumer demand. Many of our new products in the past stemmed directly from the suggestions of sales representatives.

SUMMARY OF KEY POINTS

☐ To understand and deal effectively with people in a job environment, you have to understand general principles about people that apply in a variety of situations. Here we describe some general principles of four key aspects of behavior: perception, learning, motivation, and values and beliefs.

☐ Perception, the organization of sensory information into meaningful experiences, influences job behavior. Perception is influenced by factors within the person, such as motives, needs, and goals. It is also influenced by characteristics of the stimulus, such as distinctiveness, intensity, and frequency. People take many shortcuts to perception, such as denial, stereotyping, the halo effect, expectancy, projection, and perceptual defense.

☐ Classical conditioning is the most elementary form of learning. It occurs when a previously neutral stimulus is associated with a natural (unconditioned) stimulus. Eventually, the neutral stimulus brings forth the unconditioned response. For example, a factory whistle blown just prior to the lunch break induces employees to salivate and experience hunger pangs.

☐ Operant conditioning (or instrumental learning) occurs when a person's spontaneous actions are rewarded or punished, which results in an increase or a decrease in the behavior. Much of human learning occurs through operant conditioning. Complicated sets of skills are frequently learned by modeling or imitation. Such skill repertoires are also learned by behavior shaping, a form of learning in which approximations to the final skill are rewarded. Eventually, only the final skill is rewarded.

☐ Theories of motivation attempt to explain why people behave as they do. Maslow's need hierarchy, despite its limitations, is the theory most widely used to explain work motivation. It contends that people have an internal need pushing them on toward self-actualization. However, needs are arranged into a five-step ladder. Before higher-level needs are activated, certain lower-level needs must be satisfied. In ascending order, the groups of needs are physiological, safety, social, esteem, and self-actualizing (such as self-fulfillment).

☐ Expectancy theory (ET) is a currently popular explanation of work motivation. It assumes that people are decision makers who choose among alternatives by selecting the one that appears to have the biggest personal payoff at the time. The expectancy model has three major components: effort–performance expectancy, performance–outcome expectancy, and valence (importance attached to the potential reward). Motivation is calculated by multiplying numerical values for all three.

☐ Values and beliefs influence job behavior in several ways: (1) people's values lead to goals and objectives; (2) work assignments may conflict with personal values and cause stress and inaction; (3) the assumptions we make about people, such as Theory X versus Theory Y, may influence our treatment of them.

GUIDELINES FOR PERSONAL EFFECTIVENESS

1. An important strategy for helping others to learn is to use operant conditioning, with an emphasis on positive reinforcement. The most basic approach is to give the learner encouragement when he or she makes the right response. At the same time, it is helpful to tactfully point out mistakes to the learner.
2. A generally effective way of helping people to learn complicated skills is for you to serve as an effective model. At the same time, make sure that the learner has the opportunity to observe you.
3. A generally effective strategy for motivating people is to identify the needs that they are trying to satisfy and then to give them an opportunity to satisfy those needs. An important way of improving this process is to apply expectancy theory. Do what you can to increase the expectancies and valences of the people you are trying to motivate. Specifically, you might:
   (a) Help them improve their skills so their effort-to-performance expectancies increase.
   (b) Explain how performance will lead to a reward so their performance-to-outcome expectancies increase.
   (c) Increase the attractiveness of the rewards in order to increase their valences.

DISCUSSION QUESTIONS

1. What is a "general principle of human behavior"?
2. What skills have you learned lately by operant conditioning? By modeling?
3. What kind of positive reinforcement have you received lately? What effect has it had on you?
4. What are three different perceptions people might have about a boss? Why do these differences in perceptions probably exist?
5. How do you think poor and wealthy people differ in their perception of money? Why do these differences in perception exist?

6. Suppose that an 18-year-old person with no work experience and a 50-year-old person with 25 years of supervisory experience took this course. How would their perceptions of this course probably differ?

7. What is the difference between shaping and modeling (or imitation)?

8. How do your psychological needs influence the amount of effort you put forth on the job, or in school?

9. What are your two most active psychological needs these days? How do you know they are active?

10. Give examples of two people who you think are self-actualized. Why did you reach such a conclusion?

11. How would you use expectancy theory to explain whether you will strive for an A in this course?

12. If a person has strong religious values, how might those values influence his or her job behavior?

A Business Psychology Problem
THE SOCIALLY CONSCIOUS RESTAURANT

You work as a restaurant manager for a large chain of quality restaurants. The owner says to you one day, "Let's do something good for society. We'll find 25 people recently released from prison, or on parole, who are likely to have a difficult time finding employment. We'll put them to work in one of our restaurants. You'll be the manager in this new restaurant. Your only employees will be those ex-convicts."

You ask, "Which ex-cons shall we hire?" Your boss answers, "The first 25 to show up for the job. First come, first hired. I don't care about their sex, age, race, appearance, size, schooling, or their reasons for conviction. Just put them on the payroll, train them, and run a first-class, profitable restaurant."

1. What will be your biggest challenge in this assignment?
2. What cautions should you exercise in using general learning principles in training your employees?
3. Is this any way to run a restaurant? Explain.

REFERENCES

[1] Harold J. Leavitt, *Managerial Psychology*, 4th ed. (Chicago: University of Chicago Press, 1978), pp. 25–26.

[2] The first three items on this list are based on Edgar F. Huse and James L. Bowditch, *Behavior in Organizations: A Systems Approach to Managing* (Reading, Mass.: Addison-Wesley, 1973), p. 89.

[3]W. Clay Hamner and Dennis W. Organ, *Organizational Behavior: An Applied Psychological Approach* (Plano, Texas: Business Publications, 1978), pp. 99–100.

[4]A recommended overview of classical conditioning is found in Jerome Kagan and Ernest Haveman, *Psychology: An Introduction*, 4th ed. (New York: Harcourt Brace Jovanovich, 1980), pp. 90–98.

[5]Based on similar information in James L. Gibson, John M. Ivancevich, and James H. Donnelly, Jr., *Organizations: Behavior, Structure, Processes*, 4th ed. (Plano, Texas: Business Publications, 1982), p. 66.

[6]Arnold P. Goldstein and Melvin Sorcher, *Changing Supervisor Behavior* (Elmsford, N. Y.: Pergamon, 1974), p. 26.

[7]Virtually every text about introduction to psychology, human relations, or organizational behavior has a discussion of Maslow's need hierarchy. Two original sources are Abraham H. Maslow, "A Theory of Human Motivation," *Psychological Review* (July 1943), pp. 370–396; and Abraham H. Maslow, *Motivation and Personality* (New York: Harper & Row, 1954).

[8]David J. Rachman and Michael H. Mescon, *Business Today*, 3rd ed. (New York: Random House, 1982), p. 231.

[9]The original explanation of ET as applied to work motivation is Victor H. Vroom, *Work and Motivation* (New York: Wiley, 1964). A concise explanation of ET is the following: Terence R. Mitchell, "Motivational Strategies" in Kendrith M. Rowland and Gerald R. Ferris, *Personnel Management* (Boston: Allyn and Bacon, 1982), pp. 283–285.

[10]Henry L. Tosi and Stephen J. Carroll, *Management*, 2nd ed. (New York: Wiley, 1982), p. 398.

[11]"How Good Is Values Analysis?" *Dun's Review* (March 1981), pp. 118–123.

[12]An important source of information about values clarification is Sidney B. Simon, Leland W. Howe, and Howard Kirschenbaum, *Values Clarification: A Handbook of Practical Strategies for Teachers and Students* (New York: Hart Publishing, 1972).

[13]Robert M. Fulmer, *Practical Human Relations* (Homewood, Ill.: Irwin, 1977), p. 264.

[14]Daniel Katz and Robert L. Kahn, *The Social Psychology of Organizations* (New York: Wiley, 1966), p. 184. See also the second edition of this book, 1978.

[15]Douglas McGregor, *The Human Side of Enterprise* (New York: McGraw-Hill, 1960), pp. 33–48.

SUGGESTED READING

ANDERSON, JOHN R. *Cognitive Psychology and Its Implications.* San Francisco: W. H. Freeman, 1980.

BORGER, ROBERT, and A. E. M. SEABORNE. *The Psychology of Learning*, 2nd ed. New York: Penguin Books, 1982.

BOWER, GORDON H., and ERNEST R. HILGARD. *Theories of Learning*, 5th ed. Englewood Cliffs, N.J.: Prentice-Hall, 1981.

CAELLI, TERRY. *Visual Perception: Theory and Practice*. Elmsford, N.Y.: Pergamon, 1981.

FRANKLIN, ROBERT E. *Human Motivation*. Monterey, Calif.: Brooks/Cole, 1982.

HALL, JOHN F. *An Invitation to Learning and Memory*. Boston: Allyn and Bacon, 1982.

KLEIN, STEPHEN B. *Motivation: Biosocial Approaches*. New York: McGraw-Hill, 1982.

LEVINE, MICHAEL W., and JEREMY M. SHEFNER. *Fundamentals of Sensation and Perception*. Reading, Mass.: Addison-Wesley, 1981.

NORMAN, DONALD A. *Learning and Memory*. San Francisco: W. H. Freeman, 1982.

SCHIFFMAN, HARVEY R. *Sensation and Perception: An Integrated Approach*, 2nd ed. New York: Wiley, 1982.

SMITH, MAURY. *A Practical Guide to Value Clarification*. La Jolla, Calif.: University Associates, 1977.

INDIVIDUAL DIFFERENCES
AND WORK BEHAVIOR

LEARNING OBJECTIVES

After reading and studying this chapter and doing the exercises, you should be able to

1. Understand how individual differences influence job performance.
2. Explain how human intelligence consists of many separate aptitudes.
3. Describe five different ways of improving your learning of written material.
4. Present several examples of how your personality can influence the type of work you are likely to perform well.
5. Explain how vocational interests influence job satisfaction.

Business psychology began with the awareness that individual differences in personal characteristics influence how people will perform on the job. A study of individual differences is as vital today as it was at the turn of the century. A person's basic traits and characteristics have a profound influence on his or her job behavior. The situation in which a person works is also important, but a person often influences the situation. An accurate generalization is that job behavior is always the combined influence of both the person and the situation.

How individual differences influence job performance is illustrated by the mysterious finding that a small percentage of the work force in many fields contributes to most of the extremely good or bad performances. Sales managers have claimed for many years that 20 percent of the sales force makes 80 percent of the sales. In scientific and scholarly fields, about 3 percent of the scientists are said to contribute about 90 percent of the research publications and books. A handful of the people who submit suggestions win the big awards. On the negative side, a small proportion of the work force creates most of the headaches for management, such as high turnover, absenteeism, accidents, and complaints to the union and higher management.

In this chapter we examine some basic aspects of human nuture that have a direct bearing on how well people perform in their jobs and careers. Among the topics discussed will be mental ability, reading skill, personality, and vocational interests. A common theme of the aspects of behavior studied in this chapter is that they are measurable to some extent. You will be given the opportunity to sample several of the types of measuring instruments used by psychologists to study these aspects of human nature.

MENTAL ABILITY

Intelligence, or problem-solving ability, is one of the major differences among people that affects job performance. As common sense would suggest, there is an advantage to being bright in performing a complex job. If a job is dramatically uncomplex, such as stuffing envelopes seven hours per day, being not so bright would be an advantage. The term intelligence, as it is used here, refers to problem-solving ability. Intelligence quotient, or IQ, is in reality just one measure of intelligence, just as classifying a person as having superior intelligence is a measure of intelligence. Because the particular test score called IQ is so widely known, many people regard IQ as synonymous with intelligence.

Intelligence is not a pure characteristic. It includes a variety of specialized aptitudes that contribute to problem-solving ability. At a minimum, intelligence is composed of verbal and numerical abilities. The *Employee Aptitude Survey* (EAS) is a representative, highly researched, series of tests designed to measure problem-solving ability in a job environment. An analysis of its underlying meaning shows that it measures eight different factors. These factors might be regarded as basic components of intelligence. It is worth noting these factors or components, because they are a source of individual differences related to job performance. The eight factors are as follows:[1]

1. **Verbal comprehension:** the ability to use words in thinking and in both spoken and written communications. Good verbal skills are an asset in a wide variety of occupations, including sales representatives, executives, and newspaper reporters.

2. **Numerical comprehension:** the ability to handle numbers, engage in mathematical analysis, and do arithmetic calculations. Among the occupations calling for good numerical comprehension are accounting, computer programming, tax adviser, and engineer.

3. **Pursuit:** the ability to make quick and accurate scanning movements with the eyes. Occupations calling for quick eye movements, such as proofreader, professional card player, and quality-control inspector, would require relatively high aptitude in *pursuit*.

4. **Perceptual speed:** the ability to perceive small detail in a rapid manner and "pick out" such detail from a mass of material. Most occupations do not call for considerable perceptual speed, but it would seem to be an asset for a computer programmer.

5. **Visualization:** the ability to visualize objects in three dimensions. Engineers, designers, drafting technicians, and photographers, to some extent, would need an above-average degree of the mental aptitude called visualization.

6. **Inductive reasoning:** the ability to discover relationships and derive principles by pulling together bits of information. Most higher-level and some medium-level occupations require inductive reasoning. An insurance claims adjuster uses inductive reasoning when he or she pulls together facts to reach conclusions about the probable cause of a fire. So does a mechanic when he or she diagnoses why your car keeps stalling in traffic.

7. **Word fluency:** the ability to produce words rapidly, without regard to meaning or quality. Fluency alone is not particularly helpful on the job, but it does contribute to a person's ability to communicate in speaking and in writing. Fluency appears to contribute to comprehension. It is also important in sales work.

8. **Syntactic evaluation:** the ability to apply principles to arrive at a unique solution. All higher-level occupations require a good deal of syntactic evaluation. For example, if you are a toy designer, you have to apply principles of mechanical engineering to figure out how to make a particular motorized toy operate efficiently within a certain cost limit.

Quick Thinking and Intelligence

It has long been believed that people who think quickly are more intelligent than their slower-thinking counterparts. Saying that someone has a "quick mind" implies that the person can grasp complicated ideas in a short span of time. Studies conducted by a noted psychologist, Hans Eysenck, indicate that highly intelligent people also deal quickly with elementary problems.[2] In a series of experiments conducted in England, subjects were first administered conventional IQ tests. Next they were asked to respond to dots, flashing lights, and other stimuli. In one study, subjects were shown two lines of a different length. The lines were only shown for a brief period of time. Participants in the study then were asked to judge as quickly as possible which line was longer.

The results were clear-cut. Five separate studies indicated that people with high IQs took much less time to make judgments about simple stimuli. One study showed that 4-year-old children showed a similar pattern: the higher their IQ, the more quickly they make accurate judgments on elementary stimuli.

Eysenck concluded that such results point to a biological difference that allows people with high IQs to absorb and process information more quickly than those with lower IQs. He also noted that it is unreasonable to suggest that responses to such stimuli could be biased by culture or social class. Opponents of traditional IQ tests contend that the tests favor white, middle-class children, but Eysenck reasons that there is nothing cultural about dots, lines, or flashing lights (the type of stimuli used in these experiments).

Implications for Your Career. Quick thinking is generally regarded as a desirable attribute for a person holding a responsible job. These experiments provide scientific evidence that quick thinking is most likely indicative of high-quality thinking. If you believe that mental ability can be sharpened with practice, it would be to your advantage to learn to "think on your feet." In contrast, if you regard intelligence as a relatively fixed biological characteristic, it could still be to your advantage to practice thinking quickly. It will help you to appear to have high mental ability.

At this point it may be of interest to you to sample the kind of tasks used to test your mental ability.

A Few Sample Mental Ability Test Questions

Most readers of this book have taken mental ability tests at various stages of schooling or in the process of applying for a job. Nevertheless, there is some value in examining four sample test items of the type that appear on a standardized mental ability test used in business, industry, and other work organizations. Question A measures verbal comprehension; question B measures numerical comprehension; question C measures inductive reasoning; question D measures word fluency. These questions are not taken from the Employee Aptitude Survey, but have a similar format.[3]

A. A cautious person is
   1. wealthy   2. careful   3. ignorant   4. satisfied (   )
B. In the following series, which two numbers should come next?
   16   18   17   20   18   22
   1. 19 and 24   2. 23 and 27   3. 19 and 23   4. 25 and 26 (   )

C. Read the three statements below:
A is lighter than D.
B is heavier than D.
A weighs more than C.
Who is heaviest? (   )

D. You will have three minutes to respond to the following instruction. Write down as many words as you can think of beginning with the letter T.

_____	_____	_____	_____
_____	_____	_____	_____
_____	_____	_____	_____
_____	_____	_____	_____
_____	_____	_____	_____
_____	_____	_____	_____
_____	_____	_____	_____

HOW TO MAKE GOOD USE OF YOUR MENTAL ABILITY

"I can't understand it, Darlene," said Carol. "I know my aptitude test scores are much higher than yours. Yet, you always get better grades than I do. It's certainly not a case of my not wanting to do well in school."

"I think I know the answer to that one," replied Darlene. "I know how to study and you don't. I can tell from having been your roommate for over a year. I may not be brilliant, but I'm careful to make good use of the intelligence I do have."

The conversation between Darlene and Carol points to an important fact about human intelligence. Your method of acquiring information exerts a big influence on how effectively you use your basic intellectual abilities. High intelligence makes it possible for you to learn quickly, but high intelligence does not guarantee that you will acquire good learning skills.

In the preceding chapter we explained *how* people learn. Here we will look at ten important principles of learning that will help you make good use of your basic intelligence, both in school and on the job. All these principles relate to remembering what you have learned.[4] They are based on thousands of studies conducted by experimental and educational psychologists.

1. *Concentrate.* Not much learning takes place unless you concentrate carefully on what you are learning. Concentration is basically thinking. Many failures in school are due more to poor concentration than to low mental ability. Concentration improves your ability to do both mental

and physical tasks. When your concentration increases, it is much easier to handle a cue stick in pool or balance your checkbook.

Walter Pauk, the director of a reading-study center, notes that one enemy of concentration is indecision: "Indecision about when to study and which subject to study first is not only a great time-waster, but also a sure way to create a negative attitude toward studying."[5] The same idea has relevance to the job. If you spend time wondering which job task (if any) you should do for the balance of the day, you will probably do a poor job.

Personal problems also interfere with concentration. You will not make good use of your intelligence if you are preoccupied with personal problems. After you have taken some constructive action on your problem, you will then be in a better position to learn or perform well. Personal problems carried over to the job also make for a high accident risk. One man nipped off the tip of his index finger with a paper cutter while thinking about his delinquent car payments.

2. *Use motivated interest.* You learn best when you are interested in the problem facing you. If your answer is, "This subject bores me," or "So far I don't know what interests me," this principle still applies. In any situation, you will probably be able to find something of interest to you personally. Look for some relationship between the information at hand and your personal welfare. For instance, as you read this chapter you might say to yourself, "Where do I fit in? What is my mental makeup? How extroverted am I?" and so on.

3. *Use selectivity.* William James, the famous philosopher and psychologist, said, "The essence of genius is to know what to overlook." You cannot learn everything brought to your attention in school or on the job. Be selective. Try to determine which is the most important. Your course instructor will often alert you to the most important information in a course. You boss will often alert you to the most important parts of your job.

4. *Intention to remember.* I have played cards with people who seem brilliant in terms of their ability to remember which cards in the deck have been played. One of the best of these players told me her secret of knowing which cards have been played: "As each card is turned up, just look at it carefully and try to remember it." With practice, most people can apply this simple method to their schoolwork or jobs. *Try* to remember the names of important people in your company. It will impress other people.

5. *Use meaningful organization.* When you have to learn large batches of information, the best method is to organize it into chunks that make sense to you. For instance, in studying portions of this book, you might make such arbitrary groupings as "Ideas I can use for self-development" versus "Ideas that can help me deal with other people."

6. *Rely on the magic number seven.* The immediate memory span of an adult seems fixed at about the number seven. Most people can remember up to about seven categories of most things. One researcher noted that it is probably not coincidental that we have seven days of the week, seven primary colors, seven deadly sins, and seven notes on the musical scale. When you are trying to learn new information, arrange it into seven large chunks. New bits of information can be added on to these seven chunks. An example: If you are forced to give a speech without using notes, organize it into seven major parts.

7. *Acquire the right background.* The more you know about a subject, the easier it is to acquire new information. Knowledge gives you certain "hooks" on which to hang new information. If your hobby is studying antique automobiles, it will be easy for you to learn the names and identifying information about the next generation of automobiles.

8. *Use recitation.* As Pauk states,[6] "There is no principle that is more important than *recitation* for transferring material from the short-term memory to the long-term memory." If you want to remember some information after reading it, say it out loud to yourself in your own words. Recitation interferes with speed reading, but retention is more important than speed in many situations. To illustrate, if you are trying to master a precise subject like bookkeeping or computer programming, comprehension is much more important than speed.

9. *Use distributed practice.* An effective way of learning something is a little bit at a time. Most people retain more, and thus make better use of their intelligence, when they break up learning with frequent rest periods. (Some students overdo this principle and use too many rest periods.) Assume that you are trying to learn some difficult company procedures. It would be best to study these for about 15 minutes at a time, and then do something on the job that is relatively easy for you. The principle of distributed practice helps explain why cramming for exams is inferior to studying over a longer period of time.

10. *Let things jell in your mind.* Your long-term memory is likely to improve if you allow one set of facts to jell in your mind before attempting to learn another set of facts. Psychologists call this principle *consolidation*. It helps explain the value of reviewing material immediately after your first exposure to it.

OTHER IMPORTANT APTITUDES AND SKILLS

Intellectual ability is important for many jobs, but so are other abilities or aptitudes.[7] Many higher-level jobs also call for nonintellectual abilities such as eye–hand coordination. For instance, these days many jobs require the

Many higher-level jobs call for non-intellectual abilities such as eye-hand coordination.

ability to operate a computer. People show wide individual differences in their ability to perform such tasks. For instance, some people can repair office machines by themselves, even if it is not part of their job. Others would have to call a maintenance worker to elevate a swivel chair.

Aptitude and ability are related, but not identical, ideas. An **aptitude** is basically a native ability to perform some task, such as singing, dancing, or fixing machinery. An **ability** is a current capability that is partially based on native talent and experience. You might have good aptitude for rifle shooting because of your steady hand and keen vision. But your shooting ability might not be developed because of lack of practice. The terms aptitude and ability are often used interchangeably.

Mechanical Ability

Much machinery used in offices and plants can be operated by simply pushing a button or flipping a switch. Yet many other technical jobs still call for mechanical know-how. Office machine repair technicians (sometimes called

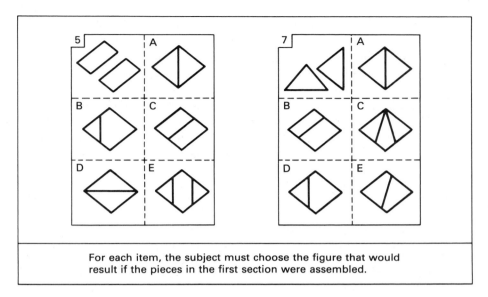

For each item, the subject must choose the figure that would result if the pieces in the first section were assembled.

FIGURE 3-1

Sample items from the Revised Minnesota Paper Form Board. (Reproduced by permission. Copyright © 1941–1970 by the Psychological Corporation, New York, N.Y. All rights reserved.)

field service representatives) are generally selected, in part, on the basis of their mechanical ability. People who do not have high mechanical aptitude can develop their mechanical skills through continued practice. It is important not to block out future learning with the defense, "I have no mechanical aptitude."

A reasonable degree of mechanical ability is also helpful in everyday office situations. It is not uncommon, for example, for a photocopying machine to jam. By "poking around" inside the machine, it can often be brought back to functioning without having to wait for a service visit. Sample test questions from a standard test used to measure mechanical aptitude are presented in Figure 3–1.

Psychomotor Abilities

Eye–hand coordination, dexterity, manipulative ability, and the like are also important in the world of work. People show extreme variations in this ability. Outstanding baseball, golf, and tennis players are often people who are gifted in eye–hand coordination. As with most human abilities, the term psychomotor can be broken down into a group of separate skills. Following are three of the many components of psychomotor ability:

- **Control precision:** tasks requiring finely controlled muscular adjustments, such as moving a gauge to a precise setting.
- **Manual dexterity:** tasks involving skillful arm and hand movements in manipulating large objects under conditions of speed. Many assembly-line jobs require good manual dexterity.
- **Reaction time:** the ability to respond to a signal. Fast reaction times are required for truck drivers and process control technicians. (The latter individual watches computerized dials, which may indicate when something like a malfunctioning machine requires immediate attention, for example.)

Visual Skills

Blind people are capable of good performance in a wide range of jobs, including those of a computer programmer or psychotherapist. Yet most jobs involve the use of vision. Visual skills are especially important to successful job performance in such jobs as production inspector, proofreader, or vehicle operator. People show a wide range of visual ability, even after wearing corrective lenses.

The importance of good vision to job success is illustrated by the information presented in Table 3–1. People with adequate vision are more likely to be considered above-average employees than people with inadequate vision. The test of vision used is the ortho-rater, an instrument similar to one you might find in an optometrist's office or a motor vehicle bureau. The "total" figures help explain the results of the study. Sixty-five percent of above-

TABLE 3–1
How visual ability influences job performance

Job Category	Percent of Above-Average Employees among Those with:	
	Adequate Vision	Inadequate Vision
Clerical and administrative	71	37
Inspection and close work	62	50
Vehicle operator	59	45
Machine operator	63	45
Laborer	67	34
Mechanic and skilled tradesman	69	57
Total	65	46

SOURCE: Ernest J. McCormick and Daniel Ilgen, *Industrial Psychology,* 7th ed., Prentice-Hall, Inc., Englewood Cliffs, N.J., 1980, p. 156.

average employees have adequate vision. In contrast, forty-six percent of employees rated above average have inadequate vision.

Physical Skills

People also show a wide range of physical abilities, and those differences can influence your ability to perform your job. An X-ray technician, for example, must have to stand up most of the work day. He or she cannot sit down while administering X-rays to patients. Many jobs inside and outside a factory or mill require good physical condition. Many postal carriers have had to resign because of bad backs or ailing feet. A butcher may be required to manipulate cuts of meat weighing up to 200 pounds.

Many physical skills, such as the ability to lift heavy objects, can be developed. In the past, women were excluded from certain occupations, such as telephone "lineman," because it was assumed that they lacked the appropriate physical skills. Now many telephone pole climbers are female. With practice, a male or female can learn to scale a telephone pole.

INDIVIDUAL DIFFERENCES AND PERSONALITY

"Gladys, we're going to have to fire you," said her boss. "You are certainly a competent X-ray technician, but the doctors and nurses in our hospital don't want to have anything to do with you. As we've discussed so many times before, you are forever fighting with others. We like your work, but we can't tolerate the way you deal with people. Come back to us when you get your personality quirks straightened out."

This anecdote illustrates an important point about human nature on the job: most failures on the job are not attributed to a person's amount of intelligence or mechanical skill (or technical ability in general), but to personality characteristics. The subject of personality must therefore be given some consideration in any serious study of business psychology.

In the popular sense, the concept of personality is used to evaluate an individual's manner of relating to people. An effective way to insult another person is to say, "Don't ask me to work with him. He has a horrible personality." A psychologist uses the term personality not to make value judgments, but to describe those "persistent and enduring *behavior patterns* of an individual that tend to be expressed in a wide variety of situations."[8] Your personality is what makes you unique as an individual. Your walk, your talk, your appearance, your speech, and your inner values and conflicts all contribute to your personality.

Most failures on the job are attributed to personality characteristics.

Personality Traits and Needs

Among the many ways to study individual differences in personality is to observe how people differ on important traits. Over 40 years ago, Henry Murray developed a list of human needs that led to personality traits.[9] **A need** is an internal striving or urge to do something. Thus, if you have a strong *need* to dominate people, a noticeable personality trait of yours will be **dominance.**

Personality traits and needs influence people to act in certain ways. The dominant person will gravitate toward leadership positions or frequently get into arguments with others. Table 3–2 describes nine important personality needs. To the right of each need is a sampling of the type of behavior that corresponds to that particular need. Each need results in a propensity to behave in a particular way. The needs we have chosen to include in this list are those most likely to influence you in your work and personal life.

TABLE 3-2
How personality traits based on needs influence behavior

Personality Trait Based on Particular Need		Example of Type of Behavior Shown by Person Who Has Strong Need
Achievement	To accomplish something difficult; to win over others	Tries hard in competitive sports; runs for political office; sets up own business
Affiliation	To seek out close relationships with others; to be a loyal friend	Joins many social groups; tries to be "one of the gang" at work
Aggression	To attack, injure, or punish others; to overcome people	Uses hard-sell tactics as a sales representative; gets into fights with people off the job
Autonomy	To act independently and be free of constraints	Takes job as insurance claims adjuster; feels uncomfortable when closely supervised
Deference	To admire and support a superior or other person in authority; to conform to custom	Prefers to call older people by title (Mister, Professor, Doctor); makes excellent soldier and respectful subordinate
Dominance	To influence others toward your way of thinking, often by forceful methods	Often takes over in meetings; volunteers to be the leader; good at the hard sell
Nurturance	To help, support, take care of weak and needy people	Works well with disadvantaged people; often overprotective of children or subordinates
Order	To put things in order; to achieve arrangement, balance, neatness, and precision	Keeps work area neat; writes careful reports; keeps good files; works well with computer
Power	Strong need to control other people and resources; wants fame and recognition	Orients life around rising to the top; likes to look and act powerful through choice of clothing and car

Two Major Dimensions of Personality

Personality is a far-reaching field of study. Each theory of personality itself could be the subject matter for an entire book. Much of what Sigmund Freud contributed to modern thought about human behavior is a study of human personality. Personality theorists have used a number of methods to study human personality. People have been observed at work, play, and love. People have been administered paper and pencil tests, interviewed, or asked to interpret ink blots, make drawings of their parents, or take drugs under controlled circumstances—all in the interest of studying personality in a systematic manner.

Personality as it relates to the job has been the most extensively studied with paper and pencil tests. Despite the fact that people can fake many personality tests if they want to, such objective measures still contribute to our understanding of how differences in personality potentially influence job behavior. Two major dimensions of human personality, emotionality and extroversion–introversion, will be discussed here. They have been singled out for two reasons. First, they are highly important in a job environment. Second, they have been the subject of extensive research. Sample items from a personality test frequently used in industry are shown in Figure 3–2.

Emotionality. Also called neuroticism, emotionality* is a broad general trait of personality that helps explain a wide range of job and personal behavior. Among the individual differences partially accounted for by emotionality are "emotional instability; changeability in mood; sensitivity to environmental stress; tendencies toward guilt, worry, anxiety, and lower self-esteem; feelings of fatigue and, more generally, concern about physical health; and experience and tension."[10]

In general, a person who is not too highly emotional makes a better worker at all job levels. Many movie directors, artists, entrepreneurs, and rock singers appear overemotional on the surface, but they have more emotional control than meets the eye. It takes good control over tension, anxiety, and environmental stress to turn in a superior performance week after week.

		Mostly True	Mostly False
1.	It is extremely difficult for me to turn down a sales representative when that individual is a nice person.	_____	_____
2.	I express criticism freely.	_____	_____
3.	Work is no place to let your feelings show.	_____	_____
4.	A weakness of mine is that I'm too nice a person.	_____	_____

FIGURE 3–2
Sample of test questions designed to measure assertiveness.

*We use the term emotionality rather than neuroticism here for an important reason. In recent years many practicing psychiatrists and psychologists have decided that the term *neurotic* is too general a label. In 1978, the American Psychiatric Association discontinued the official use of the term neurotic. Instead, it is preferable to use more specific descriptions of a person's behavior, such as "he is phobic about climbing on ladders or flying in airplanes."

The general trait of emotionality is also closely related to emotional arousal. Job effectiveness increases for most people when they are at the right state of emotional arousal. People vary markedly in what constitutes a useful amount of arousal. One woman may need to be highly aroused in order to call on sales prospects. Another woman might be able to make such calls in a state of low arousal. A person who is in a high state of arousal does not require too much pressure from the environment in order to perform well. A person already at a high state of arousal might become ineffective if too much pressure were present in the environment. Thus, a "nervous" person might perform poorly under high pressure.

Extroversion–Introversion. The most widely known dimension (or continuum) of human personality is that of extroversion versus introversion. Its technical meaning is not too different from its popular meaning. Extroversion refers to the extent to which a person wants to receive stimulation from the outside world.

Extroverts have a strong need for stimulation in the form of social activities, exciting adventures, loud colors and noises, and even drugs. Introverts desire (or require) less stimulation and tend to be more withdrawn than extroverts. There is some truth to the stereotype that most sales representatives are extroverted, whereas most chemists are introverted.

Extroversion versus introversion represents end points, or extremes, on one major dimension of personality. Most people are really **ambiverts**, a mixture of extroversion and introversion. The situation in which a person is placed influences his or her tendency toward being extroverted or introverted, despite a general leaning in one direction. It is not unheard of for a reserved, scholarly individual to shout wildly at a basketball game. Some socially introverted individuals become aggressive and outgoing on the job; they turn from a social pussycat into a business tiger.

W. Clay Hamner and Dennis W. Organ provide a concise analysis of the job implications of individual differences in extroversion and introversion. They observe,[11]

> In short, extroverts are more apt to suffer—either in terms of lower satisfaction or deterioration in performance—from sensory deprivation or understimulation; introverts more often fall prey to overstimulation, sensory overload, and excitation. As with other dimensions of personality, the differences do not become striking until one compares groups at opposite ends of the distribution.

Another important implication of differences in extroversion–introversion according to Hamner and Organ is that introverts are easier to condition. That is, they are more ready to change their behavior in a positive direction if given a worthwhile reward. An introvert, all things being equal, is more likely to improve his or her attendance if given a bonus for good attendance.

TABLE 3–3

Key personal traits of people related to combinations of emotionality and extroversion–introversion

High Emotionality Combined with Introversion	High Emotionality Combined with Extroversion
People in this category tend toward being moody, anxious, rigid, sober, pessimistic, reserved, unsociable, and quiet	People in this category tend toward being touchy, restless, aggressive, excitable, changeable, impulsive, optimistic, and active
Low Emotionality Combined with Introversion	*Low Emotionality Combined with Extroversion*
People in this category tend toward being passive, careful, thoughtful, peaceful, controlled, reliable, even-tempered, and calm	People in this category tend toward being sociable, outgoing, talkative, responsive, easygoing, lively, care-free, and assertive

SOURCE: Adapted from H. J. Eysenck, *Eysenck on Extroversion,* John Wiley & Sons, Inc., New York, 1973, p. 27.

Combinations of Extroversion–Introversion and Emotionality. People can be roughly typed by their standing on the two dimensions of extroversion-introversion *and* emotionality. H. J. Eysenck has developed a list of personality traits with four different combinations of extroversion–introversion and emotionality to characterize people. Table 3–3 summarizes his analysis. It is apparent that people with low emotionality, whether introverted or extroverted, would make good employees if placed in the right job, assuming that they were otherwise qualified.

Personality Types and Occupational Choice

Individual differences in personality can also influence our choice of occupation. According to the theory of John Holland, people tend to choose a career to match their personalities.[12] Furthermore, if people are able to find a career matching their personalities, they are likely to be happier on the job and stay longer with their work.[13] An elementary example is that, if your personality type is classified as *artistic,* you will be happier as a photographer than as an accountant. Table 3–4 lists and defines Holland's personality types and a sampling of occupations associated with each type.

One important criticism of this theory of personality type and occupational choice is that it is too simplistic. Some occupations require a combination of two or more personality types. For example, an accountant who sets up his or her own firm would need to be both "Enterprising" and "Conventional."

TABLE 3–4

Holland's personality types and corresponding sample occupations

Personality Type	Description	Sample Occupations
Realistic	Likes work requiring physical strength; tends to avoid interpersonal and verbal types of work; prefers task problems that are concrete rather than abstract	Engineer, carpenter, architect, forester, machinist, printer, agriculturist
Intellectual	Prefers tasks involving the intellectual processes such as thinking and comprehension; tends to avoid work activities that require domination and persuasion of people or close interpersonal contact; tends to be more introverted than extroverted	Physician, home economist, paramedic, anthropologist, veterinarian, biologist, medical radiographer
Social	Exhibits skill in interpersonal relations and chooses work situations requiring interpersonal relationships; prefers work activities that help other people such as teaching or therapeutic service; tends to avoid high stress, intellectual problem-solving work activities	Minister, teacher, psychologist, counselor, dental assistant, nurse, social worker
Artistic	Tends to dislike structure, to be more introverted than extroverted, and to exhibit a high degree of femininity; expresses feelings and may act on impulse	Actor or actress, musician, photographer, artist, journalist, cosmetologist
Enterprising	Desires power and status and likes work activities that involve manipulating and dominating others; tends to have good verbal skills	Attorney, salesperson, politician, manager, administrator, real estate agent, public relations worker, economist
Conventional	Prefers structure and order with rules and regulations governing the work activities; exhibits much self-control; identifies with power and status	Secretary, accountant, business teacher, clerk, data-processing worker, financial advisor

SOURCE: Synthesis of Holland's work prepared by A. Christine Parham, *Basic Psychology for the Work Life,* South-Western Publishing Co., Cincinnati, Ohio, 1983, p. 294. The original source material is from John L. Holland, *Making Vocational Choices: A Theory of Careers,* Prentice-Hall, Inc., Englewood Cliffs, N.J., 1973.

VOCATIONAL INTERESTS

An industrial psychologist was in the process of interpreting the results of his vocational interest test to a tool and die maker. The latter had recently taken the test as part of a program in career counseling. The psychologist told the tool and die maker that his test profile reflected very low interests in the mechanical, science, and mathematical scales, a very unusual pattern for a tool and die maker. In contrast, he showed dominant interests in much more socially oriented occupations, such as public speaking, social service, and teaching. With a burst of emotion, the tool and die maker exclaimed,

> That's it. You've hit it. I've hated being a tool and die maker all my life. I'll never forget the first day of my apprenticeship. As my first project, I was forced to file a metal cube. The sound made me sick. It's been a lifetime of agony. I hate coming to work, but tool and die making is all I know.

This unfortunate gentleman illustrates how a person's basic vocational interests influence job satisfaction. When people perform work that coincides with their basic interests and preferences, they tend to be happier. To work in a job not in line with your interests misdirects human energy. An interest is a relatively stable disposition about a person. Most people who make their living by inventing and developing products have had a lifelong interest in tinkering with new mechanical ideas. Vocational interests, or preferences, are another major source of individual differences on the job.

Measuring Interests

Vocational interests or preferences are typically measured by the use of interest tests. Such a measuring instrument usually requires the person whose interests are being tested to indicate the strength of his or her interests in such things as various jobs, recreational activities, or hobbies. A person might be presented three activities and asked to indicate which activity he likes the least, and which one the most. A simpler approach is to ask the person the extent to which he likes or dislikes the activity in question. Representative interest test items are shown in Figure 3–3 and 3–4.

Areas of Interest

Interest testing is a highly specialized activity. An almost infinite number of combinations of interests is possible. Computerized scoring now helps simplify the task of the counselor in scoring and interpreting interest tests. One common feature of the scoring of interest tests is that they provide you with a rating or score on a number of basic interest scales. These basic scales are labeled in a manner that fits the popular meaning of the terms used.

1. Actor	L	I	D
2. Aviator	L	I	D
3. Architect	L	I	D
4. Astronomer	L	I	D
5. Athletic director	L	I	D
6. Auctioneer	L	I	D
7. Author of novel	L	I	D
8. Author of scientific book	L	I	D
9. Auto sales representative	L	I	D
10. Auto mechanic	L	I	D

FIGURE 3–3

Type of test items found on the Strong–Campbell Interest Inventory test. In this section of the test, the subject indicates whether he or she would like (L), dislike (D), or be indifferent to (I) working in each occupation.

In other words, most of the basic scales are self-explanatory. If you scored highly on the "agriculture" scale, you could assume that your interests are similar to people in agricultural occupations. If you scored low on an "artistic" scale, you might assume that your occupational interests do not match those of people with high artistic interests. The Strong–Campbell Interest Inventory (the new version of the Strong Vocational Interest Blank) has 23 basic scales in its most widely used version. Separate scales are used for men and women. The Kuder Preference Record has 10 scales. The Vocational Preference Inventory of John L. Holland, discussed previously, has 6 basic scales. A comparison of the scales for these three interest inventories is shown in Table 3–5.

One of the many ways of interpreting your own profile is to compare it with the profile of members of various occupational groups. Average profiles of these occupational groups are provided by the developers of the in-

	Most	Least
A. Read a romantic story	_____	A. _____
B. Read a murder mystery	_____	B. _____
C. Read a science fiction story	_____	C. _____
D. Repair a broken bicycle	_____	D. _____
E. Cook a fine dinner	_____	E. _____
F. Refinish a piece of furniture	_____	F. _____

FIGURE 3–4

Type of test items found of the Kuder Preference Record, another widely used interest test. The person taking the test is asked to indicate for each set of three activities the one he or she would most and least like to do.

TABLE 3-5
Basic interest areas measured by three widely used interest tests

Strong–Campbell Interest Inventory	Kuder Preference Record	Vocational Preference Inventory
Agriculture	Outdoor	Realistic
Nature	Mechanical	Intellectual
Adventure	Computational	Social
Military activities	Scientific	Artistic
Mechanical activities	Persuasive	Enterprising
Science	Artistic	Conventional
Mathematics	Literary	
Medical science	Musical	
Music–Dramatics	Social service	
Art	Clerical	
Writing		
Teaching		
Social service		
Athletics		
Domestic arts		
Religious activities		
Public speaking		
Law–Politics		
Merchandising		
Sales		
Business management		
Office practices		

terest tests. Assume that you are a 19-year-old male who wants to enter a career in medical technology. Specifically, you want to be an X-ray technician. If your interest profile is similar to that of X-ray technicians, you can infer that such people have a pattern of likes and dislikes similar to yours. If you also have the ability to perform such work, it would seem that the field of medical technology is a realistic vocational choice for you.

IMPLICATIONS OF INDIVIDUAL DIFFERENCES ON THE JOB

Our entire book could be devoted to a discussion of the dimensions of individual differences related to job performance. We know that individual differences exist and that organizations must pay attention to those differences in order to stay competitive. Individual differences moderate or influence how people respond to many things about their job. A company might install air conditioning, considered to be badly needed by 80 percent of the work force. Twenty percent of the employees would probably grumble that the office or factory is too cold. Five of the many ways in which individual differences have important implications for running an organization will be noted here.[14]

1. *People differ in job performance.* How a person performs on a job results from many factors from within and outside the individual. Differences in job performance are often traceable to variations in some of the dimensions of individual differences described in this chapter. Lillian and Larry may be the same age and education, but Lillian may outperform Larry as a computer programmer because she is brighter and more introverted. Her characteristics combine to give her a higher aptitude for computer programming than Larry possesses.

2. *People differ in the importance that they attach to internal job rewards.* People with a love of work are looking for stimulating, exciting, or **enriched** jobs. About one-third of the work force is not looking for stimulating, exciting work. They prefer jobs that require a minimum of mental involvement and responsibility. Some people prefer to daydream on the job and find their self-fulfillment through recreational and family life. For such individuals (the opposite of work addicts), a repetitive job is the most pleasing.

3. *People differ in the style of leadership that they prefer and need.* Many individuals like as much freedom as possible on the job and can function well under such leadership. Other individuals want to be supervised closely by their manager. People also vary with respect to the amount of supervision that they require. In general, less competent, less motivated, and less experienced workers need more supervision. One of the biggest headaches facing a manager is to supervise people who need close supervision but who resent it when it is administered.

4. *People differ in their need for contact with other people.* As a by-product of their personality traits and vocational interests, people vary widely in how much people contact they need on the job to keep them satisfied. Some people can work alone all day and remain highly productive. Others become restless unless they are engaged in business or social conversation with another employee. Sometimes a business luncheon is scheduled more out of a manager's need for social contact than out of a need for discussing job problems.

5. *People differ in their amount of commitment and loyalty to the firm.* Many employees are so committed to their employers that they act as if they were part owners of the firm. As a consequence, committed and loyal employees are very concerned about producing quality goods and

services. And they maintain very good records of attendance and punctuality, which helps reduce the cost of doing business. At the other extreme, some employees feel very little commitment or loyalty toward their employer. They feel no pangs of guilt when they produce scrap or when they miss work for trivial reasons. One reason so many Japanese companies have been so productive is that they typically have a loyal and committed work force.

SUMMARY OF KEY POINTS

☐ Business psychology began with the awareness that individual differences in personal characteristics influence how people will perform on the job. A study of individual differences is still of major importance today. This chapter concentrates on dimensions of human behavior that have a big impact on job performance.

☐ Mental ability, or intelligence, is related to good performance in a wide variety of medium- and higher-level occupations. Among the most important components of human intelligence are verbal comprehension, numerical comprehension, visualization, inductive reasoning, word fluency, and syntactic evaluation. Quick thinking is usually indicative of high intelligence. One way of making good use of your mental abilities is to practice good habits of learning and remembering. Among the more important habits described here are (1) learn to concentrate, (2) use motivated interest, (3) try to remember, and (4) use recitation.

☐ In addition to intellectual ability, other important skills related to job performance are mechanical ability, psychomotor abilities, visual skills, and physical skills. Many high-level jobs call for some manual skills, particularly with respect to operating a computer.

☐ Personality refers to those persistent and enduring behavior patterns of an individual that are expressed in a wide variety of situations. Certain needs of people, such as the need to be dominant over others, are often transformed into personality traits. Such traits then influence you to behave in certain ways, such as trying to control other workers.

☐ Two major dimensions of personality that relate to job performance are degree of emotionality and extroversion–introversion. Different combinations of high versus low emotionality and extroversion versus introversion result in relatively predictable personality traits. For example, people low on emotionality but high on extroversion tend to be sociable, talkative, responsible, and assertive. Your personality type can be influential in determining the type of work that you will find satisfying, as summarized in Table 3–4.

☐ Vocational interests and preferences are also closely related to job satisfaction: work that fits your interests tends to be satisfying. Such interests can be measured accurately with standardized interest tests (assuming that the person taking the test is candid).

☐ The implications of individual differences on the job include the fact that people differ in these ways: (1) how well they perform on the job; (2) the importance they attach to internal rewards; (3) the style of leadership they prefer and need; (4) their need for contact with people; and (5) their degree of loyalty and commitment.

GUIDELINES FOR PERSONAL EFFECTIVENESS

1. If you are an exceptionally good problem solver (a very bright person), it should help you perform well in most high-level jobs. However, it is important to recognize that most problems in business call for concrete solutions rather than abstract discussion.

2. Your degree of emotionality and extroversion or introversion can have a profound influence on your job adjustment. It is important to develop a healthy degree of emotionality and an appropriate degree of introversion or extroversion for the type of work that you are or will be doing.

3. Your main concern with your basic intelligence should be in making the best use of your capability. The suggestions in this chapter about improving your retention of information should be helpful in this regard. Information presented in other chapters in this book should also help you to make the best use of your intelligence (particularly, information about communication skills and work habits).

4. One way of increasing your chances for success and satisfaction in your career is to develop intense interest in a particular occupation. It may require much exploration on your part to find such an occupation. Along the same lines, your chances of having a satisfying career increase if you find an occupation that matches your personality.

DISCUSSION QUESTIONS

1. What are three important ways in which you are different than most other people?

2. What are two occupations you think require a very high degree of problem-solving ability? Explain your answer.

3. Can you think of a fairly high level occupation that probably does not require a high degree of intelligence? Explain your answer.

4. Do you know anybody who seems to be very intelligent, yet is not effective in his or her job? What seems to be that person's problem?

5. Why is job performance so highly influenced by personality factors?

6. Where do you rate on (a) extroversion–introversion, and (b) emotionality?

7. How would you define the term "vocational interest"?

8. Which of the needs listed in Table 3–2 do you think are very important for a leader to possess? Why?

9. If you took the interest tests listed in Table 3–5, on which scales would you probably score very high? Why?

10. Describe a type of individual difference not discussed in this chapter that in your opinion influences job performance.

A Business Psychology Case
WHO WOULD BE A GOOD COUPON SORTER?[15]

The R.G. Blair Company specializes in the distribution and redemption of grocery store discount coupons. At the heart of its operation is a huge coupon sorting department. The task of sorting coupons into appropriate boxes is performed manually by men and women employees of different ages. Each coupon sorter is surrounded by a never-ending supply of thousands of coupons. Each day, each hour, the work is the same—sorting coupons into their appropriate boxes and sending the boxes on to the next department responsible for their processing.

One day Jennie Kent, manager of the coupon sorting department, was visited by Lance McGraw, her counterpart in another location of the firm. "Thanks so much for allowing me to visit your operation," said Lance. "As I mentioned over the phone, I am really curious about how you folks are running your coupon sorting department. You seem to be doing well, and we're having lots of trouble."

"Thanks for the compliment," said Jennie. "But what kind of trouble are you having?"

"Our problem is turnover. It's vicious. We're having a tough time keeping employees on the job for more than a few months. We only have three satisfactory employees in the department who have stayed with us over a year."

"Lance, what do you see as the basic problem?" said Jennie.

"It must obviously be the job itself. It's a nightmare for the average person. The job isn't even clean. After a while a lot of the ink on those coupons comes off on your hands and clothing. The employees are forced to wear smocks and gloves unless they want stained clothing and hands. The job re-

ARE YOU A HIGH OR A LOW?

To test your own sensation-seeking tendencies, try this shortened version of one of Marvin Zuckerman's earlier scales. For each of the 13 items, circle the choice, A or B, that best describes your likes or dislikes, or the way you feel. Instructions for scoring appear at the end of the test.

1. A. I would like a job that requires a lot of traveling.
   B. I would prefer a job in one location.

2. A. I am invigorated by a brisk, cold day.
   B. I can't wait to get indoors on a cold day.

3. A. I get bored seeing the same old faces.
   B. I like the comfortable familiarity of everyday friends.

4. A. I would prefer living in an ideal society in which everyone is safe, secure, and happy.
   B. I would have preferred living in the unsettled days of our history.

5. A. I sometimes like to do things that are a little frightening.
   B. A sensible person avoids activities that are dangerous.

6. A. I would not like to be hypnotized.
   B. I would like to have the experience of being hypnotized.

7. A. The most important goal of life is to live it to the fullest and experience as much as possible.
   B. The most important goal of life is to find peace and happiness.

8. A. I would like to try parachute-jumping.
   B. I would never want to try jumping out of a plane, with or without a parachute.

9. A. I enter cold water gradually, giving myself time to get used to it.
   B. I like to dive or jump right into the ocean or a cold pool.

10. A. When I go on a vacation, I prefer the comfort of a good room and bed.
    B. When I go on a vacation, I prefer the change of camping out.

11. A. I prefer people who are emotionally expressive even if they are a bit unstable.
    B. I prefer people who are calm and even-tempered.

12. A. A good painting should shock or jolt the senses.
    B. A good painting should give one a feeling of peace and security.

13. A. People who ride motorcycles must have some kind of unconscious need to hurt themselves.
    B. I would like to drive or ride a motorcycle.

Scoring

Count one point for each of the following items that you have circled: 1A, 2A, 3A, 4B, 5A, 6B, 7A, 8A, 9B, 10B, 11A, 12A, 13B. Add up your total and compare it with the norms below.

1 - 3	Very low on sensation-seeking
4 - 5	Low
6 - 9	Average
10 - 11	High
12 - 13	Very high

Although the test gives some indication of a person's rating, it is not a highly reliable measure. One reason is, of course, that the test has been abbreviated. Another is that the norms are based largely on the scores of college students who have taken the test. As people get older, their scores on sensation-seeking tend to go down.

Readers who would like to take a more precise measure and contribute to Zuckerman's need for normative data may write to him at the Department of Psychology, University of Delaware, Newark, Delaware 19711. He requests that you send a self-addressed, stamped, 8½-by-11-inch envelope, which he will return to you with the latest form for his Sensation-Seeking Scale. When you mail in the answer sheet with another stamped envelope, he will send back a complete analysis based on your own age and sex.

FIGURE 3–5
Reprinted with permission from *Psychology Today*, February, 1978.

minds me of raking leaves after a fall rainstorm. There's no end to it. Just nonstop coupons."

"What screening devices has your personnel department used for the employees?" inquired Jennie.

"We try to be as thorough as we can in terms of the type of people we hire for the job of coupon sorter. We check references. We even use personnel tests. We look for solid citizens who are fairly bright."

Jennie responded, "Lance, I think I've located your problem."

1. What do you think is the problem that Jennie has located?
2. What level of mental ability do you think would be the most appropriate for a coupon sorter?
3. What type of personality (or which personality traits) would be best suited for the job of coupon sorter?

A Business Psychology Self-examination Exercise
ARE YOU A SENSATION SEEKER?

Psychologist Marvin Zuckerman has made a long-term study of the search for high sensation[16] (see Figure 3–5). People who seek high sensation seem to crave all kinds of sensation, from drug trips and spicy foods to risky sports and sexual adventure. They also tend to crave excitement on the job. Sensation seeking is thus another dimension of personality that could influence job performance.

1. How does your score compare to your self-evaluation of your sensation-seeking tendencies?
2. Name two occupations in which high sensation seeking would probably be related to good job performance.
3. Name two occupations in which low sensation seeking would probably be related to good job performance.

REFERENCES

[1]The Employee Aptitude Survey is published by Psychological Services, Inc., Los Angeles, Calif.

[2]David Cohen, "Eysenck Finds Quick Thinkers Have Higher IQs," *APA Monitor* (June 1982), p. 29.

[3]These questions are from a standardized test used by a management consulting firm but not sold to the public. The correct answers are A: 2, B: 1, C: B, D: no particular number is correct, but the more the better.

[4]Based on information found in Walter Pauk, *How to Study in College*, 2nd ed. (Boston: Houghton Mifflin, 1974), Chapters 4 and 5.

[5]Ibid., p. 40.

[6]Ibid., p. 69.

[7]Our discussion in this section is based on information in Ernest J. McCormick and Daniel Ilgen, *Industrial Psychology*, 7th ed. (Englewood Cliffs, N.J.: Prentice-Hall, 1980), pp. 150–157.

[8]Audrey Haber and Richard P. Runyon, *Fundamentals of Psychology* (Reading, Mass.: Addison-Wesley, 1974), p. 456.

[9]Henry A. Murray, *Explorations in Personality* (New York: Oxford University Press, 1938).

[10]W. Clay Hamner and Dennis W. Organ, *Organizational Behavior: An Applied Psychological Approach* (Plano, Texas: Business Publications, 1978), p. 168. Our discussion of these two dimensions of personality is from the same source, pp. 168–176.

[11]Ibid., p. 174.

[12]John L. Holland, *Making Vocational Choices: A Theory of Careers* (Englewood Cliffs, N.J.: Prentice-Hall, 1973).

[13]A. Christine Parham, *Basic Psychology for the Work Life* (Cincinnati, Ohio: South-Western Publishing Co., 1983), p. 293.

[14]The idea for this discussion is based on Hamner and Organ, *Organizational Behavior*, pp. 186–187. The second and third items in the discussion are credited to this source.

[15]Adapted from Andrew J. DuBrin, *Foundations of Organizational Behavior* (Englewood Cliffs, N.J.: Prentice-Hall, 1984), pp. 79–80.

[16]Marvin Zuckerman, "The Search for High Sensation," *Psychology Today* (Feb. 1978), pp. 38–40, 43, 46, 96–99.

SUGGESTED READING

ANASTASI, ANNE. *Differential Psychology*. New York: Macmillan, 1970.

————. *Psychological Testing*, 5th. ed. New York: Macmillan, 1982.

EYSENCK, HANS J., and LEON KAMIN. *The Intelligence Controversy*. New York: Wiley, 1981.

FESHBACK, SEYMOUR, and BERNARD WEINER. *Personality*. Lexington, Mass.: D.C. Heath, 1982.

GATCHEL, ROBERT J., and FREDERICK G. MEARS. *Personality: Theory, Assessment, and Research*. New York: St. Martin's, 1982.

GOLEMAN, DANIEL. "The New Competency Tests: Matching the Right People to the Right Jobs," *Psychology Today* (Jan. 1981), pp. 34–46.

HAWKINS, KATHLEEN L. "How to Read More by Reading Less," *Success* (June 1982), pp. 44, 47.

HOLDING, DENNIS H. *Human Skills: Studies in Human Performance*. New York: Wiley, 1981.

HOLLAND, JOHN L. *Making Vocational Choices*. Englewood Cliffs, N.J.: Prentice-Hall, 1973.

KAPLAN, ROBERT M., and DENNIS P. SACCUZZO. *Psychological Testing: Principles, Applications, and Issues*. Monterey, Calif.: Brooks/Cole, 1982.

MINTON, HENRY L., and FRANK W. SCHNEIDER. *Differential Psychology*. Monterey, Calif.: Brooks/Cole, 1980.

"Risking It All: The Spirit of Adventure Is Alive and Well," *Time* (Aug. 29, 1983), pp. 54–59.

4

UNDERSTANDING YOURSELF

LEARNING OBJECTIVES

After reading and studying this chapter and doing the exercises, you should be able to

1. Understand yourself better than you do now.
2. Understand how your attitudes toward yourself can influence your personal and work life.
3. Be aware of several ways of gaining self-understanding.
4. Decide whether or not you want to be more open with people.
5. Acquire some tactics for increasing your self-confidence (if you think it is necessary).

A substantial number of people who are reading this book are doing so primarily because they want to become more successful in their future careers. If you are one of those people, your reaction to parts of the first chapters may have been, "Seems interesting, but how does knowledge about business psychology apply to me as an individual?" The answer is that most of business psychology applies to you, since you are one member of the general class of humans.

An important starting point in applying knowledge in general to yourself is to begin the process of self-examination. Suppose that, instead of a book about business psychology, this were a book about social dancing. It would be of immense value to you to read about what other dancers do right and do wrong. But reading about principles of dancing would be of greater benefit to you if you first took a candid look at your own style of dancing. Video taping your dance style would be helpful. You might also want to receive comments and suggestions from other people about your dancing.

Because an entire chapter is devoted to the self, it does not imply that other chapters in this book do not deal with the self. Most of this book is geared toward using business psychology for self-development and self-improvement. Only Chapters 1 to 3 and 13 deal more with general psychological information than with information specifically geared toward personal improvement and self-understanding.

WAYS OF LEARNING ABOUT YOURSELF

To achieve self-understanding, you need to gather accurate information about yourself. Much of the modern-day human potential movement is geared toward achieving self-understanding and personal improvement. Personal growth groups and encounter groups are two such examples. Everytime you read a self-help book, take a personality quiz, participate in an encounter group, or learn about your bodily sensations through a biofeedback device, you are learning something about yourself. (Feedback is bringing back information to you, about you.) Here we will discuss five general methods of gaining information for self-understanding: (1) acquiring general information about human behavior, (2) feedback from psychological tests, (3) feedback from superiors, co-workers, and friends, (4) feedback from growth groups, and (5) feedback from counselors. At the end of the chapter, you will be asked to complete the Self-Knowledge Questionnaire, a comprehensive survey of yourself.

General Information about Human Behavior

As you read about or listen to facts and systematic observations about people in general, you should also be gaining knowledge about yourself. This book, and all other books about human behavior, discuss many things that have relevance to you as an individual. At times, the author will explain how this information applies to you. At other times, it is your responsibility to relate the general information to your particular case.

Among the many general topics discussed in Chapter 2 is perception. To improve your self-understanding with respect to perception, you will have to relate that information to yourself. For example, one aspect of perception described is selective perception, a tendency to see things according to our need at the time. In reading about selective perception you might arrive at a self-insight such as, "Maybe that is why I didn't listen when people said I was too young to get married. If I had listened, I wouldn't have the problems I do today."

To cite another example: in discussing intelligence, there is evidence that the left side of the brain performs the intellectual tasks that depend on careful, logical thinking. People with the left half of their brain dominant thus tend to be logical and orderly. If you are just the opposite (more intuitive and emotional), you might say to yourself, "Perhaps part of my intellectual style is due to my heredity. I'm right brain dominant."

If you are interested in improving your self-understanding, it is worth the attempt to relate facts and observations about people in general to yourself. The danger, of course, is that you may misapply information to yourself. That is one important reason why feedback from other people is an important supplement to introspection (looking into oneself).

Feedback from Standardized Tests and Questionnaires

Methods are available for gathering systematic knowledge about your aptitudes, interests, and skills. To illustrate, thousands of people in the last two decades have discovered through aptitude testing that they had the potential to become computer programmers. Many of these people are now engaged in a satisfying career because of the self-understanding that they achieved from these tests. However, test results can also be inaccurate and misleading. You might be functioning as a confident and outgoing individual. If you take a personality test and discover that you rated low on self-confidence and high on introversion, you should not be concerned about the results. In your particular case, the test results are misleading.

In Chapter 3 we discussed several of the major types of mental tests. Should you take a battery of tests for purposes of vocational or personal counseling, you will again be exposed to such tests. The most effective way to receive self-understanding from mental ability, personality, and interest tests is to have the results interpreted to you by a professional in the field of mental measurement.

In addition to receiving feedback from standardized tests, you might derive self-understanding from other self-examination instruments. A standardized test or questionnaire has the advantage of having been constructed on the basis of scientific principles. Other self-examination instruments offer less certain results, but they are still valuable for purposes of introspection. A number of such self-examination instruments are presented in this book to help you understand yourself better. Extremely high or low scores on these questionnaires may provide useful clues to self-understanding.

Feedback from Superiors, Co-workers, Subordinates, and Friends

A valuable source of information for understanding yourself is to learn what significant people in your life think of you. Feedback of this nature sometimes hurts or makes you feel uncomfortable; but when it is consistent, it gives you an accurate picture of how you are perceived by others. In many organizations, systematic feedback is offered to people during the process of appraising their performance.

If you are seriously interested in feedback about yourself from others, it is better to act independently than to wait for a yearly performance appraisal. One problem is that not all performance appraisal systems provide candid feedback. A simple, but effective, approach is to ask people who know you for such feedback. One man enrolled in a personal improvement seminar obtained valuable information about himself on the basis of a questionnaire he sent to 15 people. His directions were:

> I am hoping that you can help me with one of the most important assignments of my life. I want to obtain a candid picture of how I am seen by others. What they think are my strengths, weaknesses, good points, and bad points. Any other observations about me as an individual would also be most welcome.
>
> Write your thoughts on the enclosed sheet of paper. The information that you provide me will help me develop a plan for personal improvement that I am writing for a course in career management. Mail the form back to me in the enclosed envelope. It is not necessary for you to sign the form.

Inevitably when this method of obtaining feedback is mentioned, a few skeptics will argue that friends will not give you a true picture of yourself. Instead, they will say flattering things about you because they value your friendship. Experience has shown, however, that if you impress others with the importance of their opinions they will generally give you a couple of constructive suggestions. Not everybody will give you helpful feedback; therefore, you may have to sample a wide range of opinion.

Feedback from Personal Growth Groups

A formal method of improving your self-understanding is to obtain feedback about yourself in the process of participating in a **personal growth group**.[1] Groups of this nature are designed to help people improve their self-awareness and learn how to express their feelings. The major reason personal growth groups (or encounter groups) have persisted over the years is that so many people recognize they need to become more open with their feelings. Too often, we are taught from early childhood to suppress our feelings. Three specialists in the area of feeling-expression put it this way:

Emotional suppression is everywhere. The social groups we live in—family, friends, work groups, and neighbors—make frequent demands on us to curb feeling-expression. These demands, rational and irrational, are frequent, at times subtle, and often extremely persuasive. Growing children learn under what circumstances feelings can be expressed fully, covertly, or not at all. Even the freest children quickly learn that many feelings must be at least partially suppressed. For example, if a child gets angry and begins to yell in a supermarket, his or her parents are liable to become extremely embarrassed. In most cases, parents will forcibly stop the child from yelling. Few will be so composed as to explain, "I need you to stop yelling. Feel angry if you want, but don't show it."[2]

As a starting point in the growth group, you usually receive feedback on how you are perceived by other members of the group. Such perceptions by others have a positive impact on self-understanding. Feedback can occur at any phase in the life of the personal growth group. A sample of the type of feedback from others that took place at an early stage of one such group is presented next.

Group leader: To get things started, everybody will tell everybody else what kind of first impression they have made. We'll do this clockwise, starting with Jeanne sitting on my left. Everybody, beginning with Jack, will tell Jeanne what he or she thinks of her. Of course, if Jeanne has made absolutely no impression on you, if she is the invisible woman, you can pass [group laughs]. Okay, Jack, look Jeanne straight in the eye and tell her what you think.

    Jack: My first impression of you, Jeanne, is that you're kind of cool. The type of woman I'd like to know better.

    Meryl: Jeanne, I would guess that you have a lot of friends. No doubt you are a nice person. But those eyes of yours give me something to worry about. They look a little shifty. I wouldn't trust you fully until I got to know you better. [Nervous laughter from the group.]

    Maggie: I think you try to give the impression that you are very casual. But underneath, you have worked very hard to create that impression. I know for sure that your jeans costs about three times as much as the usual type you find in the discount store. I'll bet you worked hours on your hair to achieve that casual look.

    George: Don't take Maggie too seriously. I think you're one fine-looking woman. You also give me the impression of being very intelligent. I like the way you talk. I think you should "go for it" in life. There's nothing stopping you.

    Terry: I can see those good points about you, too. I think the real you, however, is a fun-lover. I can see Jeanne out on a sailboat taking long weekends. I think that underneath you're the party type. Am I wrong?

    Carol: So long as we're being candid, I'll make this comment. You're kind of pushy in a nice way. I noticed it was you who manipulated things so you could be right next to the group leader. You've also got this look about you that you're superior to other people. Maybe it's that you're a natural leader.

Jeff: It's tough to be last. All the good comments have been used up. I'll have to go along with the good comments made about Jeanne. She's terrific. I wish I wasn't already engaged. Jeanne would be a lot of fun to go out with.

Group Leader: Jeanne, tell us how you feel about what has just happened to you.

Jeanne: I feel terrific. Thanks for all the compliments. Even your negative comments were helpful. Maybe I do come on a little too strong at times. I like to be on top of situations. This is the first time anything like this has happened to me. Thanks again.

How might this session have benefited Jeanne? First, she perceived the tone of the feedback to be positive. This would probably give her at least a temporary boost in self-confidence. (See the discussion of self-confidence building toward the end of this chapter.) Second, the session might give her some ideas for self-improvement, even if they are somewhat superficial. She can't do much about the alleged "shifty eyes," but she might try not to appear standoffish *when she does not want to be perceived in this manner.* If Jeanne leaves the session with a boost in self-confidence and one valid suggestion for self-improvement, we can conclude that the session was worthwhile for her.

Feedback from a Career Counselor

An advanced method of achieving self-understanding is to obtain feedback about yourself from a career counselor. College counseling centers often provide such a service. In addition, some psychological consulting firms offer career counseling to individuals.[3] Career counselors obtain their information from interviews, tests, and questionnaires. A valuable service that they provide is to collect the information that you have provided about yourself and organize it into a meaningful whole. Figure 4–1 presents a counseling report written for an individual who wanted to discuss the advisability of his pursuing a career in financial analysis. The report was written over ten years ago. The man did obtain a job as a financial analysis trainee. Today he is a middle manager in the financial department of a large corporation.

Reports of this nature are based on a combination of information gathered in an interview and from the results of psychological testing. Many of the questions asked in such an interview are of the same type that you will find in the exercise at the end of this chapter. As you read the counseling report, you will notice that the psychologist sometimes makes direct reference to a test. (See the paragraph about Interests and Motivation.)

Name: Bruce M. Larson   Age: 21

Special Counseling Report

The following evaluation report contains comments about your intellectual, personality and motivational characteristics as they relate to your expressed interest in pursuing the field of financial analysis.

Intellectual area

Your basic intelligence, as measured by a standardized test of intelligence compares satisfactorily to financial analysts. You would need to expend effort to do well in this field. One of your intellectual assets is a common sense, practical-minded approach. Your basic communication skills are also satisfactory for financial work. You would be well advised to stay one step ahead of other analysts by continuous reading and study. This might give you the competitive edge you need.

Personality

Your basic level of psychological maturity and stability appear satisfactory for this occupational choice. I suspect that your level of self-confidence can be strengthened, which would help you deal with pressure situations. Many of the minor concerns you have are not at all unusual for a young man who psychologically "levels" with himself. Don't deny your feelings, just continue to take a mature approach to their recognition.

Interests and Motivation

You appear to be strongly motivated by thoughts of financial success. You also recognize knowledge as a source of power and a way to control your own destiny. Your interest in financial analysis has endured over the years which suggests you are making a sound vocational choice. Your pattern of likes and dislikes (as measured by the Strong Vocational Interest Blank) indicates that you might find satisfactions in many fields. Your interest in working with people appears at least, if not stronger, than your interest in dealing with financial details. For example, your interests showed much similarity to those of psychiatrists, psychologists, public administrators, rehabilitation counselors, ministers, and physical therapists. However, you also demonstrate similar preferences to computer programmers. The tentative interpretation I make here is that your biggest satisfactions will probably stem from managerial work.

Relationships with People

You have better basic skills for dealing with people than you realize. You need to develop your self-confidence in this area. Perhaps early success with people in a business environment will be helpful in strengthening your self-confidence. Continuing to control your weight, and talking to successful people are two recommended courses of action. Your basic poise is good. It is not unlikely that you will feel more comfortable with business people than you have with your school peers.

Understanding Human Behavior

You appear to have good sensitivity to people. You are admirably frank in evaluating your strengths and weaknesses. It appears that you will continue to grow in your ability to understand yourself and others. I do not see this as a problem area. Your present level of insightfulness is certainly adequate for financial analysis. Your attitudes toward self-improvement are positive.

Work Habits

I don't have much to go on here, but it appears that your work habits have shown improvement in recent years. Effective work habits might very well be your path to success. Obtain a copy of Drucker's The Effective Executive and refer to it frequently.

Conclusion

You have many personal characteristics that will eventually enable you to assume leadership (managerial) positions in business. At this point you might be more concerned about becoming technically competent before pursuing supervision.

This has been an informal personal report for you, covering the essence of my findings. I cannot guarantee that all my findings are correct, nor that my recommendations will lead to success. Interview and testing suggest that you have made a sound choice in pursuing financial analysis.

ek

FIGURE 4-1

Report written for an individual seeking assistance in making a good career choice.

YOUR SELF-CONCEPT: WHAT YOU THINK OF YOU

As the opening exercise in a group meeting designed to encourage self-aware-ness and self-improvement, the members were asked to tell the other people who they were. Joe Barnes spoke first: "I guess I'm just Joe, an average guy. Nobody special." Maxine Silver, spoke second: "I'm Maxine Silver. I'm 20 years old, very talented, and ready to make a big splash in this world."

Joe and Maxine obviously have quite different views of themselves. With just this limited information, we might guess that Joe has a negative or lim-ited self-concept, while Maxine has a very positive self-concept. Such differ-ences in self-concept can often have a profound influence on your career.[4] If you see yourself as a successful person, you will tend to engage in activities that help you to prove yourself right. If you have a limited view of yourself,

If enough people tell you that you are terrific, after awhile you will have the concept of a terrific person.

you will also tend to engage in activities that prove yourself right. You will find ways to not be particularly successful.

A strong self-concept leads to self-confidence, which in turn is an important requirement for being successful as a leader. Why some people develop strong self-concepts, while others have average or weak self-concepts, is not entirely known.[5] One important contributing factor is the lifelong feedback you receive from other people. If at two years old your parents, other children in your family, and playmates consistently told you that you were great, it would probably lead to strong self-concept. A four-year-old may occasionally look in the mirror and utter statements such as "I like me," "I'm cute," or "I'm a good girl." It would appear that in later life she will have a strong self-concept (and perhaps be unbearably conceited).

In summary, much of what we call the self-concept is a reflection of what others have said about us. If enough people tell you that you are "terrific," after awhile you will have the self-concept of a "terrific" person. When enough people tell you that you are not a worthwhile person, after awhile your self-concept will become that of a not worthwhile person. People who say "I'm OK" are expressing a positive self-concept. People who say "I'm not OK" have a negative self-concept.

HOW YOUR PERSONALITY INFLUENCES YOUR SELF-CONCEPT

What you think of yourself depends in part on your basic traits and characteristics, a major part of your personality. Here is how the tie-in between the development of your personality and your self-concept might work in practice.

Keith begins life as an active human being, even before he is born. In his prenatal days, Keith made his mother quite aware of his presence through his frequent kicking and squirming. His father was often invited by his mother to rest his hand on her abdomen to feel Keith making his presence known.

Keith's high activity level continued into his crib life. His squirming and kicking made him an attractive object of affection to his mother, father, and older sister. They enjoyed playing with him because of his responsiveness to them.

The affection and attention Keith attracted through his physical movement helped reinforce his energetic action. As a toddler, his exceptional physical condition brought him continued attention from adults. Keith's personality in early life was characterized by a high energy level. As the growing (maturation) process continued, Keith learned new ways of making good use of his abundant energy. He played several sports, studied hard, and helped his parents and older sister take care of household chores.

By the time Keith was 14, he had already developed the self-concept of an energetic, confident person. A self-concept of this nature helped direct Keith toward activities requiring a high degree of energy. When Keith was 17, he had the chance to work for a distant relative as a roofer's assistant. The money offered was outstanding for a person of his age. Yet the work would be physically exhausting to most people and require extreme courage. Keith thought to himself, "Why not take the job. I'm a 'heavy' who can handle almost any tough job."

As an adult, Keith completed technical training beyond high school. Today he runs a successful home improvement business and plays semiprofessional football. He has four children and a happy wife. As Keith sees himself, he works hard and plays hard. His high natural energy level is one of the factors that has contributed to such a self-concept.

How the Self-Structure Influences Personality

Trying to explain how the personality influences your self-concept is similar to describing how the force of gravity influences the tide. We are dealing with abstractions that are difficult to visualize. James C. Coleman has developed an analysis of the close relationship between personality and the self. Both develop in tandem. He explains it this way:[6]

> As the infant grows and learns to distinguish between himself and other people and things, a part of his total perceptual field is gradually delineated as the "me," "I," or "self." As this self-structure develops, it becomes the integrating core of his personality—the reference point around which his experiences and coping patterns are organized.
>
> When a problem arises, it is perceived, thought about, and acted upon in relation to the self. That is, the individual comes to perceive himself as an active agent in determining his own behavior—as indicated by such statements as "I know," "I want," and "I will."

SELF-ACCEPTANCE: THE KEY TO A GOOD SELF-CONCEPT

Different ways of discussing the self tend to overlap. Despite their apparent fuzziness, notions about the self have a major influence on your life. Self-acceptance is one such fuzzy but critical idea.[7] When you accept yourself for who you are, when you do not reject yourself, it helps you develop a positive self-concept. People who highly regard themselves also tend to highly regard others. In contrast, the self-rejecting person tends to reject many other people. If your level of self-acceptance is high, you will find much less need to put down or discriminate against others.

Effective leaders tend to be high on self-acceptance. Since they are proud of who they are, they have less need to pull rank on subordinates. People who are self-accepting also enjoy better mental health both on and off the job.

A noted writer about the self, David W. Johnson, explains that there are two major ways of improving your self-acceptance.[8] First, you have to be willing to disclose more of yourself to others. (More will be said about self-disclosure later in this chapter.) If you keep yourself hidden from others, it is difficult to improve your self-acceptance. Self-disclosure gives you a chance to be accepted by others. Acceptance by others, in turn, leads to self-acceptance. Once you know that others appreciate you, you will tend to increase your self-appreciation.

Another method of improving your self-acceptance is to develop an appreciation of your strengths and accomplishments. A good starting point is to list your strengths and accomplishments on paper. The list is likely to be more impressive than you would have thought. (You will be asked to list your strengths and accomplishments in the Self-Knowledge Questionnaire presented later in this chapter.)

A popular exercise used in personal growth groups helps you to build self-acceptance through knowledge of your strengths. After group members have compiled their list of strengths, each person discusses his or her list with the other group members. Each person then comments about the list. Group members sometimes add to your list of strengths or reinforce what you have to say. Sometimes you may find some disagreement. One man told the other participants, "I'm handsome, intelligent, reliable, athletic, self-confident, very moral, and I have a good sense of humor." A woman in the group retorted, "And I might add that you have an inflated ego."

SELF-DISCLOSURE: BEING OPEN WITH OTHERS

A manager attended a weekend encounter group (very similar to the personal growth groups we have been talking about) with the hope of improving his ability to work with people. The feedback he received from others centered around comments such as "You are too tight-lipped," "You never react to people," "Far too cool and aloof," "Kind of unfriendly." The manager pressed for an explanation of what the people really meant by their comments. The group members were expressing the idea that the man did not react to what others said—he did not disclose his feelings to others.

After returning home from the encounter group, the manager made a deliberate effort to react to what others said. In the past when a subordinate might say, "What a busy day," the manager might simply nod in a noncommittal manner. Using a more open style of relating to others, the manager would now say, "It sounds like you have a busy day ahead of you," or "I appreciate the fact that you are working so hard."

After a year of making a conscious effort to react to people, the same manager attended another encounter group. This time the feedback he received from others did not contain references to his being tight-lipped or closed with others. Instead he was perceived as warm and friendly.

As the case history just described suggests, **self-disclosure** refers to revealing how you are reacting to the present situation.[9] It also means giving any information about the past that is relevant to the present. To be a self-disclosing person does not mean that you have to reveal intimate details about your past. To disclose yourself is to disclose your feelings about people, events, and things.

Why Is Self-Disclosure Important?

Self-disclosure helps you to build healthy, productive relationships in your work and personal life. It is thus an important survival skill if your work or personal life involves dealing with others. Research evidence has been collected indicating that healthy relationships are based on self-disclosure. Others become annoyed with one-way communicators (which closed people tend to be). A person who does not engage in self-disclosure does not give feedback to others. Honest feedback, of course, is a vital ingredient of a productive relationship with another person.

The characteristics of people who tend to be self-disclosing provide a further clue to the importance of being open with others. David W. Johnson has painted a composite picture of the self-disclosing individual based on research done on this aspect of personality:[10]

> A person willing to be self-disclosing will likely be a competent, open, and socially extroverted person who feels a strong need to interact with others. He is likely to be flexible, adaptive, and perhaps more intelligent than his less self-revealing peers. He is objectively aware of the realities of the interpersonal situations in which he is involved and perceives a fairly close congruence between the way he is and the way in which he would like to be. Finally, he views his fellowman as generally good rather than evil.

Another reason self-disclosure is so important is that it helps one develop a better integrated (well-rounded) personality. A better integrated personality, in turn, helps one become more effective in understanding others. People who are more self-disclosing tend to be more self-actualizing. Thus, if you stop hiding your feelings and attitudes, you may be on the path toward self-fulfillment.[11]

SELF-AWARENESS CHECKLIST

One problem in becoming more aware of ourselves is the problem of semantics. Think of the first time that you were asked to describe a painting, perhaps for a class in art appreciation. At first you might have been stymied in terms of what to say about the painting. Adjectives such as "interesting," "colorful," and "imaginative" might have been your first thoughts. Describing yourself, similar to describing a painting, requires skill. Describing yourself is important because it leads to more self-awareness and self-knowledge.

A useful exercise in developing self-awareness is the adjective list[12] shown in Figure 4–2. Read through this list and circle the seven adjectives that you think best describe you. You have now formed a brief self-description composed of seven adjectives such as "aggressive, courageous, extroverted, friendly, greedy, tenacious, and zestful." Next discuss your list with a friend. Your friend should be encouraged to discuss his or her list with you. The process should result in feedback about the accuracy of your self-perceptions.

Another recommended use of the adjective list is to discuss your list of adjectives with others in a group setting. Each group member has a chance to read his or her list to the other members and receive feedback from them.

THE STRUGGLE FOR SELF-ESTEEM: A DRIVING FORCE IN OUR LIVES

One way of tying together our discussion of the self is to recognize the overwhelming influence of self-esteem in our lives. According to the motivational theory developed by Abraham K. Korman, the struggle for self-esteem is the major driving force in our life.[13] A portion of his theory states that the basic motive for all acts is to keep oneself in balance or consistent with one's self-image. We try to keep our self-image whole. A major reason we try to perform in a way consistent with our self-image is that to do otherwise makes us tense and anxious. If you see yourself as an advanced tennis player, it would be predictable that you would decline an invitation to play another advanced player if you were physically exhausted. To perform poorly would make you tense.

Self-Esteem and Job Performance

The self-esteem, or consistency, theory of work behavior predicts that, when your self-image is favorable, it leads to good performance in doing tasks. *You work up to a level that fits your self-image.* You also will work down to a

able	happy	overconfident	self-aware
accepting	hard	overconforming	self-conscious
adaptable	helpful	overemotional	self-effacing
aggressive	helpless	overprotecting	self-indulgent
ambitious	honorable	passive	selfish
annoying	hostile	paternal	self-righteous
anxious	idealistic	patient	sensible
authoritative	imaginative	perceptive	sensitive
belligerent	immature	perfectionist	sentimental
bitter	impressionable	persuasive	serious
bold	inconsiderate	petty	silly
calm	independent	playful	simple
carefree	ingenious	pleasant	sinful
careless	innovative	pompous	skillful
caring	insensitive	powerful	sly
certain	insincere	pragmatic	sociable
cheerful	intelligent	precise	spontaneous
clever	introverted	pretending	stable
cold	intuitive	pretentious	strained
complex	irresponsible	principled	strong
confident	irritable	progressive	stubborn
conforming	jealous	protective	sympathetic
controlled	jovial	proud	taciturn
courageous	juvenile	questioning	tactful
cranky	kind	quiet	temperamental
critical	knowledgeable	radical	tenacious
cynical	lazy	rational	tender
demanding	learned	rationalizing	tense
dependable	lewd	reactionary	thoughtful
dependent	liberal	realistic	tough
derogatory	lively	reasonable	trusting
dignified	logical	reassuring	trustworthy
disciplined	loving	rebellious	unassuming
docile	malicious	reflective	unaware
dogged	manipulative	regretful	uncertain
domineering	materialistic	rejecting	unconcerned
dreamy	maternal	relaxed	uncontrolled
dutiful	mature	reliable	understanding
effervescent	merry	religious	unpredictable
efficient	modest	remote	unreasonable
elusive	mystical	resentful	unstructured
energetic	naive	reserved	useful
extroverted	narcissistic	resolute	vain
fair	negative	respectful	vapid
fearful	nervous	responsible	visionary
foolish	neurotic	responsive	vulnerable
frank	noisy	retentive	warm
free	normal	rigid	willful
friendly	objective	sarcastic	wise
genial	oblivious	satisfied	wishful
gentle	observant	scientific	withdrawn
giving	obsessive	searching	witty
greedy	organized	self-accepting	worried
gruff	original	self-actualizing	youthful
guilty	overburdened	self-assertive	zestful
gullible			

FIGURE 4-2
Adjective list.

level to fit your self-image. Here are three examples of research results that support the positive relationship between self-esteem and task performance:[14]

- College students who performed up to their potential were compared with people who did not perform up to their potential. The achievers were found to have more positive self-concepts than the underachievers.
- Another study with college students found a significant relationship between self-concept and grade-point average. The stronger the self-concept, the higher the grade-point average.
- A study involving self-descriptions of people was conducted with managers from a variety of companies.[15] One finding was that individuals

who see themselves as belonging to a high occupational level tend to be more proficient in their work. They also tend to engage in higher-level managerial work.

BUILDING YOUR SELF-CONFIDENCE

A practical use of knowledge about the self is to use it as a method of strengthening your self-confidence. Several of the ideas already presented in this chapter relate to developing self-confidence. For instance, hearing positive things about yourself from others is a good confidence-builder. Here we will describe four easy-to-implement tactics that will often lead to a strengthening of one's self-confidence. As you read them, look for one or two strategies that you think would make sense in terms of your personality and life circumstances.[16]

Obtain a Few Easy Victories. Self-confidence builds up as a direct result of success. The more little victories you achieve in life, the more likely it is that your self-confidence will be high. Correspondingly, the more lack of success you encounter, the more likely it is that you will have low self-confidence. A little victory could include such things as learning a new dance step, receiving a favorable grade on a term paper, or running a mile one minute faster than you did last month. The "easy victory" tactic is based on a recent theory called the **success cycle**. Each little success builds up your self-confidence, which leads to a bigger success, which leads to more self-confidence, and so on.

Enter a Less Competitive Environment. An extension of the easy-victory strategy is to place yourself in a less competitive environment after you are convinced that your present environment has you in over your head. A less competitive environment might be just what you need to establish a satisfactory level of self-confidence. Suppose you are playing in an "A" bowling league and you consistently score about average. It could help your self-confidence to switch to a "B" league where your average score might gain you recognition. (And if that doesn't work, how about a "C" league?)

Achieve Something That Stretches Your Capability. One highly recommended approach to restoring your self-confidence is to achieve something that stretches your capability. This strategy should be used after obtaining a few easy victories. You establish a goal that is significantly beyond what you ordinarily accomplish and then put considerable energy into attaining that goal. A man who had suffered a heart attack felt a strong need to elevate his self-confidence. To restore his health, he had already been walking five miles per day. He thought that if he could become a marathon runner—like some other cardiac victims he had read about—he would again become a confident person. Gradually, he improved his running until he could run five miles at a stretch. Then he hit on his real confidence builder. As he explains:

> You might call it the Big Event in my life. Pepsi Cola was sponsoring a ten-kilometer marathon. Since I had been running five miles, I figured I could add another mile to that total, which would equal ten kilometers. I practiced for thirty days, every day running a little less than one block further. Marathon Day had beautiful weather. I think I came in about fourth from last among all the finishers. What a fabulous accomplishment. I completed the race, and I wasn't last. I've felt great about myself ever since.

Raise Your Self-Expectations. Perhaps the ultimate solution to elevating your self-confidence is to expect yourself to perform well in tasks you set out to accomplish. Try to visualize yourself performing well in an activity that will give you self-confidence, such as making a good presentation in front of a group. It frequently happens that you will rise to the level of expectation you set for yourself.

SUMMARY OF KEY POINTS

☐ Methods of learning about yourself include (1) acquiring general information about human behavior and applying it to yourself, (2) obtaining feedback from psychological testing, (3) feedback from superiors, co-workers, subordinates, and friends, (4) feedback from personal growth groups, and (5) feedback from a career counselor.

☐ Your self-concept is basically your attitudes toward yourself. A positive self-concept leads to self-confidence. People have a tendency to perform up to or down to their self-concepts. Accepting yourself leads to a positive self-concept. Self-acceptance can be improved through (1) disclosing more about yourself to others, and (2) becoming more aware of your strengths and accomplishments.

☐ Self-disclosure refers to revealing how you are reacting to the present situation. The process helps you to build healthy, productive relationships in your work and personal life. A person who discloses his or her feelings to others is an open person. Self-disclosure leads to the formation of an integrated personality.

☐ According to the consistency theory of work behavior, the struggle for self-esteem is the major driving force in our lives. Thus, the basic motive for all acts is to keep oneself in balance or consistent with one's self-image. People with strong self-images tend to perform better in a variety of tasks, such as achieving high grades or being successful managers.

☐ Knowledge about the self can be used to strengthen one's self-confidence. Among the tactics for accomplishing this end are (1) obtain a few easy victories, (2) enter a less competitive environment, (3) achieve something that stretches your capability, and (4) raise your level of self-expectation.

GUIDELINES FOR PERSONAL EFFECTIVENESS

1. A major step that you can take toward improving your effectiveness as an individual is to strengthen your self-concept. A series of successes, however small, will improve your self-concept and help you to feel more self-confident.
2. Your self-concept will also be strengthened as you become more self-accepting. You can achieve increased self-acceptance by the process of being more open in expressing your feelings. Another approach to increased self-acceptance is to learn to appreciate your strengths and accomplishments.

DISCUSSION QUESTIONS

1. How would you describe your self-concept in 25 words or less?
2. When asked, "What do you do?" many people respond, "I'm just a . . . ." What does this tell you about their self-concepts?
3. Can you describe any method of learning about yourself that is not mentioned in this chapter?
4. What current fads seem closely related to people's desire for gaining self-understanding?
5. Where does astrology fit in with understanding yourself?
6. To what extent do you think many people study psychology in order to increase their self-understanding?
7. What does a person have to do before you conclude that he or she is accepting you?
8. Who is the most self-rejecting person you know? What makes you conclude that he or she is self-rejecting?
9. At what point would you draw the line in being open with people?
10. Why do some people have such low self-confidence?
11. How self-confident are you? How do you know?

A Business Psychology Self-examination Exercise
THE SELF-KNOWLEDGE QUESTIONNAIRE

DIRECTIONS: Complete the following questionnaire for your personal use. You might wish to make up a worksheet before putting your comments in final form.

I. Education
    1. How far have I gone in school?
    2. What is my major field of interest?
    3. Which are (or have been) my best subjects?
    4. Which are (or have been) my poorest subjects?
    5. What further educational plans do I have? Why?
    6. What extracurricular activities have I participated in?
    7. Which ones did I enjoy? Why?

II. Work Experience
    8. What jobs have I held since age 16?
    9. What aspect of these jobs did I enjoy? Why?
    10. What aspect of these jobs did I dislike? Why?
    11. What were my three biggest accomplishments on the job?
    12. What kind of employee am (was) I?
    13. What compliments did I receive from my bosses or co-workers?
    14. What criticisms or suggestions did I receive?
    15. What would be an ideal job for me?

III. Attitudes toward People
    16. The kind of people I get along best with are:
    17. The kind of people I clash with are:
    18. How many close friends do I have? What is it I like about each one?
    19. Would I prefer working mostly with men or women? Why?
    20. How much contact with other people do I need?
    21. My arguments with other people are mostly about:

IV. Attitudes toward Myself
    22. What are my strengths?
    23. What are my weaknesses or areas for improvement?
    24. What do I think of me?
    25. What do I worry about the most?
    26. What is my biggest problem?
    27. What things in life do I dislike?
    28. What have I accomplished in life so far?
    29. Has this been enough accomplishment?
    30. So far, what has been the happiest period of my life? Why?
    31. What gives me satisfaction in life?
    32. In what ways do I punish myself?
    33. What motivates me?

V.   How Others See Me
    34. What is the best compliment my spouse (or a good friend) has paid me?
    35. In what ways would my spouse (or a good friend) like me to change?
    36. What do my friends like best about me?
    37. What do my friends dislike about me?
VI. Hobbies, Interests, Sports
    38. What activities, hobbies, interests, sports, and so forth do I actively participate in?
    39. Which one of these do I really get excited about? Why?
VII. My Future
    40. What goals or plans in life do I have?
    41. a. Education and training.
        b. Career and job.
        c. Activities and interests.
        d. Plans and goals related to other people.

REFERENCES

[1] A helpful discussion of such groups is found in David W. Johnson and Frank P. Johnson, *Joining Together: Group Theory and Group Skills* (Englewood Cliffs, N.J.: Prentice-Hall, 1975). An analysis of some of the potential problems with encounter groups is Gerald Biberman, "Trainer Behavior in a T-Group Setting," *Small Group Behavior* (Nov. 1979), pp. 501–522.

[2] Adapted from Robert A. Pierce, Michael P. Nichols, and Joyce R. DuBrin, *Emotional Expression in Psychotherapy* (New York: Gardner Press, 1983), p. 2.

[3] Professional career counseling is discussed throughout Dean C. Dauw, *Up Your Career*, 4th ed. (Prospect Heights, Ill.: Waveland Press, 1984).

[4] Donald A. Laird and others, *Psychology: Human Relations and Motivation* (New York: McGraw-Hill, 1975), p. 209.

[5] Anthony F. Grasha, *Practical Applications of Psychology* (Boston: Little, Brown, 1978), pp. 341–344.

[6] James C. Coleman and William E. Broen, Jr., *Abnormal Psychology and Modern Life*, 4th ed. (Glenview, Ill.: Scott, Foresman, 1972), p. 97.

[7] A comprehensive discussion of acceptance of self and others is found in David W. Johnson, *Reaching Out: Interpersonal Effectiveness and Self-Actualization* (Englewood Cliffs, N.J.: Prentice-Hall, 1972), pp. 141–157.

[8] Ibid., pp. 142–148.

[9] Ibid., p. 10.

[10] Ibid., p. 11.

[11] James O. Lugo and Gerald L. Hershey, *Living Psychology*, 3rd ed. (New York: Macmillan, 1981), p. 348.

[12]Reprinted with permission from David W. Johnson, *Human Relations and Your Career* (Englewood Cliffs, N.J.: Prentice-Hall, 1978), p. 230.

[13]Abraham K. Korman, *Organizational Behavior* (Englewood Cliffs, N.J.: Prentice-Hall, 1977), pp. 66–77.

[14]The first two studies are cited in Korman, p. 69.

[15]Edwin E. Ghiselli, "Managerial Talent," *American Psychologist* (October 1963), p. 639.

[16]This section of the chapter is adapted from Andrew J. DuBrin, *Bouncing Back: How to Handle Setbacks in Your Work and Personal Life* (Englewood Cliffs, N.J.: Prentice-Hall, 1982), pp. 171–182.

SUGGESTED READING

GEIWITZ, JAMES. *Looking at Ourselves.* Boston: Little, Brown, 1976.

HAIGHT, M. R. *A Study of Self Deception.* Atlantic Highlands, N.J.: Humanistic Press, 1980.

HAMMACHEK, D. *Encounters with the Self.* New York: Holt, Rinehart and Winston, 1971.

JOURARD, SIDNEY M. *The Transparent Self.* New York: Van Nostrand Reinhold, 1964.

KEGAN, ROBERT. *The Evolving Self: Problems and Processes in Human Development.* Cambridge, Mass.: Harvard University Press, 1982.

KILEY, JOHN C. *Self-Rescue.* New York: McGraw-Hill, 1977.

MILLER, DONALD B. *Personal Vitality.* Reading, Mass.: Addison-Wesley, 1977.

NEVILL, DOROTHY D., ed. *Humanistic Psychology: New Frontiers.* New York: Gardner Press, 1977.

ROGERS, CARL R. *Carl Rogers on Personal Power.* New York: Dell, 1977.

YANKELOVICH, DANIEL. *New Rules: Searching for Self-Fulfillment in a World Turned Upside Down.* New York: Random House, 1981.

PART TWO

DEALING WITH INDIVIDUALS

In this part of the book we emphasize information that should be helpful in dealing with people one at a time, including yourself. Note carefully the use of the term "emphasize." Each section of this book has some information about dealing with people both one at a time and in groups. However, here we concentrate on such topics as motivating others, setting goals, making decisions, dealing with job stress, and handling conflict and frustration. The topic of dealing with individuals will be reintroduced in Part Five.

Another perspective to use in reading the chapters in Part Two is to regard them as a continuation of the study of basic psychology found in Part One. All the topics mentioned above are important topics within the psychology of individual behavior.

5

MOTIVATING OTHERS AND YOURSELF

LEARNING OBJECTIVES

After reading and studying this chapter and doing the exercises, you should be able to

1. Explain the meaning of work motivation.
2. Describe how your boss's expectations of you can influence your job performance.
3. Identify several important rules used in applying behavior modification on the job.
4. Recognize the conditions under which money can be motivational.
5. Describe several other useful techniques used to motivate people on the job.
6. Develop a strategy for motivating yourself toward some worthwhile end.

THE NATURE OF HUMAN MOTIVATION

We have already explored how the job behavior of people is influenced by their needs, motives, and the meaning they attach to work. In addition, two major theories of work motivation (Maslow's need hierarchy and expectancy theory) were explained in Chapter 2. An understanding of the psychology of motivation alone, however, will not enable you to motivate others or yourself to accomplish results. To improve motivation on the job, you must translate this underlying knowledge into methods and techniques. A variety of field-tested motivational methods and techniques will be discussed in this chapter. But, first, it will be helpful to explore further the nature and meaning of motivation.

The Meaning of Motivation

Motivation is concerned with the "why" of behavior, the reason behind people doing things. Many psychologists believe that all behavior is motivated behavior: there is a reason for doing everything you do. Following this logic, if you misplace your car keys it could mean that you want to be late for work. Perhaps you think today's tasks will be boring; or perhaps you are trying to punish yourself.

Human motivation, in general, can be defined as an *inner state that activates or moves a person toward a goal*. It includes all those inner striving conditions described as wishes, desires, and drives.[1] **Work motivation** is more specific. It refers to a person expending effort toward the accomplishment of a goal considered worthwhile by the organization. A drafting technician studying computer-assisted design (CAD) on her own time in order to improve her job skills shows high work motivation. Another drafting technician might spend much of his work day thinking about his boat and much of his leisure time using and maintaining his boat. The latter technician has low job motivation but high leisure motivation.

Most people are motivated to do something (even fishing or drinking beer). If you want to succeed in your career, you will have to be a well-motivated person. If you become (or are) a manager, you will often be placed in the position of trying to motivate others.

Emotions and Motivation

An emotion is basically a feeling. Whenever we have an emotion, we experience certain physiological changes inside our body, both physical and chemical. You may have noticed a change in your heartbeat the last time you felt anger, hate, lust, disgust, jealousy, surprise, failure, delight, or any other emotion. Emotions enter into almost every human process, including motivation. One link between emotion and motivation is that emotions lead to motivated behavior. Watch out for a co-worker who is in a state of emotional arousal because he or she resents your success. That co-worker may be motivated to discredit you to your boss. And, as crime detectives have long noted, "Watch out for a jealous lover."

On the positive side, you can expect a person who loves you (definitely an emotion) to be motivated to act kindly toward you. You can expect a boss who is experiencing the emotion of delight about your work to be motivated to recommend you for a salary increase or a promotion.

Emotions Sometimes Defy Logic. Emotions create many problems when you are trying to motivate people, including yourself. People are often governed more by emotion than logic. So when you use a rational tactic to try and motivate another person, and that individual is in a state of emotional arousal, the tactic may not work. One worker was told that he would be fired unless he improved his job performance. Instead of his job performance improving, it declined. After the man was fired, the boss asked him why he refused to shape up. The answer he gave was, "If I don't work, I don't have to send my former wife any money. And I'm so angry at her, that suits me just fine."

Self-Interest, the Ultimate Motivator

As Stephen P. Robbins has observed, people ask themselves, "What's in it for me?" before engaging in any form of behavior.[2] In one way or another every theory of motivation contains this underlying idea: given a choice, people act in a way that serves their self-interest. It can even be argued that when people act in a way that helps others they are doing so because helping others helps them! A person, for example, may give money to poor people because this act of kindness makes him or her feel wanted and powerful.

Both the need hierarchy and expectancy theories of motivation include the underlying idea of self-interest as a motivator. According to Maslow's theory, people strive to achieve goals that will satisfy their needs of the moment. And expectancy theory contends that people will put forth effort if they believe the outcome will benefit them in some important way.

MOTIVATING OTHER BY SETTING
HIGH EXPECTATIONS

The simplest way of motivating other people is to set high expectations for them. This mysterious phenomenon of a manager's expectations influencing employee motivation and performance has been labeled the Pygmalion effect. According to Greek mythology, Pygmalion was a sculptor and king of Cyprus who carved an ivory statue of a maiden and fell in love with the statue. The statue was soon brought to life in response to his prayer. The point of the Pygmalion effect is that you may be able to convert an under-motivated person into a high producer by the simple method of believing that he or she can improve.

The Pygmalion effect on the job works in a subtle, almost unconscious way. When a manager believes that a subordinate will succeed, that manager communicates this belief to the subordinate without realizing that the belief is being transmitted. Conversely, when a manager expects an employee to fail, the subordinate will usually not disappoint the manager. The manager's expectation of failure has become a self-fulfilling prophecy. Because the manager believed that the employee would fail, the manager contributed to the failure.[3]

Later in the chapter, we will examine the possibility that you can turn the Pygmalion effect inward. If you raise your level of self-expectations, your motivation and performance will sometimes increase.

MOTIVATION THROUGH BEHAVIOR MODIFICATION

Today many companies and many managers make use of operant conditioning, or **behavior modification**, to motivate employees.[4] The purpose of increasing employee motivation, of course, is to improve performance and productivity. The latter term refers to how much an employee produces in relation to how many resources he or she uses in the process. Productivity also takes into account the quality of the goods produced. The discussion in Chapter 2 about operant conditioning serves as the necessary background information, or underlying theory, for the present discussion.

Behavior Modification Focuses on Behavior and Its Consequences

A program of behavior modification is concerned with the actual job behavior of an employee (such as making a sale) and the consequences of that behavior (such as getting a commission for making the sale). This emphasis on behavior and its consequences is based on two important principles: (1) the law of effect, and (2) environmental determinism. According to the **law of effect**, behavior that leads to a positive consequence for the individual tends to be repeated, whereas behavior that leads to a negative consequence tends not to be repeated. A job example of the law of effect is as follows:

> Suppose that you are a programming supervisor. A woman working for you says, "I had to stay late to get it done, but I finally debugged that spare parts inventory program you gave me." If you respond, "Terrific Sandy, that's the kind of help we need around here," she is likely to work extra hard to debug a program in the future. Assume, instead, that you responded, "Be careful not to stay late when you are not authorized overtime pay. Besides, you could have debugged that program during normal working hours." The probability is that Sandy will not work hard (be strongly motivated) to debug the next snarled program.

The law of effect is a basic principle of psychology. **Environmental determinism** is a belief that stems from this principle. It contends that our past history of reinforcements (rewards and punishments) determines, or causes, our current behavior. Thus, behavior modification makes no references to internal states such as needs or motives that influence behavior. Reinforcers thus shape our lives. If doing little favors for people brought you the appreciation you craved in the past, you will do favors for people again when you want to be appreciated.

Motivating employees by giving out rewards for good performance—and occasionally punishments for poor performance—is the key ingredient to behavior modification. Since behavior modification (sometimes referred to as behavior mod) programs in work settings use rewards almost exclusively, the term **positive reinforcement** (PR) is generally preferred.

Rules for Using Positive Reinforcement

To effectively use PR on the job, certain rules or procedures must be followed.[5] Using rewards to modify the behavior of people would seem to follow the logic of common sense. Nevertheless, it is a specialized procedure requiring a systematic approach. Typically, a behavioral consultant is called in to help design a behavior mod program and train supervisors how to run the program. Despite these preceding statments, if you have a genuine interest in the welfare of people, you can learn to make productive use of PR on the job. Here we will present nine key rules of PR from the standpoint of the person being motivated (possibly you).

Rule 1: An appropiate reward must be used. Most motivational theories point to the idea that the way to motivate people is to use a reward that is meaningful to each particular person. If you were a status-hungry technician, you might work hard just for the opportunity to have a parking space adjacent to the engineering chief's parking space.

Table 5–1 lists a large group of rewards that are feasible in the workplace. Each of these rewards can be related back to the categories of needs mentioned in Chapter 2. People display individual differences with respect to which reward will satisfy which need. For example, money might not be an important reward to a person with a large family inheritance. Despite these individual differences, a couple of illustrative general statements are in order. The need for self-fulfillment or self-actualization might be partially met by rewards such as praise, recognition, receiving a favorable performance appraisal, challenging work assignments, or a promotion. Needs for belonging and affiliation might be met by approval, comradeship, or good co-workers.

Rule 2: Rewards should vary with the size of the contribution. Your boss is unlikely to do an effective job of motivating you if all your co-workers receive the same size of reward. If you have made substantial progress in reducing the production of defective parts, you should receive more recognition (or other reward) than somebody who has made only token progress.

The way to motivate people is to use a reward that is meaningful to each particular person.

TABLE 5-1
A checklist of rewards of potential use in a job setting

Feedback on good performance	Improved physical working conditions
Challenging work assignments	Better sales territory
Praise, encouragement, and appreciation	Capable and congenial co-workers
Recognition and approval	Company-paid lunch
Comradeship	Time off from work with pay
Job security	Status symbol (such as new personal computer)
Money, trading stamps	Take over for boss when boss is away
Favorable performance appraisal	Make presentation to top management
Promotion	Do more of enjoyable task
Access to confidential information	Private office
Power to influence co-workers and management	Freedom to personalize work area (such as hang a mobile)

Rule 3: Beginners should be rewarded for any effort that they make in the right direction. You have to begin somewhere in making improvements. Assume that your desk is so messy that you lose important files. Your boss is not obsessed with orderliness, but he recognizes that your sloppy work habits are interfering with your productivity. Using a PR approach, your boss should reward you whenever you make progress in keeping your desk in order.

For instance, if your boss notices that you no longer keep old coffee cups on your desk, he might comment, "I can already see the improvement in your work area. Keep up the progress." Although this process sounds elementary, *shaping* of behavior toward a planned-for objective increases the probability that you will make bigger changes in the near future.

Rule 4: You should be rewarded occasionally when you do something right. As explained in Chapter 2, intermittent reinforcement is more effective than continuous reinforcement for sustaining the right behavior. If you worked as a shoe store manager, it might be rewarding to you if, on an occasional visit to your store, your boss told you, "Everything looks just fine around here. The customers seem pleased. Your volume is up and the store looks first class. Keep this up and you'll notice a difference in your salary."

If your boss gave the same pep talk every week, the reward would lose its impact. Of worse consequence, you might come to depend on the reward to perform good work. No pep talk, no good performance.

Rule 5: You should receive your reward shortly after you do the right thing. Assuming that money motivated you, you would be more likely to work hard if hard work led to quick cash. If you were selling financial investments, you would tend to keep on prospecting much more readily if you received your commission in one month rather than six.

Rule 6: You have to know what has to be done to get rewarded. You need some kind of feedback device in your work to let you know when you have done a good job. If you were a quality control technician, it would be helpful for your boss to say to you, "I'll recommend that you be promoted to senior QC technician providing you decrease customer returns on product G-48 by 15 percent over the next four months."

One of the many reasons a sport like basketball is so motivational is that the path to a reward is clear-cut. A player can readily see that by putting the ball through the hoop a reward will be forthcoming (one, two, or in some leagues, three points). Feedback is immediate in these circumstances.

Rule 7: You have to know when you are doing wrong. If your boss patiently explains to you what you are doing wrong, you will know what needs to be done to get rewarded. Suppose a secretary is filing too many documents under the "miscellaneous" file. The secretary should be told what is specifically wrong with this technique. His or her boss might say, "It is time consuming to look in the miscellaneous file for most pieces of information. Your system needs to be more efficient. The purpose of a filing system is to be able to find information when you need it."

Rule 8: You should receive a realistic reward. An effective reward tends to be commensurate with the size of the constructive behavior. Suppose that your boss is trying to get you to be more assertive with customers. When you do behave more assertively, you should be rewarded with encouragement of a reasonable sort. Your boss would be overdoing praise if he or she said, "I think you've become the greatest sales representative in the region." Such encouragement would lose its effectiveness because the praise would seem ungenuine.

Rule 9: You may need to strive for fresh rewards from time to time. If the same reward is offered time after time, employees may lose interest in that particular reward. Once a reward grows stale, it loses its reinforcing properties. One company found that trading stamps lost their value as a reward for good attendance. As a substitute, a lottery system of rewards was installed. Employees who were in attendance for 30 consecutive workdays were eligible to put their name into a lottery. Every month a lucky number chosen from the eligible names received a $100 bonus. (In time, this reward too, may lose its attraction!)

USING MONEY TO MOTIVATE PEOPLE

Does money turn you on? A controversy has raged for several decades about the effectiveness of motivating people with money. At the one extreme are those who point to studies showing that employees rank money low in importance in comparison to such job factors as challenging work, opportunities for advancement, and recognition. At the other extreme are those who argue that people are still primarily motivated by money. Given the opportunity, most people seek out jobs paying more money than they are currently earning.

Recently, Richard E. Kopelman reviewed practically all the systematic studies available on the subject of the use of money in motivating people toward high productivity. He found overwhelming support for the traditional belief that money is still a top motivator. One conclusion reached, for example, was that "There is no more effective way to improve productivity than by financial incentives."[6]

For money to live up to its potential as an effective reward, certain conditions must exist or be met. To the extent that the several conditions described next apply to your situation, you will probably be motivated by money.

Money is a good motivator when you need it badly enough. Money has a motivational pull for most people who perceive themselves to have a strong need for money. Once people have enough money to pay for all those things they think are important in life, money may lose its effectiveness. There are tremendous individual differences in what people classify as "necessities." If, for example, somebody thinks owning three cars and having two residences is a necessity, that person will be motivated by money for a long time. The following case example sheds some insight on the use of financial rewards with a person of modest tastes:

> A supervisor was busily signing up people to work overtime hours for the holiday season. A 23-year-old woman said to not include her on the list. In disbelief, the supervisor said to her "How can anybody turn down overtime work during the holidays?" She replied, "Money is no big hassle for me. I lead a simple life. I make all my friends and relatives presents. I'd rather spend holiday time with my loved ones than working overtime in a factory, hustling a few extra dollars."

A financial incentive tends to be an effective motivator when it can change your lifestyle. Many people will work hard to earn enough money to change the way that they live, whether that change involves the purchase of a yacht or a used car. An assistant pharmacist worked about 30 hours a month selling Amway products (a line of household goods including toiletries and assorted gift items). His average compensation for his efforts was about $150 per month. Asked why he was willing to work so hard for what amounted to a minimum wage (in his part-time job), he answered, "One hundred and fifty dollars per month means the difference between my living at home versus having my own place. If it weren't for my Amway job, I wouldn't be leading the kind of life I want."

Money motivates you when your compensation is related to your performance.[7] One problem with owning a business is that the more hours you work, the more money you are likely to earn. You become addicted to receiving rewards. You know that if, for example, you keep your store open a few more hours per week you are likely to earn that much more money.

Not surprisingly, pay is directly related to results obtained in some occupations where the sales task is notably difficult to achieve. Life insurance agents and door-to-door sales representatives rely almost exclusively on commissions for compensation. Few people would persist in cold-canvassing life insurance prospects if pay were not directly related to performance.

You may find money to be a valuable reinforcer if you are tense and anxious about your lack of money. Many worries and concerns are financially based. If you have specific worries about current bills or past debts, it is relaxing (anxiety reducing) to receive money that can be used to take care of those obligations. Maybe you can recall your sigh of relief the last time you received a meaningful sum of money.

MOTIVATION THROUGH EMPLOYEE RECOGNITION

Another old-fashioned motivator, giving people recognition for a job well done, is of current interest. A report by two human resource professionals points out that recognizing employees for good performance still exerts a powerful influence on productivity.[8] Recognition, you will recall, is listed in Table 5–1 as a feasible motivator in a job setting. To maximize the power of recognition, it should be given to employees as a **contingent reward.** In other words, they should only receive the recognition award if they do something of merit. Typically, recognition awards are given for good service to the firm or strictly for seniority. The awards for seniority, then, probably have a smaller impact on motivation because they are not tied in with job performance.

Recognition Symbols. The first step in a formal recognition program is to develop an attractive symbol of service, which usually involves the company logo. The authors of the report in question note that when the symbol is "fashioned in gold and set with diamonds and other jewels to code years of service, it becomes the central focus of any award program."[9] The second element in the program is an attractive accessory or gift that carries the symbol. Among these items would be jewelry, pocket knives, pens, and key chains. Presenting these awards in a ceremony attended by a top organizational official is highly recommended.

It is also possible for managers to give recognition to good performers in a much less formal way. Assume that you achieved something very important on the job (such as handling a major customer problem or snuffing out a small fire). Your manager might then write a memo attesting to this fact and place the memo in your personnel file. Which would motivate you better? An expensive recognition pin or a memo to the file documenting your good deed?

Does Recognition Lead to Increased Motivation or Satisfaction? The study in question evaluated the results of 1,000 recognition award programs as perceived by the program administrators. According to these administrators (who were probably biased toward these programs), the five most frequent benefits were:

1. Increases employee recognition
2. Instills company pride
3. Emphasizes individual importance
4. Improves morale
5. Enhances company team spirit

Notice that these five benefits seem to relate to how people feel about themselves and the company, but not necessarily to how much effort they put forth or how productive they are. Stated in the language of business psychology, recognition award programs seem to be doing more for job satisfaction than job motivation. The same is true of many other programs designed to increase motivation: they demonstrate the fact that it is easier to make people happier than to make them work harder or smarter!

MOTIVATING OTHERS THROUGH EXCITING WORK

Many management experts contend that if you make jobs more interesting there may be less need for motivating people with external rewards. In other words, motivation and productivity can be increased by making jobs more exciting and challenging and giving workers more responsibility. **Job enrichment** is the most widely used approach to making jobs more interesting. In this section we will also discuss a related form of excitement on the job, called the **flow experience**.

Job Enrichment

The most advanced technique of modifying job design to increase worker motivation is job enrichment. A job is enriched by building into it more decision making, planning, and controlling. A worker who provides opinions to a supervisor about work methods has an enriched job. A job is considered enriched to the extent that it demands more of an individual's talents and capabilities. As the job becomes more meaningful to you, you become better motivated and it is hoped more productive. Unless you *want* an enriched job, these positive results may not be forthcoming. One angry worker had this comment to make about a job-enrichment program in his department:

> My job is more exciting, but it's also more taxing. I'm doing more things now, which means I have to learn more skills. I'm more tired at the end of the day. What really gripes me though is that my paycheck hasn't gotten any bigger. If management enriches the job, let them also enrich the paycheck. I don't want to be taken advantage of.

General Characteristics of an Enriched Job. A good deal of research and practical experience has gone into enriching jobs. Industrial psychologist, Frederick Herzberg, for example, has supervised the programs for enriching the jobs of over 100,000 employees in both the military and private industry. His work shows that an enriched job has eight important characteristics.[10]

1. *Direct feedback.* A worker should get immediate knowledge of the results he or she is achieving. This evaluation of performance can be built into the job (such as a highway patrol person catching a speeder) or provided by a supervisor.

2. *Client relationships.* An employee with an enriched job has a client or customer to serve, whether that client is inside or outside the organization. In this regard both a hair stylist and a staff photographer have enriched jobs.

3. *New learning.* An enriched job allows its incumbent to feel that he or she is psychologically growing. In contrast, an impoverished job allows for no new learning.

4. *Scheduling.* Employees should have the freedom to schedule some part of their own work, such as deciding when to tackle which assignment.

5. *Unique experience.* An enriched job has some unique qualities or features, such as the custodial assistants having the opportunity to report on building damage to management.

6. *Control over resources.* Herzberg suggests that groups of workers should have their own minibudgets and be responsible for their own costs. Or the individual workers might be authorized to order as many supplies as needed to get the job done (such as the purchase of diskettes for a microcomputer).

7. *Direct communication authority.* An enriched job allows the worker to communicate directly with other people who use his or her output, such as a quality-control technician handling customer complaints about quality.

8. *Personal accountability.* A good job makes workers accountable for their results. In this way they can accept congratulations for a job well done and blame for a job done poorly.

A superenriched job would have all eight of these characteristics, whereas an impoverished job would have none. The more of these characteristics present, the more enriched the job. High-level managers usually have enriched jobs. At times their jobs are too enriched: they have too much responsibility and too many different tasks to perform. Production workers are generally thought to have unenriched jobs, but sometimes organizing production workers into teams can lead to job enrichment.

The Team Approach to Job Enrichment. A popular form of job enrichment is to make jobs more exciting by organizing workers into small teams who have total responsibility for the production of an item. The team approach stands in contrast to the high specialization of an assembly line. In many instances, job enrichment through organizing workers into production teams has paid dividends to workers and management.[11]

Among the many products manufactured by Corning Glass are expensive, one-of-a-kind crystal sculptures. Many of these individual pieces carry a retail price of $600 to $800. The actual crystal figurines are manufactured by a team of people. During a plant tour, an industrial psychologist asked a young woman on such a team what she thought of the team arrangement. She replied:

> Most of all it's fun. It's like having your own crystal-making laboratory in your own basement. We work at a relaxed pace, yet we contribute some very important art to the world. After a few days work we can hold up a little glass duck that somebody is going to keep in their family for a couple of hundred years. I'd say that's a good feeling. A lot of things people make today are worn out by the time they are paid for.

Enriched Work through the Flow Experience

During surgery in a Chicago hospital, part of the ceiling of the operating room caved in and fell to the floor. The surgeon was concentrating with such intensity on the operation that only after surgery was completed did he ask about the plaster on the floor about him.[12] This anecdote illustrates the ultimate form of job enrichment: a task so intriguing to the job holder that it is capable of totally absorbing that individual's attention.

The **flow experience** is the term given for the phenomenon of total absorption in your work. In flow there is a sense of being lost in the action. The individual cares much more about the task itself than the potential external rewards derived from successfully completing the task. When you experience a sense of flow, you receive rewards from the work itself. A person who experiences flow is well motivated, whether or not status, prestige, or large amounts of money are associated with the job.

Flow tends to be found frequently in creative jobs and in athletics. A singer is often totally absorbed in his or her singing. A soccer player may receive total enjoyment from nimbly twirling a soccer ball on his or her foot. Fortunately, for purposes of job motivation, flow can be experienced by people in other than highly creative work or sports. A carpenter can experience flow while hammering a nail if the carpenter basically enjoys the activity of hammering nails. A secretary can experience flow in the process of carefully word processing a document.

Key Ingredients for Flow. Two essential ingredients of flow are a feeling of control and feedback. When you develop a sense of control over what you are doing, the task becomes self-rewarding. A tennis player who is "on" his or her game often feels totally in control of the ball. He or she can hit to the opponent's court with a feeling of pinpoint accuracy. A truck driver who is feeling flow can maneuver around the highway with precision.

The feedback that a person receives from doing a task correctly serves as a signal that things are going well. As the tennis player hits the ball squarely in the middle of the racket, there is an immediate sound (a delightful thud), indicating that things are going well. In addition, a pleasant vibration moves up the arm. As the truck driver maneuvers properly around a curve, he or she receives a road hugging feeling up through the wheels, indicating that the turn has been executed properly.

Despite the importance of control and feedback, the person who is experiencing flow doesn't stop to think what is happening. It is as if you are an onlooker and the precise actions are taking place automatically. Your body is performing pleasing actions without much conscious control on your part. When you are totally absorbed in reading a book, you do not realize you are turning the pages—your fingers take over for you. A pizza chef totally absorbed in twirling pizza dough gives no thought to the twirling. The dough just seems to rise up off the table into the air and above his fingertips.

MOTIVATION THROUGH EMPLOYEE PARTICIPATION

Another major strategy for increasing the motivation of employees is to allow them to participate in decisions affecting themselves and their work. (In Chapter 14, we will discuss this topic again in relation to the leader acting as a participative manager.) People tend to be better motivated when they participate in decision making because they become *ego involved* in the matter. For example, if it was your suggestion to purchase a particular machine for the office, you would probably be well motivated to use that machine. Employee participation also has a positive effect on job satisfaction. Here we will mention four different aspects of work in which an employee might be asked to provide input. Again, the practical consequence of this participation is often increased employee motivation and productivity.

Goal Setting. One widely used strategy for increasing employee motivation and performance is to have them set some of their own work goals. Because these goals reflect part of their self-concept, people put more effort into reaching these goals than they do into reaching goals arbitrarily set by management.[13] This goal-setting strategy works best with ambitious people performing complex jobs. Many people resist setting their own production goals. Some employees even regard participation in goal setting as a form of manipulation by management.

Increasing motivation through participation in goal setting can be regarded as a special case of job enrichment. If you help determine your own work goals, you would have a more responsible job than another employee who simply follows orders. Goal setting contributes so much to the psychology of work that it will be the entire subject of the next chapter.

Participation in Technical Suggestions. A natural way to encourage employee participation is to give employees a chance to make suggestions about the technical details of their jobs. Often this takes the form of employees giving their advice on how to improve the workings of the job. For instance, a waitress might be asked her opinion about what management can do to better please the customers. Bit by bit, as large numbers of employees throughout the organization contribute technical suggestions, the work force becomes better motivated and satisfied. A Westinghouse executive puts it this way: "Participative management is most of all a way of releasing the natural, inherent enthusiasm of and creativity of the entire organization."[14]

Decision Making about Administrative Matters. Many employees like to provide their input into decisions about topics that go beyond the confines of their particular job. These nontechnical matters are often termed administrative work and could involve such things as general working conditions, the assignment of offices, and department budgets. An example follows:

> An assistant professor in a department of business suggested to the department head that he purchase a small-sized copying machine for the office. The purpose of this machine would be to allow professors to make a few quick copies themselves without having to go through the central copying center. Following the professor's advice, the department head did authorize the purchase of a personal copying machine for the office. As a result, the assistant professor's satisfaction and motivation increased. The rest of the department, too, had at least a temporary surge in morale.

Participation in Setting Working Hours. Today a large number of firms grant their employees some say in setting their own working hours. Called **flexible working hours** (or **flexitime**), these programs consistently make employees happier and sometimes lead to increased motivation and productivity.[15] Flexible working hours are more frequently found in offices than in factories or mills. If you worked under flexitime, you would be expected to work certain core hours.

As shown in Figure 5–1, a core is typically from 10 A.M. to 3:30 P.M. You would then be free to choose which hours from 7 A.M. to 10 A.M. and from 3:30 P.M. to 6:30 P.M. that you wanted to work. Time-recording machines are often used to monitor whether or not employees have put in their fair share of work for the week. As with most organizations, you would be expected to work 40 or 37½ hours.

A.M.	(One-half or one-hour lunch)	P.M.
Flexible	Core	Flexible
7:00 10:00	3:30	6:30

FIGURE 5-1
Typical flexible working hours schedule.

MOTIVATION
THROUGH COMPETITION

To increase your motivation, some organizations will put you in competition against other employees. Many managers believe that a healthy degree of competition increases the motivation (and therefore performance) of individuals and groups. You are most likely to encounter motivation through competition in sales work. Sales representatives from the same company sometimes compete for cash bonuses, vacation trips, home appliances, and even trading stamps. An employee suggestion system in which only a limited number of the suggestions submitted are rewarded is also based on the principle of competition.

Competition can increase motivation, but it can also create a number of headaches for management and employees. When competition gets strong enough, some of your co-workers may try to block your work. Several case studies have shown that competition is only effective when two conditions are met:[16]

1. The reward offered is desired by all the participants. For instance, offering a color TV set as a reward might not increase your motivation if you were afraid of the radiation allegedly emitted from color TV receivers.

2. Competing groups or individuals must feel that they have a relatively good chance of winning. In the classified ad department of a newspaper, a contest was held to see who could process the most ads within a two-month period. All the other employees in the department believed that one particular woman would win because she had been the most rapid worker in the past. Employees, as predicted, were not motivated by this ad processing contest.

Motivation through competition can be regarded as a special case of positive reinforcement. However, the probability of receiving a reward for

In order to increase your motivation, some organizations will put you in competition against other employees.

any given individual or group is small. Generally, the most competitive people will exert extra effort to win. Many people will continue along with their usual amount of effort, which brings forth a more predictable set of rewards.

Good and Bad Forms of Competitiveness. A competitive spirit will generally help a person advance his or her career. For example, you will only respond to motivation by competition if you enjoy competing with co-workers. An analysis by clinical psychologist Robert Meier suggests that there are two forms of competitiveness, one healthy and the other unhealthy. The difference lies in the distinction between competing for a reasonable goal and competing for the goal of trying to outdo others for its own sake. Striving to get ahead in business in order to gain such rewards as more money, benefits, and status reflects a healthy form of competitiveness.

Unhealthy competitiveness is shown in striving to get ahead *for its own sake*, in order to feel like a superior person. Meier cautions that you may have the competitive disease if (1) you need to advance and reach higher levels in order to protect your self-esteem, and (2) you feel good only if you achieve rank and status. If you think that your competitiveness is of the unhealthy, envious variety, Meier suggests that you should forcefully ask yourself questions such as these:

> What do I actually prove by trying to being king (or queen) of the mountain?

> Is there really a contest going on around me all the time to determine who's the smartest, the richest, or the most attractive person, or is this mostly going on inside my own head?

> If I strive to be the best, don't I always end up being a slave—to the next goal, the next hurdle, the next steppingstone? Whose interests am I serving, anyway?[17]

MOTIVATION THROUGH FEAR AND PUNISHMENT

Fear

A manager attended a talk about the use of positive reinforcement to increase productivity. After the talk, the manager commented to the speaker, "Maybe what you say about encouraging people is true in some companies, but not in mine. Our company is a leader in its field. Yet fear is the only technique we use to motivate our management team. Every manager is told by the president that, if he makes a major mistake or doesn't give his all to the company, he will be canned. No excuses, no second chances. Every manager in our company is afraid of losing his job. Where does positive reinforcement fit in here?"

As this case example illustrates, there are some instances in which motivating people through fear will work. But it is a far less effective strategy in the long run than appealing to your dignity and self-worth. If you are motivated by fear, you may very well search for revenge. Production workers sometimes use sabotage in retaliation for being motivated through fear. Executives sometimes retaliate against fear motivation by joining another company and taking along trade secrets to the new company.

One reason that fear or the threat of punishment is sometimes effective as a motivator is that most individuals have some need to avoid pain or achieve financial or job security. The strength of such needs depends on individual and situational differences, but they are usually lower-level needs.

Threatening you with dismissal if you make a major mistake tends to work under three conditions: (1) You are highly self-confident and therefore can work effectively under threats. (2) You believe that no other good alternatives to working for your present organization exist at the time. (3) You are not a particularly self-motivated person and thus require strong external pressure to perform at a high level of output.

Punishment

Defined precisely, **punishment** is the negative consequence one receives as a result of some behavior or activity. Both actual punishment and the threat of punishment are still widely used on the job as motivational tactics. As mentioned earlier, punishment is rarely used in behavior modification programs in industry. Instead, punishment is used much less systematically by managers trying to control the behavior of subordinates. Behavioral scientists have studied the drawbacks of punishment as a method of motivating (or teaching) people. These drawbacks include the following:[18]

1. The results of punishment are not as predictable as those of reward. If you punish somebody for not performing the job correctly, it is difficult to predict how they will respond.
2. The results of punishment are less permanent than those of reward. Somehow, people tend to forget punishments rather quickly.
3. Punishment is frequently accompanied by negative attitudes toward the person who administers the punishment, as well as the activity itself. For instance, one young man who was punished several times by his sergeant for not having polished his own shoes came to dislike both the army and shining shoes! Once a civilian, he faithfully wore scuffed shoes, which certainly did not help his career.
4. Similar to fear, punishments and the threats of punishment are tied in more closely with lower-level needs rather than higher-level needs. As such, they are weak motivators.

Despite these reservations about punishment as a motivator, punishment is still important in maintaining discipline in a work setting. Employees should recognize that negative consequences will be forthcoming from certain kinds of counterproductive behavior such as poor performance, fighting on the job, and excessive absenteeism. More will be said about punishment in Chapter 12 for dealing with counterproductive people.

TECHNIQUES FOR MOTIVATING YOURSELF

Many students of business psychology and practicing managers often interpret theories and techniques of work motivation as a way to motivate other people. Of equal importance, a study of work motivation should help you to energize yourself to accomplish worthwhile tasks. In general, applying the techniques discussed in this chapter (and the motivation topics in Chapter 4) to yourself should help you to understand the conditions under which you are likely to work and study hard. Described next are six techniques for motivating yourself, all based on theory and research about human behavior.

Set Goals for Yourself

Goals are fundamental to human motivation. Set yearly, monthly, weekly, daily, and sometimes even morning or afternoon goals for yourself. For example, "By noontime I will have emptied my in-basket and made one suggestion to improve safety practices in our shop." Longer-range, or life, goals can also be helpful in gathering momentum in spurring yourself on toward higher levels of achievement. However, these have to be buttressed by a series of short-range goals. You might have the long-range goal of becoming a prominent architect, but first it would be helpful to earn an A in a drafting course.

Identify and Seek Out Your Motivators

Having read this chapter, combined with some serious introspection, you should be able to identify a few job elements that turn you on (your personal motivators). Next find a job that offers you them in ample supply. You might have good evidence from your past experience that the opportunity for close contact with people (comradeship or good interpersonal relationships) is a personal motivator. Find a job that involves working in a small, friendly department.

Owing to circumstances, you may have to take whatever job you can find, or you may not be in a position to change jobs. In that situation, try to arrange your work so you have more opportunity to experience the reward(s) that you are seeking. Assume that solving difficult problems excites you, but your job is 85 percent routine. Develop better work habits so that you can more quickly take care of the routine aspects of your job. This will give you more time to enjoy the creative aspects of your work.

Get Feedback on Your Performance

Few people can sustain a high level of drive without getting an objective or subjective opinion on how well they are doing. Even if you find your work exciting, you will need feedback. Photographers may be enamored with aspects of their work. Yet photographers, more than most people, want their work displayed. A display delivers the message, "Your work is good enough to show to other people."

If your boss or company does not recognize the importance of feedback (or simply forgets to tell people how they are doing), don't be hesitant to ask an occasional question such as:

"Is my work satisfactory so far?"

"How well am I doing in meeting the expectations of my job?"

"I haven't heard anything good or bad about my performance. Should I be worried?"

Apply Behavior Modification to Yourself

The information presented earlier in this chapter about others using behavior modification to motivate you can also be applied to self-motivation. To boost your own motivation through reinforcement principles, you have to (1) decide whether you should be rewarded or punished for your behavior, and (2) administer those rewards or punishments. You become both the jury and the judge.

One method of using behavior mod for self-motivation would be to decide which of the rules for the user of PR (described on pages 107 to 110) would make the most sense in your particular situation. A lot depends on the particular motivational problem you are facing. The representative example presented next will help direct you toward an approach that might work for you.

Brett keeps a sloppy desk and work area. His job is that of an automobile service manager. Customers with complaints and problems often meet with Brett in his small office. Brett and his boss both know that such a messy desk looks bad for the automobile dealership. Brett realizes that his disorganized desk also hampers his efficiency. He wastes a good deal of time looking for misplaced papers. Using the power of PR, Brett might try this approach:

First, he should make a list of all the good things that he can think about as a result of having a clean and orderly desk. Among the many items on his list might be, "I could find things in a hurry. This would decrease my so frequently being behind schedule." "I would impress my boss." "I would feel less tense because I would be in control of my job."

Second, Brett should force himself to make a logical plan for organizing his desk and keeping it organized. His plan might include getting an additional file cabinet and new in- and out-baskets. (Chapter 16 has much to say about getting organized.)

Third, Brett should reward himself for any progress he makes toward the goal of maintaining a neat and orderly desk. He might purchase himself a new fountain pen for having kept an orderly desk for an entire day; he might buy himself a new tie; or he might order an attractive wastebasket for his office. Brett should keep a chart of his progress, perhaps making simple notations on his desk calendar.

Brett, however, would not reward himself all the time. A fantasy reward now and then could be helpful. Brett might say to himself, "If I continue to keep an executive-looking desk, perhaps someday I will become an executive in a large automobile dealership."

Fourth, Brett should develop a plan of administering himself occasional punishments for lack of progress or for slipping backward to an even messier desk. A good deal of self-discipline is required to punish yourself for not moving in the direction of achieving a goal. Suppose that Brett discovers that he is procrastinating about cleaning up his work area and maintaining a sensible filing system. He might punish himself by coming to work on a Sunday morning to clean up his work area.

Many people have used a plan such as Brett's to overcome counter-productive habits such as nail biting and cigarette smoking. With some modification to suit your particular circumstances, you should be able to use behavior modification to motivate yourself toward some worthwhile end.

Increase Your Effort-to-Performance Expectancies

Expectancy theory was described in Chapter 2 as a modern general explanation of human motivation. ET can also be applied to the problem of self-motivation. The idea is for you to increase your subjective hunch that your effort will lead to good performance on a given task. One way to increase your $(E \rightarrow P)$ expectancy is to increase your level of skill with respect to a task for which you want to be highly motivated. If a person has the necessary skills to perform a particular task, that person will usually raise his or her subjective probability that he or she can get the task accomplished.

A recommended strategy for increasing your $(E \rightarrow P)$ expectancies in a wide variety of situations is to raise your general level of self-confidence. Self-confident people, by definition, tend to have high subjective hunches that they can achieve performance in many situations. Raising your self-confidence is a long and gradual process, as described in Chapter 4.

Raise Your Level of Self-Expectation

A final important strategy for increasing your motivational level has to do with the Pygmalion effect turned inward, or setting up a self-fulfilling prophecy to guide your own behavior. Instead of somebody else having high expectations of your performance, you set up these high expectations for yourself. You expect to succeed, so you do succeed. Often this same phenomenon is called developing a **positive mental attitude.** Since you expect to succeed, you do succeed, so the net effect is the same as if you increased your level of motivation.

Although the concepts of effort-to-performance expectancies and self-expectations are not identical, they are related. If you have many high $(E \rightarrow$

P) expectancies, you are a self-confident person. And if your raise your level of self-expectation, you begin to behave in a self-confident manner.

SUMMARY OF KEY POINTS

☐ This chapter examines a number of techniques and methods for increasing the motivation of other people and yourself, particularly in a work setting. Motivation, in general, is an inner state that activates or moves a person toward a goal. Work motivation refers to expending effort toward the accomplishment of a goal considered worthwhile by the organization. Emotions are linked to motivation because they often lead to motivated behavior, and they sometimes interfere with motivating a person by rational methods. Given a choice, most people are motivated by the prospects of serving their self-interest.

☐ A manager's expectations of subordinates can influence their actual performance. Employees tend to live up to (or down to) a supervisor's expectations of them.

☐ Underlying the use of behavior modification in organizations is the law of effect. According to this law, behavior that leads to a positive consequence tends to be repeated, whereas behavior that leads to a negative consequence tends not to be repeated. Nine rules have been formulated for using the positive reinforcement aspect of behavior mod on the job. Among the most important considerations are (1) choosing an appropriate reward, (2) scheduling rewards intermittently, (3) telling the person what behavior will lead to a reward, and (4) changing the rewards from time to time.

☐ Financial incentives are effective in increasing motivation and productivity, particularly under these conditions: (1) You need the money. (2) The amount of money can change your lifestyle. (c) The amount of money you receive is related to your performance. (d) You are tense and anxious about your lack of money.

☐ Giving employees recognition for a job well done can be an effective motivator and lead to increased productivity. Recognition programs involve developing an attractive recognition symbol and making formal award ceremonies. It is possible that, in reality, these programs do more for job satisfaction than motivation.

☐ Another popular motivational strategy is to enrich jobs by building into them more decision making, planning, and controlling (thus giving the job holder more responsibility). A related approach to job enrichment is to make work more exciting by organizing workers into small teams that have total responsibility for the production of an item. An ideal state of job enrichment is when the job holder experiences flow, a feeling of total absorption in the task at hand. It is characterized by intense concentration and effortlessness in performing the job.

☐ Another approach to increasing employee motivation is to allow them to participate in decisions affecting themselves and their work. Motivation is increased because employees become ego involved in the job. Areas of potential participation in decision making include (1) goal setting, (2) technical suggestions, (3) administrative matters, and (4) setting working hours (flexible working hours).

☐ Engaging employees in competition can also increase motivation. The individual should learn to differentiate between healthy and unhealthy competitiveness. Fear and punishment are two related motivational techniques. Punishment has its place in maintaining discipline, but it has several negative side effects.

☐ Six important general principles of self-motivation are (1) set goals for yourself, (2) identify and seek out your own motivators, (3) get feedback on your performance, (4) apply behavior modification to yourself, (5) increase your effort-to-performance expectancies, and (6) increase your self-expectations.

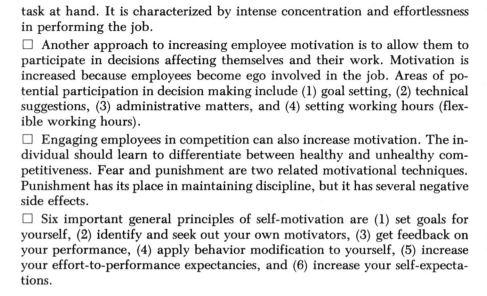

GUIDELINES FOR PERSONAL EFFECTIVENESS

1. One critical factor related to success in all occupations is motivation—the expenditure of effort toward goals. To increase or sustain your level of motivation, it is recommended that you pick and choose from the six techniques described previously.

2. A relatively easy way of increasing your motivation and performance is for others to raise their expectations of you. Raising your self-expectations might be helpful in increasing your own motivation. However, it is not easy to raise your self-expectations.

3. A well-documented and highly recommended approach to motivating others is to systematically apply positive reinforcement. The general audience book, *The One Minute Manager,*[19] presents a very simple and practical method of using PR on an informal, day-to-day basis. PR can also be helpful in self-motivation.

4. Your level of satisfaction and motivation will increase substantially if you find a job activity so interesting that you experience flow—total absorption in what you are doing.

5. Although it often works well in the short range, motivating others through fear and punishment is an ineffective long-range strategy. It leads to defensiveness and hostility.

DISCUSSION QUESTIONS

1. How strong is your work motivation? What evidence do you have to support your answer?
2. It has been said that recognition is one of the most important motivators in our society. What support can you give for this contention?
3. How might the Pygmalion effect work in terms of your performance in this course?
4. Pick your favorite sport and your favorite coach in that sport. Does the coach you picked seem to make effective use of positive reinforcement?
5. Which three of the rewards listed in Table 5–1 are the most appropriate for motivating you? How do you know?
6. Which type of workers probably do not want to participate in decision making about their jobs?
7. What evidence can you present that public personalities, such as movie stars, athletes, and TV newscasters, are strongly motivated by money?
8. What kind of work has given you, or do you think will give you, the sensation of flow? Would you take a lower paying job to get that sensation?
9. Do you think flexible working hours would be effective for the position of bank teller? Why or why not?
10. What evidence do you see that the strategy of motivation through competition is used in the classroom?
11. What do you think makes so many managers believe in motivation by fear?

A Business Psychology Problem
*HOW DO YOU MOTIVATE A COUPON SORTER?**

Lance McGraw took Jennie Kent's advice and did install new screening procedures for hiring coupon sorters. After eight months of using these procedures, it seemed that some of Lance's earlier problems were under control. Turnover was down and the newly hired employees seemed to enjoy their work. Several of the new employees even took the initiative to thank management for having given them a job that is just right for them. Lance noticed, however, that productivity within the group was below company standards. Although the coupon sorters seemed to be enjoying their work, they were too relaxed.

*Refer to the problem at the end of Chapter 3 for background information about the setting of this case.

They did not seem to pay much attention to the output figures suggested by the company.

Lance paid another visit to Jennie. The substance of his comments were, "Jennie, this time I have another tale of woe. The personnel procedures you suggested have helped me reduce turnover. And some of the new people we hired are good workers. But I think we have a bunch of contented farm animals. They like what they are doing, but they are working at a pace below what R. G. Blair Company wants.

"What advice can you give me to get these coupon sorters to hustle a little? As you know, there are strict limits on what we can pay them."

1. What program of employee motivation do you suggest be used to increase the productivity of these coupon sorters?
2. Do you think that management should adopt a philosophy of "shape up or ship out"? Why or why not?

REFERENCES

[1]Bernard Berelson and Gary A. Steiner, *Human Behavior: An Inventory of Scientific Findings* (New York: Harcourt Brace Jovanovich, 1964), p. 239.

[2]Stephen P. Robbins, *Organizational Behavior: Concepts, Controversies, and Applications,* 2nd ed. (Englewood Cliffs, N.J.: Prentice-Hall, 1983), p. 133.

[3]The original discussion of this topic appears to be J. Sterling Livingston, "Pygmalion in Management," *Harvard Business Review* (Jan.–Feb. 1969), pp. 81–89. See also, John P. McSweeney, "Pygmalion in the Plant," *Personnel Journal* (Aug. 1977), pp. 380–381.

[4]A comprehensive source of information about behavior modification in organizations is Richard M. O'Brien, Alyce M. Dickenson, and Michael P. Rosow (eds.), *Industrial Behavior Modification: A Management Handbook* (Elmsford, N.Y.: Pergamon, 1982).

[5]Several of these rules are based on W. Clay Hamner, "Using Reinforcement Theory in Organizational Settings," in Henry L. Tosi and W. Clay Hamner, *Organizational Behavior and Management: A Contingency Approach,* 3rd ed. (New York: Wiley, 1982), pp. 534–541.

[6]Richard E. Kopelman, "Linking Pay to Performance Is a Proven Management Tool," *Personnel Administrator* (Oct. 1983), p. 68.

[7]John B. Miner, cited, ibid., p. 65.

[8]David J. Cherrington and B. Jackson Wixom, Jr., "Recognition Is Still a Top Motivator," *Personnel Administrator* (May 1983), pp. 87–91.

[9]Ibid., p. 90.

[10]Frederick Herzberg, "The Wise Old Turk," *Harvard Business Review* (Sept.– Oct. 1974), pp. 70–80.

[11]Several of these programs are described in Paul Bernstein, "Using the Soft Approach for Hard Results," *Business* (April–June 1983), pp. 13–21.

[12]This section of the chapter is based on William Barry Furlong, "The Fun in Fun," *Psychology Today* (June 1976), pp. 35–38, 80.

[13]Henry L. Tosi and Stephen J. Carroll, *Management*, 2nd ed. (New York: Wiley, 1982), p. 430.

[14]E. J. Cattabiani and Randall P. White, "Participative Management," *Issues & Observations* (Aug. 1983), p. 2. Published by the Center for Creative Leadership, Greensboro, N.C.

[15]John R. Turney and Stanley L. Cohen, "Alternative Work Schedules Increase Employee Satisfaction," *Personnel Journal* (March 1983), pp. 202–207.

[16]Tosi and Carroll, *Management*, p. 429.

[17]Robert Meier, "Are You Too Competitive?" *Success* (July 1983), p. 67. The above discussion is based on the same article, pp. 28–31, p. 67.

[18]James L. Gibson, John M. Ivancevich, and James H. Donnelly, Jr., *Organizations: Behavior, Structure, Processes*, 4th ed. (Plano, Texas: Business Publications, 1982), p. 67.

[19]Kenneth Blanchard and Spencer Johnson, *The One Minute Manager* (New York: Berkley Books, 1983).

SUGGESTED READING

"A Personal Achievement Guide to Motivation." *Success* (Oct. 1981), pp. A2–A8.

BATE, PAUL, and IAIN MANGHAM. *Exploring Participation*. New York: Wiley, 1981.

DUNHAM, RANDALL B., and JON L. PIERCE. "The Design and Evaluation of Alternative Work Schedules," *Personnel Administrator* (April 1983), pp. 67–75.

FORD, ROBERT. "Job Enrichment Lessons from AT&T," *Harvard Business Review* (Jan.–Feb. 1973), pp. 96–106.

MIHAL, WILLIAM L. "Merit Pay: More Research Is Needed; Goals May Motivate Better," *Personnel Administrator* (Oct. 1983), pp. 61–67.

MOORE, LEWIS B. "Motivation through Positive Reinforcement," *Supervisory Management* (Oct. 1976), pp. 2–9.

NELSON, DAVID E. "Employee Control Is an Important Variable in Work Schedules," *Personnel Administrator* (June 1983), pp. 118–123.

ROSENBAUM, BERNARD L. *How to Motivate Today's Workers: Motivational Models for Managers and Supervisors*. New York: McGraw-Hill, 1982.

SCANLON, BURT K., and ROGER M. ATHERTON. "Participation and the Effective Use of Authority," *Personnel Journal* (Sept. 1981), pp. 697–703.

SHYNE, KEVIN. "Olympic Motivators," *Success* (March 1983), pp. 23–25, 52–53.

6

GOALS AND HUMAN BEHAVIOR

LEARNING OBJECTIVES

After reading and studying this chapter and doing the exercises, you should be able to

1. Understand the importance of goal setting in achieving satisfaction and productivity in your work and personal life.
2. Explain the basics of goal-setting theory.
3. Establish a set of goals for your present job or program of study at school.
4. Write a tentative set of career goals.
5. Recognize the problems sometimes created by goals.

THE IMPORTANCE OF GOAL SETTING

A successful attorney and author, Keith DeGreen, says, "All truly successful men or women I have met or read about have one thing in common. At some point in their lives, they sat down and wrote out their goals. The first great key to success begins with you, a piece of paper, and a pencil."[1]

This quote describes aptly the importance of goal setting in our work and personal lives. A goal gives us direction because a **goal** implies an individual's intentions to regulate his or her actions. With goals we focus our effort in a consistent direction. Without a goal our effort is often scattered in a variety of directions. We keep trying, but it leads us nowhere unless we receive more than our share of luck.

Goals and Success. Another value of goal setting is that the process increases our chances for success. Particularly so since success can be defined as the achievement of a goal! When we set goals for accomplishing a task, they serve as a standard for knowing when we have done a satisfactory job. A real estate agent might set a goal of selling $1,000,000 in one year. By November she might close a deal that places her sales for the first 11 months at $1,100,000. With a sigh of relief she can then say, "I've done well this year."

Aside from helping you become more productive, goals can contribute to success in another way. Setting goals can help you to achieve satisfaction (which is part of being successful). One important fact about human behavior is that most people derive an inner source of satisfaction from attaining a goal that is meaningful to them. Suppose that you establish the modest goal of cleaning out your desk this weekend and you accomplish it. You will achieve a temporary good feeling from that accomplishment. Assume that your goal is to graduate from business school, and you do graduate. Your feeling of personal satisfaction will be of greater intensity than if you graduated without having set an explicit goal.

Goal setting should be regarded as an extension of our discussion on motivation and performance. Virtually all programs of motivation and productivity improvement include some element of setting goals. A good example would be motivation through competition, where employees set goals of trying to outperform other employees. A review of research prepared by William Mihal points to the importance of goals in helping work organizations achieve success. He concludes that goal-setting programs are perhaps the single most effective technique for improving performance yet developed.[2]

Much of this chapter contains information about the specifics of how to set goals. It is important, however, to first understand some of the well-documented theory that underlies goal setting.

GOAL-SETTING THEORY

A large number of research studies has been conducted on the application of goal setting to human behavior on the job. Over 90 percent of these studies support the basic ideas contained in the goal-setting theory of Edwin A. Locke. The results indicate clearly that setting goals leads to improved performance, as you would probably suspect.[3]

The basic facts of goal-setting theory are shown in Figure 6–1. Underlying goal theory is the key idea that behavior is regulated by values and

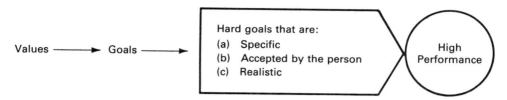

FIGURE 6-1
Basics of goal theory.

goals. A **goal** is defined as a conscious intention, or simply as what the person is trying to accomplish. Our values create within us a desire to do things consistent with them. Thus, if you value helping other people, you might establish the career goals of working in the human services field (such as managing a nursing home).

Goal-setting theory also contends that hard (difficult) goals lead to a higher level of performance than easy goals. It is also important to make goals specific rather than general, such as "do your best." The goals people work toward generally lead to improved performance whether these goals are set by them or the organization, providing the individual accepts the goal.[4] Another important consideration is that the goals set by the individual should not be so unrealistically high that they most likely result in frustration due to failure. If you want to become wealthy, it would be best to begin by setting realistic goals, such as finding a good job in a good company or starting a small business.

The basics of goal-setting theory have such a big impact on your work and personal life that they require elaboration.

Specific Goals Improve Productivity

Setting specific goals for work performance is of major value in improving productivity. Among the dozens of studies that have supported this idea was one involving unionized truck drivers.[5] A paper manufacturer faced a costly problem involving the loading of logging trucks. If the trucks were underloaded, the company lost money because of inefficient use of trucks, personnel, and diesel fuel. If the trucks were overloaded, the driver could be fined by the highway department and face losing his job. The drivers typically took the conservative choice of underloading the trucks.

To deal with this problem, six logging operations in Oklahoma were studied. Each operation consisted of six to ten people who performed one of the following operations: felling a tree, dragging the tree to a landing, loading the tree into a truck, or driving the truck to the mill where it is weighed and unloaded.

Management's first attempt to solve this problem was to urge the drivers to try harder to fill the truck to its legal maximum net weight by developing scales that could be attached to the truck. (This is called the "do your best" approach to goal setting.) The maneuver proved too costly because the scales continually broke down when subjected to the rugged terrain over which the trucks traveled. Consequently the drivers returned to their previous practice of underloading the trucks. During the three months in which the problem was under study, the trucks were rarely loaded in excess of 58 to 63 percent of the legal maximum.

The team of researchers working on the problem suggested that the company set specific weight goals for the truckers. Part of the program was that the only reward for good performance would be spoken praise, and that no penalties would be imposed for not reaching the goals. Union officials were skeptical that a tough production problem could be solved so easily. Nevertheless, they reached an agreement that a goal of 94 percent of the truck's legal weight would be assigned to the drivers.

The results of this experiment were dramatic. During the first month, performance jumped to 80 percent. After the second month, performance slipped to 70 percent. Interviews with the drivers conducted by the researchers indicated that the drivers were testing management's promise of no punishment for poor performance. The supervisors held true to this promise, and the performance exceeded 90 percent of the truck's average capacity after the third month. Seven years later, performance was still up. The results over the nine-month period during which the study was conducted saved the company an estimated $600,000 (expressed in current dollars).

Difficult Goals Improve Performance

Locke has proposed that, as long as goals are accepted by the individual, the more difficult the goals, the higher the performance. A number of laboratory and field studies have supported this maxim.[6] A limiting factor, however, is that a point of diminishing returns quickly sets in. If a goal is perceived as so difficult that it is almost impossible to attain, the result will be frustration rather than increased accomplishment. Difficult goals have a bigger impact on performance improvement when the person who faces the more difficult goals is highly self-confident. If you are self-confident, you are less concerned about not reaching a work goal. A young man from New York City explains how he improved his work performance through difficult goals:

I worked in the "pressure cooker" of a company that manufactured and sold industrial solvents. Ten of us would sit in a room filled with telephones. We would call companies all over the United States giving them our sales pitch. After a while I psyched myself up for the calling by standing up and shouting into the phone. I was doing great. Each week the company would raise my quota by two sales. After a while I thought I was becoming the best over-the-phone salesman in the city. I knew that if I sold enough chemicals over the phone, I would soon be entitled to my own office.

Participation Improves Goal Setting Indirectly

It is certain that goals lead to improved performance, but another aspect of goal-setting theory is much less certain. This uncertainty centers around the importance of employee participation in setting work goals. Based on about 12 experiments, the evidence so far suggests that:[7]

1. Participation in goal setting leads to higher performance than simply assigning goals to employees, providing the participation leads to higher goals. When given the chance to contribute to the goal-setting process, employees will sometimes have higher expectations of themselves than management might have for them.

2. Participation sometimes improves the goal setting process because it leads to high acceptance of the goal. The employee then performs better. However, if employees accepted the goal already, participation makes very little contribution to improved performance. For instance, if a government agency was told to cut costs by 10 percent or be abolished, most employees would accept the goal of cutting costs. Allowing them to participate in the cost-cutting goal would have no particular impact on goal setting—or performance.

3. How goals are set is much less important than the fact that goals *are* set. And since participation is but one method of goal setting, its importance has therefore been overexaggerated.

An experiment conducted with typists provides support for the preceding conclusions, particularly point 3. One group participated in setting goals, while the other group of typists were assigned goals. In the participative group, the employees chose to set exceptionally high goals whether or not they had attained their goal the previous week. Consistent with the theory that high goals lead to high performance, their productivity improved week to week.

In the assigned-goal group, the supervisors were purposely highly supportive of their employees. Failure to attain goals did not result in criticism. Instead, the supervisor showed support by lowering the goal after failure so that the employee could reach the goal in his or her next attempt. The goal was then raised gradually each week until the employee appeared to be reaching his or her potential. The result was feelings of accomplishment and achievement for the typists involved and improved productivity for the company.

Tabulation of the results showed that both assigned and participative goals led to substantial improvements in typing speed. It did not matter so much how the goal was set. The crucial factor was the fact that a goal was set.[8]

Now that we have presented a strong case for the value of goals, it is time to recognize that there is an art to setting goals that will lead to success.

THE NATURE OF SUCCESSFUL GOALS

"I'd like to make it big someday" is a nice thought but not likely to ensure success. A more useful goal would state specifically what you mean by "making it big" (such as being a vice-president of a bank). It would also state when you expected to make it big (such as December 31, 1993). However, setting a goal that leads to success is not so simple. The following paragraphs offer some suggestions for establishing goals that are likely to result in successful outcomes.

1. Formulate clear, concise, and unambiguous goals. A useful goal can usually be expressed in a concise statement much like a telegram. Such a goal might be, "Develop an inventory control system that reduces inventory costs by 25 percent by June 30 of this year."

2. Describe what you would actually be doing if you reached your goal. A vague goal for a data-entry clerk would be "to become a better data-entry clerk." A more useful goal would be "to increase current speed to 100 lines of data per hour" or "increase the average number of discs filled per week." The meaning of "better data-entry clerk" needs to be narrowed down as much as possible.

3. The goal must be consistent with organizational policies and procedures. A goal that violates company policy only leads its setter into trouble. One caseworker established the objective of making night calls to agency clients in order to facilitate communication with them. She was later reprimanded by higher management for violating an agency restriction about after-hours work.

4. Set interesting and challenging goals whenever possible. It is important to recognize that trivial goals are not motivational. At the same time, goals that are too far beyond your capability may lead to frustration and despair because there is a good chance you will fail to reach them. As implied earlier, realistic goals fall somewhere between the two. An income tax specialist might find challenging a goal that stated, "Successfully complete income tax returns for two small businesses by April 15 of this year."

5. Specify what is going to be accomplished, who is going to accomplish it, when it is going to be accomplished, and how it is going to be ac-

complished. Establishing the "what," "who," "when," and "how" in your goals reduces the chance for misinterpretation. Here is a work goal meeting these requirements: "The waterbed sales manager will increase sales by 50 percent within 12 months. Returns will be subtracted from the dollar amount of sales. Waterbeds will not be offered to the public at or below cost."

6. *Review your goals from time to time.* An experienced goal setter realizes that all goals are temporary to some extent. In time, one particular goal may lose its relevance for you, and therefore may no longer motivate you. At one period in your life you may be committed to earning an income in the top 10 percent of the population. Along the way toward achieving that goal, some other more relevant goal may develop. You might decide that the satisfactions of being self-employed are more important than earning a particular amount of money. You might therefore open a retail store with the simple financial goal of "meeting my expenses."

Psychologist David Campbell expresses the desirability of flexible goal setting in this way:

> Practically all goals tarnish with time if not renewed in some way. A job that is exhilarating during the first year becomes less so after five years; without renewal it becomes an automatic activity after ten years, and a prison after twenty. The same for a marriage. The divorce rate, perhaps the best indication of a marriage failure, continues to climb and demonstrates that even relationships of love ("till death do us part") can weaken and change with time if there are no changes.[9]

SETTING GOALS FOR DIFFERENT TIME PERIODS

Many of the goals mentioned in this chapter include a date for their attainment. It also helps the goal-setting process to classify goals into a time frame roughly as follows: long range, medium range, short range, daily, and immediate.[10]

Long-range goals relate to the overall lifestyle that you wish to achieve, including your highest level of career accomplishment and the family situation you hope to have. A hospital might set the long-term goal of becoming "the biggest and most influential general hospital in this region by the year 2000."

Medium-range goals relate to events that will take place in the next five years or so. They concern things such as the type of education or training you plan to undertake and the next step in your career. An example of a medium-range goal is, "Become a supervisor within this company within four years." You usually have more control over medium- than long-range goals and you can tell how well you are achieving them. If you are falling behind in reaching a medium-range goal, you can adjust your actions accordingly.

Short-range goals cover the period from about one month to one year into the future. Many short-range goals are used on the job, as illustrated in the preceding section.

Daily goals relate to what you intend to accomplish today. Most successful people establish daily goals for themselves in the form of a "do list" (see Figure 6–2). We will return to this topic in Chapter 16.

Immediate goals are concerned with the next 15 minutes to an hour. No one can accomplish long-range, medium-range, short-range, or daily goals without paying attention to immediate goals. A successful philosophy of goal setting contends, "The only kind of planning you have direct control over are the modest little goals; the trick of planning a successful life is to stack together these smaller goals in a way that increases your chances of reaching the long-range goals you really care about."

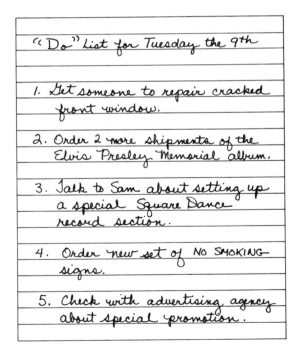

"Do" List for Tuesday the 9th

1. Get someone to repair cracked front window.

2. Order 2 more shipments of the Elvis Presley Memorial album.

3. Talk to Sam about setting up a special Square Dance record section.

4. Order new set of NO SMOKING signs.

5. Check with advertising agency about special promotion.

FIGURE 6–2
Daily work goals of assistant manager of record store.

EVERY GOAL NEEDS
AN ACTION PLAN

Suggestion 5 for establishing successful goals included the idea that you should specify *how* you are going to accomplish the goal in question. The accepted way of answering how is to develop an **action plan**—a series of steps that will be taken in order to achieve your goal. The major reason you need an action plan for most goals is that, without a method for achieving what you want, the goal is likely to slip by. Goal-setting programs on the job usually encourage the individual to draw an action plan to support the goal being pursued. Action plans are also important in personal life.

One of the goals mentioned in the preceding section concerned a data-entry clerk who intended to "increase current speed to 100 lines of data per hour" or "increase the average number of discs filled per week." Action planning to achieve this goal might include such things as (1) taking a refresher training course, (2) participating in a stress management workshop to improve mental concentration, and (3) getting more sleep on a regular basis to increase mental alertness.

Do You Always Need an Action Plan? Some goals are so difficult to reach that your action plan might encompass hundreds of separate activities. You would then have to develop separate action plans for your major subgoals. If your goal were to lead a rewarding and satisfying career, the techniques presented in this book could help you formulate many of your action plans. Among these skill-building techniques are assertiveness, resolving conflict, solving problems and making decisions, and developing good work habits.

Some very short term goals do not really require an action plan. A mere statement of the goal may point to an obvious action plan. If your goal were to get your computer account number from your school or employer today, it would not be necessary to draw up a formal action plan, such as "Go to office of student services, speak to clerk, ask for computer account number form, take ball pen from pocket, fill out form, return same."

GOAL SETTING ON THE JOB

"We're in a tough line of work. If we can't account for what we've done with our time and money, we'll be put out of business. Everybody in this place knows what's expected of him or her. And everybody has to produce."

The person just quoted is not a sales manager nor a factory manager. He is the executive director of a neighborhood center that provides services to the community, such as day care for children and unemployment counseling. His center operates under a system of **management by objectives** (MBO). Everybody in the agency has specific objectives to reach that he or she helped to establish. An objective in this context is a lesser goal that contributes to the larger goals of the total organization. The goal of an organization might be to increase profits by 10 percent. A department objective to help reach that goal might be to decrease department operating costs by 10 percent.

Goal Setting in an MBO Program. MBO is fundamentally an application of goal-setting theory to help individuals and organizations to be more productive. Since it is used in such a wide variety of profit and nonprofit organizations, MBO lacks a format that is uniformly applied in every organization.

A key element, however, can be found in most programs. An MBO program typically involves people setting many objectives for themselves. However, management frequently imposes important objectives on people. The top management of a hospital might impose the following objective on all ward personnel: "All prescription drugs must be accounted for with 100 percent accuracy."

A sample set of objectives is shown in Figure 6–3. The caseworker who set these objectives took into account the requirements of her boss and the agency. Even if you set objectives by yourself, they still take into account the needs of your employer.

Job Title and Brief Job Description

Caseworker: Responsible for interviewing welfare applicants for public assistance. Serve as liaison person between agency and client. Provide clients assistance on matters of managing personal resources.

Objectives for Wanda Benjamin

1. By December 31, 1986, fifteen percent of my clients will be able to live adequately without benefit of public assistance. I will accomplish this by helping them to find employment or additional help from close relatives.

2. Improve my handling of hostile clients by using transactional analysis to achieve this end. I will attend a week-long TA workshop in February.

3. Decrease by 75 percent the number of case reports that I submit to my manager past their due date.

4. Increase by 20 percent the number of clients that I serve by spending less time with my most troubled clients.

5. Will coordinate my efforts more closely with utility company to ensure that my clients do not spend cold nights without heat.

FIGURE 6–3
Memo form used in social agency for statement of objectives.

Ethical Concerns about MBO Programs. Later in this chapter we will examine some of the problems associated with goal setting in general. The MBO approach to goal setting has aroused a good deal of controversy, despite the many solid contributions it has made to organizations. Among the criticisms of MBO is that it manipulates employees and is therefore unethical. MBO programs are sold to employees as being organization-wide programs of participative management. Yet, in practice, not much participation takes place.

After interviewing several hundred managers in an MBO program, one researcher reached this conclusion: "Managers may feel forced to accept objectives that they honestly feel are unrealistic or undesirable because they are unable to argue effectively against them."[11] The argument here is that your input is important if you are going to be measured in terms of how well you achieved these objectives.

A stronger ethical argument against MBO is that they are systems of phony participation. The fiction is maintained that the subordinate is making a real input into planning work goals and procedures. Yet he or she is forced into setting goals that fit exactly what the company wanted in the first place.[12]

Of course, not all employees working under an MBO (or similar) system feel they are being manipulated. Do you see any ethical problems with management by objectives?

SETTING GOALS FOR YOUR CAREER

A person's chances of finding career satisfaction increase if he or she establishes clear-cut goals. The opposite of the goal-setting process is referred to as **occupational floundering.** It occurs "when an individual enters the labor market seeking full-time work without having a chosen commitment to an occupational goal or for one reason or another does not adapt to that goal once it is attained."[13] A fortunate few flounderers find their way into rewarding jobs and careers. One vice-president of marketing began employment in his company as a draftsman. A sales manager asked him to try his hand at selling because he was familiar with the workings of the machines sold by the company. Ultimately, this individual rose to the vice presidency, having no early goal that related to marketing or sales. For most people, goal setting is crucial for success.

The two types of career goals we are concerned with here are (1) levels of responsibility (or career pathing), and (2) financial goal setting.

Levels of Responsibility

After a person finds a field compatible with his or her interests, and then finds an entry-level job, the process of career-goal setting becomes meaningful. Career-goal setting is also referred to as **career pathing** because the goals

A person's chances of finding career satisfaction increase if he or she establishes clear-cut goals.

establish a path to important destinations in your career. In some organizations there is a logical path from beginning jobs to higher-level jobs, such as rising from first lieutenant to colonel in the army, or from management trainee to department head at General Electric. Of course, not everybody can make it to the top.

A career path should include several contingency plans or alternatives you will accept if you run into detours in your career. An ambitious graduate of a business school with a major in secretarial sciences who wants to rise to the top in his or her field might establish goals and contingency plans such as these:

1. Word-processing technician for two years in large firm.
2. General (nonprivate) secretary in large department for four years.
3. Private secretary to middle manager for two years.
4. Executive secretary for three years.
5. Administrative assistant to executive for four years.
6. Manager of word-processing department for five years.

7. Second-level office manager for six years.
8. Owner and operator of boutique until physically and mentally unable to continue.

Contingency Plans for These Goals

1. Will seek new employment if by stage 2 not promoted to private secretary.
2. If not promoted to manager of word processing (or comparable position) by stage 6, may set up own word-processing firm.
3. If develop stress disorder at any point (such as bad heart), will retreat to job as word-processing technician or clerk in smooth-running (nonhectic) firm.

This person's career goals include the time element, which, as mentioned earlier, is crucial to sound career management. Your long-range goal might be clearly established in your mind (such as owner of an automobile dealership). It is also necessary to establish short-range goals (for example, get any job connected with the automobile business) and intermediate-range goals (sales manager of an automobile dealership by age 30). Most people cannot rely on long-range goals exclusively because they cannot wait that long for satisfaction. It is motivational to pursue some shorter-range goals because they yield quicker satisfaction.

Financial Goal Setting

Some people establish income goals rather than focus on the kinds of work they want to do. Today, for example, it is said that you are achieving financial success if you "earn your age in thousand dollar units." Therefore many people set the goal of earning $25,000 by age 25; $30,000 by age 30, and $55,000 by age 55. One problem with this financial rule-of-thumb is that it does not take into account the effects of inflation or the differences in wage rates in different fields.

A career goal set by some money-motivated people is to double their salary every seven years. Such an accomplishment is supposed to signify career success. Although this goal sounds fanciful, it is realistic if you take into account inflation and the fact that salary increases are compounded. That is, the income base on which you get a raise keeps increasing. One year you earn $20,000. The next year you receive a 10 percent increase, thus earning $22,000; the next year with another 10 percent increase, you will receive $24,200, and so forth.

If a person reading this book takes on a job at $22,000 in 1986, the same person will be earning $176,000 per year by the year 2007, assuming a doubling of salary every seven years. What are you going to name your yacht?

A *Nonfinancial Way of Setting Financial Goals.* Financial goals expressed in dollar figures have several disadvantages. First, it is difficult to predict accurately the effects of inflation. You must therefore use a standard such as, "By 1992 I would like to earn $35,000 per year expressed in 1985 dollars." Second, financial goals do not point you toward work in which you will necessarily be successful. People who earn high incomes usually do so because they are successful in their work. Third, financial goals may seem too shallow to some people. For those people it is preferable to strive to earn enough money to support a particular lifestyle. An example would be, "By the year 2000, I want to earn enough money to own my own home, plus a large camper, and take two vacations a year."

Despite these reservations about financial goals, they do have two potential advantages. If your financial goals are modest, it gives you more flexibility in choosing a field; you don't have to be concerned much about salary when choosing a career or a job. Also, if your financial goals are high, it can help point you toward fields that give you a chance of meeting your goals. For example, companies in the business equipment field tend to pay better than public utilities.

SETTING GOALS FOR YOUR PERSONAL LIFE

Personal goals enter heavily into the formulation of career goals. For this reason alone, it is well worth setting personal goals and objectives in conjunction with career goals. Ideally, there would be an integration or meshing of career and personal goals. Several examples are in order.

One young man may have a strong interest in visiting museums, shopping at retail stores, dancing at discotheques, and dining at a variety of restaurants. One personal goal that he formulates is to have enough money and to live in an area where he can lead such a cosmopolitan life. His occupational goals should then include developing job skills that are needed in large cities. The same man may set a personal goal of dating a large number of women for many years into the future. His career planning might then focus on obtaining employment in a geographic location such as Washington, D.C., where there are many more single women than men.

A young woman might develop an early preference in life for the outdoors, with an emphasis on hunting, fishing, and camping. She might also be interested in raising a large family. Part of her career planning should include developing skills that are in demand in rural areas where her preferences are easier to satisfy than in a city. She then learns that in recent years many manufacturing facilities have been developed in rural and semirural areas. Her career planning might then include the goal of developing job skills that are in demand in a factory or mill. Secretarial skills, of course, are in demand everywhere. Another alternative for her would be to develop technical and professional skills that would enable her to find a manufacturing job. For instance, she might seek a job as a manufacturing technician.

Career Goals Can Influence Personal Goals. In many situations a person's career goal exerts a heavy influence on personal goals. One 22-year-old male decided that he wanted to become a commercial artist. One of his major personal goals was to become a successful motor cross (motorcycle racing) racer. After careful deliberation, he decided to give up on his motorcycle goals. The reason he offered was this: "Without a good right hand and a good mind, I'll never make it as a commercial artist. Too many of my buddies have been smashed up racing their bikes. My art means more to me, so I'll find some other off-the-job thrills. Maybe golf or model airplane racing."

Similarly, many other individuals have postponed marriage or raising families in order to better establish themselves in their career. A heavy travel schedule, for instance, might place too many strains on a young marriage or a young family. Some people with heavy travel schedules have postponed raising a family until that phase of their career has passed.

Fantasy and Personal Goal Setting. Some people find it exciting to add an element of fantasy to their personal goal setting. A fantasy goal is usually a goal that is way beyond attaining at your present stage in life, but someday it may become a realistic goal. At one time fantasy goals were thought to be wasteful, but current information indicates that fantasies may help both career and personal life. Fantasies are supposed to help with personal adjustment and reduce stress.[14] As long as a person continues to believe that life will be wonderful one day, that person finds it easier to be optimistic about life. Specifically, it is easier to cope with everyday frustrations when you believe that a magnificent future awaits you. Fantasy goals often bridge the gap between personal and career goal setting. Here is a sampling of fantasy goals found in the career reports of young adults:

"Someday I would like to own a stable of horses and have one of them win the Kentucky Derby."

"I would like to take a year off from work and go big-game hunting in Africa."

"Once my children are grown, I would like to travel around the world taking nature photographs for fun and profit."

"Before I retire I would like to be a millionaire and buy a major league hockey team."

PROBLEMS SOMETIMES
CREATED BY GOALS

Despite the positive aspects of goals discussed in this chapter, they are not without flaws. As one woman expressed it, "I have never taken goal setting too seriously. I like to live my life spontaneously." Two major criticisms of goal setting will be discussed next.

Goals Often Neglect Achieving a Balance between Quality and Quantity. If you set difficult goals on the job, quantity may be given priority over quality. You might, for example, turn out numerous shoddy products just to meet your quota. An example from personal life is that you might set an arbitrary goal of dating six new people over the next three months. In your quest to date six people you might fail to recognize that the fifth person you date

IT'S SMICKLEY AND PERKINS FROM ACCOUNTING. THEY DO THIS EVERY CORPORATE CHARTER.

Some people find it exciting to add an element of fantasy into their personal goal setting.

would make an excellent long-term companion for you. In short, in addition to setting goals, you should set priorities as to the relative importance of quantity and quality.

Goals Sometimes Become Obsessions. In some instances people become so obsessed with reaching particular goals that they cannot react to emergencies or fail to grasp real opportunities. Many sales representatives neglect to invest time in cultivating a prospective customer simply because of the pressure to achieve a specific sales quota.

Short-range goals sometimes backfire for another reason. Long-term negative consequences are sometimes ignored for the sake of the short range. The argument has been advanced, for example, that saving the taxpayer money by cutting back on youth programs could incur more expense in the long run. Some of the young people no longer enrolled in the youth program might turn to crime. It can cost society as much as $35,000 per year to imprison one convicted criminal.

When goals become obsessions, they lead to neglect in another way. Sensing that reaching goals is the only thing the company cares about, an individual might neglect other important aspects of his or her job. Suppose you are a salesperson in a furniture store. You are paid strictly on a commission basis. To maximize your pay, you might concentrate on selling fast-moving merchandise (such as inexpensive desk lamps). In the meantime you might neglect trying to sell slower-moving items such as high-quality bedroom sets. Some students find themselves facing a similar situation when taking a course. They might be tempted to concentrate their efforts on the details they think will be on a forthcoming test and neglect to review other important aspects of the course.

Despite the problems that can arise in goal setting, goals appear to be a valuable tool for managing your work and personal life. Used with common sense and the ideas presented in this chapter, goals can have a major impact on your life.

SUMMARY OF KEY POINTS

☐ A goal is an individual's conscious intention to regulate his or her actions. Goal setting increases your chances for attaining satisfaction and productivity. According to goal-setting theory, a person's intentions regulate his or her actions. Specific goals lead to a higher level of performance than do abstract or generalized goals such as "do your best." Difficult (hard) goals consistently lead to higher performance than do easy goals. Participation leads to higher performance in goal setting only to the extent that it leads to (1) higher goals and (2) greater goal acceptance.

☐ A successful (effective) goal has the following characteristics:

1. Clear, concise, and unambiguous.
2. Describes what person will be doing when the goal is reached.
3. Consistent with organizational policies and procedures.
4. Interesting and challenging, thus motivational.
5. Specifies "what," "who," "when," and "how."

☐ It is also helpful to set goals for different time periods, such as long range, medium range, short range, daily, and immediate. Every goal should be backed up by an action plan—a series of steps or actions that will be taken in order to achieve the goal.

☐ Goal setting on the job often takes the form of a management-by-objectives (MBO) program. It involves both individual and organizational goals and can also be considered a system of management. MBO programs have been criticized as being unethical because they impose goals on people while pretending to be participative.

☐ Career goals play a significant role in achieving career success and satisfaction. When you set career goals, or a career path, it is advisable to also set contingency plans. Two types of career goals are (1) levels of responsibility that you hope to attain and (2) amounts of money you hope to earn. Personal goals should be kept in mind when establishing career goals. Setting fantasy goals can both help your career and be beneficial to your outlook on life.

☐ Despite their advantages, goals sometimes create problems. These potential problems include (1) neglecting quality at the expense of quantity, (2) not taking care of emergencies or using opportunities, and (3) ignoring activities not tied in with the established goals.

GUIDELINES FOR PERSONAL EFFECTIVENESS

1. A major improvement that you can probably make in your career or personal life is to set realistic goals. In addition, you must develop action plans for attaining these goals.
2. Even if your place of work does not have a formal system of goal setting, you will personally benefit for setting work goals for yourself. Such goals will generally lead to improved performance.
3. Although goals are very beneficial, be careful not to become obsessed with attaining them. The obsession, in turn, will limit your flexibility in exploring new opportunities and alternatives.

DISCUSSION QUESTIONS

1. What do you see as the relationship between psychological needs and goals?

2. What relationship do you see between goal-setting theory and the theories and programs of motivation discussed in previous chapters?

3. A 22-year-old man wrote in a career report that his goal was to become president of the United States. His job at the time was floor manager in a department store. If you were his instructor, what comments would you have made about his goal?

4. What similarity do you see between learning objectives (of the type found in the beginning of each chapter in this book) and work objectives?

5. Do ambitious and well-motivated people really need goals on the job? Or will they do their job just as well without goals?

6. What are three personal goals you have set for the future? How will you know when you have reached them?

7. What are two potential disadvantages of having career goals?

8. It has been observed many times that many wealthy people never set financial goals for themselves. What kind of goals do you think they set that led to their wealth?

9. What is your fantasy goal?

10. How useful has goal setting been to you in your personal and work life?

A Business Psychology Problem
THE WHIZ KID LOOKS AT HIS FUTURE[15]

Question: Can a 19-year-old young man be successful and happy selling real estate?

Answer: Yes, if he is Scott Cohen, who turned 20 a few days ago but not before he had sold $2 million worth of residential housing in one year.

And happy he is. Also enthusiastic. And hard-working.

This young man has to be one of the legitimate whiz kids of local real estate.

He looks four or five years older than his age, but he is a verified 20 and he is making a mark for himself on the real estate scene with the enthusiasm of youth and the results that come from long hours and a dedication to his craft.

Curiously enough, he is an exponent of the "soft sell" technique, which you might not expect from someone who has made such a spectacular success of a brief career.

"I love to work. I've worked hard and I really enjoy giving my time and energy to the people with whom I deal. I think it is an absolutely fascinating profession, and I guess that's why I've done so well."

Scott had taken some economics and political science courses at a college in San Francisco and took some more real estate schooling at a local college. He obtained his real estate salesman's license and joined the firm of A. J. Petranto in March of last year.

He "did well" with the Petranto firm, selling about $1,500,000 worth of houses in 10 months. "It was a tough decision for me to change, but I wanted a broader marketing base, so I left and went with Town Crier."

He apparently wasted no time making his mark with the new company. In his first month he won the top-salesman award for the entire company (it has 15 branches, 300 salespeople), and then for three months in a row won the top award for his office (22 salespeople).

Amazingly, the majority of his sales are in the city rather than the suburbs, and his sales usually run in dollar amounts between $20,000 and $52,000.

"I'd rather sell four houses at $50,000 each than have one going for $200,000, because if that latter deal falls through you are nowhere. The other way you always have something cooking."

Cohen, as you might expect, is already shooting for his broker's license. A state law decrees that a person must be 21 years old to get one.

He admits that he works long hours. "I'm out of the house by 8:30 every morning, and I usually don't get back until 10 P.M. I try to work Monday through Thursday, but I'm always still working the rest of the time, too. Or at least part of it."

Cohen was a Junior Achievement winner. "I said at one time I'd never go into sales, but I sure changed my mind. It's dynamite."

"The day for the pushy salesman is over. That's no good. I believe in giving a lot of service and working hard for people. I feel comfortable with the younger crowd, and I try to dress conservatively, but stylishly, so I make sense to older people, too. I give as much service to people for a $50,000 sale as for someone with a house that goes for $200,000."

He is enthusiastic about his job, and about the city. "The trend is toward city properties. There are some beautiful areas of the city that are overlooked, I have found."

"I'm doing about 90 percent of my deals now through VA- and FHA-insured mortgages; I guess I've really become an expert on the forms and paperwork involved, so I can show people the advantages of these programs. You know, it's an excellent way for people to get started in home owning without having to come up with a big down payment, so they don't have to hold off and wait until they have enough money to make their 'big' buy, which takes too many years."

Cohen, who is getting married in July, has a goal. "I want to retire at thirty-five."

Retire? Well, he has just bought his first house, a double, for investment purposes. He is "dealing around" for vacant land. If he "retires" at thirty-five, you can bet he will continue in real estate investments and property management. "I just think the whole field is wonderful." Even though, he just turned 20, he had to pay income taxes last year on something like $60,000!

1. What evidence do you see of goal setting on the part of Scott Cohen?
2. What do you think are several of Scott Cohen's major personality traits?
3. How realistic is Cohen's stated goal, "I want to retire at thirty-five"?

A Business Psychology Exercise
GOAL SHARING AND FEEDBACK

Each person writes down one occupational (or school) and one personal goal that he or she would be willing to share with other members of the class. In turn, every class member presents these two goals to the rest of the class exactly as they are written down. Other class members have the privilege of providing feedback to the person sharing his or her goals. Here are some questions you should ask yourself about the goals you have written down to avoid common errors in goal setting:

1. Is the goal too lengthy and complicated? Is it really a number of goals rather than one specific goal?
2. Is the goal so vague that the person will be hard pressed to know if he or she has reached that goal? (Such as, "I intend to become successful.")
3. Does the goal sound sincere? (This is admittedly a highly subjective judgment on your part.)

REFERENCES

[1]"Goal-Setting Guide," *Success* (Jan. 1983), p. A–10.

[2]William L. Mihal, "Merit Pay: More Research Is Needed; Goals May Motivate Better," *Personnel Administrator* (Oct. 1983), p. 67.

[3]A thorough review of this topic is Gary P. Latham and Gary A. Yukl, "A Review of Research on the Application of Goal Setting in Organizations," *Academy of Management Review* (Dec. 1975), pp. 824–845. An update of similar information is found in Gary P. Latham and Herbert A. Marshall, "The Effects of Self-Set, Participatively Set and Assigned Goals on the Performance of Government Employees," *Personnel Psychology* (Summer 1982), pp. 399–401.

[4]Miriam Erez and Frederick H. Kanfer, "The Role of Goal Acceptance in Goal Setting and Task Performance," *Academy of Management Review* (July 1983), p. 458.

[5]Gary P. Latham and J. James Baldes, "The 'Practical Significance' of Locke's Theory of Goal Setting," *Journal of Applied Psychology* (April 1975), pp. 122–124.

[6]Gary P. Latham and Timothy P. Steele, "The Motivational Effects of Participation Versus Goal Setting on Performance," *Academy of Management Journal* (Sept. 1983), pp. 406–407.

[7]Ibid.

[8]Gary P. Latham and Edwin A. Locke, "Goal Setting—A Motivational Technique That Works," *Organizational Dynamics* (Autumn 1979), p. 74.

[9]David Campbell, *If You Don't Know Where You're Going, You'll Probably Wind Up Somewhere Else* (Niles, Ill.: Argus Communication, 1974), p. 12.

[10]Based on ibid., pp. 36–40.

[11]Charles D. Pringle and Justin G. Longenecker, "The Ethics of MBO," *Academy of Management Review* (April 1982), p. 306

[12]Ibid.

[13]Lou Varga, "Occupational Floundering," *Personnel and Guidance Journal* (Dec. 1973), p. 225.

[14]Stephen Sprinkel, "Not Having Fantasies Can Be Hazardous to Your Health, Counselor Says," Rochester *Democrat and Chronicle* (April 10, 1982), p. 12B.

[15]Bill Beeney, "Whiz Kid at 19—$1 Million in Sales His First Year in Real Estate Business," Rochester *Democrat and Chronicle* (May 7, 1978), p. 1H. The dollar figures cited are updated to reflect current real estate values. Scott Cohen now has his own real estate firm.

SUGGESTED READING

CHACKO, THOMAS I., and JAMES C. MCELROY. "The Cognitive Component in Locke's Theory of Goal Setting: Suggestive Evidence for a Causal Attribution Interpretation," *Academy of Management Journal* (March 1983), pp. 104–118.

COVELSKI, MARK A., and MARK W. DIRSMITH. "MBO and Goal Directedness in a Hospital Context," *Academy of Management Review* (July 1981), pp. 409–418.

FORD, GEORGE A., and GORDON L. LIPPITT. *Planning Your Future: A Workbook for Personal Goal Setting.* La Jolla, Calif.: University Associates, 1976.

HUGHES, CHARLES L. *Goal Setting.* New York: AMACOM, 1965.

LATHAM, DONALD R., and DAVID W. STEWART. "Organizational Objectives and Winning: An Examination of the NFL," *Academy of Management Journal* (June 1981), pp. 403–408.

LATHAM, GARY P., and LISE M. SAARI. "The Importance of Union Acceptance for Productivity Improvement through Goal Setting," *Personnel Psychology* (Winter 1982), pp. 781–787.

————Timothy P. Steele, and Lise M. Saari. "The Effects of Participation and Goal Difficulty on Performance," *Personnel Psychology*. (Autumn 1982), pp. 677–686.

Murray, Richard K. "Behavioral Management by Objectives," *Personnel Journal* (April 1973), pp. 304–306.

Odiorne, George S. *MBO III: A System of Managerial Leadership of the '80s.* Belmont, Calif.: Fearon-Pitman Publishers, 1979.

7

SOLVING PROBLEMS AND MAKING DECISIONS

LEARNING OBJECTIVES

After reading and studying this chapter and doing the exercises, you should be able to

1. Make more effective decisions on the job and in everyday life.
2. Understand the underlying factors that influence a person's decision making.
3. Understand why decision making is not an entirely rational process.
4. Understand how creativity influences solving problems and making decisions.
5. Develop a plan for improving your own creativity.

Three business associates and friends, Barry, Lani, and Rick, are comfortably employed by a large corporation. All three are relatively satisfied with their careers, but each person is to some extent a thrill seeker. In past discussions Barry, Lani, and Rick have shared with each other their eagerness to do something exciting and challenging with their business lives. At Rick's initiative, one evening the three of them meet to discuss a topic of profound significance. Rick informs Barry and Lani:

"I think I finally have the idea for an opportunity of a lifetime. Let me hit you full blast with my idea to make us rich. You know that vacant car dealership on Alpine Avenue? I drive by it about every day on the way to work. Last week as I glanced at that vacant property it flashed across my mind that the site would be ideal for a night club. Later that evening, I came up with a good idea for the motif. Why not place the shell of a mammoth fiber-glass yacht around the present building? We could then have a club with a yacht motif throughout. The ticket takers would dress like yachtsmen and yachtswomen, including captain's hats and fishnet stockings for our waitresses and coat room attendants. We could call the place The Pleasure Cruise. What do you think gang?"

Barry, Lani, and Rick have a heavy decision to make if the idea for The Pleasure Cruise goes beyond the fantasy stage. The process by which they will make this *decision* is similar to the *decision-making* process at all levels in business and personal life. A **decision** is a choice among two or more alternatives. There are many alternatives facing these three friends. **Decision making** is the "process of thought and deliberation that leads to a decision."[1] Much of our chapter will be devoted to information that has a direct bearing on making effective decisions.

DECISION-MAKING STAGES

Your decision-making effectiveness tends to increase when you use a systematic approach to solving problems and making decisions. The diagram presented in Figure 7–1 is one such generally accepted approach. It summarizes our explanation of solving problems and making decisions. Much of the information presented throughout this chapter is an elaboration of the elements contained in Figure 7–1. The diagram is based on the assumption that decision making should take place in an orderly flow.

We begin with an awareness of a problem, try to clarify the problem, search for creative alternatives, weigh the alternatives, choose one of the alternatives and implement it, and evaluate the outcomes. At any stage of the decision-making process, certain factors influence our thinking. The decision faced by Barry, Lani, and Rick will be used to illustrate the mechanics of solving problems and making decisions.

Awareness of Problem. The process of solving a problem and making a decision begins with an awareness that a problem exists. A problem has been defined as something that begs to be worked on. That "something" is a gap or discrepancy between an existing and a desired situation. By this definition, a problem is not limited to an observed situation that requires repair. It could also mean an opportunity waiting to be taken, including the possibility of improving an already acceptable condition.[2]

Rick has found a problem or perhaps an opportunity. He believes that he and his two friends should decide whether or not to open The Pleasure

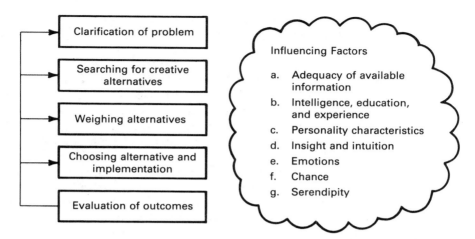

FIGURE 7-1
Stages in solving problems and making decisions.

Cruise. A decision of this nature is really a major decision composed of dozens of smaller decisions. If the group decides to pursue the idea further, they will have to make decisions about who to contact for help, where to get legal advice, where to get financing, which contractors to approach, and so forth. Of major importance, they will also have to decide whether or not to quit their regular full-time occupations.

In most instances of decision making, problems are *given*. Somebody hands us a problem for which a decision has to be made. The check-out woman in the supermarket says to her boss, "This gentleman wants a refund on his leg of lamb. He says it tasted peculiar." The grocery store manager must decide whether or not to grant the refund. An employee brought or gave a decision situation to him. He did not find the problem. Similarly, the loan officer at the bank has to decide whether or not she will loan a credit applicant $1000 to remodel his garage. Your instructor has to decide whether to grant or deny your request for an incomplete grade in a course. Or the traffic cop has to decide whether or not to give you a ticket for running a stoplight. He or she makes the decision, but it was brought to his or her attention.

Influencing Factors. The "cloud" in Figure 7–1 contains a list of factors that can influence a person's ability to solve problems and make decisions. For example, an individual's ability to discover a problem is related to many traits and characteristics, such as perceptiveness and intelligence. Those same factors are closely related to a person's ability to make a decision. In combination, these influencing factors help to account for individual differences in decision-making ability. Some people are much better at making decisions than others and because of this achieve a higher quality of work and personal life.

a. Adequacy of available information. People who have ready access to current, relevant information are in a good position to find problems and make decisions. Barry, Lani, and Rick would need a supply of good information about the launching of night clubs and their profitability. They would also need reliable market data about the potential demand for a lavish club with a novel motif. Could the neighborhood support another club for dancing? Would people drive across town to frequent their club? Would the crowd that they might attract dance too much at the expense of purchasing drinks?

Barry, Lani, and Rick would also need accurate information about the costs of erecting The Pleasure Cruise. Contractors might have a difficult time giving construction estimates on this unusual project. Our three potential entrepreneurs (people who start enterprises) would also have to know for sure whether or not they would be granted a full liquor license for their venture.

b. Intelligence, education, and experience of decision maker. In general, intelligent, well-educated, and experienced people are more likely to find problems and make good decisions than their counterparts of lesser intelligence, education, and experience. Common sense would suggest that this statement would go unchallenged because it is obviously true. Subtle exceptions, however, are known to exist. People without a well-developed facility for abstract reasoning (those of average intelligence or below) will sometimes see a problem or opportunity in the most rudimentary form.

> A company was embarking on a study to determine the root causes of low morale and high turnover in the organization. A worker at the very bottom level of the company made a spontaneous comment that proved to be the crux of the problem: "There's only one thing wrong with this place. The president is a cheap S.O.B. He tries to squeeze every penny he can out of the workers. He has us skimp on ridiculous things like making it almost impossible to replace a broken broom."

Let us assume that Rick is an intelligent person with a good background in the marketing end of business. His education includes two years of college plus a heavy program of company-sponsored courses. His work experience is mostly in sales and marketing, which should help in making a decision about the club. Lani and Barry have comparable backgrounds. A concern is that none of the three has made a real-life decision about a business venture in the past. An experienced night club owner—all things being equal—might be in a better position to make the right decision about The Pleasure Cruise. Many a successful business has been started by somebody who made a wrong decision in the past. They profited from the knowledge gleaned from past failures.

c. Personality characteristics of the decision maker. Traits and behavioral characteristics of an individual can also influence his or her ability to find problems and make decisions. Rigid people will have difficulty finding problems even when they are intelligent, well educated, experienced, and have access to good information. Perfectionism can also inhibit problem finding. A scientist was hired because of his presumed inventive talents. After one year had passed, this man had not only discovered nothing, he had failed to even completely define what kind of project he would like to pursue. His perfectionistic tendencies led him to rework one fundamental experiment until (in his words) its "scientific integrity is unquestionable." Similarly, cautious individuals have some difficulty in finding problems. Discovery of new opportunities requires an entrepreneurial or risk-taking flare.

Back to Barry, Lani, and Rick. Rick is the type who would find a problem. He is intellectually energetic and is forever looking for new ways to improve his work and personal life. He frequently prods his boss to spark the company's interest in carrying new lines of merchandise. Lani is a reflective type of person. In this decision situation, she will probably ask a number of good questions that need to be asked, such as, "Will the idea of a yacht lose its appeal very quickly?" or "Will people be attracted to a yachting theme all year around?"

Barry will balance out the decision-making team. He has an underlying quality of pessimism. He likes to play the devil's advocate. Perhaps that's why he's a financial analyst in his company. He is likely to ask questions such as, "Suppose the idea doesn't work? Who do you think would be interested in purchasing a used disco in the shape of a yacht? We could be paying for the wrong decision for the rest of our lives." Perhaps the blend of personality characteristics represented by Barry, Lani, and Rick will help them to arrive at a good decision.

d. Insight and intuition of the decision maker. Another important intervening variable that influences whether or not problems will be found (or effective decisions made) is insight and intuition. Finding problems or opportunities requires a person to make interpretations of trends that have not already been made. Two young men on the West Coast thought that the world was ready for a chain of restaurants in the form of converted railroad cars. They were right, as their legendary success (and their imitators) indicates. No matter how well schooled and intelligent the decision maker, intuition, insight, or "instinct" is important. As people say in so many businesses, "You have to have a feel for this business, otherwise you cannot be a success." Later in this chapter we will take a closer look at the importance of intuition in decision making.

Rick thinks he has good intuition. He has already shown good intuition in sizing up customer needs. As in most decision-making situations, you need the combination of facts and intuition to arrive at an effective decision. No matter how perceptive Barry, Lani, and Rick might be, if they cannot obtain accurate facts about bank financing for this project, they will most probably fail.

e. Emotional factors. Emotion plays a key role in problem finding and in all stages of decision making. Problem finding and decision making are not entirely rational processes. Have you ever decided to take a weekend vacation instead of studying for an exam, although all the facts in the situation suggested that you stay home and study? Intellect, reason, *and* emotion enter into most decisions. Even when decisions appear to be based almost entirely on hard data, *which* data are selected for inclusion in the decision-making process is influenced to some degree by emotion and feeling.

A strong emotional factor that our trio must contend with is that they want to find an exciting new business opportunity in life. It is difficult to be entirely rational when you are infatuated with an idea, person, or thing. As a prominent marriage counselor and psychotherapist, Albert Ellis, once said, "Just because you love someone it's not a good reason for marrying that person."

f. Chance factors. Problems and opportunities are sometimes found or correct decisions made on the basis of luck or other unpredictable factors. One foreman became a millionaire because of his investments in Xerox stock. Asked how he made such a shrewd decision, he replied, "It was mostly luck. I was there when the company was still small. It seemed like investing in the company that was putting food on your table was the right thing to do. The stock just multiplied like wildfire during the early days. I had no idea I was making a good investment at the time."

Research conducted at the Center for Creative Leadership confirms the idea that there is a good deal of luck involved in decision making. A researcher there notes that the all-knowing decision maker who decides on the basis of logic alone and with knowledge of all the facts simply does not exist. Decisions made by managers have been and will continue to be a product of judgment and luck, as well as expertise.[3]

g. Serendipity, the gift of finding valuable things not sought for, is another unpredictable factor that enters into problem finding and decision making. It is rumored that at one time New York State decided to charge an additional fee for special-order license plates, such as those with an owner's initials. The purpose of the fee was to discourage state residents from making these special orders. Word spread that the New York State Motor Vehicle Department was now offering personalized plates for a modest fee beyond that charged for the regular plates. Demand for this service has continued to be strong and has proved to be a worthwhile source of revenue.

Rick's suggestion about The Pleasure Cruise is partially attributable to serendipity. If the car dealership had not moved to a newer location, Rick would not have seen on his route to work an empty building with the potential of being converted into a club. It might be argued that, if Rick was not in some way looking for a new opportunity, he would not have noticed the building. All these influencing factors interact (act in combination) with each other.

Decision-Making Stages

Solving a problem and making a decision should proceed along a series of overlapping stages. For ease in understanding the process, problem solving and decision making are divided into five stages as shown in Figure 7–1.

1. Clarification of the Problem. The three potential entrepreneurs need to clarify the problem about which a decision has to be made. They must determine specifically what decision they are facing. Among the possibilities are these: (a) Should we investigate this site along with others as a potential club? (b) Should we think of converting this desirable site into a club or another type of business? (c) Are we talking about quitting the company and jumping into this venture full time? (d) Are we thinking of financing this venture and hiring other people to operate it? (e) Does Rick want to be in charge of the project full time, while Lani and Barry work on the project part time? (f) Are we limiting our thinking to investing in this site?

Part of good decision-making practice is to clarify the true decision being faced. Many decisions prove to be poor decisions because a decision was not made about the real problem. Management might observe that company morale is low. The antidote that they choose to boost morale is to build a new company cafeteria, at a cost of $500,000. After completion of the project, morale might decrease. The underlying cause of low morale might be that employees have so little voice in the affairs of the company. Constructing a new cafeteria without consulting the employees simply aggravated the problem.

2. Searching for Creative Alternatives. Intellectual free swinging is called for at this stage. All kinds of possibilities are explored here even if they appear unrealistic at the outset. Suppose that management is trying to encourage employees to obey speed signs to and from work and adhere to all safety regulations in the plant and office. (Management is genuinely interested in employee health and welfare, but they are also interested in lowering their accident insurance premium.) Among the many alternatives to choose from are these:

Plaster the walls with elaborate safety posters.

Fine or suspend employees involved in careless accidents.

Put the names of people who have no accident for 12 months into a lottery. Prizes of $300 and $200 will be awarded based on a random selection of the names of the accident-free people.

If insurance premiums go down because of a good accident record, the company might distribute some of the savings to employees.

Form an employee safety committee to study the problem further.

Hire two more safety engineers to design more effective safety systems.

If our trio decides to go ahead with The Pleasure Cruise idea, their creativity might be applied to such things as ways of financing the project or different ways of implementing The Pleasure Cruise motif. As a case in point, Lani suggested that the disk jockey sit in a glass-enclosed booth styled after a captain's station. Among the other ideas suggested were using portholes for windows and deep-sea fishing gear as wall decorations.

One specific decision requiring creative alternatives was how the group should approach entering this business. Should they jump in full time? Part time? The reader will note that during the clarification of the problem stage these alternatives were mentioned. In practice, decision-making stages often overlap. Information sought in one stage might be retained for use in a later stage. Barry, Lani, and Rick decided "yes," that they would explore further The Pleasure Cruise concept.

3. *Weighing Alternatives.* This stage refers simply to examining the pros and cons of the various alternatives developed in the previous stage. In facing a major decision, each alternative would have to be given serious consideration. Barry, Lani, and Rick face a major decision. Giving up their regular jobs to jump into this venture full time seems a little risky, even to adventuresome Rick. They mull over such thoughts as going bankrupt and having no good job to fall back on. However, they also recognize that a venture as big as The Pleasure Cruise may need full-time attention to launch it successfully.

A mechanical, but useful method of weighing alternatives is to list each alternative on a sheet of paper. The sheet is then divided into two columns. Advantages are listed on the left side and disadvantages on the right. An alternative that has many more advantages than disadvantages would be considered a favorable alternative in most situations. Once in a while, a disadvantage could be so striking that it would outweigh the larger number of advantages. Hiring an outside manager to run The Pleasure Cruise might have two such striking disadvantages: (a) finding a competent outside manager would be very difficult; (b) the cost involved would be prohibitive for a small new business.

4. *Choosing an Alternative and Implementation.* At the next to the final stage of the decision-making process, a choice must be made among the alternatives specified. In this situation, Barry, Lani, and Rick have decided to launch their enterprise on a part-time basis. For now (all good decisions

should be subject to change) the group will devote evening and weekend time to planning for the opening of The Pleasure Cruise. Once the club opens, the situation will be reevaluated.

In this decision-making situation, action was taken. Another alternative open in any decision-making situation is to take no action. Deciding not to go ahead with a plan is different than ignoring the problem from the outset. As within any of the three previous decision-making stages, the outcome in the final stage is somewhat dependent on the intervening variables. Had the three would-be entrepreneurs been more impulsive, they might have simultaneously quit their jobs.

5. *Evaluation of Outcomes.* The decision-making sequence is not complete until the decision has been evaluated. Evaluation, however, may take a considerable period of time. Many decisions made by managers cannot be evaluated for a long time. If a manager decides to fire Harry and replace him with Jack, it may take four months to learn if Jack is really an improvement over Harry. Personal decisions also frequently take a long time to evaluate. If you decide to purchase a four-cylinder car instead of a six-cylinder car, it may take many months, perhaps years, to know if you made a good decision. To carefully evaluate your decision, you would need to learn how well the four-cylinder car performed when you had to get out of a tight spot while driving up a hill. The trade-in value of the "four" versus the "six" would be another factor to consider.

As things worked out for our adventuresome trio, they made an eminently correct decision. The Pleasure Cruise construction and financing proceeded relatively smoothly. Opening night was a big success. Three months later the biggest problem facing Barry, Lani, and Rick was that of finding adequate parking space for the glut of customers streaming into their posh club. Within five months the trio resigned from their regular jobs to devote full time to their new business venture.

SIGNIFICANCE AND TIME PRESSURE OF DECISIONS

A student exposed to the decision-making schema said, "You mean I have to go through all that to decide which movie to go to?" The answer is no. The decision-making schema is designed to provide a systematic method of making decisions about major, important, or significant decisions. A manager, or any other employee, should spend the most time on significant decisions. The late William F. Glueck, a successful writer of management texts, has developed three commonsense measures of the significance of decisions:[4]

- *Number of people affected.* The more people affected by a decision, the more significant the decision. If one bank employee is sent home because he shows up to work in jeans, that is a relatively insignificant decision. Should the company pass an edict that anybody who wears jeans to work will automatically be suspended for the day, that is much more significant. Perhaps thousands of employees would be affected. (The company might also have a class-action civil rights suit issued against them.)

- *Relative impact of dollar amounts involved.* "A decision is significant if it affects the survival or profitability of an enterprise." One division of a major corporation was sold to another company because it only produced an annual profit of about $10,000. When asked why the parent company sold off his division, the division president said, "I guess we're just a fly speck from the overall corporate viewpoint. They don't want to bother with us any longer." Yet many small businesses would be happy to produce an annual profit of $10,000.

- *Time needed.* Significance can also be measured by the amount of time involved in acquiring the knowledge necessary to make a proper decision. Four years of apprenticeship training might be needed before a diamond cutter develops enough confidence to make the right decision about where to place the chisel on a large stone. One day of on-the-job training might provide sufficient knowledge about where to dig a hole for planting a bush. The concept of time needed can also include time spent in school to attain the appropriate knowledge or certification. Some decisions require that the decision maker be a CPA (Certified Public Accountant). One year in a specialized program might give you enough knowledge to make proper decisions about choosing the best hair style for a customer.

Time pressure is another important factor influencing decision making. When a manager, or any other decision maker, is harassed by time, the quality of the decision making may suffer. An exception is the manager who works best under heavy pressure. Under too much pressure, it is difficult to identify enough alternatives to make a good decision. Most people think more clearly when they are not rushed.

Perhaps you have had the experience of clothes shopping with another individual, and he or she says, "Please hurry, I have to be home within one hour." You wind up selecting an ill-fitting garment, a purchase decision you probably would not have made if you had taken more time. A laboratory study of business students forced the subjects to make decisions under varying degrees of pressure and distraction.[5] Under heavy time pressure and many distractions, the students placed much more weight on negative than positive evidence in arriving at decisions. The particular decision that they faced was something of interest to most people about to graduate from business school: making an automobile purchase.

INTUITION AND DECISION MAKING

Before the first edition of this book was accepted for publication, the editorial committee of the publisher had established the fact that a market existed for business psychology books. They had gathered the necessary facts about this demand in a logical and orderly manner. When the decision had to be reached about whether or not this particular book, *Effective Business Psychology*, could meet the demands of that market, facts had to be abandoned. Subjective opinions of knowledgeable people had to be pooled. Each person had to contribute his or her intuitive judgment about whether or not this particular manuscript would be of interest to students and instructors.

Intuition, or educated hunch-making, enters into most decision making about nonroutine matters.[6] When a decision is repeated frequently and is not

Intuition, or educated hunch-making, enters into most decisions about non-routine matters.

particularly complex, it can be programmed. Banks program many decisions about the issuance of small loans. If you meet certain fixed criteria of occupational stability and income, you automatically qualify for certain small loans. Some decisions are so programmed that they are made entirely by computer. A bank's computer has the decision-making authority to reject payment on a check if your balance is zero.

Henry Mintzberg studied the decision-making habits of hundreds of managers. He also pulled together evidence compiled by other management researchers. Among his many conclusions were that intuition still plays an important part in the making of management decisions. The actual program (decision-making process) that managers use remains locked deep inside their brains. Mintzberg observes:[7]

> I was struck during my study by the fact that the executives I was observing—all very competent by any standard—are fundamentally indistinguishable from their counterparts of a hundred years ago (or a thousand years ago, for that matter). The information they need differs, but they seek it in the same way—by word of mouth. Their decisions concern modern technology, but the procedures they use to make them are the same as the procedures of the nineteenth-century manager. Even the computer, so important for the specialized work of the organization, has apparently had no influence on the work procedures of general managers. In fact, the manager is in kind of a loop, with increasingly heavy work pressure but no aid forthcoming from management science.

CREATIVITY IN DECISION MAKING

Creativity is the processing of information in such a way that the result is new, original, and meaningful. Decision making calls for such an ability primarily at the stage termed "searching for creative alternatives." It requires creativity to think of a variety of potential solutions to your problem. (Decision making is one kind of problem solving.)

A creative decision maker or problem solver lets his or her imagination wander. In addition, he or she makes deliberate jumps in thinking and welcomes chance ideas whenever they come along. He or she ventures beyond the constraints that limit most people. In contrast, the conformist or less creative person "proceeds in an orderly way from point to point. Each step is supported by the preceding step, as if a computer program were being written, a mathematical proof were being derived."[8]

What Is Your Creative Potential? A logical starting point in understanding how creativity fits into decision making is to gain a tentative awareness of your creative potential in comparison to other people. Psychologists have developed standardized tests (not for use by the general public) to measure creativity. Here we will confine our measurement of creative potential to the two illustrative exercises in Exhibits 7–1 and 7–2. Do not be overly

Exhibit 7-1

WORD HINTS TO CREATIVITY[9]

The object of this exercise is to find a fourth word that is related to all three words listed below. For example, what word is related to these?

| cookies | sixteen | heart | _____ |

The answer is "sweet." Cookies are sweet; sweet is part of the word "sweetheart" and part of the phrase "sweet sixteen."
What word is related to these words?

| poke | go | molasses | _____ |

Answer: slow.

Now try these words:

1. surprise	line	birthday	_____
2. base	snow	dance	_____
3. rat	blue	cottage	_____
4. nap	rig	call	_____
5. golf	foot	country	_____
6. house	weary	ape	_____
7. tiger	plate	news	_____
8. painting	bowl	nail	_____
9. proof	sea	priest	_____
10. maple	beet	loaf	_____
11. oak	show	plan	_____
12. light	village	golf	_____
13. merry	out	up	_____
14. cheese	courage	oven	_____
15. bulb	house	lamp	_____

If you were able to think of the "correct" fourth word for ten or more of these combinations of words, your score compares favorably to that of creative individuals. A very low score (about one, two, or three correct answers) suggests that performing such remote associations is not yet a strength of yours. Here are the answers:

1. party	5. club	9. high	13. make
2. ball	6. dog	10. sugar	14. Dutch
3. cheese	7. paper	11. floor	15. light
4. cat	8. finger	12. green	

Exhibit 7-2

THE CREATIVE PERSONALITY TEST

Creative Personality Test.[10]   The following test will help you to determine if certain aspects of your personality are similar to those of a creative individual. Since our test is for illustrative and research purposes, proceed with caution in mind. Again, this is not a standardized psychological instrument. Such tests are not reprinted in general books.

	Mostly True	*Mostly False*
1. Novels are a waste of time. If you want to read, read nonfiction books.	⎯⎯⎯	⎯⎯⎯
2. You have to admit, some crooks are very clever.	⎯⎯⎯	⎯⎯⎯
3. People consider me to be a fastidious dresser. I despise looking shabby.	⎯⎯⎯	⎯⎯⎯
4. I am a person of very strong convictions. What's right is right; what's wrong is wrong.	⎯⎯⎯	⎯⎯⎯
5. It doesn't bother me when my boss hands me vague instructions.	⎯⎯⎯	⎯⎯⎯
6. Business before pleasure is a hard and fast rule in my life.	⎯⎯⎯	⎯⎯⎯
7. Taking a different route to work is fun, even if it takes longer.	⎯⎯⎯	⎯⎯⎯
8. Rules and regulations should not be taken too seriously. Most rules can be broken under unusual circumstances.	⎯⎯⎯	⎯⎯⎯
9. Playing with a new idea is fun even if it doesn't benefit me in the end.	⎯⎯⎯	⎯⎯⎯
10. As long as people are nice to me, I don't care why they are being nice.	⎯⎯⎯	⎯⎯⎯
11. Writing should try to avoid the use of unusual words and word combinations.	⎯⎯⎯	⎯⎯⎯
12. Detective work would have some appeal to me.	⎯⎯⎯	⎯⎯⎯
13. Crazy people have no good ideas.	⎯⎯⎯	⎯⎯⎯
14. Why write letters to friends when there are so many clever greeting cards available in the stores today?	⎯⎯⎯	⎯⎯⎯
15. Pleasing myself means more to me than pleasing others.	⎯⎯⎯	⎯⎯⎯
16. If you dig long enough, you will find the true answer to most questions.	⎯⎯⎯	⎯⎯⎯

Scoring the Test. The answers in the *creative direction* for each question are as follows:

1. Mostly False	7. Mostly True	13. Mostly False
2. Mostly True	8. Mostly True	14. Mostly False
3. Mostly False	9. Mostly True	15. Mostly True
4. Mostly False	10. Mostly True	16. Mostly False
5. Mostly True	11. Mostly False	
6. Mostly False	12. Mostly True	

Give yourself a plus one for each answer you gave in agreement with the keyed answers.

How Do You Interpret Your Score? As cautioned earlier, this is an exploratory test. Extremely high or low scores are probably the most meaningful. A score of 12 or more suggests that your personality and attitudes are similar to that of a creative person. A score of 5 or less suggests that your personality is dissimilar to that of a creative person. You are probably more of a conformist (and somewhat categorical) in your thinking, at least at this point in your life. Don't be discouraged. Most people can develop in the direction of becoming a more creative individual.

1. How does your score on this test compare to your own evaluation of your creativity?
2. Describe a person who you think would probably score 15 or 16 on this test. Identify him or her.
3. Do the same for a person whom you think would score 0 or 1 on this test.

encouraged or dejected by the result that you achieve on these tests. They are research instruments designed to give only preliminary insights into whether or not your thought process is similar to that of people who think of creative solutions to problems.

The Creative Personality

People known to behave in a creative manner tend to have different personality characteristics than their less creative counterparts. A large number of studies point toward one distinguishing overall characteristic. Creative people are in general more emotionally loose and open than their less creative counterparts. This emotional looseness is often manifested in practical jokes and other forms of playfulness. A case in point is Terry, a physician's assistant. One Halloween he encouraged three of his friends to join him in an outlandish prank. The first part of their prank was to borrow a coffin from an undertaker known to Terry. He also arranged to borrow four operating room uniforms. On Halloween day the four pranksters carried the coffin around downtown Cleveland during midday. Terry's playful idea worked. The foursome brought laughter to some people and shock to others.

Conclusions about the Creative Individual. Twelve conclusions can be reached about the personality characteristics and behavior of the creative individual, based on research and expert opinion.[11] As you read these traits and behaviors, try to compare them to your own traits and behaviors.

- Creative people tend to be bright rather than brilliant. Extraordinarily high intelligence is not required to be creative, but creative people are good at generating many different ideas in a short period of time.
- Creative people tend to have a positive self-image; they feel good about themselves but are not blindly self-confident.
- Creative people are emotionally expressive and sensitive to the world around them and the feelings of others.
- Creative people, almost by definition, are original and imaginative in their thinking.
- Creative people tend to be interested in the nature of the problem itself; they are stimulated (motivated) by challenging problems.
- Creative people usually suspend judgment until they have collected ample facts about a problem. Thus they are more reflective than impulsive. (A slight disclaimer here is that creative people do follow their hunches and are willing to take chances.)
- Creative people are frequently nonconformists. They value their independence and do not have strong needs to gain approval from the group.
- Creative people lead a rich, almost bizarre, fantasy life. They are just "crazy" enough to serve their creative ends.
- Creative people tend to be flexible and not authoritarian. Faced with a problem, they reject black and white, either–or (categorical) thinking and look for nuances.
- Creative people are more concerned with meanings and implications of problems than with the small details. They are able to choose the more fundamental aspects of problems and cast the superfluous aside.
- Creative people tolerate ambiguity and complexity rather than preferring predictability and order. For example, creative executives have been observed to be suspicious of pat explanations and have developed a healthy respect for groping around for the unknown when dealing with an unusual problem.

• Creative people have a youthful curiosity even when they are in their seventies and eighties. Their curiosity is not centered just on their own field of expertise. Instead, the range of interests of creative people encompasses many areas of knowledge, and they generate enthusiasm toward almost any puzzling problems.

A general picture emerges from this list of the creative person as being more loose than tight, open than closed, flexible than rigid, playful than always serious. Also, several of these characteristics support the popular stereotype of the creative person as somewhat of a maverick, both intellectually and socially. Later, we will present some suggestions from a creativity expert for helping you develop into a more creative person.

The Brains of Creative People Are Different. Some evidence exists that people who frequently find creative solutions to problems rely more on the right side than the left side of their brains. About 20 years ago it was first discovered that one's characteristic problem-solving style may depend on which hemisphere (side) of one's brain is dominant.[12] The left hemisphere of the brain controls analytical and logical tasks, such as that used in conducting a chemistry experiment or programming a computer. The right hemisphere of the brain controls intuition. It specializes in detecting patterns and meanings rather than breaking things down into analytical bits. The right side of the brain is also responsible for creative, imaginative thought, such as that necessary to think of a good idea for a new business. Creative people therefore tend to be right-brain dominant.

One implication of this type of brain research is that left-brain-dominant people tend to perform better in logical, analytical assignments. Conversely, right-brain-dominant people tend to perform better in assignments calling for intuitive, creative thought. Another implication is that each of us has both analytical and intuitive capabilities. Through practice, you can develop your creative, intuitive thinking or your logical, analytical thinking.

Most people tend to be biased in one direction or the other. It would therefore be helpful to your career to develop more fully the nondominant side of your brain. If you are too right-brained, you could develop your analytical skills (as is normally done in the majority of courses in a business curriculum). If you are too left-brained, you might consider the creativity-enhancing exercises presented later.

What Triggers Creativity?

An individual with the characteristics and brain makeup of a creative person will not inevitably bring forth creative solutions to problems. Triggering creativity from an individual requires the right interaction between that person and the environment. Support for this conclusion comes from the work of a psychologist who has conducted several studies on job creativity.[13] He concludes that the appropriate condition for creativity has five ingredients. When they are all present, creative behavior is almost a certainty.

First, you need a person of sound intelligence, someone who has a high capacity for learning, for abstracting, for solving problems, and for detecting differences. Second, the potentially creative person must have a strong ego and be confident that he or she can overcome problems. Third, the person must be faced with a need (environmental condition) that stimulates the setting of a goal. (To quote an old adage, "Necessity is the mother of invention.") Fourth, a barrier must exist to reaching this goal, and a standard solution to overcoming the barrier should not be available. Fifth, the person must have insight (defined here as a broad awareness of the self and environment).

Improving Your Creativity

Creativity can sometimes be improved through formal training programs. One of them, group brainstorming, will be described in Chapter 13 about working within a group. At other times, do-it-yourself techniques can be equally beneficial. Here we summarize 12 exercises and principles suggested by Eugene Raudsepp as a guide to creative growth.[14]

1. *Keep track of your ideas at all times.* Keeping an idea notebook at hand will help you to capture a permanent record of flashes of insights and good ideas borrowed from others.

2. *Pose new questions every day.* If your mind is questioning and inquiring, it will be creatively active. It is also a mind that constantly enlarges the circumference of its awareness. "Have fun, and enjoy your creative probings and experiences."

3. *Maintain competence in your field.* The information explosion makes knowledge become obsolete quickly. Having current facts in mind gives you the raw material to form creative links from one bit of information to another.

4. *Read widely in fields that are not directly related to your field of interest.* Look for the relationship between what you read and what you already know. Once you learn how to cross-index the pieces of information you gather, you will be able to cross-fertilize seemingly unrelated ideas.

5. *Avoid rigid patterns of doing things.* Strive to overcome fixed ideas and look for new viewpoints. Experiment and always generate several alternative solutions to your problems. Develop the ability to let go of one idea in favor of another.

6. *Be open and receptive to your own as well as to others' ideas.* Seize on tentative, half-formed ideas and hunches. A new idea seldom arrives

in finished form. Entertain and generate your own far-fetched or silly ideas. If you are receptive to the ideas of others, you will learn new things that can help you behave creatively.

7. *Be alert in observation.* Search for the similarities, differences, and unique features of things and ideas. The greater the number of new associations and relationships you form, the greater your chances of arriving at creative and original combinations and solutions.

8. *Engage in creative hobbies.* Develop hobbies that allow you to produce something with your hands. You can also keep your brain tuned up by playing games and doing puzzles and exercises. "Creative growth is possible only through constant and active use of your mind."

9. *Improve your sense of humor and laugh easily.* Humor helps to relieve tension, and most people are more productively creative when they are relaxed. (In this author's opinion, humor is an everyday expression of creativity.)

10. *Adopt a risk-taking attitude.* The fear of failure suppresses creativity, so be willing to fail on occasion.

11. *Have courage and self-confidence.* Move ahead on the assumption that you can solve your problems or achieve your goals. Many people surrender just when they are on the brink of a solution, so persist when you are seeking a creative solution to a problem.

12. *Learn to know and understand yourself.* "Creativity is an expression of one's uniqueness. To be creative, then, is to be oneself."

An underlying message to these suggestions is that self-discipline is required to develop more creative behavior. The advice offered also assumes that you have sufficient control over your emotions and intellect to develop new habits and break old ones. Assuming you have such control, following these suggestions over time would most likely help you to become a more creative person.

POLITICAL ASPECTS OF DECISION MAKING

A serious discussion of decision making would be incomplete, if not naive, if it ignored the importance of **political factors**. A political factor in the sense used here refers to the potential reaction to the decision by an influential person. A nonpolitical factor would be the strict objective merits of a decision. You have to make allowances for political considerations if you want your decision to be accepted. "Politics" is particularly important at two stages in decision making: (1) choosing an alternative and (2) evaluation of outcomes.

Choosing an Alternative. Politics plays a major role in determining which alternative is chosen from among the many possible alternatives. One office supervisor decided not to request the dismissal of her most inept employee. Two of the employee's co-workers finally approached the supervisor, asking her why this ineffective and unmotivated employee was kept on the payroll. In frustration the supervisor replied, "You two find me a tactful way of requesting that I fire the president's son and I'll do it."

The alternative chosen in a decision also takes into account values and ideals, which are closely related to political factors. Sometimes an alternative is a sound one, but it is rejected on the basis of human values. An industrial psychologist published an article in *Psychology Today* that demonstrated how employee larceny can be a useful form of job enrichment. Allowing people to steal on the job, according to his research, keeps them happy and relieves boredom.[15]

The article was acceptable from a scientific standpoint and certainly of high reader interest. *Psychology Today* therefore made a "yes" decision with regard to its publication. Previous to submitting the article to *Psychology Today*, the author had sent it to the highly respected *Harvard Business Review*. An editor at HBR wrote the psychologist a polite letter explaining why his article was finally rejected. He explained: "To be perfectly frank, the consensus is that your conclusions—especially the idea of a tolerable amount of theft—aren't consistent with the ideals of HBR."

Evaluation of Outcomes. Another stage of the decision-making process particularly susceptible to political considerations is evaluation of outcomes. Political factors are sometimes more influential than hard data or objective facts in determining whether a decision was good, just acceptable, or unacceptable. Many people in work organizations are more concerned about what management thinks of their decision than the usefulness to the organization of the decision chosen. A counterargument might be that no decision is a good decision if the people in power dislike that decision. The author's position is that a person with professional integrity arrives at what he or she thinks is the best decision. A diligent attempt should then be made to convince management of the merits of the alternative chosen. The political factor in evaluating outcomes is illustrated by the case of Dustin, a financial analyst in a factory.

> Dustin was given the assignment of making a "make or buy" decision for a component of a smoke detector alarm. His recommendation was that the company should make the component themselves, even though it was more expensive when all direct and indirect costs were evaluated. One month after his analysis was completed, a colleague asked Dustin if his decision was a good one, and how he knew if he had made the right recommendation to the company.

Dustin replied, "I made the best possible decision. After I presented my recommendation that we make the component, I saw the manufacturing vice-president's eyes light up. He wants to keep our staff as large as possible. He doesn't care a diddly about a small difference in cost. I told them what they wanted to hear. As a result of my helping them reach what they consider the right decision, they've given me another assignment."

SUMMARY OF KEY POINTS

☐ A problem is a gap between an existing and a desired situation. And a decision is a choice among two or more alternatives to solve that problem. At any stage of identifying a problem or making a decision, certain factors can influence our thinking. These influencing factors include adequacy of available information, a variety of personal characteristics of the decision maker, and chance or luck factors.

☐ The decision-making process consists of five overlapping stages: (1) clarification of the problem, (2) searching for creative alternatives, (3) weighing alternatives, (4) choosing an alternative and implementation, and (5) evaluation of outcomes of the decision.

☐ The amount of time and effort that should be put into making a decision is influenced by the significance of that decision. Three considerations that influence significance are (1) number of people affected, (2) relative impact of dollar amounts involved, and (3) time needed to prepare for the decision.

☐ Time pressures influence decision-making effectiveness. In general, people make less effective decisions when they are harassed by time pressures. Despite advances in information processing, intuition still plays a major role in decision making at all levels. Good decision makers have good intuition.

☐ Creativity is the processing of information in such a way that the result is new, original, and meaningful. Being creative allows us to find several alternative solutions to problems. Creative people are in general more emotionally loose and open, and more playful, than their less creative counterparts. Creative people also tend to be right-brain dominant. Among the important conditions for triggering creativity is the existence of a problem that stimulates the setting of a goal.

☐ People can improve their creativity on their own by engaging in certain exercises and following certain principles. Following these exercises and principles requires considerable self-discipline. One such suggestion is to avoid rigid patterns of doing things and to generate several alternative solutions to your problems.

☐ Politics enters into many decisions because so many people making a decision attempt to please higher-ranking people with the outcome of their decisions.

GUIDELINES FOR PERSONAL EFFECTIVENESS

1. Use a deliberate systematic approach, such as following the stages in the decision-making process, when making major decisions in business and personal life. An impulsive, hasty decision will often neglect some important information that should have been included before you reached your decision.

2. Indecisiveness hampers many decision-making situations. To deal with this problem, you might try a suggestion offered by William Glueck: "Set a time limit for making decisions. More failure results from no decision than from making the wrong one."[16]

3. Although a systematic approach to decision making is highly recommended, it does not mean that you should avoid using your insight and intuition. Intuition is particularly helpful in finding a problem to work on and in selecting from among the available alternatives. Top-level decision makers still rely heavily on intuition.

4. Improving your creativity can improve your chances for success in your career. When faced with a problem or decision, discipline yourself to search for several alternatives, since this is the essence of creative behavior.

DISCUSSION QUESTIONS

1. What are two of the biggest decisions people face in their personal lives? By what criteria did you measure "bigness"?

2. What are two of the biggest decisions people face in their careers? By what criteria did you measure "bigness"?

3. Assume that a person is highly intelligent and very well educated. How might that person's intelligence and education hamper his or her ability to make decisions?

4. Granted that hunches are important in decision making, how can you improve the quality of your hunches?

5. Think of the most creative person you know. How well does he or she fit the characteristics of a creative person summarized on pages 166 to 171?

6. Suppose you decide that you are not an effective decision maker. How do you think you might be able to improve your decision-making ability?

7. What do you think might be a potential negative consequence of being a highly creative employee?

8. If you are given the responsibility of hiring a creative person, how do you determine if a particular job applicant is creative?

9. What similarities do you see between the method by which humans make decisions, and computers provide the user with information?

10. Suppose your instructor in this course met you socially and asked you, "How are you enjoying the course so far?" How would political factors influence the alternative you chose in answering his or her question?

A Business Psychology Problem
THE NEW VENTURE TASK FORCE

Your company is experimenting with a form of organization structure designed to motivate young people and increase its own sphere of influence. The New Venture Task Force consists of a group of people (with you as task-force head) given the assignment to investigate new business opportunities. Your group reports to Bart Meadows, the vice-president of finance. He requests that you meet with him in your office. After a brief exchange of pleasantries, Meadows informs you:

"So far, we like the way you conduct yourself and we like the way the New Venture Task Force is progressing. But we really haven't given you an opportunity to test your initiative and wisdom. As you know, we are a creative organization, noted for its adventuresome spirit. We are going to try something that we think has so far not been tried in industry.

"We are giving your group $650,000 to play with. We want you to invest the money wisely. The only restrictions are that you do not purchase stocks, bonds, or interest-bearing notes of any kind. Also, you cannot do anything illegal with the company money. Report back in 30 days with your progress."

1. What kind of questions would you ask Meadows?
2. Explain how you would use the decision-making schema to make a sound investment decision.
3. Would you accept such an assignment? Why or why not?

A Business Psychology Case
WHY CAN'T OUR PEOPLE BE MORE CREATIVE?

Ralph Benson, president of Mainline Food Service, Inc., looked forward with anticipation to his Monday morning staff meeting with his five key subordinates. Ralph spoke to his secretary, "I hope this morning will be it. We certainly need a breakthrough in our thinking about Mainline. I've keyed up the staff for today's meeting."

After the usual exchange of pleasantries on Monday morning, Ralph introduced the major topic of the meeting: "I'm glad you could all be here today. We have some heavy thinking to do. The way I see the problem, Mainline Food Service needs to diversify a bit. For over 30 years we've been offering vending machine and cafeteria service on a nationwide basis. As you all know this is a tough, competitive business with very slim margins of profit.

"Because of the many cost-cutting procedures I've suggested—sometimes over your objections—we've been able to stay profitable. Our profit as a percentage of sales is two percent, which may not sound like much to the person on the street, but we're doing much better than our competitors. Yet it's obvious to me that we have to diversify. We're too heavily concentrated in the food service business. As I see the problem, we should be using some of our capital to get into the restaurant business.

"And that's why I have called this meeting. As I informed you in my memo, the purpose of today's meeting is to decide upon what type of restaurant business we should enter."

Naomi Miller, manager of customer service, spoke first: "Ralph, you've made the assumption that we should be entering the restaurant business. Isn't that kind of limiting our choices? Suppose I said we should be opening up a chain of garden stores? Why are we restricting ourselves to restaurants?"

"Naomi, enough of your philosophizing," replied Ralph. "It only takes common sense to realize that a company in the food business should stick to the food business. As my father told me many times, 'Shoemaker, stick to thy last'."

"Could be, Ralph, but we don't find too many shoemakers around anymore. Maybe they stuck to their lasts too long."

Appearing mildly irritated, Ralph asked for somebody to make the first specific suggestion about Mainline entering the restaurant business. Buzz Owens, institutional sales manager, complied: "Let's go all the way Ralph. I'm suggesting we open up a chain of ten posh restaurants called the Executive Club. You could only eat there if you had a membership card that cost about fifty dollars per year. All our waitresses would be well spoken and physically attractive. Grand dining has sort of slipped by the wayside, but I think there is still a big demand for that kind of fine, elite restaurant."

"Buzz, I would hardly call that a novel idea. It's been tried many times in the past and failed," answered Ralph. "Does anybody else have a more novel idea?"

Chuck Adams, manager of vending operations, spoke next: "Ralph, you asked for a novel suggestion, so I'm taking you at your word. My brainstorm for a new restaurant chain would be to set up a franchise of fast-food restaurants called Jet Service. Each restaurant would have a fiberglass front that would look like the nose cone and cockpit of a Boeing 747. The help would all wear airplane personnel uniforms. We'd have travel posters on the walls, and jet-turbine-shaped salt and pepper shakers. Even our rest rooms would be styled after those found in an airplane."

"Thanks so much, Chuck. If we ever merge with Eastern Airlines or Pan Am, I'll be back in touch. Maybe you need an airplane trip yourself. Maybe you've been working too hard. Next suggestion please."

John Rubright, operations manager, looked around at his colleagues self-consciously before making his suggestion. "Ralph, I've given a lot of careful thought to our problem. I detect a new era of conservatism and nostalgia sweeping the country. I'm recommending that we open a chain of simple country restaurants called G.O.F.F. That stands for Good Old Fashioned Food. Get it? We would have knotty pine chairs and tables and our waitresses would wear colonial uniforms. Even though the Bicentennial has passed, the interest in America should not pass away for years."

"Thanks for the suggestion," said Ralph, "It's not half-bad, but it seems to me that type of restaurant has been tried in New England for many years. It stands no more chance of succeeding than the average roadside beanery. We haven't heard yet from Dinah Malone. As director of quality control, she should have a good idea about the restaurant business."

"My idea is so basic, that it might be dismissed as too simple," said Dinah. "Yet I think I'm on to something very important. The United States is tired of McDonald's and the like. But most people can no longer afford to eat in first-class restaurants. I'm saying let's bring back the old-fashioned, aluminum exterior diner. But let's do it in a big way with smiling porters and authentic railroad whistles. Let's call this chain, 'Dinah's Diner.' Kind of tricky, don't you think?"

"I could see why you would want a chain of restaurants named after you, Dinah, but is the Ford Motor Company bringing back the Model T? Maybe we've gone far enough in today's meeting. Let's all try again next Monday. During the week try to be at your creative best. I'm eager to get some new suggestions."

As the last member left the room, Ralph said to his secretary, "Why can't our people be more creative?"

1. In what way might Ralph be discouraging creativity?
2. Whose suggestion do you think is the most creative? Why?
3. What approach should Ralph take to bringing forth creative suggestions for a new business venture from his subordinates?
4. Do you see Ralph as rigid or flexible? Why?
5. Should Ralph have offered a prize for the best suggestion? Why or why not?

REFERENCES

[1] William F. Glueck, *Management* (Hinsdale, Ill.: Dryden Press, 1977), p. 384.

[2] Morgan W. McCall, Jr., Robert E. Kaplan, and Michael L. Gerlach, "The Stream of Decisions," *Issues & Observations*, Center for Creative Leadership, (Aug. 1982), p. 3. The original source of this definition is W. Pounds, "The Process of Problem Finding," *Industrial Management Review* (Jan. 1969), p. 5.

[3] "The Stream of Decisions," p. 5.

[4]Glueck, *Management*, p. 388.

[5]Peter Wright, "The Harassed Decision Maker: Time, Pressures, Distractions, and the Use of Evidence," *Journal of Applied Psychology* (Dec. 1974), pp. 555–561.

[6]Bernard M. Bass, *Organizational Decision Making* (Homewood, Ill.: Irwin, 1983), p. 77.

[7]Henry Mintzberg, "The Manager's Job: Folklore and Fact," *Harvard Business Review* (July–Aug. 1975), p. 54.

[8]"Jumping to Solutions," *Psychology Today* (Dec. 1977), p. 75. Based on information in Eugene Raudsepp with George P. Hough, Jr., *Creative Growth Games* (New York: Harcourt Brace Jovanovich, 1977).

[9]This test, developed by Eugene Raudsepp, is quoted from "Ideas: Test Your Creativity," *Nation's Business* (June 1965), p. 80.

[10]From Andrew J. DuBrin, *Human Relations: A Job Oriented Approach*, 3rd ed. (Reston, Va.: Reston Publishing, 1984), pp. 74–75.

[11]Based on several sources, including the author's own observations in working with creative people. The sources include Eugene Raudsepp, "Are You a Creative Executive?" *Management Review* (Feb. 1978), p. 15; Donald W. MacKinnon, "The Nature and Nurture of Creative Talent," in *Readings in Managerial Psychology* (Chicago: University of Chicago Press, 1965), pp. 22–23.

[12]Our discussion here is based on the synthesis of the literature in Thomas V. Bonoma and Gerald Zaltman, *Psychology for Management* (Boston: Kent, 1981), pp. 111–112.

[13]Daniel G. Tear, as quoted in *Issues & Observations* (Feb. 1981), p. 5.

[14]This listing is paraphrased from Eugene Raudsepp, "Exercises for Creative Growth," *Success* (Feb. 1981), pp. 46–47. The italicized statements are quotes, along with the several brief quotes.

[15]Lawrence R. Zeitlin, "A Little Larceny Can Do a Lot for Employee Morale," *Psychology Today* (June 1971), pp. 22, 24, 26, 64.

[16]Glueck, *Management*, p. 404.

SUGGESTED READING

GUNN, HARRY E. "Test Your Creativity," *Success* (July 1981), pp. 24–28.

HUBER, GEORGE P. *Managerial Decision Making*. Glenview, Ill.: Scott, Foresman, 1980.

LEBOEF, MICHAEL. *Imagineering: How to Profit from Your Creative Power*. New York: McGraw-Hill, 1982.

MCALINDON, HAROLD R. "Toward a More Creative You: Developing the Whole Person," *Supervisory Management* (March 1980), pp. 31–35.

OXENFELDT, ALFRED R. "Effective Decision Making for the Business Executive," *Management Review* (Feb. 1978), pp. 25–28, 41–44.

RADFORD, K. J. *Modern Managerial Decision Making*. Reston, Va.: Reston Publishing, 1981.

RAUDSEPP, EUGENE. *More Creative Growth Games.* New York: G. P. Putman's Sons, 1980.

―――――. "Trust That Hunch," *Success* (Aug. 1982), pp. 26–30.

SCOTT, DRU. "Decisions: How You Can Make Them Faster," *Success* (May 1981), pp. 20–22, 54.

TURLA, PETER A., and KATHLEEN L. HAWKINS. "Self-Test: How Decisive Are You?" *Success* (March 1983), pp. 26–28.

8

MANAGING STRESS
AND BURNOUT

LEARNING OBJECTIVES

After reading and studying this chapter and doing the exercises, you should be able to

1. Describe how stress influences job behavior and performance.
2. Explain why some people are predisposed to experiencing job stress.
3. Identify at least ten sources of stress in personal and work life.
4. Understand the nature of burnout.
5. Develop a program for managing stress in your own life.

WHAT IS STRESS?

One window washer decided to quit his job after four years of good service. His parting comment to his boss was, "I can't take it anymore. I just don't want to wind up splattered all over the sidewalk. Those heights are just too much for me right now."

The same day, in the same office building, a company president stood up during a meeting with the board of directors and announced, "I'm asking for a demotion to a staff specialist of some kind. My doctor tells me I have a bleeding ulcer. She has warned me that if I don't get some relief from the pressure-cooker I'm in, it could mean my life. If you can't honor my request, I'll have to ask for a medical leave of absence."

These incidents illustrate the important fact of work life that nobody, from the window washer to the company president, is immune from the kind of job pressures that may create negative stress. To achieve satisfaction and be productive in your career, it is necessary to manage job stress—to make it work for you rather than against you.

In recent years, stress has become one of the most widely used terms about human behavior. Almost anything that creates a strong reaction can produce stress. There are several technical meanings of the term stress. As used here, **stress** refers to *your internal reaction to any force that threatens to disturb your psychological or biological balance.*[1] You may experience stress

From the window washer to the company president, nobody is immune to job stress and frustration.

as you get set to ride a big wave to shore on your surfboard. And you may experience stress when you are being interviewed for a job you really want.

In everyday language, stress is the term given to the force bringing about the internal reaction. In technical language, a **stressor** is the force that brings about the reaction called stress. Your perception influences whether or not a given situation, event, or thought acts as a stressor. Some people find analyzing data with statistics to be a source of unsatisfying stress. Others may find it to be a pleasant challenge and therefore a source of satisfying stress.

THE PHYSIOLOGY AND SYMPTOMS OF STRESS

This chapter highlights techniques for managing negative stress and its closely related condition, burnout. An important preliminary step is to look at the physiology of stress and to explain how we know when we are experiencing stress. If you have faced a crisis or high excitement in your life, you may recall symptoms such as dry mouth, sweaty palms, a rapid heartbeat, or mild dizziness.

Basic Physiology of Stress

Stress experts agree that the physiological changes within the body are quite similar in response to most stressors. Narrowly escaping being fired or receiving a passionate kiss make you feel about the same inside. The reason is that all types of stress produce hormonal (chemical) changes within the body. In turn, these changes in body hormones produce a short-term physiological reaction. Among the most familiar are an increase in heart rate, blood pressure, breathing rate, perspiration, and blood clotting, and sometimes a ringing sensation in the ears.

The body functions become so accelerated under heavy stress that some people carry out feats of strength they would not be able to accomplish under ordinary (nonstressful) circumstances. A case in point is the 125-pound woman who dragged her unconscious 225-pound husband out of their burning house. After the event was over and the husband was saved, the woman joked with the firefighters that she could not ordinarily even roll her husband over to stop his snoring. She was able to accomplish this feat of strength because of the spurt of adrenaline (also referred to as epinephrine) accompanying her stress.

The body's battle against the stressor is referred to as the **fight-or-flight response**. The person either tries to cope with adversity in a head-on battle or tries to flee from the scene. Famous stress researcher, the late Hans Selye, showed that when the fight-or-flight response persists over a long period of time, long-term chemical changes occur. These changes can be both annoying and life-threatening. Among them are high blood pressure, heart disease, an increased rate of arteriosclerosis, increased cholesterol level, migraine headaches, ulcers, allergies, and colitis.[2] Unfortunately, chronic (prolonged) stress also leads to a weakening of the body's immune system, which makes recuperation from all illnesses difficult. It has even been said that one of the contributing factors to the disease AIDS is a series of stressful situations in life.

Despite all the problems just mentioned, the right amount of stress reaction prepares us for meeting difficult challenges and spurs us to new heights of physical and mental performance.

Symptoms of Stress

Placed under unsatisfying or negative stress, people display many different symptoms of distress. Selye says that people should heed these symptoms because they signal that it is time to take constructive action against the effects of stress. For example, you might have to improve your education and training to ward off the stress that accompanies worrying about being laid off. At times the symptoms of negative and positive stress are quite similar, particularly when the positive emotion is intense. Signals of distress (or extremely positive emotion) include:[3]

- Anxiety (a feeling of fear not directed at any particular object).
- Constant tension (a general feeling of nervousness and uneasiness).
- Dryness of the throat and mouth.
- Impulsive behavior and unstable emotional reactions.
- Difficulties in concentration and rapid changing of thoughts.
- Accident proneness. Accidents are the most frequent under extreme stress, whether the stress be satisfying or unsatisfying.
- Predisposition to fatigue and a loss of general happiness about life.
- Stuttering and other speech difficulties.
- Insomnia (usually associated with positive stress).
- Frequent need to eliminate body wastes.
- Extremes in appetite. Some people become less hungry because of turmoil in their intestines. Others eat excessively as a diversion from the stressful situation.
- Lower back or neck pain usually attributed to increases in muscular tension.
- Increased cigarette smoking, use of alcohol, and intake of illegal drugs.
- Increased use of prescription drugs such as tranquillizers or amphetimines (uppers or pep pills).

A MODEL OF STRESS
AND JOB BEHAVIOR

A summary explanation or model of the difference between the right and wrong amounts of stress is shown in Figure 8–1. Sometimes the type of stress can be as influential as the amount of stress. For example, being constantly criticized by a boss or knowing that one has a dreaded disease is a harmful type of stress for virtually everyone. It is helpful also to view the right type of stress as satisfying and the wrong type of stress as unsatisfying. An industrial physician put it this way: "It is satisfying when you are running around achieving goals. It is unsatisfying when everything gets out of control. That's when people develop symptoms such as headaches, diarrhea, and heart palpitations."[4]

Cognitive evaluation. The starting point in the stress model shown in Figure 8–1 is our subjective analysis of the situation. It is based on a cognitive

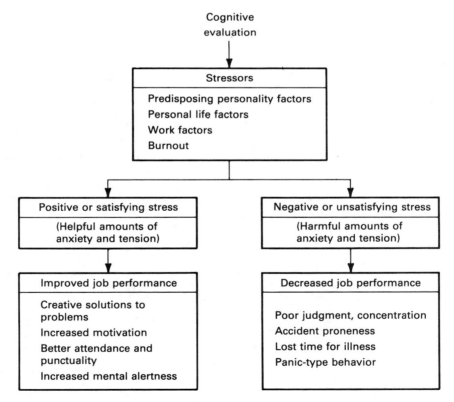

FIGURE 8–1
How stress influences job behavior and performance.

(or intellectual) evaluation of the event. An everyday illustration of the subjectivity of stress is the stimulus of a German shepherd dog. Many people would experience stress if an unleashed "police dog" came into view. A minority of people would find the same event to be peaceful and enjoyable, and would probably respond, "Here boy."

Stressors. Almost anything that frustrates, aggravates, annoys, or puts a person in conflict can lead to stress. The stressors listed in the left-hand box of Figure 8–1 will be explained in the following pages. It is important to recognize that stressors change from time to time, both for individuals and groups. Many people today, for example, worry about nuclear waste contaminating them. In the past, they did not have such a worry. And being fired is much more of a stressor to some people than to others.

Positive stress and its consequences. Few people can escape stress in their lives, which is fortunate, because escaping all forms of stress would be

The right amount and kind of stress can make you come alive.

undesirable for most people. Selye says that the right amount and kind of stress makes us come alive. He calls this positive force in our lives **eustress.** It is the equivalent of finding excitement and challenge in your life.[5] Too little stress and a person runs the danger of becoming lethargic and unstimulated. The type and amount of stress you need to derive a beneficial experience vary from person to person. A sky diver might thrive on the routine of one sky dive a month. Another individual engaging in the same sport might succumb to a heart attack.

Negative stress and its consequences. Stress and its accompanying tension can also have an adverse impact on job performance, as depicted on the right-hand side of Figure 8-1. People under substantial amounts of unsatisfying stress often have difficulty concentrating on their work and their judgment suffers. In a fit of anger, some workers have physically attacked another employee (or their bosses) and consequently have lost their jobs. An example of panic-type behavior is the company president who fires several much needed employees in response to a downturn in business conditions.

PERSONALITY FACTORS CONTRIBUTING TO JOB STRESS

Some people are more susceptible to the adverse consequences of job pressures than others because of some factor within their personality. One important example would be emotional insecurity and low self-confidence. If you worry a lot about making mistakes, any demanding job will prove to be stressful. Two important personality factors predisposing people to job stress are Type A behavior and a belief that much of their life is controlled by external forces.

Type A Behavior

People labeled as displaying Type A behavior have a basic personality that leads them into stressful situations. It is these impatient, demanding, overstriving types that often wind up with heart disease at an early age. Cardiologists Meyer Friedman and Ray Rosenman have studied Type A personalities extensively.[6] The distinguishing characteristics and behaviors of Type A individuals are as follows:

1. Chronic and severe sense of time urgency, making them impatient and demanding. For example, such people become particularly frustrated in traffic jams.

2. Constant involvement in multiple projects subject to deadlines. These people delight in the feeling of being swamped with work.

3. Tend to neglect all aspects of life except work; thus many of these people are termed **workaholics** (an addiction to work combined with a dislike of nonwork).
4. A tendency to take on excessive responsibility, combined with a feeling that "Only I am capable of taking care of this matter."
5. Explosiveness of speech and a tendency to speak faster than most people. Type A personalities are thus prone to ranting and swearing when upset.
6. Basically hostile and angry people who channel much of their anger into work.

One possible reason so many people with Type A behavior have heart attacks is that they experience unsatisfying stress. Many hard-working, impatient people remain relatively free of stress disorders. They love their work and it serves as a source of satisfying stress.

Type B Behavior. The vast majority of people reading this book probably are Type B personalities—those with a more relaxed, casual attitude toward life. If you display the Type B behavior pattern, the following conditions are typical of your life:

1. You are free of the habits and exhibit none of the Type A characteristics just listed.
2. You rarely suffer from a sense of impatience or time urgency.
3. You harbor no hostile attitudes and you have no desire to brag about your accomplishments, unless the situation calls for such actions.
4. You play for the fun of it, not to exhibit your superiority at any cost.
5. You can relax without guilt and work without agitation.

Keep in mind that many people, in fact, exhibit a combination of Type A and Type B behaviors. Before making a final analysis of your personality, recognize that you might be Type A in some situations and Type B in others. I know one man who is definitely Type A in the office or when stuck in traffic. When washing his car or dining at a restaurant, he is definitely Type B.

Belief in External Locus of Control

Some evidence has been gathered that if you believe your fate is controlled more by external than internal forces, you are more susceptible to job stress. People with an **internal locus of control** believe that their fate is pretty much under their control. Conversely, people with an **external locus of control** believe that external forces control their fate. The link between locus of control and job stress works in this manner: If people believe that they can control potential adverse forces in their job setting, they are less prone to the stressor of worrying about them. At the same time, the person who believes in an internal locus of control experiences a higher level of job satisfaction.[7] Work is more satisfying and less stressful when you perceive it to be under your control.

What about your locus of control? Do you believe it to be internal? Or is it external?

SOURCES OF STRESS IN PERSONAL LIFE

Almost any form of frustration, disappointment, setback, inconvenience, or crisis in personal life can be a stressor. The different sources of stress encountered in everyday life can be placed into these categories: daily hassles; social and family problems; disappointments with hobbies, interests, and sports; physical and mental health problems; financial problems; school-related problems; terrifying experiences; and significant changes in general.

Daily Hassles. Researchers have known for years that catastrophic life events can have major consequences on personal health. But now scientific evidence is mounting that daily hassles—and the way they are managed—may have more significant health effects than major life events. It's sweating the small stuff that brings you down! Evidence along these lines was gathered in a long-term study of 100 people in California. Using a hassles scale developed for the study, subjects rated 117 daily irritations. The daily hassles cited most frequently were concerns about weight, the health of a family member, inflation, home maintenance, overcrowded schedules, yardwork and outside maintenance, taxes, crime, and physical appearance. Several of these hassles will be discussed as separate categories.

The major finding was that the more hassles people experienced, the more stress-related physical ailments they had, including dizziness, headaches, and upset stomachs. It was reported that "hassles were a more powerful predictor of psychological symptoms than life events in every comparison made."[8] Sex differences were discovered in these findings. For men, the working hassles were associated more strongly with poor health. For women, working hassles were not so clearly associated with poor health. Instead, home hassles such as cooking and shopping were more strongly associated with physical health problems. (It may help in interpreting these findings to recognize that working women often do more than their share of housekeeping and child rearing.)

A secondary finding in the study has important implications for stress management. People who were able to cope well with daily hassles tended to have good health. They were able to tailor-make a coping strategy for each hassle they faced, such as overcoming a billing error made by a store or credit-card company.

Social and Family Problems. Friends and family are the main source of love, affection, and emotional support in one's life. But they can also be a powerful stressor. Most acts of physical violence are committed among friends and family members. One of the many reasons we encounter so much conflict with friends and family is that we are emotionally involved with them.

Disappointments with Hobbies, Interests, and Sports. People take their pastimes seriously in our culture. The greater the emotional involvement, the higher the probability that setbacks in this area will create stress for the individual. One young man attempted suicide with an overdose of an assortment of medications he found in the family medicine cabinet. Upon revival, he offered an explanation for his attempted self-destruction: "Our soccer team lost one to nothing last night. I was the goalie who let the winning goal go by me."

Physical and Mental Health Problems. Prolonged stress produces physical and mental health problems, and the reverse is also true. Physical and mental illness can act as stressors. A related problem is that the stress from the act of being hospitalized can be almost as severe to some patients as the stress from the illness or injury that brought them to the hospital. Being incapacitated can also be a blow to one's self-confidence, creating more tension and anxiety.

Financial Problems. A major source of friction (and therefore stress) in life is financial problems. Although you may not be obsessed with money, not having enough money to take care of what you consider the necessities of life can lead to tension and anxiety. A health-care provider made this comment about financial problems and stress:

> We have about 40,000 members enrolled in our health-maintenance organization, so I'm in a good position to judge problems in the community. When unemployment goes up and people get into a financial fix, we are busier than ever. A lot of patients develop ulcers or other intestinal disorders when they are financially squeezed. I think money worries tear them apart inside even more than marital problems.

School-Related Problems. Among the stressors students have to cope with are taking exams in subjects they do not understand well, having to write papers on unfamiliar topics, working their way through the complexities of registration, and having to cope with competing demands on their time from several courses. On most campuses you will find several students who work full-time, go to school full-time, and have families. This type of three-way pull often leads to marital problems. You do not have to be a middle-aged executive to develop ulcers!

Terrifying Experiences. Among these once-in-a-lifetime experiences are being involved in a house fire or serious automobile accident, being caught in a tornado, being raped or shot at, or having your house washed out from under you in a flood. Much of the early knowledge about stress was derived from studying the war condition called "shell-shock" or "battle fatigue." It has been observed that people involved in terrifying experiences frequently show psychological shock reactions.[9]

The extent to which you deteriorate after a terrifying experience depends partly on how strong a person you were before the catastrophe struck. Your reaction also depends on how much emotional first aid you received from friends or professionals right after the terrifying experience. As a result, a relatively new procedure is for mental health workers to counsel hostages immediately after they are released by their captors.

Significant Life Changes. A general stressor that encompasses both work and personal life is having to cope with significant change in any aspect of one's life. For example, the stressor called financial problems could be interpreted as having to cope with the change associated with trying to manage a large debt. A pioneering series of studies on stressful life events was conducted by Thomas Holmes and Richard Rahe over a period of 25 years. Their research, and similar studies, showed repeatedly that the necessity of significant change in the life pattern of an individual was the common denominator for stress. The tension associated with stress seems to accelerate a disease process. For example, Holmes discovered that the onset of tuberculosis generally followed a group of disruptive events: a death in the family, a house purchase, or marriage.[10]

The research on life changes resulted in the assigning of scale values to the impact of changes in 42 life events. These values, called **life-change units**, were taken to represent the average amount of social readjustments considered necessary to cope with a given change. Here is a sampling of life-change events and their values:

Death of a spouse, 100 points
Divorce, 73 points
Marital separation, 65 points
Pregnancy, 40 points

Buying a house, 31 points

Change in residence, 20 points

Christmas, 12 points

Minor violation of the law, 11 points

The more of these life-change units a person has to absorb in a short period of time, the more likely that person is to experience a physical health problem. For example, by adding up the life stress of healthy college football players, Holmes and Rahe made accurate predictions about which ones would be injured in the upcoming season. (Perhaps the overstressed players suffered concentration problems that predisposed them to injury.)

SOURCES OF STRESS IN WORK LIFE

Almost any job situation can act as a stressor for some employees but not necessarily for others. To repeat, a person's subjective interpretation of the event generally determines whether or not it is stressful. Three o'clock one afternoon, a secretary might be handed a set of scribbled notes by her boss, accompanied by the order, "Have this report back to me before you leave this afternoon." This secretary might experience distress over the situation. Another secretary might welcome the challenge and therefore experience positive stress—and high performance.

Here we will examine six job stressors that adversely affect a large number of people: exorbitant work demands, confusing directions and conflicting demands, job insecurity and unemployment, computer shock, underutilization of abilities, and frustrated ambitions.

Confusing Directions and Conflicting Demands. Two well-documented sources of stress and frustration are role ambiguity and role conflict. **Role ambiguity** exists when you are uncertain of your true job responsibilities. One engineering aide expressed it this way: "I often wonder why the company hired me. When I volunteer to help the engineers, they act as if I'm butting into their jobs. When I don't volunteer, I'm not kept very busy. The people think I'm goofing off."

Role conflict exists when you are caught in the middle between competing demands. If you obey one order, you are automatically disobeying another. Suppose that you worked as an aide in a mental hospital and your boss was the head aide. He might tell you to be very strict with the patients, because if you didn't they would soon take advantage of you. His boss, the psychiatric nurse on the ward, might suggest to you that you treat the patients with warmth and kindness. A situation such as this would make most people tense. Role conflict is thus a legitimate source of stress.

Exorbitant Work Demands. Many people feel that they are overworked and underpaid. When you do face unusually heavy demands (referred to as **role overload**), it can be a stressor. The same situation leads to frustration because you may be blocked from participating in as much family or leisure activity as you would like.

A work schedule tends to be perceived as exorbitant when the job requires long hours of heavy-pressure work. One notable characteristic of a demanding job is that competing demands are placed on your time (**role conflict**). One youth worker described his stressful job demands in these terms: "My job really gets ridiculous when school isn't in session. Must be about twenty-five kids waiting to see me. Then my boss wants to see me, but the kids won't go away. Also the paper work starts to build up. By the time I get home, I'm beat. I'm not home but an hour when the phone starts ringing. More problems, it never lets up."

Job Insecurity and Unemployment. People worry about losing their jobs for many reasons, including a poor economic climate and the arrival of new technology in the workplace. A survey was made of large companies, 98 of which already used some form of electronic equipment, including word processors, video display terminals, and electronic mail systems. More than half of the companies reported that employees were apprehensive prior to automation. Twenty-six percent specifically mentioned concern over job security as their primary reason for being apprehensive. Clerks were found to be more apprehensive than any other office workers.[11] Intense job insecurity of this type is a source of distress.

Unemployment itself generates more stress than the threat of job insecurity. Unemployed people, in comparison to employed people, have much higher rates of depression, suicide, homicide, child abuse, and spouse abuse. One study of joblessness showed that people unable to find jobs express low self-esteem, feelings of powerlessness, and many forms of psychosomatic illness.[12] Part of the problem is that the identity of many people is related to their occupation. Being unemployed is thus a blow to their self-identity.

Computer Shock. Working intensely with computers can lead to a modern form of job stress called **computer shock**. It is defined as an intense negative reaction to being forced to spend many more hours behind a computer than one desires. Among its symptoms are a glassy-eyed, detached look, aching neck muscles, and a growing dislike for high technology. The application of human engineering to the design of computer systems may be helpful in minimizing the physical problems that contribute to computer shock. Nevertheless, working closely with computers can still create job dissatisfaction for some people. As told by Mindy, a manufacturing specialist:

> The reason I majored in business was so I could get a job working with people. I never minded doing my share of writing reports and crunching numbers. I put up with it so I could spend most of my time relating to people. After graduation I took an interesting sounding job as an inventory-control specialist. Little did I know I would be sitting behind a computer almost all day, every day. I hardly talk to anybody. I'm even supposed to communicate with my boss by sending messages on the computer. Now the company is telling me to get more advanced computer training. I'm looking for another job. Especially one that involves working with people.

Underutilization of Abilities. While attending school it might be satisfying to work as a night clerk in an unbusy motel. You would be able to study during your working hours. However, you probably would quickly become frustrated if you held that job while no longer a student. Your goal of becoming a productive member of society would be blocked. The blow to your self-esteem from making so little use of your capacities would most likely make you tense and anxious.

One young man took employment as a management trainee in a supermarket. Three months later he developed a severe skin rash. A comment he made to his family doctor about his job led to the eventual cure of his rash: "I'm beginning to hate my job. They told me I was going to be a management trainee. All I do is unload boxes and check to see that the produce department is well stocked. I wonder why I even bothered to get a business degree." The young man's discussion with his doctor gave him the insight to demand more job responsibilities on the job. The supermarket manager obliged and within two months the trainee's rash had disappeared. He also felt much less tense.

Frustrated Ambitions. If you decide that you must have a 30-foot yacht for yourself by age 30, you might be setting yourself up for some heavy frustration. Not everybody can have a high-paying, high-ranking job. Most organizations need large numbers of people who are content to work hard at their assignments without worrying about climbing the organizational ladder. Approximately 1 percent of jobs in any organization are truly executive (policy-making) positions. Thus, when a person is bitterly frustrated because he or she fails to become an executive, the organization should not always be blamed. It is frequently a problem of a person aspiring toward a goal with an exceedingly small chance of success.

Before describing techniques individuals and organizations can use to manage stress, we will devote separate attention to a condition that is both a product and a cause of negative stress.

JOB BURNOUT

As a consequence of experiencing a big discrepancy between the rewards they expected from work and the rewards they are receiving, many conscientious people experience *job burnout*. Originally, this condition was observed primarily among people helpers, including teachers, nurses, social workers, and police workers.[13] It then became apparent that managers and specialists of many kinds could develop burnout. It was even observed that world-class professional athletes could suddenly burn out at the peak of their careers. Bjorn Borg is a classic case. He dropped out of major tournament play at about the time he was being described as the greatest tennis player of all time.

Burnout, as used here, is defined as *the general discomfort, fatigue, cynicism, feelings of helplessness and hopelessness, and apathy stemming from not receiving the rewards you anticipated.* According to a recent analysis, there are three major signs indicating that burnout is present:[14]

1. Emotional exhaustion. A burned-out employee is emotionally exhausted. When asked how they feel, burned-out employees typically answer that they feel drained or used up, at the end of the rope, and physically fatigued. Often the burnout victim dreads going to work in the morning despite the fact that he or she was once enthusiastic and idealistic about what could be accomplished.

2. Depersonalizing relationships. The burnout victim tries to cope with emotional exhaustion by depersonalizing relationships with the boss and co-workers. "She or he develops a detached air, becomes cynical of relationships with others, and feels callous toward others and the organization." Managers suffering burnout hurt the organization because they create a ripple effect, spreading burnout to their subordinates.

3. Low personal accomplishment. The third and final aspect of burnout is a feeling of low personal accomplishment. The once idealistic employee begins to realize that there are too many barriers to accomplishing what needs to be done. One customer service technician described his problem with burnout in these terms: "What difference does it make if I hustle everyday? My customers just keep on misusing their equipment. No matter how many I fix, there's an endless amount of rework. People just won't listen about taking proper care of their equipment. And I get most of the blame for machine failure."

How is burnout related to stress? One tie-in between the two conditions is that burnout is said to be the end product of prolonged stress. Being deprived of the rewards you are seeking acts as a stressor that leads to burnout.

Also, some cases of burnout, such as that experienced by firefighters and high school teachers exposed to student violence, are caused by prolonged job stress. Burnout can also be a cause of stress. For example, if you feel depleted and unhappy everyday, it creates stress.

Causes, Consequences, and Treatment of Burnout

The causes and consequences of burnout are similar to those described for job stress in the preceding sections. Both the individual and the organization share some responsibility for creating employee burnout. As shown in Figure 8–2, certain organizational conditions contribute to burnout. These include the company not giving the employee sufficient rewards and support to get the job done. Yet it is the individual's idealistic expectations and a feeling of personal responsibility for what goes wrong that lead to burnout. For example, the customer service technician mentioned previously seemed to take machine breakdowns personally.

The management of burnout follows many of the same approaches as the management of stress, to be described in the following two sections. One reason is that burnout is accompanied by so many stress symptoms. Another reason is that the organization should improve conditions that contribute to burnout, which is also a major tactic for stress management. Despite these general similarities, two specific approaches to dealing with burnout are worthy of mention here.

An important method for both preventing and overcoming burnout is to develop realistic expectations. One of the reasons employees develop burnout is that they try to be "miracle workers." If you establish realistic expectations in any job, you are less likely to be crushed when you achieve modest goals. For instance, an administrative assistant might say to herself, "If I get

Causes	Psychological Reactions	Consequences

Organizational conditions:
    Lack of rewards
    Lack of control
	Emotional exhaustion	Withdrawal

Lack of clarity Lack of support	Depersonalization	Interpersonal friction
		Declining performance
Personal conditions:	Low personal accomplishment	
Idealistic expectations		Family problems
Personal responsibility		Health suffers

FIGURE 8–2

Causes and consequences of employee burnout [From Susan E. Jackson and Randall S. Schuler, "Preventing Employee Burnout," *Personnel* (March–April 1983), p. 60].

two good suggestions a month across to my boss, I'll consider my job a success."

A second important suggestion is to "stroke" yourself. Burnout is in reality a mild form of mental depression. A useful antidote is therefore to reward yourself, such as purchasing a new stereo tape, when you accomplish something worthwhile. In short, take care of yourself, rather than waiting for others to reward or "stroke" you.

WHAT INDIVIDUALS CAN DO TO MANAGE STRESS

Unless stress is managed properly it may lead to harmful long-term consequences, including disabling physical illnesses and career retardation. Managing stress refers to controlling stress by making it become a constructive force in your life. Managing thus refers to both preventing and reducing stress. However, the distinction between methods of preventing and reducing stress is not clear-cut. For example, physical exercise not only reduces stress; it also contributes to a lifestyle that helps you prevent stress.

Methods of stress management under your control vary from highly specific techniques (such as the relaxation response) to general strategies that reflect a lifestyle. Included in the latter would be maintaining a diet that is low in caffeine, alcohol, sugar, and nonnutritious food. Here we will mention a half-dozen do-it-yourself techniques of stress management. It should be recognized, however, that your stress symptoms may be so overwhelming that self-remedies will not work. In that case, you should seek the help of a mental health professional. Your family doctor or school counselor might be a good starting point for such a referral.

Take Constructive Action. The prime step in coping with stress is to take constructive action about the stressor-creating problems for you. Your stress symptoms will continue to gnaw at you unless you modify the conditions that underly your problem. In other words, you must in some way make your environment less hostile. Here is an example:

> Hank, a production supervisor for a commercial printer, noticed that his smoking and drinking were approaching the danger level. With the encouragement of his wife, Hank enrolled in separate clinics for smokers and drinkers. He was able to stop smoking and control his drinking, but he still felt that too much stress existed in his job. His tension level remained annoyingly high.
>
> Hank then discussed his problem with an employee counselor. He encouraged Hank to confront management about the fact that he (Hank) did not have enough authority to carry out his responsibility—the true stressor. For example,

one time Hank was told to accomplish a major printing job in one week less time than it ordinarily took. Yet he was not authorized overtime help. Hank was given more authority and some of his stress symptoms began to subside.

Talk out Your Problems. Many stress symptoms, particularly tension and anxiety, are reduced by the mere process of talking to somebody else about the problem bothering you. Almost everybody knowledgeable about human behavior recognizes this adage, but few people put it to good use. Talking about your problem with a sympathetic listener is a good start toward dissipating stress. An important by-product of letting out your feelings and talking about your problem is that it may lead to constructive action that resolves the problem. Hank accomplished this by talking to an employee counselor.

Get Ample Physical Exercise and Rest. It is well known that being in good physical shape helps you to cope with job-related stress. A person with a cardiac system beautifully toned by constant exercise is less likely to have a heart attack when overworked than a person whose heart is already weak from lack of exercise. It is also well accepted by many people that physical exercise helps prepare your mind for taking on tough mental tasks. Finally, being in good physical shape makes you more resistant to fatigue; thus, you can handle a bigger mental or physical workload.

Physical exercise is acknowledged today as an effective way of dissipating tension. A national survey indicated that physical exercise is the most frequently used constructive method of reducing tension.[15] A related fact is that jogging is also known to reduce mental depression.[16] It therefore could be beneficial in coping with employee burnout. Since exercise releases the natural pain killer called endorphine, it further contributes to a feeling of well being. This is true because pain itself creates tension.

Rest is closely related to exercise as a method of stress management. If you rest well, you are better able to exercise; and if you exercise well, you are better able to rest. Rest, itself, also helps the body deal with the ravages of heavy stress, whether it be of the satisfying or unsatisfying variety. Finally, rest accompanied by change is also recommended as an antidote to burnout.[17]

Use Everyday Relaxation Methods. People with Type A behavior characteristics (and tense, overworked people in general) continue to be urged by their physicians, friends, spouses, and gurus to relax. The simple expedient of learning to relax is apparently still an important method of reducing the tensions brought about by stress. Ten everyday suggestions for learning how to relax are presented in Table 8–1. If you can accomplish these, you may not

TABLE 8-1
Thirteen suggestions for relaxation and tension reduction*

1. Plan to have at least one idle period every day.
2. Learn to listen to others without interrupting them.
3. Read books and articles that demand concentration, rather than trying to speed-read everything.
4. Learn how to savor food by taking your time when eating pleasant food.
5. Have a quiet place for retreat at home.
6. Plan leisurely vacations so that virtually every moment is not programmed.
7. Concentrate on enriching yourself in at least one area other than work or school.
8. Live by the day or week, not by a stopwatch.
9. Concentrate on one task at a time rather than thinking of what assignment you will be tackling next.
10. Avoid irritating, overly competitive people; they tend to bring out the worst in another competitive person.
11. Stop drinking so much coffee, soft drinks, or alcoholic beverages. Try fruit juice or water instead.
12. Stop to smell the flowers, make friends with a preschool child, or play with a kitten once in awhile.
13. Smile at least five minutes every day.

*The first ten suggestions are based on Meyer Friedman and Ray H. Rosenman, *Type A Behavior and Your Heart* (Greenwich, Conn.: Fawcett Crest, 1975), pp. 207–271.

need formal methods of tension reduction, such as psychotherapy or tranquilizing medication.

Use the Relaxation Response. Cardiologist Herbert Benson has developed a simple technique for reducing tension and other stress symptoms. If practiced 10 to 20 minutes a day, this simple exercise can make your life healthier by evoking what he calls the *relaxation response* (RR). The response can be brought about in several ways, including meditation, exercise, or prayer. The RR is designed to counteract the fight or flight response of the stressed individual. Within 3 to 5 minutes after beginning, the individual experiences an altered state of consciousness, slower respiration and heart rates, lowered blood pressure, and lowered metabolism.[18]

According to Benson, four things are necessary to practice the RR: a quiet environment, an object to focus on, a passive attitude, and a comfortable position. The response can be evoked in many ways, and the particular technique is not so important. You try several until you find one that is the most comfortable. RR is quite similar to the form of deep physiological rest called transcendental meditation. It is also similar to short prayers found in the major religions.

To evoke the relaxation response, Dr. Benson advises you to "Close your eyes. Relax. Concentrate on one word or prayer. If other thoughts come to mind, be passive and return to the repetition."[19] One striking advantage of the relaxation response is that it is absolutely harmless and not time consuming.

Muscle Monitoring. An important part of many stress management programs is to learn to relax your muscles. You learn to literally loosen up and be less uptight. **Muscle monitoring** involves becoming aware that your muscles have tightened and then consciously relaxing them. If your jaw muscles are tightening up in a tense situation, you learn to relax your jaw enough to overcome the stress effects.

It is helpful to determine whether muscle tautness occurs in association with some recurring event. If it does, pay attention to the tautness of your muscles on those occasions.[20] For example, you might experience a tightening of your neck muscles whenever you are about to ask somebody a favor. Take a few moments to be aware of that muscle tension. After a while you will learn to relax when you are about to ask another person a favor.

Concentrate on Your Work or Hobby. For those individuals who do not want to bother going through formal exercises to relieve stress, an alternative exists. Learning to concentrate on a meaningful activity for 30-minute periods can be stress reducing. For example, you might concentrate so hard on what you are studying that the book in front of you (and its contents) is your only touch with reality. Intense concentration on an activity such as needlecraft or bowling should achieve similar results.

The principle underlying concentration as a method of reducing stress is probably similar to the relaxation response. Despite the fact that you are physically active, key bodily processes such as blood pressure decrease. Of major importance, your muscles assume the right degree of tautness, particularly when you are busily engaged in a sport.

A logical question at this point is, "Which method of stress management should I choose?" The best answer is that no one method of stress management is best for everybody. For example, people obsessed with power have a hard time dealing with rest and relaxation. Similarly, very impatient people may not enjoy the ritual of the RR. They are better off engaging in vigorous physical exercise as a way of reducing stress. It is recommended that you begin with one or two methods of stress reduction that you think would fit your preferences. If they work, continue. If not, try another stress-management technique until you find one that is comfortable and effective.

WHAT ORGANIZATIONS CAN DO TO MANAGE STRESS

Financial reasons alone make it important that employers be concerned about job stressors. Conservative estimates of stress-related costs are over $100 billion annually.[21] This figure includes such things as benefits paid to employees who are ill with stress-related disorders and lost productivity due to absenteeism. Humanitarian reasons also figure into helping reduce and prevent negative stress in the workplace. One of the most significant ways of keeping employees happy and healthy is to help them keep stress under control. Here we will describe two organizational approaches to managing stress: (1) practicing good management and (2) formal stress-management programs.

Practice Good Management

Since many forms of job stress are caused by poor methods of management, practicing good management will prevent many instances of negative stress. What constitutes good management is a book-length subject in itself. One example of the relationship between stress management and good management will suffice for now—the use of participative decision making in helping prevent and reduce both stress and burnout.

Participative Decision Making and Stress. Some employees find it stressful to be left out of important decisions that directly affect their work. Therefore, a managerial action capable of reducing stress is the use of participative decision making—encouraging input from the employee on meaningful matters. However, participation in routine and trivial decisions is transparent to employees and might increase rather than decrease job stress.[22]

The underlying psychology to participative decision making as a stress reducer relates to the idea that not having control over your environment is very stressful. For instance, many people do not mind working long hours providing they can control when they do this extra work. The inconvenience and indignity that go along with not being able to control your own fate also act as stressors. Participating in decision making is one way of gaining more control and thus reducing stress.

Participative Decision Making and Burnout. A similar argument for the value of participative decision making in managing burnout is offered by Susan Jackson and Randall Schuler. They note that current studies of burnout suggest that increasing employees' inputs into decision making, and thus increasing their control, often prevents burnout. Participation also may help prevent burnout by reducing confusing directions and conflicting demands (one of the stressors mentioned earlier).[23] Under participative decision making, the employee has a chance to iron out some of these rough spots with the boss. And it is these areas of ambiguity and conflict that often bring about the exhaustion characteristic of burnout.

Stress-Management Programs

Executive awareness of the hazards of too much stress in the work environment has lead to the establishment of stress-management programs in many large firms. The most basic form of these stress-management programs is an alcoholism clinic for employees whose alcoholism surfaces in response to job pressures. The most elaborate facilities have exercise rooms, meditation rooms, and biofeedback systems. The latter is a device that teaches you how to control physiological symptoms of stress. Under a typical biofeedback system, the person is connected by sensor wires to a machine with a computer-like screen that feeds back information on physiological indicators of stress. Among them are blood pressure, breathing rate, tension in the facial or neck muscles, and skin temperature (the colder the more tense). The saying about an apprehensive person getting "cold feet" thus has scientific validity.

By learning how to loosen their muscles, breathe deeply, or let their minds wander, stressed employees learn how to control their stress responses. After six to ten sessions with the biofeedback machines, patients are able to elicit the relaxation response at home or on the job without being wired to the machine.[24] Not every stressed employee can benefit from biofeedback training, but many employee health facilities find it to be an important part of managing stress symptoms.

An important current trend in stress-management programs sponsored by companies is to emphasize health improvement or improving one's lifestyle. Five key elements are included that will serve as a summary guide to anyone interested in managing stress:[25]

1. Exercise regularly but not excessively.
2. Achieve an appropriate amount of relaxation (too much relaxation on the job and the employee becomes lethargic).
3. Control your weight and eat nutritious food and beverages. Being underweight, as well as being overweight, can hamper your ability to combat job stress.
4. Find rewarding recreation and hobbies for yourself.
5. Reduce your dependency on chemicals ingested into the body including alcohol, caffeine, tobacco, marijuana, and cocaine.

SUMMARY OF KEY POINTS

☐ Stress is your internal reaction to any force that threatens to disturb your psychological or biological balance. A stressor is the force that brings about stress. The physiological changes within the body are quite similar in response to most stressors. When stress is chronic, it may lead to physical and mental health problems. Anxiety and tension are the two most frequent stress symptoms. A person's subjective evaluation of an event or situation heavily influences whether or not it will serve as a stressor.

☐ The right amount of stress can lead to improved job performance through such means as improved motivation and creativity. The wrong amount and kind of stress can lead to decreased job performance through such means as poor judgment and concentration.

☐ People with Type A behavior are impatient, demanding, and hostile, which predisposes them to job stress and cardiac disease. People who believe that external events control their fate (external locus of control) are also predisposed to stress. Sources of stress in personal life include these: daily hassles; disappointments with hobbies, interests, and sports; physical and mental health problems; financial problems; school-related problems; terrifying experiences; and any sort of significant life change. Among the major sources in work life are these: confusing directions and conflicting demands, exorbitant work demands, job insecurity and unemployment, computer shock, and underutilization of abilities.

☐ Job (or employee) burnout is both a cause and a by-product of stress. It refers to the discomfort, fatigue, and apathy stemming from not receiving the job rewards you anticipated. Three major signs or stages indicate the presence of burnout: emotional exhaustion, depersonalizing relationships, and low personal accomplishment. Burnout can be managed in ways similar to managing stress. One important specific strategy, however, to both prevent and overcome burnout is to develop realistic expectations. Individuals can do many things themselves to manage stress. Recommended strategies include:

1. Take constructive action about your true stressor.
2. Talk out your problems.
3. Get ample physical exercise and rest.
4. Use everyday relaxation methods, such as plan to have an idle period everyday.
5. Use the relaxation response (a simple form of meditation).
6. Muscle monitoring (learn how to relax your muscles).
7. Concentrate on your work or hobby.

☐ Organizations, also, can be helpful in managing stress. Practicing good management prevents many sources of stress. One such approach is to encourage participative decision making, which is said to decrease both stress and burnout. It works because the employee gains control over his or her environment. Stress-management programs are widely used in large organizations. They include training in biofeedback control, physical exercise, and weight-control classes.

GUIDELINES FOR PERSONAL EFFECTIVENESS

1. Find out through trial and error what appears to be the optimum (right amount) of job stress for you. If you avoid all stress, you might become lethargic and complacent. On the other hand, too much stress over a prolonged period of time can have detrimental consequences to your physical and mental health. Your job performance might also suffer.
2. To be successful in today's competitive world, you are strongly urged to maintain an active program of managing your stress. At an absolute minimum, it is important to take constructive action about your problems and learn to relax.
3. There is no one best technique for reducing your job-related stress. If you feel tense owing to work pressures, experiment with different methods of stress reduction and prevention.
4. If you are beginning to experience burnout either as a student or an employee, it is a signal to make some changes in your life. These could take the form of new experiences on and off the job.

DISCUSSION QUESTIONS

1. What is the major stressor where you work or attend school? What can be done to improve the situation?
2. What stress symptoms are you experiencing these days? How do you know they are stress symptoms?
3. Can you identify two jobs that you think would be particularly stressful for most people?
4. Can you identify two jobs that you think would have a minimum of stress for most people?

5. How has stress actually improved your life?
6. Can you think of an example of role ambiguity in the life of a student?
7. Can you identify several occupations or professions that are essentially in the business of reducing and preventing stress?
8. Do you have a Type A personality? Or is it Type B? Give the reasoning behind your answer.
9. What do you see as the difference between burnout and just being tired with the work you are doing?
10. What techniques of combating stress and/or burnout have you already used in life? How well do they work?

A Business Psychology Problem
KEEP THE HELP ON THEIR TOES

Marlene, a hotel administration major, found summer employment at White Mountain Inn, a Rocky Mountain resort. Two weeks into the summer, Marlene noticed that the waiters, waitresses, and busboys spent considerable time bickering with each other about the use of cups and saucers. Apparently, when the inn was filled to near capacity, there were not enough cups and saucers for everybody. Marlene immediately brought this problem to the attention of Cyrus, the dining room manager.

"Are you aware, Cyrus," explained Marlene, "that we have useless fighting over this easily rectified problem?"

"Young lady," replied Cyrus, "I intentionally have a shortage of cups and saucers. I've been doing that for years with pretty good results."

"You mean it saves the hotel money on cups and saucers?"

"I don't know that," answered Cyrus, "but it's good for the help. It keeps them on their toes. This way they come into the dining room early just to get their share of cups and saucers. Kind of a clever ploy on my part, don't you think?"

1. How should Marlene respond to Cyrus? What should be her recommendations?
2. What do you think of Cyrus as a boss?

A Business Psychology Exercise
HOW MUCH STRESS ARE YOU FACING?

Here's a brief questionnaire to roughly estimate if you are experiencing too many negative consequences of stress (or too much distress). Apply each question to the last six months of your life. Answer each question Mostly Yes or Mostly No.

	Mostly Yes	*Mostly No*
1. Have you been feeling uncomfortably tense lately?	_____	_____
2. Are you engaged in frequent arguments with people close to you?	_____	_____
3. Is your romantic life very unsatisfactory?	_____	_____
4. Do you have trouble sleeping?	_____	_____
5. Do you feel lethargic about life?	_____	_____
6. Do many people annoy or irritate you?	_____	_____
7. Do you have constant cravings for candy and other sweets?	_____	_____
8. Is your cigarette consumption way up?	_____	_____
9. Are you becoming addicted to soft drinks or coffee?	_____	_____
10. Do you find it difficult to concentrate on your work?	_____	_____
11. Do you frequently grind your teeth?	_____	_____
12. Are you increasingly forgetful about little things like mailing a letter?	_____	_____
13. Are you increasingly forgetful about big things like appointments and major errands?	_____	_____
14. Are you making far too many trips to the lavatory?	_____	_____
15. Have people commented lately that you do not look well?	_____	_____
16. Do you get into verbal fights with other people too frequently?	_____	_____
17. Have you been involved in more than one physical fight lately?	_____	_____
18. Do you have more than your share of tension headaches?	_____	_____
19. Do you feel nauseated much too often?	_____	_____
20. Do you feel light-headed or dizzy almost everyday?	_____	_____
21. Do you have churning sensations in your stomach far too often?	_____	_____
22. Are you in a big hurry all the time?	_____	_____
23. Are far too many things bothering you these days?	_____	_____

Scoring: The following guidelines are of value only if you answered the questions sincerely:

0–5 Mostly Yes answers: You seem to be experiencing a normal amount of stress.

6–15 Mostly Yes answers: Your stress level seems high. Become involved in some kind of stress management activity, such as the activities described later in this chapter.

16–23 Mostly Yes answers: Your stress level appears much too high. Seek the help of a mental health professional or visit your family doctor (or do both).

REFERENCES

[1]Based on definition from Terry A. Beehr and John E. Newman, "Job Stress, Employee Health, and Organizational Effectiveness," *Personnel Psychology* (Winter 1978), p. 668.

[2]Rose Mary Rummel and John W. Rader, "Coping with Executive Stress," *Personnel Journal* (June 1978), p. 305.

[3]Hans Selye, "Stress," *The Rotarian* (March 1978), p. 25.

[4]Quoted in Lee Smith, "What Kills Executives," *Dun's Review* (March 1976), p. 37.

[5]Hans Selye, "On the Real Benefits of Eustress," *Psychology Today* (March 1978), pp. 60–63.

[6]Meyer Friedman and Ray H. Rosenman, *Type A Behavior and Your Heart* (New York: Fawcett, 1975), pp. 100–103.

[7]Carl R. Anderson, Don Hellriegel, and John W. Slocum, Jr., "Managerial Response to Environmentally Induced Stress," *Academy of Management Journal* (June 1977), p. 260.

[8]Research reported in Sally Squires, "Daily Hassles May Add Up to Poor Health," Newhouse News Service reprint in *Democrat and Chronicle*, Rochester, N.Y. (Aug. 21, 1981), p. 1C.

[9]James C. Coleman, James N. Butcher, and Robert C. Carson, *Abnormal Psychology and Modern Life*, 6th ed. (Glenview, Ill.: Scott, Foresman, 1980), p. 183.

[10]A summary of this research is reported in "Stress: Can We Cope?" *Time* (June 6, 1983), p. 49. For more details on this topic, see Rabi S. Bhagat, "Effects of Stressful Life Events on Individual Performance and Work Adjustment Processes within Organizational Settings: A Research Model," *Academy of Management Review* (Oct. 1983), pp. 660–671.

[11]Marsha Taylor, "Office Workers Worry about Losing Their Jobs to Automated Equipment," Newhouse News Service reprint in *Democrat and Chronicle*, Rochester, N.Y. (Nov. 23, 1982), p. 8D.

[12]Joan Wolinsky, "Black Jobless Suffer Despair, Self-Blame," *Monitor* (Oct. 1982), p. 21. See also, H. G. Kaufman, *Professionals in Search of Work: Coping with the Stress of Job Loss and Underemployment* (New York: Wiley, 1982).

[13]Cary Cherniss, *Staff Burnout: Job Stress in the Human Services* (Beverly Hills, Calif.: Sage Publications, 1980).

[14]Susan E. Jackson and Randall S. Schuler, "Preventing Employee Burnout," *Personnel* (March–April 1983), p. 59.

[15]Patricia A. Renwick and Edward E. Lawler, "What Do You Really Want from Your Job?" *Psychology Today* (May 1978), p. 54.

[16]Margot Slade, "Emotional Pain of the Athlete's Physical Injuries," *New York Times* reprint in *Democrat and Chronicle*, Rochester, N.Y. (Jan. 25, 1983), p. 1C.

[17]Barry A. Farber, ed., *Stress and Burnout in the Human Service Professions* (Elmsford, N.Y.: Pergamon, 1982). The suggestion for resting appears in many of the selections in this book.

[18]Herbert Benson, *The Relaxation Response* (New York: Morrow, 1975).

[19]Reported in Joseph Carey, "You Can't Fight or Flee—So Relax," *USA Today* (Oct. 20, 1983), p. 4D.

[20]John M. Ivancevich and Michael T. Matteson, *Stress and Work: A Managerial Perspective* (Glenview, Ill.: Scott, Foresman, 1980), p. 222.

[21]Data gathered by Michael T. Matteson and John M. Ivancevich, "Note on Tension Discharge Rate as an Employee Health Status Predictor," *Academy of Management Journal* (Sept. 1983), p. 540.

[22]John M. Ivancevich and Michael T. Matteson, "Organizations and Coronary Heart Disease: The Stress Connection," *Management Review* (Oct. 1978).

[23]Jackson and Schuler, "Preventing Employee Burnout," p. 65.

[24]"Stress: Can We Cope?" p. 53.

[25]Randy Weigel and Sheldon Pinsky, "Managing Stress: A Model for the Human Resource Staff," *Personnel Administrator* (Feb. 1982), p. 59.

SUGGESTED READING

ANSON, SEERS, and others. "The Interaction of Job Stress and Social Support: A Strong Inference Investigation," *Academy of Management Journal* (June 1983), pp. 273–284.

CHARLESWORTH, EDWARD A., and RONALD G. NATHAN. *Stress Management: A Comprehensive Guide to Wellness.* Houston, Texas: Biobehavioral Publications, 1983.

FREUDENBERGER, HERBERT, and GERALDINE RICHELSON. *Burn Out: The High Cost of High Achievement.* Garden City, N.Y.: Doubleday, 1981.

FRIEND, KENNETH E. "Stress and Performance: Effects of Subjective Work Load and Time Urgency," *Personnel Psychology* (Autumn 1982), pp. 622–633.

GMELCH, WALTER H. *Beyond Stress to Effective Management.* New York: Wiley, 1982.

MASLACH, CHRISTINA. *Burnout—the Cost of Caring.* Englewood Cliffs, N.J.: Prentice-Hall, 1982.

MATTESON, MICHAEL T., and JOHN M. IVANCEVICH. *Managing Job Stress and Health.* New York: Free Press, 1982.

MORANO, RICHARD A. "How to Manage Change to Reduce Stress," *Management Review* (Nov. 1977), pp. 21–25.

NOVIT, MITCHELL S. "Mental Distress: Possible Implications for the Future," *Personnel Administrator* (Aug. 1982), pp. 47–53.

SAILER, HEATHER R., JOHN SCHLACTER, and MARK R. EDWARDS. "Stress: Causes, Consequences, and Coping Strategies." *Personnel* (July–Aug. 1982), pp. 35–48.

9

MANAGING CONFLICT
AND FRUSTRATION

LEARNING OBJECTIVES

After reading and studying this chapter and doing the exercises, you should be able to

1. Understand the meaning of conflict and frustration and how they relate to each other and stress.
2. Understand why so much frustration and conflict are found on the job.
3. Explain several of the helpful and harmful consequences of job conflict.
4. Be aware of a variety of approaches for resolving conflict.
5. Develop a strategy for managing your next important conflict.

THE MEANING OF CONFLICT
AND FRUSTRATION

"I just about cannot take it anymore," complained Marv to his sympathetic wife. "For thirteen years I've been selling insurance for the company, and they've let me down again. I had one of the biggest premium packages put together that our branch has seen in a good many years. Underwriting fouls me up again. I ask them for quick service, and they tell me not to be pushy. I told the restaurant chain I had on the hook that our company would love to have their business. Underwriting next tells me that they may not want to take this line of insurance. It's a helluva lot easier doing battle with my customers than with the people inside our company."

Marv's conflicts are not unusual. People in responsible jobs often find themselves locked into disputes with people inside their own organization. Conflict is an inevitable part of life when your job involves contact with a variety of people, whether they be people directly in your chain of command, people from other parts of the organization, or outsiders.

Conflict. In technical terms, a conflict is the simultaneous arousal of two or more incompatible motives or demands. Since conflict acts as a stressor, it is usually accompanied by unpleasant emotions and feelings such as tension and anger.[1] In Marv's situation, he is in conflict with his company. He seems unable to satisfy both the company and the customer at the same time.

A more general or popular definition of conflict is "a hostile relationship among individuals or groups."[2] The technical and popular definitions of conflict are not incompatible. Your relationship with another person tends to become hostile when you both cannot satisfy your demands at the same time. If you and a co-worker are in competition for the same job, both of your demands cannot be met simultaneously. Therefore, the two of you may develop mutual hostility and antagonism.

Frustration. Conflict typically leads to frustration, a blocking of need or motive satisfaction by some kind of obstacle. You experience a sense of frustration when something stands in the way between you and the goal you want to achieve. Marv's frustration came about because of his perception that the underwriting department was blocking his path to satisfying his customers (an important need of Marv's). Note that it is usually your perception of an event, situation, or thing that determines whether or not it is an obstacle. If Marv perceived the underwriting department to be simply doing its job, he would not have experienced a sense of frustration.

Conflict, frustration, and stress are interrelated. Conflict (an incompatibility of motives) leads to frustration (a blocking of motives). And both serve as a source of stress. The following diagram summarizes these relationships:

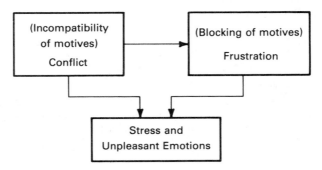

The major purpose of this chapter is to explain the nature of job conflict and how to manage it to your advantage. However, it is also important to devote some attention to frustration since conflict is the most common form of frustration.[3]

FRUSTRATION AND JOB-RELATED BEHAVIOR

Frustration is most likely to arise when we are ego involved in reaching a particular goal. Suppose that you are sitting in the waiting room of a dentist's office. You begin to solve a crossword puzzle because there is little else to do. You find the puzzle difficult, and you are unable to finish it. However, you do not feel frustrated because you have no personal stake in finishing crossword puzzles.

While seated in the dentist's chair, you learn that you will need extensive root canal work. It will be both painful and expensive. You now experience frustration because you were hoping to purchase a motorcycle for a cross-country trip this upcoming summer. This motorcycle trip is very important to you. The expense of the root canal work blocks your pleasure path—at least for the time being.

As shown in Figure 9-1, job frustrations are of many types. Anything that prevents you from reaching a goal that is important to you is a potential source of frustration. If you are discriminated against because of factors beyond your control, such as your age, race, religion, sex, or height, you will probably experience frustration. One woman found employment as a market research assistant in an advertising agency in Vancouver. When asked how she liked her new position, she claimed that she was frustrated: "Oh the work is fine, and I'm on my way in my career at long last. But it's awfully frustrating being cooped up inside an office building during the day. I'm an outdoors type. I miss the freedom to roam about. Maybe I should try for a sales position."

High-Frustration-Tolerance People

If you are a person who can tolerate high frustration, there is a good chance that you will do something constructive about your frustration. In other words, you will use an effective coping method. Among these are changing your goals if you are frustrated. If you cannot become the manager of manufacturing after years of trying, why not be content with a general foreman's or forewoman's position? People with high frustration tolerance often use a systematic approach to solving the problem that is causing them frustration. A man might be looking for a particular book in the library. He cannot locate it because he does not understand how to use the microfiche reader which

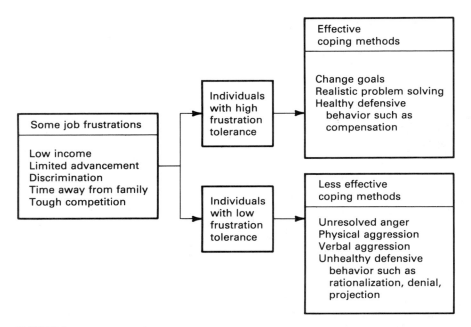

FIGURE 9–1
Relationship between frustration and job-related behavior.

has replaced the card catalogue. A person with low frustration tolerance might swear at or slam the microfiche reader. A problem solver would ask the librarian for help.

One healthy defensive act in response to frustration is **compensation.** Because you are frustrated in reaching a specific goal, you work overly hard to reach a related goal. One woman who was denied admission to medical school eventually wound up as an owner of a dental hygiene school. One man who couldn't make his high school football team became the team equipment manager.

Low-Frustration-Tolerance People

A person who cannot tolerate much frustration usually responds to frustration with anger, verbal and physical aggression (for instance, kicking a car when it won't start), or counterproductive defensive behavior. Virtually every reader of this book is already somewhat familiar with the human tendency to become defensive when a person receives a threatening blow to the ego. Three such defense mechanisms are common when people with low frustration tolerance are blocked in reaching their goals.

Rationalization is the most frequently used defense mechanism. A person who rationalizes finds a plausible reason for doing something when he or she cannot face up to the real reason. A woman who was passed over for a supervisory position might rationalize, "Who needs the aggravation anyway? In this company a supervisor winds up taking home problems almost every night." Her defense is not particularly constructive, because she still has an unresolved longing to become a supervisor.

Denial is a straightforward defense mechanism in response to frustration. The person with low frustration tolerance simply blocks out or denies that a particular event has taken place. By denying the reality of what happened, the individual blocks out the aggravating tension and anxiety associated with the event. One custodial worker left an office window unlatched. During the night a wind storm blew open the window. The mixture of rain and wind did severe damage to the office. Afraid that he would lose his job, he denied responsibility for the act: "When I left that office I double checked to see that it was locked. Besides that, I didn't clean that floor last night."

Projection means that we attribute our own undesirable desires, traits, and impulses to another individual. We are also using projection when we blame others for our own failures. People use projection when they are frustrated, because it temporarily decreases some of the discomfort associated with failing to reach an important goal. A teen-age girl failed the road test for her driver's license for the second time. The reason she failed is that she put the car into reverse when the examiner motioned her to proceed forward. While attempting to park the car, she did the opposite and bumped into a car parked in front of her. When asked by her mother why she failed, the girl projected: "The stupid examiner made me fail. He was so confused, he didn't know if he wanted me to go forward or backward."

WHY SO MUCH JOB CONFLICT EXISTS

A number of reasons create conflicts in organizational life. We shall discuss six of the most common sources of conflict here. All these reasons or *sources* of conflict stem from the same underlying theme of two incompatible motives, demands, or events. You and another person, or your department and another department, cannot both have what you both want at the same time.

Competition for Limited Resources

A fundamental reason that you might experience conflict with another person is that not everybody can get all the money, material, and human help he or she wants. You might have an important idea you want to present to your boss before he or she leaves for vacation. Upon asking to see the boss before he leaves, he says, "I'm sorry but I have already agreed to meet with Debbie and Mike. Why don't you catch me first thing after vacation?"

At that moment you will probably feel frustrated because your goal of presenting your idea to the boss is blocked. You might also be in conflict with Debbie and Mike, who have monopolized your boss's time for the balance of the day. The limited resource in this situation is the boss's time.

Differences in Goals and Objectives

When two individuals or two groups have major differences in objectives, the potential for conflict is high. Although one might argue that everybody working for the same organization should have the same ultimate goal—the success of the organization—this does not always happen in practice. Frequently, individuals and departments have different aspirations than does management.

Conflict between instructors and students sometimes reflects a difference between goals and objectives. An instructor might look on his or her course as a valuable contribution to each student's career. His or her goal is for students to maximize their effort in study and classroom participation. Some of the students may have the goal of receiving the maximum grade for the minimum amount of study and participation. When an examination question is posed based on a minor point made in supplementary reading, conflict occurs. If the students shared the goal of maximizing learning, they would not object to the question. If the instructor shared the goal of maximum grade for minimum effort, he or she might not have asked the obscure question.

Different Methods Proposed to Reach a Common Goal

There are usually alternative approaches to achieving almost any goal. Consequently, individuals and groups often enter into conflict over the best method of accomplishing a goal.[4] A continuing conflict of this nature took place in one company between Alice, the head of the word-processing center, and her boss Jack, the manager of office services.

> Jack believed strongly that the word-processing center should produce high-quality work but also be run as economically as feasible. His strategy was to urge Alice to hire mostly student and part-time help. He reasoned that their low wages would reduce operating costs. Jack thought that with close supervision these young word-processing technicians could produce high-quality work. Alice shared Jack's goal of running a department with high-quality work at low cost. Her solution was to pay good wages to experienced word-processing technicians and secretaries. She reasoned that by paying high wages to mature women a stable work force could be established. Alice thought that the savings on turnover costs would more than compensate for high wages.

Alice and Jack frequently argued about which strategy would best achieve their shared goal. Jack finally imposed his formal authority and basically ordered Alice to use a compromise strategy: an attempt was made to strike a balance between hiring trainees and experienced workers.

Personal Differences

You may encounter conflict with another person on the job simply because the two of you are radically different types of people. A variety of personality and cultural differences among people contribute to incidences of conflict in the office. Difference in age is one such factor. The **generation gap** can lead to conflict because members of different generations may not accept each other's values. Cooperation is sometimes difficult to achieve between older and younger members of a department because older workers question the seriousness of purpose of the younger workers. Simultaneously, the younger workers may believe that the older workers are resistant to change and blindly loyal to the company.

Hostile and Aggressive People

Some people enter into frequent conflict on the job simply because of their naturally hostile or aggressive nature. They use the office as a battleground for expressing their undesirable impulses. A cameraman in a TV studio earned the nickname Pete the Fire Spitting Dragon because of his antagonistic attitude toward the television directors, hosts, and talk-show guests. On one occasion he told a local politician that her dress looked wretched on television. The Dragon was finally transferred to a position in the control room where he did not have contact with directors, hosts, or guests.

Some Jobs Breed Conflict

If you were a collection agent for a finance company, an investigator of welfare fraud, or an auditor for the Internal Revenue Service, you could expect to enter into frequent interpersonal conflict. Some job conflict is thus more related to the roles that people occupy than to their differences in personality. (A **role** is a set of behaviors a person is supposed to engage in because of his or her job or situation.) Certain jobs have built-in conflict in the sense that people tend to resent the activities performed by the holder of that job (his or her role).

An informal survey of students on one college campus revealed that many of them disliked the campus security officers. One student expressed the very nature of role conflict in her comments about the security officers: "It's nothing personal. Those guys are paid to be bastards. Most students can't afford the type of cars that you can count on to start when you want them

Some people enter into frequent conflict on the job simply because of their naturally hostile or aggressive nature.

to. The result is that during a cold spell we often have to abandon our cars for a couple of days. Often you get a ten-dollar ticket that you can't afford. Worse is when you get the car towed away."

Sexual Harassment

A substantial number of employees find themselves in conflict because they are sexually harassed by a superior. **Sexual harassment** can be generally defined as "any unwanted attention of a sexual nature from someone from the workplace that creates discomfort and/or interferes with the job."[5] It can include something as violent as rape or as subtle as a sexually oriented comment about somebody's body or appearance.[6] A legal definition of the term stipulates that unwelcomed sexual advances, either verbal or physical, become a form of harassment when:

- Submission to the advances is a term or condition of employment.
- Submission to or rejection of the advances is used as the basis for making employment decisions.
- Such conduct interferes with an individual's work performance or creates an intimidating, hostile, or offensive working environment.[7]

Sexual harassment against women is a frequent occurrence, with one estimate suggesting that 70 percent of women are sexually harassed at some point in their careers.[8] A survey of more than 17,000 federal employees conducted by the Merit Systems Protection Board found that 42 percent of women and 15 percent of the men surveyed had been harassed.[9] As these figures would suggest, sexual harassment usually takes the form of an unwanted action by a male toward a female, but may also include female against male, male against male, and female against female. Brief case examples of the two most frequent categories of harassment are presented next.

Male against Female. An investment analyst asked her boss that she be considered for promotion to senior investment analyst. She pointed out that she was eligible for promotion on the basis of her good job performance and length of service. He suggested that they have dinner together the next Thursday evening to discuss the matter. Over dinner, the boss stated explicitly that he would be much more receptive to recommending her for promotion if they became romantically involved that evening. The woman rejected her bosses advances and asked to be escorted home immediately after dinner. Her boss was disappointed but granted her request. Two weeks later when the woman again brought up the issue of promotion, he responded, "I told you that uncooperative employees do not get promoted in my department."

The woman went around her boss and complained to her boss's boss that she was being treated unfairly because she refused to date her boss. A transfer to another office was arranged for the woman and she received her promotion to senior investment analyst.

Male against Male. A group of building maintenance employees in New York City filed a complaint about their boss to a city agency whose function it was to hear such complaints. The superintendent of a building insisted that the employees who worked for him have sexual relations with him. He implied that if they did not comply their job would be in jeopardy. The building superintendent also had them photographed in compromising positions to prevent them from complaining. The men complained anyway and the superintendent was fired.[10]

Tie-in with Conflict and Frustration. Sexual harassment creates conflict because the harassed person has to make a choice between two incompatible motives. One motive is to get ahead or at least keep the job. But to satisfy this motive, the person is forced to sacrifice the motive of holding on to his or her moral values or preferences. Frustration takes place because the sexual harasser becomes a barrier preventing the individual from reaching his or her goal.

Employer Responsibilities. Sexual harassment is classified as a form of sex discrimination because those subordinates who do comply with the boss's sexual demands are given preferential treatment. Equally important, those individuals who do not comply may be denied something they deserve, such as a salary increase. This reason is illegal because it is unrelated to job performance. The major piece of relevant legislation is Title VII of the 1964 Civil Rights Act. Preliminary Guidelines were issued to employers in 1980 by the Equal Employment Opportunity Commission, which explained the latter's role in preventing harassment.

The Guidelines require that employers take all necessary steps to create an environment that prevents sexual harassment. The suggested actions include "affirmatively raising the subject of sexual harassment, expressing strong disapproval, developing appropriate sanctions, informing employees of their rights to raise the issue of sexual harassment under Title VII, and developing methods to sensitize all concerned."

The individual also has responsibility for taking action against sexual harassment. He or she is advised to use an appropriate method of resolving conflict (to be described in the next several pages), including making an appeal to a third party.

THE GOOD AND BAD SIDE OF CONFLICT

It follows logically that, since conflict is a source of stress and similar to stress, it can have both beneficial and detrimental consequences to the individual. First, we will examine a number of helpful aspects of conflict. Probably you can recall an incident in your life when conflict proved to be beneficial in the long run. Perhaps you and your boss hammered out a compromise to a problem troubling you only after you bitterly complained about working conditions. Properly managed, moderate doses of conflict can be beneficial. Some of the benefits that might arise from conflict are summarized next.

    1. Talents and abilities may emerge in response to conflict. When faced with a conflict, people often become more innovative than they would in a tranquil situation. Assume that your company told you that they would no longer pay for your advanced education unless you used the courses to improve your job performance. You would probably find ways to accomplish such an end.

2. Conflict can satisfy a variety of psychological needs. Among them are a desire to express aggressive urges and to be aroused by something in the environment. As a socially acceptable substitute for attacking others, you might be content to argue over work responsibilities.

3. Conflict can lead to worthwhile innovation and change. The history of the labor movement contains numerous examples of conflict over such matters as reducing the work week from six to five days and shortening working hours from 60 to 50 hours per week. You might be in conflict with a living partner about dividing up household responsibilities. The net result might be a more equitable sharing of tasks.

4. Many individuals are bored with their jobs, and thus find squabbles with other people and other departments a refreshing pause in their day. Office conflicts tend to add sparkle to coffee break conversations, even if the discussants are not personally involved in the dispute.

5. Conflict can provide diagnostic information about problem areas in the firm. When management learns of conflict, an investigation is sometimes initiated that will lead to the prevention of many similar problems. One example would be that many companies have taken a very positive stance against sexual harassment after a conflict of this nature was brought to their attention.

6. As an aftermath of conflict, unity may be reestablished. The drama of childhood is frequently reenacted in large and small companies. Two adolescents engaged in a fist fight may emerge bloodied but good friends after the battle. Two warring supervisors may also become more cooperative toward each other as an aftermath of confrontation.

As common sense would suggest, conflict can also have a multitude of harmful consequences to the individual and the organization. War, sabotage, homicide, suicide, and alcoholism are among the harmful consequences of conflict between people. It is the harmful consequences of conflict that make it important for people to learn how to resolve conflict.

1. Prolonged conflict between individuals can be detrimental to some people's emotional and physical well-being. Many individuals have suffered psychosomatic disorder as a consequence of the intense disputes that take place within their companies. One foreman had a heart attack on the shop floor in the midst of an argument with his boss over the necessity of replacing a machine.

2. Conflict often results in extreme demonstrations of self-interest at the expense of the larger organization. Individuals or departments will place their personal welfare over that of the rest of the organization or customers. Several times in recent years air-traffic controllers were in dispute with their management about salary and miscellaneous working conditions. The controller group expressed their conflict by literal com-

pliance with every air-traffic regulation on the books at the time. As a result, air traffic slowed down to almost a standstill because regulations that had been liberally interpreted in the past were now strictly enforced.

3. Time and energy can be diverted from reaching important goals (such as making a profit) when people are in conflict. In addition, money and material can be wasted. It is not uncommon for two managers in conflict to spend time writing memos proving each other wrong in a particular dispute.

4. The aftermath of conflict may have high financial and emotional costs. Sabotage might be the financial consequence. At the same time, management may develop a permanent distrust of many people in the work force although only a few of them are saboteurs.

5. Too much conflict is fatiguing, even if it does not cause symptoms of emotional illness. People who work in high-conflict jobs often feel "spent" when they return home from work. When the battle-worn individual has limited energy left over for family responsibilities, the result is more conflict. (For instance, "What do you mean you are too tired to go to the movies?" or "If your job is killing your sex drive, find another job.")

Knowing When Conflict
Has Been Harmful or Helpful

David W. Johnson has developed four guidelines to help you to determine when a conflict has had helpful or harmful results. These four things are well worth looking for after the conflict has subsided. The conflict has been beneficial:

- If the two of you can work better together.
- If both you and the other person feel better about each other and your jobs.
- If both you and the other person are satisfied with the results of the conflict.
- If the ability of you and the other person to resolve future conflicts with each other has been improved.[11]

RESOLVING CONFLICT THROUGH
NEGOTIATING AND BARGAINING

So far we have explained the nature of conflict and frustration. The next important step in managing frustration and conflict is to learn practical ways of resolving conflict with others. In this and the following section we describe a number of techniques for dealing constructively with conflict in the workplace. The same techniques can be applied to personal life. (The previous chapter described ways of managing the stress associated with conflict and frustration.)

Another way of understanding conflicts is to regard them as situations calling for negotiating or bargaining. When you are trying to negotiate a fair salary for yourself, you are simultaneously trying to resolve a conflict. At first the demands of both parties may seem incompatible, but through the negotiation process a salary may emerge that satisfies both parties. This is referred to as a **win–win philosophy** or **integrative bargaining** (the demands of both sides are integrated into the final solution). A settlement in which one side wins at the other's expense is called **win–lose** or **zero-sum bargaining** (what one wins is at the other's expense). It is also possible to have **lose–lose** solutions to conflict situations.[12] The negotiating tactics described in this section, as well as the other methods of conflict resolution described in the following section, are designed to achieve win–win outcomes.

Compromise

In this most widely used form of negotiation, one party agrees to do something if the other party agrees to do something else. "I'll get my reports to you on time if you agree to get them back to me with your suggestions within ten days." Compromise is a realistic approach to resolving conflict and is almost inescapable in our culture. People enter into negotiation and bargaining sessions expecting a compromise solution, both in work and personal life. For example, when negotiating a divorce settlement, neither party expects all of his or her demands to be met, but that a compromise solution will be found.

The major problem with compromise is that the two parties may wind up with a solution that pacifies both but does not adequately solve the problem. One example would be buying two department heads half the equipment each one requests. As a result, neither department really shows a productivity gain that would have been possible if the full request had been granted to either side.

Allow Room for Negotiation

The basic strategy of negotiation and compromise is to begin with a demand that allows you room for compromise and concession. Anyone who has ever negotiated for the price of an automobile, house, or used furniture recognizes this vital strategy. If you think your ten-speed bicycle is worth $300, you might put it on sale for $400. A potential buyer makes an initial offer of $250. After negotiation you wind up with an offer of $300, precisely what you anticipated.

Make Small Concessions Gradually

Research conducted at a center for dispute settlement suggests that making steady concessions leads to more satisfactory agreements in most situations.[13] Gradually you concede little things to the other side, such as throwing in an air pump and a back pack if the person agrees to move up the offer for the ten-speed bike. The small-concession tactic is described as a soft approach to bargaining. The hard-line approach is to make your total concession early in the negotiation and grant no further concessions. In our example, "My bike is for sale at $300 including an air pump and a back pack. I will keep the bike rather than let it go for less."

Use Deadlines

Giving the other side a deadline is often helpful in winning a negotiation or resolving a conflict. Deadlines often force people into action because they require some type of external control or motivation. Here are two examples of how you might be able to use deadlines to gain advantage in your negotiation:

- "Will I be receiving a promotion to restaurant manager by December 31? If not, I will be forced to accept employment at another restaurant that has offered me such a promotion."
- "I am willing to paint your house for $2,000 if you agree to sign the contract by July 15. After that date my price will go up to $2,500."

Maintain Emotional Control

A good general rule for success in business is to appear cool under pressure. Negotiating sessions are a source of pressure in which this rule is particularly applicable. You might pound the table, speak loudly, or wave your hands to display enthusiasm and sincerity. Nevertheless, try to avoid becoming so emotional that you make an irrational decision. A secretary was offered a promotion to administrative assistant, a job she wanted very much. When told that the job would pay only $35 more per month, she became enraged and quit. Since the woman wanted the job, a preferred strategy for her would have been to try and negotiate a better raise.

Negotiate on Your Own Turf

When trying to negotiate or resolve conflict to your advantage, it is helpful to place yourself in a powerful position. One subtle way of having more power is to conduct the negotiations on your own turf. The rationale for this tactic stems partially from the fact that athletic teams usually win a higher proportion of games at home than away. Among the ways of conducting negotiations on your own turf would be:

- Try to get your boss to visit you at your work station when you want to negotiate some extra time off.
- When you are buying something from somebody, try to get that person to visit you at your residence.
- When you are trying to get a broken romance back together, invite your former partner over to your place to discuss the conditions of the reconciliation.

Famous negotiator Herb Cohen suggests a variation of the "own turf" technique, which he labels, "Be the caller, not the callee."[14] When you are the person initiating the call, you somehow have slightly more power. In our example, you might call your ex-partner and say, "I miss you, and I want to see if we can work things out."

Make a Last and Final Offer

In many instances, presenting a final offer will break a deadlock. You might frame your message something like this, "All I am willing to pay for your used refrigerator is $110. Call me when you can let me have it for that price." Sometimes the strategy will be countered by a last and final offer from the other side: "Thanks for your interest. My absolute minimum price for this refrigerator is $150. Call me if that should seem OK to you." One of you will probably give in and accept the other person's last and final offer.

Allow for Face-Saving

We have saved one of the most important negotiating strategies for last. Negotiating does not mean that you should try to humiliate the other side, particularly when you believe in the win–win philosophy. You should try to create circumstances that will enable you to continue working with the other side if it is necessary. People prefer to avoid looking weak, foolish, or incompetent during negotiation or when the process is completed. If you do not give your opponent an opportunity to save face, you will probably create a long-term enemy. An example of face-saving took place in a real-estate transaction.

Annette and her brothers were in the business of buying and rehabilitating old buildings, and then later renting and/or selling them. They did this on a part-time basis. Annette learned that one of her co-workers at the office was trying to sell a dilapidated building she owned in town for $38,500. After several tries at negotiating the price, Annette's final offer of $24,000 was accepted.

She was able to get the property at this low price because the owner was badly in need of cash. To help ease the sting of having obtained the property at such a low price, Annette later told the owner (and co-worker): "Joe, I think you made a smart move unloading your property when you did. The city building codes are so tight they make it just about impossible for landlords to keep their places up to standard. My brothers and I have a big job cut out for us."

GENERAL METHODS
OF RESOLVING CONFLICT

Negotiation and bargaining strategies are important, but they are not the only workable methods of resolving conflict (and therefore eliminating a major source of frustration). Also of importance are methods of resolving conflict that can be used when dividing up resources is not particularly an issue. Seven of the techniques to be described here are geared toward individual action. When you use them you rely on yourself, rather than on a formal mechanism set up by the organization. An example of the latter is an "open-door policy" whereby any employee can bring a complaint to top management. The last technique to be described here, appeal to a third party, requires the combination of individual initiative and a formal mechanism. (Using the open-door policy to resolve your conflict would fit this category.)

Gentle Confrontation

The art of gentle confrontation leads all contenders as the best way of dealing with person-to-person conflict, particularly when the person with whom you are in conflict has a power advantage. In this technique you make a candid statement of the problem facing you without hinting at any form of violence or retaliation. Here is how it works:

Suppose that you find out that a co-worker of yours is being paid $125 more per month than you. Yet he is doing the same job and has the same amount of experience and education as you. Using gentle confrontation, you would tactfully discuss this problem with your boss, asking if the inequity could be resolved. One statement you might make would be, "I wonder if there has been a mistake in setting my salary. The fellow I work with is being paid $125 dollars more per month than another person doing the same job."

The Problem-Solving Principle. Gentle confrontation includes the important principle of resolving conflict by placing things on a problem-solving basis. First you confront the problem, and then you try to fix the problem rather than fix the blame! This is the rational way to resolve conflict. But people are frequently so emotional when trying to resolve conflict that it takes them a while to calm down enough to think and behave rationally. The conflict-resolution tactics described in this section either include the problem-solving principle directly, or help move the conflict toward problem solving.

Disarm the Opposition

When engaged in conflict, the armament you should take away from the opposition is his or her negative criticism of you.[15] You can capitalize on the same principle that children often use in handling conflict (or potential conflict) with their parents: "I broke a lamp by mistake. Go ahead and beat me. I deserve it."

Disarming the opposition has widespread application. It works more effectively than launching a counterattack against the person with whom you are in conflict. Assume that your boss is angry with you because your sales are 25 percent below target. You recognize that your boss might even be angry enough to threaten you with an ultimatum—improve sales or leave the company. Your worst strategy would be to marshal an immediate counterattack during a meeting with your boss. Do not try to dazzle him or her with a long list of reasons why sales have been below forecast.

Instead, disarm your boss with a statement such as, "You are probably upset because my sales are 25 percent below target. I agree that I should not be proud of my performance. Maybe you can help me develop a plan of attack to improve my sales situation."

Exchange Images with Your Antagonist

The essential point to this advanced method of resolving conflict is that you and your antagonist make it clear that you understand the other person's point of view. Empathy of this kind may then lead to a useful and productive compromise. A convenient application of this method is for you to list on a sheet of paper (1) your side of the argument and (2) what you think is his or her side of the argument. Next, he or she does the same for you. Table 9–1 is an example of how images might be exchanged. Each person makes up his or her image sheet without consulting the other person. After the images are exchanged, discussion (and sometimes fireworks) begins.

Mock the Opposition in a Nice Way

A conflict is difficult to win until your adversary recognizes that perhaps he or she may be in the wrong (or at least partially wrong). Telling somebody else, "You're absolutely wrong. Why can't you see it my way?" is consistently ineffective strategy. Much more can be gained by sharpening your ability to mock gently—or point out good-naturedly the inconsistencies in—your adversary's logic.

TABLE 9-1

An image exchanging list between you and your boss based on a conflict about punctuality

You: My Side of the Story	What I Think Is Your Side of the Story
a. I'm usually on time for work.	a. I'm not very dependable.
b. I live on the other side of town.	b. I live too far from the office.
c. Public transportation is unreliable in this city.	c. I take the last possible bus.

Your Boss: My Side of the Story	What I Think Is Your Side of the Story
a. You are late too often.	a. I'm as punctual as most people in the office.
b. If you cared more about your job, you would consider moving closer to the office.	b. I think you don't take my transportation problems seriously.
c. If you got out of bed earlier, you could take an earlier bus.	c. I try hard to get here on time. It's not my fault that I'm late sometimes.

Gene, a sales manager in a small chemical company, is facing a win–lose situation with Baxter, the head of manufacturing. If Baxter loses, Gene wins, and vice versa. Gene wants a 100-pound sample of a chemical compound made to the specifications of one customer. To complicate matters further, he wants the material delivered in 30 days. Baxter, upset by Gene's request, tells him, "Gene, it just won't work. Our production facilities are set up for the large-batch customer. We need business in large volume. The small occasional order just gets in our hair. It's a losing proposition for us to stop the production line just to run your order for 100 pounds of gunk."

Gene intensifies the conflict by angrily responding. "Do you think we're in business to please our customers or to please your people? Ram this order through for me, or I'll be talking to the president about your lack of cooperation."

A preferred approach for Gene: To lessen the tension and win his point, Gene might have said, "Okay, we marketing people have been bad boys again. We're out soliciting new business without accepting only customers who'll order 100,000 barrels and who won't need it for a year. I'll try harder next time, but I think this 100-pound sample could lead to substantial orders next time."

Capitalize on Your Anger

One by-product of office conflict is that people get angry, including you. Your anger could lead to your demise if you physically assault your opposition or you tell your boss that he or she is a stupid fool. In contrast, you can make constructive use of your anger if properly managed. Anger is an energizer,

Point out good-naturedly the
inconsistencies in your adversary's logic.

and this increased energy can be used to goad you on toward higher levels
of achievement. Anger can also be used for dramatic effect—to illustrate by
action that you are a person who does not care to be taken advantage of.

> An office custodian was in continuous disagreement with some of the workers
> in his office who did not take off their overshoes and umbrellas before entering
> the lobby. This resulted in mud stains on the floor that required several wash-
> ings per day. The offenders did not seem to take his pleas seriously. One snowy
> Monday morning, the custodian stood in the office lobby waving a mop over
> his head. He shouted, "Anybody who messes this floor once more with boots
> is going to get down on his hands and knees and do the mopping for me. I've
> taken enough of your messing up my floor for the rest of my life." Few people
> violated the "leave your overshoes outside rule" thereafter.

Dissipate the Other Person's Violence

Watching a professional hockey game, I noticed that the referee and other
players did not intervene until a fight between two players had lasted about
three minutes. Seated next to me was an avid hockey fan and former player.

I asked the gentleman about the delay before the fighting hockey players were separated. He replied, "If you break them up too soon, they'll get right back to fighting. You have to let them blow off most of their steam before you try to separate them."

Similarly, if your conflict with another person in the office is so intense that he or she is verbally violent, play it cool. Let most of the violence dissipate before you return with a counterargument. Until the other party has expressed most of his or her angry feelings, he or she won't listen to your side of the story. Once the person has ventilated his or her feelings, you can begin the process of effectively working out your problem.

Let the Problem Go Away

Procrastination is a subtle and usually unproductive method of resolving conflict. Nevertheless, there are times when doing nothing about a conflict will be to your advantage. The situation may change and the conflict will resolve itself. One computer programmer was particularly irked by a newcomer to the department who lectured to the other programmers about how behind the times they were. In addition to his arrogance, the new programmer did not seem to be carrying his full share of the work. The more experienced programmer decided to do nothing about the problem. He basically ignored the newcomer. Within two months, the new programmer quit and took a new job that he thought would be more technically challenging.

The first programmer defended his strategy of procrastination: "I've seen people like that come and go before. They seem to flit around from company to company, trying to create a good impression. I figured he wouldn't last, so why waste my time and my boss's time trying to straighten the guy out?"

Appeal to a Powerful Third Party

At times you may be placed in a conflict situation where the other party holds the major share of the power. Perhaps you have tried techniques such as gentle confrontation or disarming the opposition, yet he or she still won't budge. In these situations you may have to enlist the help of a third party with power—more power than you or your adversary has. Among such third parties are union stewards, personnel managers, a highly placed relative in the organization, or your boss's boss (when you are convinced that you have been served an injustice).

In some situations, just implying that you will bring in that powerful third party to help resolve the conflict situation is sufficient for you to gain advantage. One woman felt she was repeatedly passed over for promotion because of her sex. She hinted that if she were not given fairer consideration she would speak to the Equal Employment Opportunity Commission (EEOC). She was given a half-step promotion shortly thereafter.

CHOOSING A TACTIC
FOR RESOLVING CONFLICT

How does a person know which tactic or strategy of those presented in this chapter will work best for a given problem? The best answer is to consider both your personality and the situation. With respect to your personality, or personal style, pick a tactic for resolving conflict that you would feel comfortable using. One person might say, "I would like the tactic of using deadlines because I like to control situations." Another person might say, "I prefer gentle confrontation because I'm an open and up-front type of person." Still another person might say, "I'll avoid disarming the opposition for now. I don't yet have enough finesse to carry out this technique."

In fitting the strategy to the situation, it is important to assess the gravity of the topic for negotiation or the conflict between people. A woman might say to herself, "My boss has committed such a blatant act of sexual harassment that I had best take this up with a higher authority immediately" (appeal to a powerful third party). Sizing up your opponent can also help you choose the best strategy. If she or he appears reasonably flexible, you might try to compromise. Or if your adversary is especially upset, give that person a chance to simmer down before trying to solve the problem.

SUMMARY OF KEY POINTS

☐ A conflict is the simultaneous arousal of two or more incompatible motives or demands. It may also be considered a hostile relationship among individuals or groups. People in conflict usually experience tension, anxiety, and frustration (the blocking of need or motive satisfaction by some kind of obstacle). Anything that prevents you from reaching a goal that is important to you is a potential source of frustration.

☐ People with high frustration tolerance generally use effective coping methods to deal with frustration, including compensation (finding a substitute goal for the one that is blocked). People with low frustration tolerance usually respond to frustration with anger, verbal and physical aggression, or counterproductive defensive behavior.

☐ Some degree of job conflict is almost inevitable because so many different factors breed conflict. Seven major reasons for or sources of conflict are (1) competition for limited resources, (2) differences in goals and objectives, (3) different methods proposed to reach a common goal, (4) personal differences such as age and values, (5) the presence of hostile and aggressive people, (6) the fact that some jobs breed conflict, and (7) sexual harassment of employees. Sexual harassment is considered illegal because it is a form of job discrimination.

☐ Conflict, in the right amount, can be helpful to individuals and the organization. Among these potential benefits are (1) increased innovativeness, (2) satisfaction of psychological needs, (3) relief of boredom, and (4) a feeling of unity after conflict. Conversely, too much or too intense conflict can be harmful to individuals and the organization. Among its disadvantages are (1) impaired mental health, (2) demonstrations of self-interest, (3) waste of time and energy, (4) financial and emotional drain, and (5) excessive fatigue.

☐ Negotiating or bargaining is necessary in resolving conflict over dividing up resources. Ideally, both sides should retain something of value after negotiations are completed and conflict is resolved (the win–win philosophy). The negotiating tactics and strategies described here are:

1. Compromise.
2. Allow room for negotiation.
3. Make small concessions gradually.
4. Use deadlines.
5. Maintain emotional control.
6. Negotiate on your own turf.
7. Make a last and final offer.
8. Allow for face-saving.

☐ The eight general tactics, methods, and strategies for resolving conflict described in this chapter are:

1. Gentle confrontation: present your gripe in a tactful but honest and explicit way, thus placing the conflict on a problem-solving basis.
2. Disarm the opposition: agree to the criticism made of you.
3. Exchange images: each side states its and the other side's point of view.
4. Mock the opposition in a nice way: gently mock the incongruity in the other side's demands.
5. Capitalize on your anger: let anger energize you to greater heights. Also, use anger for a dramatic effect.
6. Dissipate the other person's violence: let the other person ventilate.
7. Let the problem go away: while you are procrastinating, the conflict may resolve itself.
8. Appeal to a powerful third party: take your problem "upstairs" if gentler approaches will not work.

☐ In choosing a tactic for resolving conflict, consider both your personality or style and the nature of the situation facing you. The situation includes such factors as the gravity of the conflict and the type of person you are facing.

GUIDELINES FOR PERSONAL EFFECTIVENESS

1. If your job involves dealing with people, it is almost inevitable that you will experience person-to-person or group-to-group conflict from time to time. Rather than suppress or ignore conflict, it is to your advantage to learn effective techniques to cope or deal with conflict.

2. Underlying most techniques of resolving conflict is being able to face up to (confront) the real issues. Thus, to resolve conflict, you must face your opponent and candidly discuss the problem between the two of you.

3. A general plan for using techniques of conflict resolution is to begin with a tactful, low-key approach and see if that works. If not, try an approach with more power and force. To illustrate, it might be worth your while to begin with gentle confrontation. If that does not work, appeal to a more powerful third party. As with any strategy for dealing with people, you have to use techniques that you find fit both your personality and the circumstances.

DISCUSSION QUESTIONS

1. Is a prize fight a conflict? Why or why not?

2. What do you think are the three most common frustrations facing students?

3. More murders and other physical assaults are committed among family members than among strangers. What causes such heated conflict among and between family members (including opposite-sexed partners)?

4. Aside from buying and selling, what is another situation or two in which negotiating skills are required?

5. Suppose that you are driving 60 in a 55 mile per hour zone. A traffic officer in a police car motions to you to pull over to the side of the road. After the two of you have stopped, the officer says sternly, "I've caught you speeding." What should be your response?

6. To what extent do you think negotiating tactics are manipulative in nature? In other words, do they get people to do things against their will?

7. In what way can money be used to resolve conflict?

8. What technique(s) do you use to resolve conflict with your boss? Your girl friend, boy friend, spouse, or other intimate friend?

9. Assume that you and the instructor of this course exchanged images over the amount of work assigned. Write down what you assume would be his or her perception of students about this issue. Also write down your perception of the instructor's stand on this issue.

10. Lawyers have often said that when a divorce case goes to court (tried before a judge) it represents a negotiation failure. Can you explain what they mean?

A Business Psychology Problem
THE UNCOMFORTABLE BUSINESS TRIP

Tammy worked very hard for two years as a marketing assistant at Biotronics, a manufacturer of electronic equipment for the health field. She was then promoted to sales representative, covering the entire state of Indiana. Tammy brought the good news home to her husband, Rick. As she explained the details of the promotion to him, Tammy noticed that Rick developed a glum expression. When asked why he was so unenthusiastic about her promotion, Rick replied:

"You may think that I'm being old-fashioned, but I can see a lot of trouble ahead for you in your new job. You'll be forced into a good deal of overnight travel. In the process, you'll find yourself in some touchy situations with men from your company; and also with strangers."

"Rick, I agree with one thing you said. You are being old-fashioned. A woman who isn't looking to get involved with a man on a business trip will have no problem. I just read an article to that effect in *New Woman,* a magazine for career women."

Rick and Tammy continued their discussion for 15 more minutes and then shifted to a talk about plans for the weekend. Two weeks later Tammy's boss arranged a business trip for himself and Tammy to attend a medical conference in Indianapolis. Tammy told Rick that she would be gone for three days on this important trip with "several people from the office."

Duane, Tammy's boss, invited her to have dinner with him the first night of the convention. Tammy mentioned that she was so tired from the day's excitement that she would prefer to have a snack by herself and then retire to her room. But Duane persisted, and not wanting to offend her boss, Tammy met Duane for dinner.

During dinner, Duane shifted quickly from a discussion of business topics to questions about Tammy's hobbies, personal interests, and how well she was getting along with Rick. Toward the end of dinner, Duane extended another invitation to Tammy: "Let's you and I go dancing next. The evening is young, and we're both adults free to do what we want. Besides that, I feel a lot of good chemistry between us. And if you and I were compatible, I would be more willing to get you assigned to some of our major customers in your territory."

Tammy felt a surge of uneasiness. She thought quickly to herself, "What should I do now? If I turn down Duane, this trip could turn into a disaster. But if I go out with him, I'm sure I'll be facing another kind of disaster—fighting off the advances of my boss. And then if I tell Rick about this fiasco, he'll say 'I told you so' and ask me to quit my job. I've got to say something to Duane right now, but I don't know what."

1. Precisely what conflicts is Tammy facing?
2. What on-the-spot tactic of conflict resolution can you recommend to Tammy?
3. What should Tammy do as a long-range solution to the problem of men trying to convert business occasions into social occasions, when she wants to keep them business occasions?
4. Should Biotronics develop a policy to cover the scenario just described?
5. Can this problem be classified as a case of sexual harassment?

A Business Psychology Role Play
THE UNCOMFORTABLE BUSINESS TRIP

The case problem just presented lends itself naturally to role playing in order to practice methods of conflict resolution. Reread the scenario presented above and imagine yourself in the role of Tammy, Duane, or Rick. Role-plays can then be conducted, of about 15 minutes duration each, for these three situations:

Situation A: Tammy and Duane are in the restaurant trying to work out their differences of opinion about what direction the evening should take next. One person plays Tammy, the other Duane.

Situation B: Tammy agrees to have one dance with Duane and then retire to her room. The first dance is completed, but Duane insists on "just a few more dances." Two people role play the situation as if you were on the dance floor.

Situation C: Tammy and Rick are having a discussion a week later about what took place in the restaurant. Rick wants Tammy to quit, but she wants to continue with her job. One person plays Tammy, the other Rick.

Caution: In each of these situations, do not simply carry out an argument, but use a specific negotiating or general method of resolving conflict.

REFERENCES

[1]Jerome Kagan and Ernest Haveman, *Psychology: An Introduction*, 4th ed. (New York: Harcourt Brace Jovanovich, 1980), p. 383.

[2]W. Jack Duncan, *Essentials of Management*, 2nd ed. (Hinsdale, Ill.: Dryden Press, 1978), p. 528.

[3]Kagan and Haveman, *Psychology*, p. 383.

[4]Anthony F. Grasha, *Practical Applications of Psychology*, 2nd ed. (Boston: Little Brown, 1982).

[5]Definition provided by the Working Woman's Institute, reported in Kay Bartlett, "Is Sexual Harassment in the Work Place the 1980s Glamour Cause?" Associated Press story printed in Rochester *Democrat and Chronicle* (Feb. 28, 1982), p. 1C.

[6]Ibid.

[7]Donald J. Petersen and Douglass Massengill, "Sexual Harassment—A Growing Problem in the Workplace," *Personnel Administrator* (Oct. 1982), p. 79.

[8]C. A. MacKinnon, *Sexual Harassment of Working Women* (New Haven, Conn.: Yale University Press, 1979).

[9]Reported in Robert H. Faley, "Sexual Harassment: Critical Review of Legal Cases with General Principles and Preventive Measures," *Personnel Psychology* (Autumn 1982), p. 584.

[10]Reported in Bartlett, "Is Sexual Harassment," p. 2C.

[11]Adapted from David W. Johnson, *Human Relations and Your Career: A Guide to Interpersonal Skills* (Englewood Cliffs, N.J.: Prentice-Hall, 1978), p. 251.

[12]Michele Stimac, "Strategies for Resolving Conflict: Their Functional and Dysfunctional Sides," *Personnel* (Nov.–Dec. 1982), p. 64.

[13]This and several of the strategies presented in this section of the chapter are described in Chester L. Karass, *Give & Take: The Complete Guide to Negotiating Strategies and Tactics* (New York: Thomas Y. Crowell, 1974). Some of the strategies, however, are also found in most of the current books on negotiating.

[14]Herb Cohen, *You Can Negotiate Anything* (New York: Bantam Books, 1982), p. 215.

[15]This technique is similar to assertiveness training methods of coping with criticism, particularly "fogging." See Manuel J. Smith, *When I Say No, I Feel Guilty* (New York: Bantam Books, 1975), Chapter 6.

SUGGESTED READING

COLLINS, ELIZA G. C. "Managers and Lovers," *Harvard Business Review* (Sept.–Oct. 1983), pp. 142–153.

EWING, DAVID W. "How to Negotiate with Employee Objectors," *Harvard Business Review* (Jan.–Feb. 1983), pp. 103–110.

FILLEY, ALAN C. *Interpersonal Conflict Resolution.* Glenview, Ill.: Scott Foresman, 1975.

GRAHAM, JOHN L., and ROY A. HERBERGER, JR. "Negotiators Aboard—Don't Shoot from the Hip," *Harvard Business Review* (July–Aug. 1983), pp. 160–168.

JOHNSTON, ROBERT W. "Negotiation Strategies: Different Strokes for Different Folks," *Personnel* (March–April 1981), pp. 36–44.

KING, DENNIS. "Three Cheers for Conflict," *Personnel* (Jan.–Feb. 1981), pp. 13–22.

LIKERT, RENSIS, and JANE G. LIKERT. *New Ways of Managing Conflict.* New York: McGraw-Hill, 1976.

"Negotiating: A Master Shows How to Head off Argument at the Impasse" (Interview with Gerald J. Nierenberg), *Success* (Oct. 1982), pp. 48–53.

RAIFFA, HOWARD. *The Art and Science of Negotiation.* Cambridge, Mass.: Harvard University Press, 1983.

WHITNEY, GARY C. "When the News Is Bad: Leveling with Employees," *Personnel* (Jan.–Feb. 1983), pp. 37–45.

PART THREE

PERSONAL RELATIONSHIPS ON THE JOB

A substantial part of this entire book is concerned with personal relationships on the job. It would be difficult to study business psychology without dealing directly with interpersonal relationships. The three chapters in this section of the book, however, are concerned with special problems in dealing with others in a work setting. Chapter 10 examines a variety of tactics and techniques for building better relationships with your peers and immediate boss. Chapter 11 provides information about making such adjustments as becoming a team player, being less shy, and reentering the work force. Chapter 12 deals with one of the touchiest problems of all in the workplace—dealing with counterproductive people.

10

GETTING ALONG
WITH CO-WORKERS
AND SUPERIORS

LEARNING OBJECTIVES

After reading and studying this chapter and doing the exercises, you should be able to

1. Recognize the importance of effective interpersonal relationships on the job.
2. Decide on several sensible strategies and tactics that you might use in developing good relationships with your superiors.
3. Decide on several sensible strategies and tactics that you might use in developing good relationships with your co-workers.

Anyone who wants to prosper in his or her career must have good working relationships with three groups of people: superiors, co-workers, and lower-ranking employees. To receive a decent salary increase, be promoted, or receive a favorable transfer you almost always need the endorsement of your immediate boss. By having good relationships with your co-workers, you will usually receive the kind of cooperation you need to get your job done. Also, with increasing frequency, the opinion of your peers is asked when you are being considered for promotion.

People of lower rank than yourself have about the same impact on your career and your ability to get your job done as do peers. We will therefore confine our discussion of building constructive relationships on the job to dealing with superiors and co-workers. It is also important to recognize that the behaviors that contribute to good working relationships at one level usually work at the other levels. For example, being courteous will hold you in good stead with high-level managers, your immediate boss, your co-workers, and people at job levels below you.

BUILDING GOOD RELATIONSHIPS WITH SUPERIORS

The starting point in building a good relationship with your superiors is to perform well on the job. Any rational boss is impressed more by good performance than by office politics, good appearance, or any other consideration. Good performance refers to not only being able to do your job, but to being well motivated and displaying initiative—looking for problems to work on and getting started working without being told to do so. The seven strategies and techniques described next must rest on a bedrock of solid job performance. Otherwise, they may backfire by bringing attention to the fact that the individual is more show than substance. Several of the ideas presented will help you to achieve good job performance. Thus they will assist you in impressing your boss through merit.

Clarify Expectations

Some people perform poorly on the job simply because they have an incomplete understanding of what their boss expects of them. At times, the individual has to take the initiative to find out what is expected because the boss neglects to do so. One highly regarded manager explains how he clarifies expectations:

> Whenever I get a new boss, I sit down with that person and ask that his or her expectations be made explicit. We try to list not my job activities but the main purposes of my job. To do that, we continue each statement of activity with "In order to . . . ," and try to complete the sentence. By recording my job purposes, we get a clear picture of what I should be accomplishing; and that's what counts—results.[1]

Using this tactic, one department secretary found out that she was supposed to take care of her boss's work first. Once her boss's work was done, she would be free to do work for other professionals in the department. Before the secretary in question asked for clarification, she was trying to give everyone's work equal attention. (Your reaction might be, "The boss should have told her that at the outset." Unfortunately, not all managers are aware of the importance of clarifying work expectations.)

Establish a Relationship of Trust

A fundamental way of impressing superiors is to behave in a trustworthy manner. Trust is established over the long range through such behaviors as meeting deadlines, following through on promises, having good attendance and punctuality, and not passing along confidential information to the wrong people. Management psychologist Eugene Jennings views four conditions as being necessary for trust to develop:[2]

1. *Accessibility.* An accessible subordinate is a person who takes in ideas freely and gives them out freely. A subordinate who does not respect the boss's ideas will not be trusted and will not receive help in developing his or her own ideas.

2. *Availability.* The trusted subordinate is attentive and available physically, mentally, and emotionally when the manager is under pressure and needs support.

3. *Predictability.* Jennings refers here to being a predictably good performer and to being dependable about getting things done on time. A subordinate who does not get things done on time quickly loses the trust of his or her boss.

4. *Personal loyalty.* An important way of showing loyalty is to support your boss's ideas. For example, your boss may want to purchase an industrial robot. You could display loyalty by investigating on your own the advantages of robots in factories and then talking about those advantages to others. Loyalty can also mean not misusing inside information given to you by the boss. In short, loyalty breeds trust.

Help Your Boss Succeed

When caught up in the pressures of pursuing your own ambitions, it is easy to forget the primary reason that you were hired. Your boss or the person who hired you originally thought that you could make a positive contribution to helping him or her to accomplish the department's mission. Even if you were hired into the company through nepotism (family relationships), the person who accepted you into the department believed that you would contribute directly or indirectly to his or her success. Most of your job activities should be directed at this vital success strategy of helping your boss succeed.

> George learned through the grapevine that a representative from company headquarters would be visiting his plant, where he worked as the chief manufacturing engineer. George had also learned from casual conversations with his boss, Gus, that the home office was concerned about the physical appearance of some of the company plants. A few stockholders had complained that the company image was suffering because of the filthy conditions at some of the mills and plants.

George swung into action without first conferring with his boss. He organized a clean-up committee to remove trash and repaint badly smudged doors and walls. The entire clean-up operation took four days—precisely the four days that Gus was out of town on a business trip. When Gus returned he was pleasantly surprised to see the good housekeeping that had taken place in his absence. When the inspection team visited the plant shortly thereafter, Gus was praised for keeping up the company image.

Gus then asked his secretary the name of the person who initiated the clean-up campaign. After being informed that the person was George, Gus said to his secretary, "Write me a note of commendation to place in George's personnel file. After I sign it, we'll send one copy to George and place one in his personnel file. We need more company-minded people around here."

Appear (and Be) Cool under Pressure

A good way to impress higher-ups is to assume the role of a polished executive. Although this strategy is obvious, many people trying to create a favorable impression make no particular effort to appear poised and in control of themselves or the situation. In recent years, management has been alerted to the importance of people honestly expressing their feelings. However, it is still to your advantage not to appear distressed when the pressure mounts.

Throwing adult temper tantrums when things do not go your way is also ill-advised. Bursts of emotion are more permissible on the shop floor than in the executive office. Such outbursts are more accepted when directed downward or sideways than upward. Eric, now a marketing executive in the machine tool industry, made a big impression on a company president by remaining cool under pressure. His secretary relates the incident:

Eric had newly arrived as the sales manager at one of our biggest divisions. About the day he finished unpacking, sales in the machine tool industry plummeted. There was a lot of talk about a depression sweeping the world, so naturally people were holding back on buying new machines. It was very difficult to place an order. Also, a number of customers were trying to cancel contracts for new machinery.

Three months after Eric was on the job, not one new order had been placed. The vice-president of marketing from corporate headquarters visited our division. He asked Eric in my presence how things were going. I'll never forget his reply:

"Everything is in good shape except for orders. We have a good sales force and excellent clerical support and equipment repair. Once demand picks up, we'll be in great shape."

You could tell the vice-president of marketing was very impressed. Instead of Eric acting defensive and flustered, he made a factual statement of business conditions. You have to admit it is unusual for a sales manager to create a positive impression when his department is selling nothing but a few replacement parts.

Talk Big, Shun Trivia

Small talk can keep you placed in a small job. If you have a predilection for talking about the weather, your sinuses, or the food in the company cafeteria, save these comments for the right occasion. The right occasion is when you are spending time with people who enjoy small talk. The wrong occasion is when you are trying to impress higher-ups (and also your boss). When you have the chance to talk to an influential person, some trivia may be necessary for an initial warmup. But quickly shift the topic to "big" talk.

Here is an example of the difference between making small talk and big talk over the same issue when meeting a high-ranking official from your

Small talk can keep you placed in a small job.

organization. The person talking is the manager of a branch motor vehicle department. The visitor is the state commissioner of motor vehicles.

Manager (using small talk): Look at that rain outside. It's been like this for three days. This sure is the rainiest place I've ever lived. I guess it's fine if you're farmer or a plant.

Commissioner: Did you say something?

Manager (using big talk): This rain creates an interesting problem for the Motor Vehicle Department at the branch level. Common sense would suggest that our workload would decrease when it rains. My calculations and those of my staff indicate that we are extra busy on rainy days. I think a good number of people wait for a rainy day to take care of their routine business with us. I wonder if this is a national trend?

Commissioner: You have raised an important issue about our workload. I think the problem warrants further study.

Express Constructive Disagreement

At one time the office politician thought an effective way of pleasing the boss was to be a "yes-person." Whatever the boss thought was right, the yes-person agreed with. A more intelligent tactic in the modern business world is to be ready to disagree in a constructive manner when you sincerely believe the boss is wrong. In the long range you will probably earn more respect than if you agree with the boss just to please that person. Constructive disagreement is based on a careful analysis of the situation and is also tactful.

Walter St. John advises that the right way to disagree means not putting your superior in a corner or embarrassing your superior by confronting him or her loudly or in public.[3] If you disagree with your boss, use carefully worded, inoffensive statements. In this way you minimize the chances of a confrontation or hostile reaction. St. John suggests statements of this type:

- "Boss, I'm able to agree with you on most things, but on this matter I wonder if you would be willing to reconsider for these reasons."
- "I like your basic idea and wonder if I could make a suggestion that I think would make it work even better."

The reason constructive disagreement helps you build a good relationship with most bosses is that the boss comes to respect your job knowledge and your integrity. However, if you are working with a very insecure boss, he or she may be taken back by disagreement. In that case you have to be extra tactful in expressing disagreement.

Exhibit 10-1

COMMUNICATING WITH YOUR BOSS

An important general strategy for building a constructive relationship with your boss is to understand that person. Walter St. John points out some questions that needed to be answered in order to size up one's boss:

1. What is your supervisor's position in the company pecking order? What are his or her relationships with his or her bosses?
2. What are your supervisor's blind spots, prejudices, pet peeves, and sore spots? What are positive and negative words to your boss?
3. Does your boss understand better as a reader (should you send a memo) or as a listener (should you tell him or her in person)?
4. Is your supervisor a morning or an evening person? When is the best time of day to approach your boss?
5. What is your supervisor's preference for getting things done?
6. What is most important to your supervisor?
7. What does your supervisor expect of you?
8. What nonverbal signals does you supervisor communicate to you? (See Chapter 15.)

Common Fears

When sizing up your boss, it's essential to realize that your supervisor has the same concerns, fears, and anxieties as anyone in the organization. Some of the most common fears that need recognition, understanding, and coping are:

1. Looking bad to their own bosses; losing face in front of others; being proven wrong or shown up; and being criticized or ridiculed.
2. Not being respected as a person and not having his or her effort appreciated.
3. Personal or on-the-job inadequacy or obsolescence, and insecurity regarding the future.
4. Rejection as a leader.
5. Sharp, aggressive subordinates who make him or her feel insecure.

Source: Excerpted and adapted from Walter D. St. John, "Successful Communications between Supervisors and Employees," *Personnel Journal* (Jan. 1983), p. 76. Reprinted with permission.

Think Carefully about
Socializing with Your Boss

A real concern of employees at any level is how much to socialize with the boss and what effect this could have on the boss's evaluation of your performance. Many young people in the work force express the belief that socializing with the boss builds a friendship that leads to a good working relationship on the job. Thus the supervisor and employees dine and drink together and engage in sports. Older workers place less emphasis on this kind of socializing, but do tend to entertain superiors in their home and be entertained by them.

Despite these positive results that do come about from socializing with superiors, there are some real dangers. The biggest issue relates to role confusion. If you are fishing with the boss on Sunday afternoon, you are acting in the role of a friend. On Monday, the same boss has to evaluate your job performance and recommend a salary increase for you. Now you are in a subordinate role. Some people complain that bosses will go out of their way to give stringent salary increases to friends just to avoid charges of favoritism.

The biggest role confusion and role conflict comes about when a person becomes romantically involved with the boss. If the relationship is alive, working together in the office is difficult. If the relationship terminates, relationships on the job become unbearably tense. As one 20-year-old man put it, "I dated one boss, but I'll never do it again. We split, and from that point on she acted like a zombie toward me in the office." One way a dating relationship between superior and subordinate can be handled is for the subordinate to request a transfer to another department.

In summary, there are no absolute principles about the influence of socializing with the boss on your relationship with that person. A tentative guideline is that you must carefully evaluate the pros and cons of anything more than ceremonial socializing (office parties, company picnics, and so forth) with the boss. It leads to a conflict of roles that can work to your disadvantage.

BUILDING GOOD RELATIONSHIPS
WITH CO-WORKERS

Anyone with work experience is aware of the importance of getting along well (or at least satisfactorily) with co-workers. If you are unable to work cooperatively with those around you, it will be difficult for you to do your job. Mutual cooperation among employees must exist for a department to be productive. Furthermore, the chief reason people are fired is not poor technical skill, but inability (or unwillingness) to form satisfactory interpersonal relationships on the job. In this section of the chapter, we will describe eight tactics and strategies designed to help you gain favor or avoid disfavor with peers. As obvious as these suggestions may seem, many people violate them. So many people think they are experts at human relations that they do not bother to think systematically about their behavior in relation to others.

Express an Interest in Their Work

Almost everybody is self-centered to some extent. Thus, their favorite topic is themselves or topics closely related to themselves, such as their children, hobbies, or work. Sales representatives rely heavily on this fact in cultivating

Express an interest in their work.

relationships with established customers. They routinely ask the customer about his or her hobbies, family members, and work activities. You can capitalize on this simple strategy by asking peers questions such as these:

> How is your work going? (highly recommended)
> How did you gain the knowledge necessary for your job?
> What's new on your job?
> How is the output from your department used by the company?
> What's the best part of your job?
> What's the biggest headache on your job?

A danger in asking questions about other people's work is that some questions may not be perceived as well intended. There is a fine line between honest curiosity and snooping. A high school business teacher asked a guidance counselor in her school "What did you do today?" The guidance counselor interpreted the question as intimating that guidance counselors may not have a full day's work to perform.

Be a Good Listener

After you ask questions, you must be prepared to listen to the answers. The simplest technique of getting along with co-workers within and outside your department is to be a good listener. The topics that you should be willing to listen to during working hours include job problems and miscellaneous complaints. Lunch breaks, coffee breaks, and after hours are better suited to listening to people talk about their personal lives, current events, sports, and the like.

Listening can also be an effective tool for developing a good relationship with your boss. Few people are listened to, or taken seriously enough, at home or on the job. Active listening to your boss can take a number of forms: asking for suggestions and then following them, nodding with enthusiasm when the boss speaks, or taking notes when your boss is giving you instructions. If your boss seems so inclined, be willing to listen to his or her personal problems.

Becoming an effective listener takes practice. As you practice your listening skills, try the suggestions offered in Chapter 15. The payoff is that listening builds constructive relationships.

Maintain Honest and Open Relationships

Modern psychology attaches considerable importance to maintaining *honest* and *open* relationships with other people. Giving co-workers frank, but tactful, answers to their requests for your opinion is one useful way of developing

MR. GREMLEN SAID YOU HAD A TALENT FOR LISTENING!

The simplest technique of getting along with co-workers is to be a good listener.

open relationships. Assume that a co-worker asks your opinion about a memo that he intends to send to his boss. As you read it, you find it somewhat incoherent and filled with spelling and grammatical errors. An honest response to this letter might be:

"I think your idea is a good one. But I think your memo needs more work before that idea comes across clearly."

As described in Chapter 4, accurately expressing your feelings also leads to constructive relationships. If you arrive at work quite upset over a personal problem and appearing obviously fatigued, it may cause some reaction. A peer might say, "What seems to be the problem? Is everything all right?" A dishonest reaction would be, "Everything is fine. What makes you think something is wrong?" In addition to making an obviously untrue statement, you will also be perceived as rejecting the person who asked the question.

If you prefer not to discuss your problem, an honest response on your part would be, "Thanks for your interest. I am facing some problems today. But I think things will work out." Such an answer will not involve you in a discussion of your personal problems. Also, you will not be perceived as rejecting your co-worker.

Display a Helpful, Cooperative Attitude

Many jobs require teamwork. If you display a willingness to help others and work cooperatively with them, you will be regarded as a good team player. Organizations are designed with cooperation in mind. If people do not cooperate with each other, the total system breaks down. Not all your co-workers are concerned about the smooth functioning of the total organization, but they do want cooperation from you.

When evaluating your work performance, many companies include a rating of your cooperativeness. Both management and peers value cooperative behavior on your part. The following question is reproduced from a rating form used by many companies.

COOPERATION AND CONTACTS

Goal: Rating ability to work for and with others.

Criteria: Willing to follow directions? Accept suggestions? Does he or she consider others' viewpoints? Adapt to changing situations? What is his or her attitudes toward others? Does he or she respect them and earn their respect? Successful in dealing with others?	☐ Best; upper 10% ☐ Next 20% ☐ Normal; 40% of group ☐ Next 20% ☐ Bottom 10%

Give Recognition to Others

The least expensive method of cultivating people, in terms of money and time, is to give them attention, kindness, affection, or any appropriate form of recognition. "Show people how important you think they are," contend most books about getting along with people. Similar to warnings about the importance of driving carefully, the number of people who understand the concept far exceeds the number who drive carefully. Yet investing a small amount of time in recognizing a co-worker can pay large dividends in terms of cultivating an ally.

Be Courteous

Many people are rude to co-workers both in business and nonprofit organizations.[4] Consequently, if you show common courtesy to other employees, you may be at a substantial advantage in gaining their respect and support.

Two elementary suggestions are in order to help the reader avoid the discourtesy trap.

- *Answer memos and letters.* Many an employee answers memos and letters according to the rank of the sender. Correspondence from the highest rank is answered promptly; correspondence from medium-ranking personnel is answered within one week; correspondence from lower-ranking people is often ignored and discarded. Answer the memos of lower-ranking people promptly and you will be at an advantage in cultivating their support. It generally requires only a little more time to give a quick answer to a memo than to earmark it for later action. A modern technique is to handwrite a quick response on the bottom of a typewritten memo. A photocopy is then made for your files and the original is returned to the sender.
- *Return telephone calls.* Neglecting to return telephone calls of sales representatives and job applicants is a common practice in many organizations. Even if you are not interested in the message that the caller has for you, saying "No thank you, I'm not interested" will at least end the matter. Also, you will not be branded as another discourteous person. The message sender may prove to be somebody who can someday help you.

Adhere to Group Norms

The basic principle to follow in getting along with co-workers is to pay heed to group **norms**. These refer to the unwritten set of expectations or standards of conduct that tell group members what they ought to do.[5] Norms become a standard of what each person should do within the group. Employees learn about norms both through simple observation and direct instruction from other group members. If you do not deviate too far from these norms, much of your behavior will be accepted by the group. If you deviate too far, you will be subject to much rejection. Here is one example of how group norms influence work output:

> Kathy worked as a receptionist–secretary for the county government. She was one of five women occupying a similar job in the same division of the county. The women had developed the procedure whereby if one receptionist–secretary was overloaded with work, she would ask one of the other women to help her. This was accomplished by calling each of the other receptionist–secretaries in turn to see if one of them had some slack time. It became apparent that Kathy frequently asked for help, but never assisted any of the other women. During a coffee break one day, two of the other receptionist–secretaries confronted Kathy. They told her that if she didn't soon do her share of overload work she would be bad-mouthed to her boss. In addition, they would refuse to have

coffee or lunch with her. Within a few days, Kathy was volunteering to help the other women.

Group norms also influence the social aspects of behavior in work settings. Many of these norms relate to such things as the people to have lunch with, getting together with other employees for an after-hours drink on Friday, joining a department team, and the type of clothing to wear to work.

If you deviate too far from work or social norms, you run the risk of being ostracized from the group. In some instances you might even be subjected to physical abuse if you make the other employees look bad. The risk of conforming too closely to group norms is that you lose your individuality. You become viewed by your superiors as "one of the guys or gals" rather than a person who aspires to move up in the organization. Getting along too well with peers has its price as well.

Avoid Being Abrasive

Abrasiveness is an important behavior to avoid when trying to develop good relationships with other workers. An abrasive person is one who creates mental abrasion upon contact or someone who literally "rubs people the wrong way." Harry Levinson, who coined the phrase "abrasive personality," says this kind of person "like the proverbial porcupine seems to have a knack for jabbing others in an irritating, sometimes painful way."[6] Abrasive personalities are frequently fired from high-level positions. On the way up, they make irritating, annoying, and uncomfortable co-workers. The primary characteristics of the abrasive personality are self-centeredness, isolation from others, perfectionism, contempt for others, and a tendency to attack people.

The abrasive person is a source of irritation to superiors, co-workers, and lower-ranking employees. It is not uncommon for the abrasive person to be less abrasive in upward than in sideways or downward relationships. This would suggest that the abrasive individual can exercise some control over his or her abrasiveness. The tendency to be less abrasive toward superiors would also indicate that abrasive people are not completely naive as office politicians.

Most abrasive persons do not really understand how upsetting they are to peers. An advantage of participating in personal growth groups is that you will find out quickly if others consider you to be abrasive. Here is a representative example of abrasiveness on the job:

- *Employee asking for help:* Excuse me, but could you please help me retrieve the loss prevention file in the computer? I can't seem to get it right.
- *Abrasive employee:* What's the matter, didn't you learn how to use a computer in school? Besides, I'm too busy now to do your work.

SUMMARY OF KEY POINTS

☐ To prosper in your career, it is essential to have good working relationships with superiors, co-workers, and lower-ranking employees. The starting point in building good relationships with superiors is to perform well in your job. Other important strategies include:

1. Clarify expectations: find out what your boss expects of you.
2. Establish a relationship of trust: be accessible, available, predictable, and loyal.
3. Help your boss succeed.
4. Appear (and be) cool under pressure: be able to handle problems in an emotionally controlled manner.
5. Talk big, shun trivia: keep small talk to a minimum, and engage in some talk about important organizational concerns.
6. Express constructive disagreement: disagree with your boss when necessary, but be tactful.
7. Think carefully about socializing with your boss.

☐ Although some of the above tactics are helpful in developing constructive relationships at all levels, the following suggestions are particularly geared toward developing good relationships with co-workers.

1. Express an interest in their work.
2. Be a good listener.
3. Maintain honest and open relationships.
4. Display a helpful, cooperative attitude.
5. Give recognition to others.
6. Be courteous; for example, answer memos and letters and return telephone calls.
7. Adhere to group norms; follow group standards of conduct.
8. Avoid being an abrasive person; don't rub people the wrong way.

GUIDELINES FOR PERSONAL EFFECTIVENESS

1. Although job knowledge is indispensable for performing well in your job, it is not sufficient to make you a high performer. Another important set of behaviors necessary to perform well on the job is maintaining constructive relationships with other

employees at all levels. Other important behaviors contributing to job performance (such as high motivation and work habits) are discussed elsewhere in this text.

2. Similarly, if you ignore the strategies presented in this chapter, you do so at great risk of not gaining a wide base of support in your present or future place of work. An important success strategy is to make a deliberate effort to form constructive working relationships with co-workers.

DISCUSSION QUESTIONS

1. How can you tell if your boss trusts you?

2. How can you use the tactic Talk Big, Shun Trivia to help you get ahead in school?

3. How do personal values enter into choosing among the tactics and strategies mentioned in this chapter?

4. What are the risks involved in being one of the gang?

5. What did you learn from your study of stress and burnout that will help you be cool under pressure?

6. People who become top executives of business organizations have been with their firms an average of 22 years. How does this fact relate to any of the information presented in this chapter?

7. One reviewer who read this chapter said, "A lot of ruthless people get ahead in this world. So cultivating peers and subordinates may not really be all that important." What do you think?

8. What would happen if you went out of your way to violate every suggestion in this chapter?

9. What are three good questions you might ask the instructor of this course to show that you are interested in his or her work?

10. What makes so many people act discourteously on the job?

A Business Psychology Problem
THE UNPOPULAR ADMINISTRATIVE ASSISTANT

While shopping one day, you run into Marlene, a former classmate of yours. Happy to see her, you comment, "Marlene, good to see you. How are things going? Last I heard you were promoted from secretary to administrative assistant. How do you like your new job?"

Marlene answers: "Thanks for asking. That's true, I was promoted to administrative assistant. I work in a different department now. My boss is the director of public relations. The job is exciting. I'm in on a lot of important things and I get to meet a lot of important people. But things in the office aren't going as well as I would like."

Your curiosity aroused, you ask, "What do you mean?"

Marlene continues: "I don't think the other women in the office care too much for me. I feel kind of left out of things. I'm almost never asked to join the 'girls' for lunch or coffee breaks. I don't know what I'm doing wrong. Sometimes I think it could be jealousy over my job. But that isn't such a plausible reason. Being an administrative assistant isn't *that* impressive. Also, I'm a few years older than most of the women in the office. They should be glad to see that experience and hard work pay off.

"Sometimes I feel like the woman in those TV ads who loses out with friends because she needs breath freshener. That certainly isn't the case with me. I don't recall having a problem making friends either at school or in my other jobs.

"If you come up with any ideas that might help me, please let me know. I would feel awkward asking the 'girls' in the office why they don't like me."

1. What should Marlene do (if anything) to discover what she might be doing wrong?
2. Do you have any general suggestions as to how Marlene might become better accepted by the group?

A Business Psychology Role Play
CRITICIZING YOUR BOSS

To prepare for this role-play, first review the information presented earlier about expressing disagreement with your boss in a constructive manner. Then get mentally set to assume one of the roles described next. The rest of the class will observe the role play and serve as a source of feedback about how well the tactic was implemented.

Boss: You have a meeting shortly with one of the key employees in your department. You are excited about your ideas for a new product for the company—a coffee pot with a built-in tape device that plays the national anthem when the pot is turned on. You believe there is both a large domestic and international market for your idea. You intend to bounce these ideas off your subordinate before bringing them to higher management.

Subordinate: You like your boss, you value your relationship with that person, but you think the idea for the singing coffee pot is strictly off the wall. You also think it is your duty to save the company from investing in this idea. Tactfully, try to get the boss to bury the idea for a singing coffee pot.

REFERENCES

[1]Norman C. Hill and Paul H. Thompson, "Managing Your Manager: The Effective Subordinate," in J. B. Ritchie and Paul Thompson, *Organization and People* (St. Paul, Minn.: West Publishing, 1980), p. 298.

[2]Eugene E. Jennings, *The Mobile Manager* (New York: McGraw-Hill, 1967), pp. 47–50. As abridged in Hill and Thompson, "Managing Your Manager."

[3]Walter D. St. John, "Successful Communications Between Supervisors and Employees," *Personnel Journal* (Jan. 1983), p. 77.

[4]Research about the problem of courtesy in business is reported in Eugene H. Fram and Herbert J. Mossein, "High Scores on the Discourtesy Scale," *Harvard Business Review* (Jan.–Feb. 1976), pp. 5–6.

[5]W. Jack Duncan, *Management: Progressive Responsibility in Administration* (New York: Random House, 1983), p. 198.

[6]Harry Levinson, informal quote. His ideas on this topic are presented in his article, "The Abrasive Personality at the Office," *Psychology Today* (May 1978), pp. 78–84.

SUGGESTED READING

CARNEGIE, DALE. *How to Win Friends and Influence People.* New York: Pocket Books, reprinted every several years.

DuBRIN, ANDREW J. *Winning at Office Politics.* New York: Ballantine Books, 1978.

FORSYTH, DONELSON R. *An Introduction to Group Dynamics.* Monterey, Calif.: Brooks/Cole, 1983.

HABER, AUDREY, and RICHARD P. RUNYON. *Psychology of Adjustment.* Homewood, Ill.: Dorsey Press, 1984.

HEGARTY, CHRISTOPHER. *How to Manage Your Boss.* New York: Rawson-Wade, 1981.

RAUDSEPP, EUGENE, and JOSEPH C. YEAGER. "How to Win at Office Politics," *Administrative Management* (May 1981), pp. 26–28, 40–44.

ROSEMAN, ED. "How to Become a Better Teamworker," *Product Management* (Jan. 1976), pp. 17–20.

STEIL, LYMAN K., JOANNE SUMMERFIELD, and GEORGE DEMARE. *Listening: It Can Change Your Life.* New York: Wiley, 1983.

WINTER, CARYL. *Present Yourself with Impact: Techniques for Success.* New York: Ballantine Books, 1983.

11

ADJUSTING TO THE ORGANIZATION

LEARNING OBJECTIVES

After reading and studying this chapter and doing the exercises, you should be able to

1. Recognize that you have to adjust to the informal rules of conduct in any place you work now or in the future.
2. Understand how dress, appearance, and manners can influence your career success.
3. Know what has to be done to become a team player.
4. Develop a strategy for becoming more outgoing if shyness is a problem for you.
5. Appreciate the challenges facing a mid-life woman who enters or reenters the work force.

"I just can't hack it. It's too much for me. You're expected to cater to everybody else. Not only that, they won't let you just sit in a corner and do your job. After the company fired me, the personnel manager told me I wasn't aggressive enough. That I was supposed to reach out to people and sell them my ideas. Maybe I'm not the corporate type."

The 22-year-old male who made these remarks faces a dilemma that many other people face, although usually to a lesser extent. He is experiencing difficulties adapting his personal style to the demands of a work organization. Somehow his lack of ability or willingness to adjust has made him an unfit employee in the eyes of his company.

Adjusting to the organization includes many things discussed in this book, such as managing job stress, resolving conflict, getting along with co-workers and superiors, and taking the initiative to manage your career. In this chapter we highlight four problems of consequence in adjusting to organizational life: (1) making a good appearance, (2) following business manners and etiquette, (3) becoming a team player, and (4) overcoming shyness. We also look at the unique adjustment problems of a growing segment of the work force, the reentry woman.

Formal versus Informal Rules

Adjusting to formal rules is often easier than adjusting to informal rules. Formal rules are part of the formal organization that tells you the official, sanctioned way of doing things. The formal organization tells you who reports to whom (see the organization chart). It also tells you how various problems should be handled (see the policies and procedure manual). The formal organization is said to be composed of "job descriptions, organization charts, procedures, and other written documents which describe and define how individuals should work with each other."[1]

The informal organization is much more subtle. It refers to two complicated aspects of the organization. One is the pattern of relationships that develop to both satisfy people's social needs and get work accomplished (more will be said about this in our study of groups). Another is custom and tradition that develop in the firm. Informal rules stem from the informal organization. Examples of informal rules governing behavior on the job include: (1) An office supervisor should never invite the chief executive officer out to lunch. (2) A production employee should never wear a pin-striped suit to work. Examining codes of dress and appearance is a good starting point in understanding adjustment to the organization.

STANDARDS OF DRESS AND APPEARANCE

Some formal standards of dress and appearance exist in most places of work. A typical one would be, "Employees must wear suitable attire to the office, and clothing must not violate safety codes." However, the informal codes of dress and appearance have a far greater impact on your career. Business and secretarial schools have always emphasized the importance of good grooming and dress. A burgeoning of interest in this topic during the last decade was created by two books written by John T. Molloy, *Dress for Success* and *The Woman's Dress for Success Book.* Some general guidelines can be drawn that will help the career-minded person look successful. However, the advice of Molloy and other dress-experts should not be taken too literally. If every white-collar worker followed these suggestions, they would all look like clothing salespersons in a posh retail store. An example of the rigidity of some of these tips is Molloy's warning to men that if they take any of his advice seriously, "You will never, ever, as long as you live, wear a short sleeve shirt for any business purpose, no matter whether you're the office boy or the president of the company."[2]

In reality, many well-adjusted, successful men at all job levels wear short-sleeved shirts. Here we will present some general guidelines for dress and appearance, all based on the premise that the situation must be taken into account in choosing clothing and appearance. Five important factors influencing your choice of clothing are:[3]

1. The products and services sold (the industry in question).
2. The type of customer or client served.
3. The desired image projected by the firm.
4. Geography.
5. Your comfort and self-image.

Products and Services Sold. Restaurant A sells expensive food with elegant service, including setting tables with linen and fine silverware. Restaurant B sells ranch-style food and seats people on picnic benches. You would dress quite differently as the manager of each restaurant. Similarly, if you are selling financial services you would expect to wear formal business attire, that is, suits (both males and females) or conservative dresses. If you are selling sports equipment, casual attire (including golf and tennis shirts) would be appropriate.

Type of Customer or Client Served. Closely related to the preceding is the idea of choosing clothing that fits the expectations of the people served by your firm. A woman working as a veterinarian's assistant in a rural area would be appropriately attired in casual, "down-home" clothes. If the same woman worked as a veterinarian's assistant in a large city, it would be more appropriate for her to wear traditional business-style clothing. We are assuming, of course, that the veterinary office does not require assistants to wear medical clothing.

Desired Image Projected by the Firm. Clothing and appearance are used to control the image projected by a firm. A contemporary illustration is the image physical fitness centers try to project. All employees who serve the public in these firms are expected to appear physically fit (ideally, trim and muscular) and wear athletic-style clothing, and not smoke in front of customers. Consider also that a firm that serviced expensive, imported automobiles—and charged high fees—might impose a dress code. The service manager would wear a dress shirt and tie, and the mechanics would start each day with clean clothing, perhaps wearing a smock.[4]

Geography. Regional differences in dress and grooming standards should be taken into account in choosing work attire. For example, a receptionist working in a Los Angeles office might be able to wear much more casual attire than his or her counterpart in New York City. In southern Florida, shirt-sleeved executives are found more frequently than in Boston, where the conventional, conservative look is more in fashion.

Your Comfort and Self-Image. Another important consideration is to choose clothing that fits your self-image and is therefore comfortable. (Size and fabric also influence comfort.) When you are comfortable in your clothing, you project the desired image of appearing self-confident. Conversely, when your clothing is uncomfortable, you are likely to appear ill at ease and low in self-confidence. Dress codes imposed by the organization usually allow you enough latitude to choose outfits that you will find comfortable. An informal expectation in one company might be that sales representatives who are male wear dress shirts, ties, and suits or jacket and slacks. In reality, a salesman for the company can select from thousands of different combinations and still adhere to the code.

The same company might approve of casual attire for office employees. A woman might not be able to wear tennis shorts and a fishnet "see-through" blouse to work. However, she might choose from thousands of other combinations of casual attire that are within the bounds of the code.

In summary, the most helpful guidelines for dress in business center around the idea that you must size up the situation in making appropriate choices. Nevertheless, a number of conclusions can be reached that should prove useful in many situations, as shown in Exhibit 11–1.

MANNERS AND ETIQUETTE

Manners and etiquette are even more strongly linked to informal rules than are dress codes. Similar to clothing and appearance, you often learn about what is considered correct only after you have committed an error. One man-

Exhibit 11–1

HOW TO DRESS FOR IMPACT

1. Dress to reflect the competent person you are now or expect to be.
2. Resist fads in styles, clothes, and fabrics. (They may become out of date while they are still new.)
3. Dress to look as if you mean business. (Look serious about what you are doing—don't wear running shoes to the office the day you are making a presentation to management.)
4. Dress to make an impression, not to cause a stir about the way you look. (Overdressing is often the sign of an insecure person.)
5. Follow your company's dress code or follow your company's leaders. (Also check out the way the "fast-trackers" dress.)
6. Be aware that you are representing your company through your style of dress. (The public often evaluates companies by the appearance of their employees.)
7. Wear fabrics that travel well and won't make you look rumpled. (A real problem with cheap clothing is that it rumples readily.)
8. Buy clothes from a salesperson whose style you admire. (That individual is likely to show good taste in helping you make clothing selections.)
9. Look and buy for quality. (High-quality clothing can often be purchased at off-price stores who specialize in name brands.)
10. Choose clothes the way you should choose people—for durability and dependability.
11. Dress for comfort. (If you are comfortable, you are likely to feel more confident and be able to concentrate on your work better.)

SOURCE: The statements not in parentheses are adapted from Caryl Winter, *Present Yourself with Impact: Techniques for Success* (New York: Ballantine Books, 1983), p. 199.

agement trainee was sharply criticized by his boss for having clipped his nails during a staff meeting. The young man innocently replied, "I didn't know I was doing anything wrong. In my last job, my boss clipped his nails during meetings." Our discussion of manners and etiquette will cover (1) the problem of informal socializing on the job and (2) a sampling of minor habits and practices that could influence your image in the firm.

Doing the Right Amount of "Schmoozing"

Sociologist Robert Schrank has made a serious study of the employee practice of schmoozing.[5] A schmoozer engages in such activities as telling jokes, lingering at the water cooler, telephoning a friend on company time, wandering around the plant, office, or lab, or taking a long lunch break. The general purpose of schmoozing seems to be to relieve boredom or tension. It is a normal type of social interaction on the job.

No company procedure manual will tell you that work breaks of this nature are taboo, but they are certainly not welcomed. On the other hand, if you do not schmooze at all, you may miss out on establishing rapport with co-workers. The adjustment problem relates to finding out how much to schmooze. Too much social interaction, and you are wasting your own time and company resources. Too little, and you may not get the cooperation you need from co-workers to accomplish your job. If you are intent on advancing in your career, I would recommend the minimum amount of social interaction (schmoozing) necessary to keep you on good terms with peers.

Modern Business Etiquette
and Manners

What is considered proper manners and etiquette in business changes over time. At one time, men almost always kept their suit jackets on while working in the office. And no self-respecting employee would remain alone in an office with a person of the opposite sex if the door was closed. One important generalization about proper business etiquette, both past and present, is to be considerate of other people. Every other specific guideline stems from this key general principle. Former White House social secretary, Letitia Baldridge, says that these days business etiquette is largely a matter of being considerate of one's co-workers:

> When anyone is having trouble carrying something down the hall, when anyone's arms are full and thus can't open the door, when anyone needs help hailing a taxi, women and men should help women and men. Consideration for each other, regardless of gender, is a very important aspect of a person's ability to get along with people, and part of his or her success and rise in the corporate world.[6]

Below are 12 specific suggestions about business manners and etiquette that should be considered in the context of a specific job situation.[7] For example, point 12 about severely limiting smoking on the job would be less important if you worked for a tobacco company.

1. *Names should be remembered.* It is both good manners and good human relations to remember the names of work associates, even if you see them only occasionally. If you make a deliberate effort to do so, you can improve your skill in remembering names. Make sure you learn the person's name in the first place.

2. *Respect other people's senses.* Any assault on other people's senses—sight, sound, smell, or touch—should be avoided. Thus strong cologne and perfume are unwelcome, as are grotesque color combinations in your clothing, pinching co-workers, and making loud noises with chewing gum.

3. *Avoid vulgarities.* As George Mazzei says, "It is rude to use what we still call four-letter words in any business context. If you are tough, you don't have to prove it by falling back on the "F" or the "S" word."[8]

4. *Males and females should receive equal treatment.* Amenities extended to females by males in a social setting are minimized in business settings today. During a meeting, a male is not expected to hold a chair or a door for a woman, nor does he jump to walk on the outside when the two of them are walking down the street. Many women workers resent

being treated differently than males with respect to minor social customs.

5. *Shouting is out.* Emotional control was mentioned in the previous chapter as an important way of impressing superiors. Following the same principle, shouting in business is said to detract from your image. (Except if you are a commodities broker shouting out orders on the exchange floor.)

6. *Coats can be removed in the office.* Today it is considered appropriate to take off your coat, and keep it off, not only in your own work station or office, but when moving to other parts of the building.

7. *The host or hostess pays the bill.* An area of considerable confusion about etiquette surrounds business lunches and who should pay the check, the man or the woman. The new rule of etiquette is that the person who extends the invitation pays the bill. (Do you think this same rule should be extended to social life?)

8. *Address superiors and visitors in their preferred way.* As the modern business world has become more informal, a natural tendency has developed to address people at all levels by their first name. It is safer to first address people by a title and their last name (such as Mr. Baxter or Ms. Leon) and then wait for them to correct you if they desire. If you say, "Ms. Leon, may I call you by your first name," she may feel forced to consent.

9. *Make appointments with high-ranking people rather than dropping in.* Schmoozing may be all right with co-workers, but a taboo in most firms is for lower-ranking employees to casually drop in the office of an executive.

10. *Stand up only for infrequent visitors.* It is still considered polite to stand up when an infrequent visitor of either sex enters the office. However, if another worker enters your work area frequently, such as a file clerk who needs regular access to your files, standing up is not required.

11. *Sexiness in the office should be muted.* Women are strongly advised to avoid looking overly sexy or glamorous in the office. Thus waist length hair should be avoided and so should dangling jewelry, five-inch high heels, and heavy eye makeup. Men, too, should not appear too sexy, and thus tight pants and shirts are to be avoided.

12. *Watch out for smoking on the job.* Smokers are beginning to believe increasingly that their civil rights are being violated in many public places. Nevertheless, good business etiquette these days is to avoid smoking in meetings and in the work areas of other people. In some firms, smoking is restricted to certain limited areas, such as restrooms, locker rooms, and the parking lot.

Although all the preceding points could have some bearing on the image you project, violation of any one of them would not necessarily have a negative impact on your career. It is the overall image you project that counts the most. Therefore, the general principle of being considerate of work associates is much more important than any one act of courtesy or etiquette.

BECOMING A TEAM PLAYER

An important part of adjusting to the organization is learning how to work as part of a team. At every level of the organization, it is important to work cooperatively with others. You will have to work cooperatively with others even if you reach the pinnacle of power in your company. Chief executive officers who cannot get along with their immediate subordinates face the threat of being overruled or overthrown by them.

An important adjustment to organizational life is to become a team player.

The idea has been advanced that a major reason relatively few women make it to the top of organizations is that they are inexperienced in team play.[9] Men, according to this reasoning, are at an advantage because so many of them played team sports early in their lives or spent time in the military. Whether or not you accept this observation, it does emphasize the importance of becoming a good team player if you want to adjust to the organization and advance. Male or female, you can improve your status as a team player if you share credit with co-workers, give information and opinion to them, and touch base with them on important issues.

Sharing credit with co-workers is a direct method of promoting the team concept. Instead of focusing on yourself as the person responsible for a work achievement, you point out that the achievement was indeed the product of a team effort. A salesman, Frank, is a good example of the team concept in action:

> "We won team, we won," said Frank excitedly to his four lunchmates. "The world's largest manufacturer of air conditioners is going to use our new electronic switch in every one of their units. I just received the good news today. Thanks to all of you for giving me so darn many good suggestions for explaining the merits of our switch. I know that the big boss will be thrilled with our sales department."

Giving information and opinions to co-workers shows that you are teamminded. This is true because one of the benefits of group effort is the fact that members can engage in a sharing of ideas. The result is often a better solution to problems than would have been possible if people worked alone. (**Synergy** is the name given to this phenomenon of group effort whereby the whole is greater than the sum of the parts.)

Touching base on important issues refers to such things as keeping your co-workers informed about plans you have that could affect them. One example of this concept in action is to inform your peers about a suggestion that you are planning to make to management. In this way, if your proposal is accepted, you are more likely to gain the support of your co-workers in implementing your idea than if your suggestion was a big surprise.

> Sharon, a computer repair specialist, worked for a computer store. Both she and her co-workers made occasional visits to customers to service their equipment. Sharon thought that if the store purchased a colorful van with the name of the store imprinted on it the result would be more repair business for the store. Before bringing this idea to the store management, Sharon discussed it with her teammates individually. One of them added the suggestion that the sign on the truck should state, "Repairs in your own office or home." When management later discussed Sharon's idea with the group, each of the repair technicians expressed enthusiasm. By touching base with her co-workers, Sharon won acceptance for her ideas.

OVERCOMING SHYNESS: BECOMING MORE ASSERTIVE ON THE JOB

A problem many people have in adjusting to a large organization is that of overcoming a quiet, reserved, and shy disposition. Reserve of this type is not necessarily a negative character trait in all situations. Many technical, scientific, and scholarly people are socially shy. During working hours their attention is focused more on their work and inner thoughts than on others. For many other workers, such as sales representatives, managers, coordinators, and a variety of staff specialists, it is important to be socially aggressive.

Causes of Shyness

The traditional view of shyness is that it stems from a learned pattern of low self-confidence. If in the process of growing up a person is dominated by a parent, close relative, or sibling, he or she may develop a pattern of feeling and behaving submissively in the presence of others. Another contributor to shyness could be an early lack of success in attempts at dealing with strangers. For instance, if a person was rejected several times by potential playmates, or was turned down by several potential dates, he or she may become inhibited with others.

Recent research suggests that shyness may be inherited. Psychology professor Jonathan Cheek has found strong evidence that about one-half of shy people inherit this personal characteristic that inhibits social activity at critical times. Responses of identical and fraternal twins to a questionnaire indicated a much closer relationship of shyness levels between identical twins (those with the same genetic composition). Both groups of twins in the study shared the same school and home environment. Cheek points out that his findings of a genetic propensity for shyness does not destine certain people to lives of social discomfort and underachievement. Instead, it offers hope because shyness becomes a predictable problem that can be monitored and managed. Because a behavior pattern is inherited, it does not mean that it cannot be changed through new learning. According to Cheek, nobody has to be shy, and shy persons can generally become more relaxed and assertive in social situations given the right kind of emotional support from their friends or family.[10]

Consequences of Shyness

Before discussing methods of overcoming shyness, it is helpful to examine the scope of the problem. Philip Zimbardo and his co-workers found that about 40 percent of 800 students in their study considered themselves to be shy.[11]

Among those who reported feeling shy, three-fourths said that they did not like being shy. Being socially reserved and withdrawn (a major facet of shyness) is also a problem among people engaged in higher-level occupations. A substantial proportion of evaluations of managers written by psychologists recommend something like "Jack should learn to become a more socially outgoing person." Many performance appraisal reports written by a person's boss make the same type of comment.

Zimbardo reports that most people think of shyness as a definite personal problem. People break down the consequences of shyness into seven categories.[12]

1. Difficulties in meeting new people and making friends or getting the most out of relationships
2. Negative emotional feelings, such as feeling depressed and lonely.
3. Difficulty in being assertive enough or expressing personal opinions and values.
4. Creating a false negative impression upon others. Shyness often clouds a person's true assets.
5. Creating a poor initial impression. A shy person is often interpreted as being weak, unfriendly, or tense.
6. Difficulty in thinking clearly and communicating effectively in the presence of others.
7. Self-consciousness and an overpreoccupation with one's personal feelings and thoughts.

Techniques for Overcoming Shyness

Since so many people are concerned about their shyness, a number of methods have been suggested for dealing with the problem. If a person is introverted and is not concerned or anxious about becoming less introverted, these suggestions can be disregarded. The following suggestions, if carefully implemented, can be considered an action program for those people who are uncomfortable about their shyness.[13]

1. *Set a goal.* Clearly establish in your mind how you want to behave differently. Do you want to date more often? Speak out more in meetings? Be able to express dissatisfaction to co-workers? You can only overcome shyness by behaving differently; feeling differently is not enough.
2. *Relax physically.* Use the tension reduction of relaxation before entering into a difficult social situation. Just before a job interview or any other socially demanding situation, breathe deeply and stretch your neck and shoulder muscles.

3. *Talk positively about yourself.* Shy people tend to put themselves down too much. Try to think positively about your ability to deal with situations involving people. (For example, "I know I can make as good a class presentation as the last student who went up in front of the room.")

4. *Appear warm and friendly.* Shy people often communicate to others through their *body language* that they are not interested in reaching out to others. To overcome this impression try smiling, lean forward, uncross your arms and legs, and unfold your hands.

5. *Make legitimate phone calls to strangers.* Telephone conversations with strangers that have a legitimate purpose can help you start expressing yourself to people you do not know well. You might call numbers listed in classified ads to inquire about articles listed for sale. Try a positive approach like, "Hello, my name is _____ . I'd like to know about the condition of that 1958 Mercedes-Benz you have for sale."

6. *Anonymous conversations.* Try starting a conversation with strangers in a nonthreatening or neutral setting such as a ticket line for a concert, a political rally, the waiting room in a dental office, or a laundromat.

7. *Greet strangers.* For the next week or so, great every person you pass. Smile and make a neutral comment such as "How ya doing?" "Fine day, isn't it." You may receive a few quizzical looks, but many other people may smile and return your greeting.

8. *Dress and groom for assertiveness.* Dressing in comfortable clothing that fits your self-image can help you overcome shyness for several reasons. The right attire can project the image that you feel good about yourself and are interested in relating to others. If you are satisfied with your appearance, your confidence might be boosted just enough to help you make that all-important initial contact with another person.

9. *Rehearse difficult situations.* If you find certain social situations frightening, practice them beforehand. Ideally, role play the situation with a friend. Think through a script of what the other people might say and how you might respond. An important work example would be to rehearse how you would go about asking for a job transfer when you know your boss is gruff.

10. *Observe and model self-confident people.* Note their posture, tone of voice, choice of words and gestures. How do they approach people? How do they change the subject when they want to avoid answering a delicate question? After you have identified what these people are doing right, model some aspects of their behavior.

11. *Help other shy people.* Zimbardo notes that two out of five people in any social setting are probably shy. If you are one of those two, find the other shy person and make him or her feel comfortable by starting a conversation, smiling, or shaking hands. "To the extent that you're not preoccupied with your own worries, you're automatically going to be less shy."[14]

12. *Attend shyness workshops and training programs.* Formal programs for overcoming shyness are found in many places. College counseling centers and placement offices generally have information about these workshops. Often these programs are called "assertiveness training" because they help you become more assertive in expressing your feelings and thoughts and more outgoing in your behavior. Shyness workshops typically cover many of the activities incorporated in the previous 11 suggestions.

WOMEN REENTERING THE WORK FORCE

A major adjustment to the organization is that faced by a mid-life woman who has (1) never held full-time employment in the past or (2) not worked in over ten years. The number of mid-life women entering the work force has increased steadily in recent years for three major reasons. First, the women's movement has spurred job opportunities for women. Second, the increased divorce rate in recent years has forced more women to take over primary financial support of their families. Third, many families require two incomes to keep pace with inflation. Most women who reenter the job market face one or more of the problems described next.[15] Each of these problems requires some adjustment to the organization.

We are devoting some attention to the specific problems of the mid-life woman entering the work force for an important reason. These women face special problems that do not apply to the male or female student who is just graduating from business school, secretarial school, or college. The older male who is changing jobs also does not face some of the problems encountered by mid-life women.

Capitalizing on Life Experiences

A major challenge facing the reentry woman is to find a field that makes use of her extensive experience as a full-time homemaker and perhaps volunteer worker. Running a household that includes children and a spouse involves many managerial skills including planning, supervising, and resolving conflict! Since it is not always easy to sell prospective employers on this fact, the reentry woman still needs to acquire new training or retraining. Two career specialists suggest that the best opportunities for women entering a job market for the first time are in fields that require a modest amount of formal education and training. Equally important, the field should be one where knowledge gained from life experiences can be used. Among these careers are fund raising, public relations, sales of large ticket items such as real estate, office machines, and automobiles, and financial services.[16]

The subjects of finding a field and then a job within that field will be discussed in Chapter 17. This information applies equally well to the reentry woman and to people who are entering the working world for the first time (or at any other point in their careers).

Competition with Younger Women

Mid-life women are often overly concerned that they are unequal competition to their younger counterparts. Such women believe that younger women have a better chance of being hired, and that once hired they have a better chance of getting better assignments. Younger women carry the cultural stereotype of being more physically attractive. But more mature women carry the stereotype of having better records of attendance and punctuality and represent a smaller turnover risk. One 51-year-old returnee to the work force put it this way: "What I had to sell was my age. Any employer knew that I planned no more children. Besides, I desperately needed the money. I still do and that's a real asset."

Relating to Younger Superiors

A substantial adjustment for many mid-career women is learning how to be supervised by a male or female young enough to be their child. Adjustments also have to be made in the other direction. Young supervisors sometimes feel awkward supervising women old enough to be their mother. Exposure to the situation is the best antidote to such feelings of awkwardness. After awhile it may seem natural for the mid-life woman to be supervised by a much younger individual.

Another helpful approach to bridging the age gap in such relationships is for the mid-life woman to recognize that technical qualifications and job experience have determined the balance of authority. If you are 50 years old and female, you generally have few problems in consulting a tax advisor who is 25 years old and male. In a work setting, age is a weak source of authority.

Unequal Advancement Opportunities

Many mid-life women find employment. But the more ambitious of these women find out shortly that there are informal barriers to their advancement opportunities. Although women have made important strides in overcoming discrimination by sex, many subtle sexist barriers still exist. "Ageism" (discrimination against people based on age) also frequently works against the mid-life woman who wants to advance.

A frank discussion with management about her interest in advancement may be helpful. Many managers probably think that a mid-life woman has limited interest in moving up the organizational ladder. A general strategy an ambitious mid-life woman might use to advance is to pay careful attention to the type of career-boosting strategies discussed in Chapter 18. For instance, a woman looking for advancement might work extra hard at documenting her accomplishments or becoming a highly valued subordinate.

In short, a woman (or man) who enters the work force late in life will have to outperform her (or his) younger counterparts in order to be considered a likely candidate for promotion. (We recognize that all forms of job discrimination are illegal. However, when a person is not considered eligible for promotion, it is difficult to document that she is being discriminated against. Most criteria for promotion relate to intangible factors such as leadership ability.)

Balancing Career and Family Demands

A major adjustment problem for the return-to-work woman is adjusting to the dual demands of career and family. Women who do not have a man at home to help with family responsibilities face an even more difficult adjustment. Women who begin their careers at mid-life often double their workload, running a household and holding down a job. Poor performance in both the homemaker and career roles can be the net result.

Positive, constructive approaches have to be taken to prevent this problem. Clear arrangements with husbands or boy friends (if one is available) and older children should be made with regard to homemaking chores. Subcontracting homemaking chores to domestic help is a luxury few mid-life women can afford. Suitable day-care arrangements for children are essential. Adolescent children who are too old for day-care facilities but too young to spend many hours unsupervised represent a special problem. Women preoccupied with concerns about the welfare of their children cannot fully concentrate on the job.

Women, however, should not be expected to make all the adjustments. The flextime arrangements discussed in Chapter 5 are helpful to the working woman with heavy family responsibilities. A woman or man with children, but without a partner, is particularly in need of a work schedule that provides flexibility for taking care of family demands.

Job sharing is a constructive way of redesigning a job that will allow two women who can only work part time to have an exciting job challenge. Job-sharing arrangements are slowly working their way into business. One such successful application involves two mid-life women.

Gladys and Janice share an advertising manager position in a photographic supply company. An outstanding advantage to such an arrangement is that the company gets an output in excess of the equivalent of one full-time person. Two people working half-time will usually produce more than one person working full time, particularly in creative work. As Gladys explains:

> Both Janice and I will admit it. The job calls for coming up with new ideas. Usually the big ideas pop into view when your mind is fresh. Neither of us comes back to work feeling sluggish after a two-martini lunch, and we have no time to fritter away in water-cooler or coffee conversations with other people. I'm a morning person, and Janice is an afternoon person. If one of us has a family obligation to take of, the other one covers for her. Our job is always covered and the company usually gets us at our peak period of productivity.

SUMMARY OF KEY POINTS

☐ Adjusting to the organization refers to many things that you have to do in order to get along on the job. Several of these major adjustments are described in this chapter. Adjusting to formal rules is often easier than adjusting to informal rules that stem from the informal organization. The latter includes the customs and traditions that develop in the firm.

☐ Standards of dress and appearance are governed by both formal and informal rules, and both may require adjustments by the employee. It is more helpful to use general guidelines for proper dress and appearance than to adhere closely to detailed suggestions about specific items of clothing. Five important factors influencing your choice of clothing are (1) products and services sold, (2) type of customer or client served, (3) desired image projected by the firm, (4) geography, and (5) your comfort and self-image.

☐ Manners and etiquette are even more strongly linked to informal rules than are dress codes. Knowing how much schmoozing (informal socializing) to engage in is part of adjusting to the manners and etiquette of the firm. An important generalization about proper business etiquette is to be considerate of other employees. Most specific rules stem from this general principle.

☐ Another important part of adjusting to the organization is to learn how to work as part of a team. Three important strategies for promoting the team concept are (1) share credit with co-workers, (2) give information and opinions to them, and (3) touch base with them on important issues.

☐ Shyness is a personal problem for about two-fifths of the adult population. It is frequently perceived as a negative trait in a job setting and may therefore require change in order to make a good adjustment to the organization. Although about one-half of shy people may have inherited this characteristic, shy people can take a number of steps to become more assertive. It is important to set a specific goal for improvement and to practice a variety of techniques for dealing more openly with people in live settings. Shyness workshops, including assertiveness training, are also useful in overcoming shyness.

☐ A unique set of adjustment problems is faced by a mid-life woman entering the work force for essentially the first time. The adjustments described here are (1) finding a field compatible with life experiences, (2) competing with younger women, (3) relating to younger superiors, (4) dealing with unequal advancement opportunities, and (5) balancing work and family demands.

GUIDELINES FOR PERSONAL EFFECTIVENESS

1. An important strategy of adjusting to the organization is to be aware of the informal expectations made of you in such areas as dress codes, socializing on the job and appropriate business etiquette. To learn of these expectations, both make observations and delicately ask questions.
2. It is important in general to be a good team player if you want to work for an organization. However, do not carry this approach so far that you lose your personal identity or become "one of the gang." Such behavior could decrease your chances for promotion.
3. If you and others consider yourself to be overly shy, it would help your career to work toward becoming a more assertive person. This is particularly true if your job involves much contact with people.
4. If you are a family person, female or male, it is important to establish a workable plan for balancing career and family demands. If home matters are poorly attended to, it is difficult to concentrate properly on your job.

DISCUSSION QUESTIONS

1. What are the three biggest adjustments that you have already had to make or that you think you will have to make in the future?
2. What alternatives are there for people who believe that they can never adjust to organizational life?
3. To what extent do you think executives (high-level managers) schmooze?

4. If you were (or are) a supervisor, how much schmoozing would you (or do you) allow on the job?

5. Suppose a person says, "I'm not interested in paying attention to company manners or following business etiquette." What type of work would you recommend for that person?

6. To what extent do you believe that being a member of an athletic team is good training for becoming a team player on the job?

7. In what department of a firm do people tend to dress the most fashionably? The least fashionably?

8. Can you think of five different symptoms (indicators or signs) of shyness?

9. How could being shy prevent you from receiving credit for some of your work?

10. What would be a good field for a 55-year-old woman entering the work force for the first time?

A Business Psychology Problem
THE LOST JOB OPPORTUNITY

"So long, Skip," said Jason, the branch manager at Cosmopolitan Insurance Company, "you'll be hearing back from me in a few days. The next step in hiring you for this job will be to meet with Mr. William Shields, our regional manager. He's my boss." "Thanks a lot," replied Skip. "I'll wait for your call."

Four days later, Skip did hear from Jason. To his surprise, a three-way luncheon was arranged with Jason, Bill Shields, and Skip. The lunch was held at an attractive Italian restaurant two blocks from where Skip would be working, if hired. At lunch the three men talked about the nature of claims work and how bright the future looked for Cosmopolitan. As Skip finished his spumoni dessert, Mr. Shields commented, "And remember one thing, young man. A claims examiner for Cosmopolitan must be capable of meeting the public in a dignified manner."

Later that afternoon, Bill Shields informed Jason, "I do like your candidate for the open claims examiner spot. But you will have to do better. Skip's manners are just not suited for meeting the public. Did you see how he sucked up his spaghetti? Did you see how he held his fork in his left hand? He just won't do for our company."

"Are you sure you won't change your mind, Bill?" asked Jason. "Skip has a lot of potential. I think we can teach him manners. There must be a charm school we can send him to."

"Sorry, Jason. My decision is final. We have a certain image to uphold at Cosmopolitan Insurance."

The next day Jason wrote Skip a note informing him that the job in question had been filled by a candidate with more appropriate experience. When Skip read the letter he was stunned.

1. Do you think Shields was justified in refusing to hire Skip because of his table manners?
2. What criticisms might you have made of the way Jason informed Skip about his not being hired?

A Business Psychology Role Play
THE REJECTED JOB CANDIDATE

As things worked out, Skip did not take his rejection easily. He called Jason and requested an in-person interview to review why he was turned down for the job when it appeared that he was just about hired.

One person plays Skip, who is convinced that he can handle the claims job. Furthermore, he is upset that he was turned down. Another person plays Jason, who decides that in the interest of decency, he will explain to Skip why he was really turned down. Yet at the same time Jason does not want the company to appear foolish. Nor does he want the company to be sued.

REFERENCES

[1]Henry L. Tosi and Stephen J. Carroll, *Management: Contingencies, Structure and Process* (Chicago: St. Clair Press, 1976), p. 13.

[2]John T. Molloy, *Dress for Success* (New York: Warner Books, 1976), p. 70.

[3]Barry L. Reece and Rhonda Brandt, *Effective Human Relations in Business* (Boston: Houghton Mifflin, 1981), pp. 246–249.

[4]Ibid., p. 247.

[5]Robert Schrank, "How to Relieve Worker Boredom," *Psychology Today* (July 1978), pp. 79–80.

[6]Quoted in Richard Michaels, "Manners," *Success* (Aug. 1982), p. 43.

[7]Based primarily on two sources: George Mazzei, *The New Office Etiquette* (New York: Simon & Schuster, 1983); Richard Michaels, "Manners," pp. 40–43.

[8]Mazzei, *Office Etiquette*.

[9]One such book is Betty L. Harragan, *Games Mother Never Taught You* (New York: Rawson Associates, 1977).

[10]Paper presented at 1983 American Psychological Association Meeting, Ana-

heim, Calif. As reported in the *Boston Globe* and reprinted in the Rochester *Democrat and Chronicle* (Nov. 16, 1983), pp. 1A, 9A.

[11]Philip Zimbardo, *Shyness: What It Is, What to Do about It* (Reading, Mass.: Addison-Wesley, 1977), p. 14.

[12]Ibid., p. 22.

[13]Based on two sources: Zimbardo, *Shyness*, pp. 220–226, and Kevin Shyne, "Shyness: Breaking Through This Invisible Barrier to Achievement," *Success* (July 1982), pp. 14–16, 36, 37, 51.

[14]Quoted in Shyne, "Shyness," p. 51.

[15]See information about re-entry women in Patricia W. Lunneborg and Vicki M. Wilson, *To Work: A Guide for Women College Graduates* (Englewood Cliffs, N.J.: Prentice-Hall, 1982).

[16]Charlotte R. Tatro and Jacqueline Boles, "Developing New Careers and Financial Independence," in *Women in Midlife—Security and Fulfillment*, paper submitted to the Select Committee on Aging, U.S. Government Printing Office, Washington, D.C., 1978, p. 201.

SUGGESTED READING

FARLEY, JENNIE, ed. *The Woman in Management*. Ithaca, N.Y.: ILR Press, 1983.

HEGARTY, CHRISTOPHER. *How to Manage Your Boss*. New York: Rawson-Wade, 1981.

MOLLOY, JOHN T. *Molloy's Live for Success*. New York: Bantam Books, 1982.

PHILLIPS, GERALD M. *Help for Shy People*. Englewood Cliffs, N.J.: Prentice-Hall, 1981.

POWELL, BARBARA. *Overcoming Shyness: Practical Scripts for Everyday Encounters*. New York: McGraw-Hill, 1981.

RAUDSEPP, EUGENE, and JOSEPH C. YEAGER. "How to Win at Office Politics," *Administrative Management* (May 1981), pp. 26–28, 40–44.

ROSEMAN, Ed. "How to Become a Better Teamworker," *Product Management* (Jan. 1976), pp. 17–20.

STEIL, LYMAN K., JOANNE SUMMERFIELD, and GEORGE DeMARE. *Listening: It Can Change Your Life*. New York: Wiley, 1983.

WALLACE, PHYLLIS A. *Women in the Workplace*. Cambridge, Mass.: Auburn House, 1982.

A Woman's Guide to Business and Social Success. Bronx, N.Y.: MPC Educational Press, 1983.

12

DEALING WITH COUNTERPRODUCTIVE PEOPLE

LEARNING OBJECTIVES

After reading and studying this chapter and doing the exercises, you should be able to

1. Understand the nature of the influence process.
2. Acquire insights into how to confront and criticize counterproductive (or difficult) people.
3. Appreciate the role of recognition and affection in dealing with counterproductive people.
4. Be aware of game playing by counterproductive people.

People in a work environment can be counterproductive or "difficult" for a number of reasons outside of intelligence or ability. From the standpoint of a manager, a counterproductive or difficult person can be anybody who turns in substandard performance, yet who could perform well if he or she wanted to. From the standpoint of the individual worker, a peer is classified as counterproductive or difficult if he or she is uncooperative, touchy, defensive, hostile, or even very unfriendly. From the standpoint of any subordinate, a counterproductive or difficult boss is similarly any boss who is uncooperative, insensitive, touchy or defensive, aggressive, hostile, or very unfriendly.

In this chapter we explore some of the psychological techniques that a person might use to deal more effectively with people who are counterproductive or difficult, but not necessarily unintelligent or incompetent. We are dealing primarily with the situation in which the difficult person is a co-worker rather than a subordinate. However, if you have formal authority over another individual (you're the boss), the same techniques can be used to advantage. Also, if the difficult person is your boss, several of the techniques can be used, but with considerable sensitivity and tact.

Several patterns of difficult behavior are presented in Exhibit 12–1. Although not scientifically developed, they do provide some insight into the nature of counterproductive people on the job.

Exhibit 12–1

PATTERNS OF DIFFICULT BEHAVIOR

Based on his experiences in both private companies and public agencies, consultant Richard M. Bramson contends that about 10 percent of office workers are relentlessly difficult. He classifies difficult behavior into the following seven patterns. They merit your attention as one way of understanding the nature of counterproductive people.

Hostile-aggressives. These people try to bully and overwhelm co-workers by bombarding them, making cutting remarks, or throwing temper tantrums when things don't go the way they would like them to. Hostile-aggressives make few pretenses at being nice guys or gals.

Complainers. People in this category gripe incessantly, but never try to take constructive action about the source of their complaints. They either feel powerless to take action, or do not want to bear responsibility for so doing.

Silent and unresponsives. Such people respond to every question you might have, or every request for help, with "a yep, a no, or a grunt." Energetic and spirited people often get the urge to physically shake silent and unresponsives.

Superagreeables. In your presence, these people are typically personable, funny, and outgoing. The problem is that they do not produce what they say they will, and they act contrary to the way they have led you to suspect.

Negativist. When a project or idea is proposed, negativists will inevitably object with statements such as "It won't work," "It's impossible," or "It's been tried before and failed." Unfortunately, they all too often deflate the optimism of others.

Know-it-all experts. These self-proclaimed superior people believe, and want you to recognize, that they "know everything there is to know about anything worth knowing." They are condescending when they do know the subject matter at hand and pompous when they do not. Know-it-all experts are often effective at making you feel inferior.

Indecisives. People exhibiting this behavior pattern stall until the decision is made for them, or won't let go of anything until it is perfect, which means never.

Bramson notes that complainers don't always complain, indecisives sometimes do come to a decision, and so forth. Yet, there are common patterns in the behavior of difficult people that can be identified and described.

SOURCE: Adapted from Robert M. Bramson, *Coping with Difficult People* (New York: Ballantine, 1981), pp. 4–5.

THE INFLUENCE PROCESS

A logical starting point for understanding how to cope with difficult people is to recognize that we are talking about influencing or changing others. If a co-worker becomes hostile any time that you ask him about his input to a team effort, your goal is to influence (change) him into a less hostile person, at least in your dealings with him. If your subordinate habitually returns late from lunch on Fridays in an obvious state of partial intoxication, you want to influence him or her to not consume alcohol during the Friday lunch break. Harold Leavitt suggests that we keep five concepts in mind as we go about trying to influence or change people.[1] Understanding these concepts will improve your ability to influence others toward the worthwhile end of becoming less difficult and more productive. If your ends are not worthwhile, you should not be exerting influence on others.

Influence Is an Emotional Process

A person rarely listens to reason when the subject matter is himself or herself. One construction estimator pleaded with a co-worker of his to stop playing his radio so loudly during working hours. The changer (from here on A is the changer) said to the changee (from here on B is the changee), "Don't you realize that you're behaving like an adolescent? An adult shouldn't be playing a radio when there's work to be done." However logical A thought his plea was, B did not want to listen to reason. Instead he issued the rejoinder, "I'll do what I damn well please. It's my civil right to play my radio." The relationship between A and B only worsened after that incident. If A had been aware of the role of emotions involved in changing people, he would have

People rarely listen to reason when the subject matter is themself.

tried a more tactful method of getting B to turn off his radio (or A might have used earphones).

Recognize Your Motives

When A is trying to change B, the reasons A gives B for the change are sometimes not the real reasons. Sam, an industrial engineer, may say to the plant superintendent, "I wish you would adopt my program of redesigning the work layout in your area. It could raise your department efficiency and help you get the recognition you deserve from management." Sam believes that the plant superintendent is being difficult because he flatly rejects his offer.

If Sam would look more closely at his motives, he would recognize that he is as much concerned about himself looking good as he is concerned about the superintendent. Maybe Sam is pushing the superintendent too fast on a program that really isn't that sound. Maybe Sam would be better off in the long run if he waited to suggest a program to the superintendent that would really make the latter look good. Right now A seems to be more concerned about looking good than he is about his long-term relationship with B. Leavitt offers a rule of thumb for a person trying to bring about change in another individual:[2]

> Let him examine his own reasons for wanting to effect a particular change before plunging into the effort. Let him examine his own motives. If he does, he may be more likely to effect change successfully because he will be more clear-headed about what he wants to do; or he may alter or give up his efforts altogether if such an examination brings the realization that changing other people would not satisfy the needs he most wants to satisfy.

All Change Is Self-Change

An important principle of trying to influence or change other people is that virtually all change by psychological methods comes from within B. A therapist does not cure a patient or client. The latter arrives at some understanding that helps him or her see the way and the path toward change. You cannot make a co-worker stop blowing smoke in your face by clever manipulation. That person has to somehow perceive that not blowing smoke in your face is more pleasant, or less unpleasant, than blowing smoke in your face. You encourage the change, but he or she makes the actual change.

Change Is Uncomfortable

Little wonder it is difficult for A to influence B to change. For most people, change is an uncomfortable, even painful process. Barbara worked in a pub-

For most people, change is an uncomfortable, even painful experience process.

lic relations department as a copywriter. One of her co-workers persisted in referring to Barbara as "Barb." A (Barbara in this relationship) told B several times that she much preferred the name "Barbara" to "Barb"; B somehow persisted in referring to A as "Barb." A had again reminded B of her preferred name. Subsequently, B simply turned her head when she saw A or used no name at all. She found the trivial change of calling A by her preferred name to be an uncomfortable experience.

People often feel more uncomfortable when you try to bring about a major change in their behavior. Trying to get someone to become well organized whose disorganization is causing you difficulties amounts to a major change in that person. He or she may find the situation uncomfortable and make statements such as, "I hate being so obsessed with details."

Responsibility for Change
Should Be Shared

Changing counterproductive people is much less difficult if both A and B share responsibility for the change. Unfortunately, B sometimes does not want any part of the change. The importance of shared responsibility can be understood from the example of a compulsive gambler. His preoccupation with gambling and his problem of paying off creditors begin to adversely affect his ability to concentrate on his job.

The gambler's boss may want him to change this difficult behavior pattern. A may make the suggestion that B join the local Gambler's Anonymous group. If B does not feel a shared responsibility for this change, A's efforts will fail. Yet if A takes no responsibility (does not even make constructive suggestions to B), B may not have the encouragement he needs to overcome his gambling compulsion.

CONFRONTING
THE DIFFICULT PERSON

A good starting point for overcoming problems created by a difficult person is to confront that individual with his or her annoying or counterproductive behavior. In some instances, simply confronting the problem will make it go away. One co-worker said to another, "Please stop suggesting that we take two-hour lunch breaks every payday. It makes me tense to have to reject you." The requests for the luncheon sojourns stopped immediately.

A fundamental reason why we resist confronting another person, particularly a subordinate, about a sensitive issue is that we recognize how uncomfortable *we* feel when confronted by a boss about a sensitive issue. A manager who is about to confront a subordinate about irregularities on an expense account might say to himself: "I know how bad I would feel if I were told by my boss that I had been overcharging the company on trips. Maybe if I let it pass one more time, Jack [the subordinate] will shape up by himself."

Another reason many people are hesitant to confront another person is fear of reprisal. What specific kind of reprisal might be chosen by the confronted person (should the roles be reversed) is usually unknown, which makes the confrontation seem all the more hazardous. One member of a task force was going to confront another with the opinion that the latter was not carrying her fair share, thus increasing the burden for other members of the task force. The would-be confronter backed off, thinking that the woman confronted might tell lies about her to their mutual boss.

Helpful Confrontation Techniques

Five suggestions are in order to ease the confrontation process.[3] Since confrontation of some sort is a vital step in attempting to influence the behavior of another individual, they are worth giving serious thought.

1. Attempt to relax during the confrontation session. If you appear overly tense, you might communicate the message in body language that you are not confident of the position that you are taking about the individual's negative behavior. Sometimes a role-playing or rehearsal interview with a friend will be helpful in reducing your tension about the confrontation.

2. Get to the central purpose of your meeting almost immediately. Too often when people attempt to confront somebody else about something sensitive, they waste time talking about unrelated topics. Discussions about vacations, the company parking lot, professional sports, or business conditions have some small value as warm-up material for *other* kinds of interviews, but that's all.

3. Avoid being apologetic or defensive about the need for the meeting. You have a right to demand constructive relationships with other people in your work environment. For instance, there is no need to say, "Perhaps I may be way off base, but it seems like you slam the door shut every time I can't process your request immediately." Let the door-slamming co-worker correct you if you are "way off base."

4. Confront the other individual in a nonhostile manner. Confrontations about counterproductive behavior should be conducted with feeling (particularly sincerity), but not with hostility. Confrontations are associated with bitter conflict so frequently that the concept of confrontation connotes hostility. Yet all forms of confrontation need not be conflagrations. Hostility begets hostility. Confrontation mixed with hostility comes across to the person being confronted as an attempt at retribution or punishment.

Our suggestion about avoiding hostility does not mean that all emotion should be ruled out of a confrontation session. An appropriate amount of displeasure, annoyance, disapointment, and controlled anger should be conveyed. A confrontation session stripped of legitimate feeling would appear sterile to the person being confronted.

The following statements illustrate the difference between hostile and nonhostile confrontations over the same issue:

Hostile: I don't care if you have no natural teeth and you are forced to wear dentures. Stop that wretched clicking of your teeth when you're around me.

Nonhostile: I have something very delicate to talk about with you. I'm having trouble concentrating on my work because of the clicking sound that you are making with your teeth. Maybe you aren't aware of doing it, but it disturbs me.

5. *Confront job-related behavior.* The essential skill to be acquired in constructive confrontation is to translate counterproductive behavior into its job-related consequence. Once the counterproductive or difficult behavior is translated into its consequences in terms of actions, the situation is placed on a problem-solving basis. Instead of confronting a person about his or her feelings, attitudes, or values, you discuss their job-related consequences. These consequences are much easier to deal with than internal aspects of people. Two examples follow, designed to illustrate the difference between confrontation related to job behavior and confrontation unrelated to job behavior.

Manager to subordinate (job-related): I wish you would smile at customers more frequently. They are likely to purchase more goods when they receive a warm smile from the store clerk.

Same manager to subordinate (not job-related): I wish you would smile at customers more frequently. If your attitude isn't right you'll never make a good sales clerk.

One forewoman to another (job-related): I can't help but overhear you use all those four-letter words. If you keep that up you may lose the respect of your employees. Then they won't listen to you when you need something done out of the ordinary.

One forewoman to another (not job-related): I can't help but overhear you use all those four-letter words. There's nothing worse than a foul-mouthed female supervisor.

6. *Show that you care.* Human resource consultant Pamela Cole suggests that the word "carefrontation" be substituted for confrontation. She says, "You have to care enough to confront because it's easier not to confront and to avoid the problem. Caring enough to confront increases the likelihood

that the situation will be resolved. When I do not confront a situation, I can be pretty much assured that it will go on the way it is or get worse."[4]

Communicating the fact that you care can sometimes be done by the sincerity in your voice and the concerned way you approach the difficult person. Using the words "care" and "concern" can be helpful. To illustrate, "The reason I'm bringing up this problem, is that I *care* about our working relationship. And I'm *concerned* that things have been a little rough between us."

THE ART OF CRITICIZING CONSTRUCTIVELY

Confrontation and criticism are closely linked. Confrontation precedes the actual criticism, and both are part of the same process of trying to get other people to change their behavior. It is difficult to criticize productive people in a constructive manner. The challenge multiplies when you try to criticize counterproductive people. One of the problems in criticizing anybody in a job setting is that the person being criticized may have put considerable emotional energy into the job. The person therefore interprets the criticism as an attack on his or her ego.[5]

A second problem is the sense of competitiveness that typically develops among co-workers. If you criticize a peer, your criticism may be interpreted as an attack on his or her work just so your work seems better in comparison. A copywriter in an advertising agency made this comment about the criticisms he was exchanging with a peer:

> Everytime I came up with an idea, Steve managed to find something wrong with it. Of course, we were both playing the same game—every time Steve made a suggestion I found a reason to downgrade and reject it. We were not only competing to see who could come up with the better idea, we were competing to see who could find the most flaws in the other fellow's ideas.[6]

Presented next are several suggestions for criticizing a difficult person in a constructive manner. Recognize, however, that these suggestions also apply to criticizing anybody on the job.[7] (Several may also be used when making criticisms in personal life.)

Be sensitive to the setting. A primary principle of good human relations is to criticize in private. The counterproductive person will only become more defensive if you confront and criticize him or her in the presence of peers. It also may prove to be less threatening to criticize the person away from his or her work area. The company cafeteria, parking lot, or vending machine area may prove to be a reasonable place to confront and criticize.

Base the criticism on objective facts. In criticizing anybody, it is important to base your criticism on objective facts rather than on subjective perceptions. Much criticism is rejected because it is thought to be invalid. When you use facts to aid your case, you have a better chance of getting through to the counterproductive person. Assume that you are dealing with a superagreeable who has failed to supply you some information that you need to accomplish your job. A criticism based on subjective interpretation would be, "Your unwillingness to cooperate has messed things up for me." An objective—and potentially more effective—criticism would be, "Because I did not get the information you promised me, I was unable to finish my report for our boss."

Express your criticism in terms of a common goal. As just implied, if your criticism points toward the accomplishment of a purpose that both of you are trying to achieve, it may get across to the difficult person. Weisinger and Lobsenz recommend the use of words that emphasize cooperation rather than competitiveness and blame. For example, "*We* can get the report done quickly if *you'll* firm up the statistical data while I edit the text," will be more effective than "Unless you get moving faster on the statistics I won't be able to finish the report on time."[8]

Avoid playing boss. Most employees resent a co-worker assuming the boss's role while criticizing them. Difficult people will resent it all the more because most of them are defensive. "Playing boss" means that you act as if you have formal authority over the other person when, in reality, you are a peer or subordinate. One manifestation of playing boss would be to tell a co-worker, "If you don't get that program written for me by this afternoon, you'll have to work overtime to get it done."

When criticizing your boss, relate it to your work performance. It takes extra tact to do a good job of criticizing your boss, particularly if he or she is a difficult person. An important guideline is to show how your boss's behavior, however well intended, is hampering your job performance. A case in point took place in a retail-store chain. The loss-prevention managers in each store were supervised by a zone manager, who in many ways behaved in a counterproductive manner. One of his worst practices was to swear at loss-prevention managers (LPMs) when losses were above average at their store. One of the LPMs decided that she could no longer tolerate her boss's tirades. Confronting him after one of his verbal reprimands, she said calmly, "Mr. Gifford, when you swear and scream at me, it interferes with my ability to perform my job well. My records show that I make by biggest mistakes in counting inventory soon after you have screamed at me for something that is not even my fault." Mr. Gifford did temper his criticism in the future.

Although the tactics we have described so far for dealing with difficult people are important, sometimes the opposite of criticism may be the best strategy.

GIVING RECOGNITION
AND AFFECTION

Counterproductive or difficult people, similar to misbehaving children, are sometimes crying out for attention. By giving them recognition and affection, their counterproductive behavior will *sometimes* cease. If their negative behavior is a product of a deeper-rooted problem, recognition and affection alone will not work. Other actions, as previously discussed in this chapter, will need to be taken. The most direct strategy is to give the misbehaving individual attention and affection. If the negative behavior stops, you have found the proper antidote. The successful resolution of such a problem took place in a photo studio.

> Rich, one of the commercial photographers, had an annoying habit of interrupting the conversation of other people during staff meetings or with customers. In one instance during negotiations with an important customer, Rich blurted out, "I'm the local expert on nature photographs. If you want anything done along those lines, your best bet would be for me to shoot the job."
>
> Mandy, Rich's boss, then tried spending a few minutes each week telling Rich how great a photographer he was and how much the studio needed him (not a lie because Rich was talented and valuable). In addition, Mandy arranged for Rich to have some of his work put on display at a local photo show.
>
> Rich changed his behavior toward that of a more subdued and contented individual. In the words of one of his colleagues, "I can't understand what happened to Rich. He's become much easier to live with."

INTERPRETING THE GAMES
OF COUNTERPRODUCTIVE PEOPLE

In Chapter 15 we will take a broad look at the use of transactional analysis (TA) in organizations. One concept about human behavior popularized by TA is particularly relevant in dealing with counterproductive or difficult people—game playing. A considerable amount of game playing takes place on the job. A **game** is a repeated series of exchanges between people that appears different on the surface than its true underlying motive. A game always has a hidden agenda or purpose. The game player acts in a way that is superficially plausible, but there is a concealed motivation.[9]

With a little practice, you can become sensitive to games that a counterproductive person might be playing. Once you think that you have his or her game pegged, you can confront that person with the game. The game player might then stop the game and deal with you more honestly. Some games are so simple and so frequently used that they have not been given formal labels. In the following example, a co-worker tries to play a game with you. You finally interpret his game and the game ends.

Co-worker (sniffling, and holding his hand to his head):	Do you possibly have any aspirin? I feel so sick this afternoon, I just don't know how I'm going to last through the afternoon.
You:	Yes, I happen to have a bottle of aspirin in my desk. Here, would you like two?
Co-worker:	You really didn't have to do that. It's so kind of you. I hope I'm not seriously sick. I have so much work to do. I would be letting the department down if I went home sick. I know how busy you are this afternoon. You have all the work you can handle by yourself. Don't you?
You (interpreting his game):	I sure do. I'm very busy this afternoon. If you are really that sick, you should get permission to visit the company medical department. I would imagine Jack (your boss) can make some arrangements to get your share of the work done this afternoon. If I recall correctly, this isn't the first time you've asked me to cover for you on a hectic afternoon. But I do hope you get well sooner.

Dozens of appealing names have been given to games that people play frequently. Following are four games often observed on the job.

Blemish

This is an extremely simple game to play and is often used by superiors to keep subordinates in line. All that is required is for the boss to find some small flaw in every assignment completed by subordinates. The game-playing boss stays one up with comments such as, "Smith, you did a great job on that report except for your conclusion. It just didn't seem to fit the body of the report."

A tactful rejoinder to this Blemish-playing boss might be, "I notice that you usually find one thing wrong with an otherwise acceptable job of mine. Is it your policy to always find at least one fault? Knowing the answer to this question would be very helpful to me in my work."

If It Weren't for That Other Person

A convenient way of avoiding responsibility for our errors is to find somebody else to blame. The person who habitually plays If It Weren't for That Other

Person tries to con someone else into being sympathetic. A subordinate of yours might say to you, "I'm sorry to let you down by being one hour late for work. If it weren't for that preposterous rush hour traffic, I would have been here before the office even opened."

One way of stopping such a game player (and a counterproductive individual) in his or her tracks is to retort, "You've been traveling the same route as long as I've known you. Why don't you leave thirty minutes earlier? If you do arrive at the office early, you can read the paper and have a cup of coffee. Why blame the traffic for your lateness? Blame yourself."

The Setup

Some bosses like to see you fail. A technique that they use is to set goals so unrealistically high for you that you are unlikely to reach them. Frustration and discouragement are the predictable results.[10] Your boss can then criticize you both for not reaching your objectives and for having a "poor attitude." Here is a portion of a review session where The Setup is being played:

Boss: I see that you only cut the cost of cleaning our guest rooms by 8 percent during the last six months. Your goal was to cut costs by 12 percent.

You: But with inflation, it was almost impossible to cut costs by 12 percent. I think the chambermaids did an enormous job of improving their productivity. I made all the savings I could find without letting service suffer.

Boss: Nevertheless, you failed to reach your objective. I therefore cannot recommend you for a good salary increase this year.

The best way around this type of game playing is to negotiate any unrealistic goals handed you by your boss. If you think the goal is unrealistically high, carefully explain your position.

Low-balling

Employees play their games too during a performance review. For instance, you might purposely set objectives at an unrealistically low level. At the time of performance review, you can then "prove" what an outstanding performer you are.

Suppose that you are working as a collection agent for a loan company. You might set a goal of increasing your total amount of dollars collected by 10 percent during the next quarter. In the meantime, you are aware that one of your largest delinquent accounts is ready to settle. That account alone will increase your collections by 9 percent. With very little effort, you can exceed your objective.

Game playing during performance review is generally a destructive process. It is much better for you and your supervisor to be straightforward and honest about the performance review process.

SUMMARY OF KEY POINTS

☐ Counterproductive or difficult people are found in most places of work, perhaps to the extent of 10 percent of employees. Such people include those who are uncooperative, touchy, defensive, hostile, unfriendly, and substandard performers. The difficult employee is not necessarily of low intelligence or ability.

☐ Dealing effectively with counterproductive people often involves an attempt to change their behavior. Influencing or changing another person is a complex process. Among the complexities are: (1) Change is an emotional process. (2) The changer's motives must be examined. (3) Change must really stem from within. (4) Change makes people uncomfortable. (5) The responsibility for change must be shared.

☐ A major aspect of dealing with counterproductive people is to confront them with the job-related consequences of their behavior. Confrontation is difficult for most people because it makes them feel uncomfortable. Suggestions for effective confrontation include (1) attempt to relax during the session, (2) quickly get to the core topic, (3) avoid being apologetic or defensive, (4) be nonhostile in your confrontation, (5) confront job-related behavior, not personal traits, characteristics, and motives, and (6) show that you care.

☐ Criticism and confrontation are both part of the same process of trying to get other people to change their behavior. Criticizing difficult people is especially difficult because they are usually defensive. Suggestions for constructive criticism include (1) be sensitive to the setting, (2) base the criticism on objective facts, (3) express criticism in terms of a common goal, (4) avoid playing boss. When criticizing your boss, show how the boss's behavior is interfering with your work performance.

☐ Counterproductive people are sometimes seeking attention. By giving them recognition and attention, their counterproductive behavior will therefore sometimes decrease. Another approach to dealing with counterproductive people is to interpret their games. A game is a repeated series of transactions between people with a concealed motive. Many of these games have been labeled by specialists in transactional analysis. The four described here are Blemish (finding flaws in another's work), If It Weren't for That Other Person (blaming somebody else), The Setup (setting somebody else up to fail), and Low-balling (underpredicting your performance in order to look good when you perform well).

GUIDELINES FOR PERSONAL EFFECTIVENESS

1. Counterproductive people tend to take up a disproportionate share of an individual worker's or manager's time. You should therefore give serious thought to developing effective strategies for dealing with such people. Ideally, you should help counterproductive people to become more productive.

2. The most essential skill for dealing with counterproductive people is confrontation. It is important to examine your own attitudes and feelings toward confrontation in order to determine if you are avoiding it. Confrontation will bring forth less resistance if you confront people with the job-related consequences of their behavior. You will receive more resistance if you discuss their personal traits, characteristics, and motives.

3. At times it is necessary to "call" (interpret) the game somebody is playing with you in a work setting. If you do not call their game, they might play the game indefinitely. Yet calling their game may lead to more hostility. Proceed with caution and tact.

DISCUSSION QUESTIONS

1. Why shouldn't as many counterproductive people as possible be fired?
2. In your opinion, does an employee have the right to criticize another employee?
3. What are several potential problems in criticizing your boss?
4. Some managers take a subordinate out for a few drinks when they want to confront the subordinate. What do you think are the advantages and disadvantages of this practice?
5. Suppose you think that a co-worker is rude. How can you relate that rudeness to objective facts rather than a subjective interpretation?
6. Suppose a student annoys classmates by monopolizing class discussion. What common goal might you bring to that person's attention?
7. In what way does giving a difficult person recognition and affection go against reinforcement theory?
8. What is counterproductive about "playing games" on the job?
9. How might an instructor play The Setup with students?
10. How might a student play Low-ball with an instructor?

A Business Psychology Problem
THE HOSTILE LOSS-PREVENTION MANAGER

Mel Gifford, the zone loss-prevention manager (LPM) at Keystone Stores, prided himself in his skill as a manager. As he explained to the person who researched this case, "I'm in complete control all the time. And control is the name of the game in the loss-prevention field. Inventory shrinkage is a big problem with us. We therefore have to keep an accurate account of our inventory. If a piece of merchandise has not been sold, and it is not on the shelf or the storeroom, we can assume that it's been stolen.

"If I find an error in an audit coming back from one of my stores, I demand an answer right away. And I don't pussyfoot. I let the local LPM know right away that a mistake has been made that must be corrected. My LPMs respect me for my toughness as a manager."

Later, the case researcher spoke to several of the loss-prevention managers to learn of their perspective on the working relationship between the LPMs and their zone manager. Bud, a 24-year man in charge of security at the highest volume store in his zone, offered these observations:

"I'm afraid for Mel Gifford. No doubt in my mind he's a Type A personality whose headed for an early heart attack. He takes his job too seriously. If Gifford finds one little error, he goes bananas. Sometimes he swears at me as if I've stolen some missing merchandise. I don't take it personally, I guess it's just his way. But overall I think Gifford gets the job done. No big complaint on my part."

Melissa, an LPM at another store in the zone, had this view of her boss, Mel Gifford:

"So long as this is confidential, I can tell you with a straight face that the man is a lunatic. When things are going fine, he's fine. But when he sees a problem, he flies off the handle. He's a fire-spitting dragon who spits too much fire at the wrong people. Somedays he swears at me over the phone. It ruins my whole day. In fact, I've got to do something about the problem soon. But I wouldn't want to lose my job over complaining to my boss."

1. How should Melissa deal with this problem?
2. Should Bud speak to Mel Gifford about his method of criticizing him?
3. What type of difficult behavior pattern best fits Mel Gifford (see Exhibit 12–1)?

A Business Psychology Role Play
CONFRONTING YOUR BOSS

The case just presented serves as the necessary background information and setting for this role play. The information about confrontation and criticism found in the chapter should be consulted before assuming the following roles.

Situation A. One person plays Bud, who is legitimately concerned about the health of his boss, Mel Gifford. As Bud, you think that your boss's ranting and raving will lead him to an early grave. Try to communicate this message to him without damaging your working relationship. At your initiative, you are meeting with Mr. Gifford today to discuss your concerns about how he handles his anger in dealing with you.

Another person plays Mel Gifford. You are meeting today with one of your LPMs, Bud. You wonder what's on his mind. If it's one thing you dislike, it's subordinates trying to tell you how to be a manager.

Situation B. One person plays the role of Melissa. At this moment you think you have experienced a last straw. Your boss, Mel Gifford, is screaming at you over the telephone. He is ranting and raving about a discrepancy in the loss reports at your store. It almost seems as if he is accusing you of stealing some merchandise yourself.

The other person plays Mel Gifford. You are really upset about a needless error in the loss-prevention audit. You firmly believe that the best way to communicate your displeasure to subordinates is to be as honest and candid as possible in expressing your feelings. You also believe that in a heavy-pressure business like yours, it is OK to use profanity.

REFERENCES

[1]This section of our chapter follows closely the ideas presented in Chapter 11 of Harold J. Leavitt, *Managerial Psychology*, 4th ed. (Chicago: University of Chicago Press, 1978), pp. 127–135.

[2]Ibid., p. 130.

[3]For information about confronting people with bad news, see Gary G. Whitney, "When the News is Bad: Leveling with Employees," *Personnel* (Jan.–Feb. 1983), pp. 37–45.

[4]Quoted in Priscilla Petty, "Shortest Route to Good Communications Is Often a Straight Question," Gannett News Service story printed in Rochester *Democrat and Chronicle* (Oct. 18, 1983), p. 8D.

[5]Hendrie Weisinger and Norman M. Lobsenz, *Nobody's Perfect: How to Give Criticism and Get Results* (New York: Warner Books, 1981), p. 204.

[6]Ibid., p. 212.

[7]Based on information in ibid., pp. 198–230.

[8]Ibid., p. 214

[9]Two sources of information about game playing are Abe Wagner, *The Transactional Manager: How to Solve People Problems with Transactional Analysis* (Englewood Cliffs, N.J.: Prentice-Hall, 1981), pp. 63–67; Muriel James, *The OK Boss* (Reading, Mass.: Addison-Wesley, 1975), pp. 105–121.

[10]The basic idea of games being played in the setting of performance review stems from Heinz Weihrich, "MBO: Appraisal with Transactional Analysis," *Per-

sonnel Journal (April 1976), p. 175. The game labels Setup and Low-balling are coined by the present author.

SUGGESTED READING

ANTHONY, WILLIAM P. *Managing Incompetence.* New York: AMACOM, 1982.

BENNETT, DUDLEY. *TA and the Manager.* New York: AMACOM, 1976.

BERNE, ERIC. *Games People Play.* New York: Grove Press, 1964.

DRAPELA, VICTOR J. *The Counselor as Consultant and Supervisor.* Springfield, Ill.: Charles C. Thomas, 1983.

FOURNIES, FERDINAND F. *Coaching for Improved Work Performance.* New York: Van Nostrand Reinhold, 1978.

HENDERSON, RICHARD I. *Performance Appraisal.* Reston, Va.: Reston Publishing, 1980.

ROSEMAN, EDWARD. *Managing the Problem Employee.* New York: AMACOM, 1982.

STEWART, VALERIE, and ANDREW STEWART. *Managing the Poor Performer.* Brookfield, Vt.: Gower Publishing Company, 1982.

PART FOUR

DEALING WITH SMALL GROUPS

In this part of the text we emphasize information that focuses on dealing with work groups. However, the previous section also dealt with work groups in the sense that personal relationships on the job come about as a result of group effort. Chapter 13 examines such key considerations as the nature of work groups and making decisions through group effort. Chapter 14 is about leadership, the process of influencing other group members to achieve worthwhile results. Chapter 15 examines interpersonal communication, the basic process by which anything gets done in a work group (and in the larger organization).

13

WORKING WITHIN
A GROUP

LEARNING OBJECTIVES

After reading and studying this chapter and doing the exercises, you should be able to

1. Understand the difference between a formal and an informal group.
2. Explain some of the advantages and disadvantages of group effort.
3. Understand how decisions are made and problems solved by groups.
4. Conduct a group brainstorming session about a real problem facing you.
5. Conduct yourself more effectively in a meeting.

WHY ARE GROUPS IMPORTANT?

Groups are vital to the understanding of business psychology because they are the building blocks of the larger organization. The department you are assigned to, the division your department belongs to, the people you share a rest break with, and the special meeting you are asked to attend are among the many groups found within a firm. Since so much of modern organizational life involves group effort, much of your time on the job will be spent working with a small group of people. If you understand how groups behave, you will be better able to capitalize on the benefits of belonging to a group.

Also, you will be better able to avoid some of the problems that a group might create for you.

A **group** is a collection of people who interact with each other, are aware of each other, are working toward some common purpose, and perceive themselves to be a group.[1] Two state troopers seated in a patrol car, watching for speeders and accidents, would thus be a group. So would the head of a company copy center and her staff. In contrast, 12 people in an airport waiting for the same plane would not be a group in the technical sense. Although they might talk to each other, their interaction would not be on a planned or recurring basis. Nor would they be engaged in collective effort, a fundamental justification for forming a group.

An important consideration for understanding groups is that people often behave and perform differently as a group member than they would individually. A group of people may laugh at a comment that its members individually would not find humorous. A group can accomplish a task, such as building a house, that could not be accomplished by combining the individual contributions of its members. And, unfortunately, a group of people will sometimes commit acts of vandalism and physical violence that the individual members would never do.

In this chapter we will discuss some aspects of working within a group that virtually every reader of this book is likely to encounter. Our frame of reference is from the viewpoint of the group member, but the same information is useful to group leaders.

FORMAL VERSUS INFORMAL GROUPS

Many different schemes have been developed to classify the many types of groups found in work organizations. One particularly useful distinction is that drawn between formal and informal groups. Unless you understand the difference in functioning between formal and informal groups, you will have a difficult time adjusting to almost any place of work.

Formal Groups

A formal group is one deliberately formed by the organization to accomplish specific tasks and achieve objectives. The most common type of formal group is a department, such as accounting, shipping, quality control, or payroll. People assigned to work on one ward in a hospital are members of the same formal group. Formal groups can also be committees or special-purpose task forces.

Formal groups are designated by the organization chart. At other times they are indicated on the bulletin board or through office memos (for example, "The undernamed people are hereby assigned to the safety committee"). Several different types of formal groups are defined in Exhibit 13–1.

Informal Groups

An organization cannot be understood by studying its organization chart alone. A large number of groups evolve naturally in an organization to take care of people's desires for friendship and companionship.[2] If you do not belong to any informal group at work, it probably means that you have not formed any friendships. Informal groups are generally thought of in relation to production and clerical workers, but they can form at any level in the organization. Here are three examples of informal groups.

1. Five secretaries from the marketing department meet once a month for lunch to discuss mutual concerns and to seek relief from the tedious aspects of their job.
2. Four computer operators form a jogging club that meets three days per week at lunch time to run two miles.
3. Three managers from different parts of the company commute to work together every business day when they are all in town. Often discussing current events and the stock market, they also discuss company business while commuting to work.

As illustrations 1 and 3 suggest, informal groups are often work related. One function of the informal organization is to fill in the gaps left by the formal organization. Few organizations have a job description written for the "coffee pot tender," yet such a person arises on a rotating basis in many offices. Similarly, when somebody in your department is absent for legitimate reasons, you might take care of his or her emergency work, even though it is not a formal part of your job. Jill, an advertising copywriter, describes an apt example of the potential contribution of an informal group:

> I work in a very creative "shop." We are paid to be creative idea people. We don't dare bring an idea forward to one of the agency heads unless it's a good one. Before submitting an idea to management, we try it out on each other. We use the simple code of "thumbs up" or "thumbs down" to give candid feedback to each other on creative ideas.
>
> Once I was doing work for an Australian Trade Association. I was supposed to come up with a slogan that would help promote Australian merchandise in the United States and Canada. I went to three of my colleagues with the slogan, "Why not bring a little kangaroo spirit into your life?" I received three downturned thumbs. I came back with "Up from Australia." That received three thumbs up from my colleagues and an accolade from my boss. Best of all, the client was sold on the idea.

Exhibit 13-1

A SAMPLING OF FORMAL WORK GROUPS

Since organizations are composed of work groups, many types of work groups can be found in a modern organization. Quite often an employee belongs to both a permanent work group (such as a department) and a temporary work group (such as a labor-management participation team). The following is a sampling of six important types of formal work groups.

Department. A basic unit within the firm that carries out a specific task over an indefinite period of time. For example, it is the job of the maintenance department to keep company equipment running smoothly and to keep the building and grounds in good shape.

Committee. A small group of people from different parts of the organization who are asked to study a particular problem and then make recommendations to management. Standing committees are permanent, while ad hoc committees are temporary groups set up to study a nonrecurring problem.

Staff meeting. A meeting composed of a department head and key department members (the staff). Its purposes include solving a particular problem and communicating information from the manager to the staff members, or in the opposite direction.

Project team. A group of people called together by the firm to accomplish a particular purpose or mission (such as building a space station or launching a new product). It involves a temporary group of specialists from diverse disciplines working together under the same project leader.

Quality circles. Teams of workers, including supervisors and employees, who meet regularly to solve production and quality problems and sometimes to think of new ways to improve productivity. QCs are a form of participative management developed and popularized by Japanese industry, but originated by an American quality-control expert.

Labor-management participation teams. Groups composed of management and labor (usually union members) who jointly try to solve production and morale problems. They represent a high level of cooperation between management and labor and are based on a belief in group decision making and employee participation.

HOW BEING A GROUP MEMBER CAN HELP YOU

Grouping of people both at work and in social gatherings would not be so common if groups did not offer some benefits over individual effort. Even if you prefer working alone to a team effort, it is still of value to look critically at some of the advantages that groups can offer. Groups also offer benefits to the organization, such as efficiency in getting work accomplished and a natural way of training new employees. Here we are more concerned about what groups can do for the individual.

Assistance in Solving Problems

When you are faced with a difficult job problem, a logical source of help is another member of your work group—including your boss. Working alone, it is more difficult to get help. Early in your career, when you are the most likely to need help, it is particularly beneficial to work in a group. Sometimes just talking over a difficult problem with a co-worker will help lead to its solution.

The concept of **synergy** is directly related to the problem-solving advantages of group effort. Synergy means that the productivity of a group often exceeds the contribution that would have been possible by having the group members working separately. The analogy of five people being able to build a house if they worked as a group (but not if they worked alone) is an example of synergy. Intellectual tasks also benefit from the synergistic effect. Five people working together to solve a business problem might accomplish more than the combined output of the same five people working independently. Many advertising firms claim that they are synergistic; the unique combination of talents gathered in their firm produces a certain chemistry that could help clients.

Economic Benefits

It could be to your economic benefit to belong to a group.[3] In a nonunion company, workers might nevertheless band together to ask management for higher wages and benefits. In one law office, the three legal secretaries presented an ultimatum to their employer asking for a $20 per week salary increase. Their request was taken seriously enough that they were granted a $16 increase. In both examples, an informal group emerged to take care of a specific need.

Feeling of Safety

Many people feel much safer and more secure acting in a group than they would acting alone. As labor unions have long contended, there is safety in numbers. People are less concerned that management will retaliate when they present their demands collectively rather than individually. Many people will sign a petition for a cause that they would not endorse as an individual. In one yachting club, the manager was asked to resign by the board of governors. One member initiated a petition to get the manager rehired. When asked why he did not first simply talk to the board of governors himself about the forced resignation, the man replied, "I thought they might cancel my membership if I acted alone. But they can't ask 50 members to resign all at once."

Satisfaction of Psychological Needs

When you are a member of a work group, it is possible for you to satisfy more of your needs than if you worked alone.[4] Among these are needs for affiliation (belonging), security, self-esteem, and self-fulfillment. A few paragraphs of explanation are in order because of the importance of this idea.

Affiliation needs are met directly through belonging to the "office gang," a term of endearment implying that your co-workers are an important part of your life. Many people prefer working in groups to individual effort because of the opportunity the former provides for socializing with others and being part of the office gang.[5] One man who switched positions from an insurance underwriter to a field claims investigator was asked how he liked his new assignment. He commented, "It's all right, but I miss the give and take that goes on among the crew in the office. It's kind of lonely out here in the field."

Satisfaction of **security needs** is possible because of the emotional support provided by group membership. Particularly when a person is establishing himself or herself in the world of work, the group offers a source of help. It is more comfortable for some people to consult peers rather than a boss about minor work-related problems.

Esteem needs can be satisfied in at least two important ways by group membership. First, your work group often provides positive feedback when you do something right. The player who hits a home run receives a good deal of congratulatory pats on his (or *her* in some leagues) back (or backside) immediately after the acomplishment. When a new-car salesperson chalks up a banner month, he or she might be named "salesperson of the month" by the dealership. Such recognition satisfies a need for recognition, but it also adds to a person's worth in the eyes of others—a major source of esteem.

Improving your skills and knowledge leads toward **self-fulfillment.** Work groups add to a person's professional or technical development by providing the person with a chance to communicate about job-related skills. If you are a photographer who works with a group of photographers, you can converse with these people about new developments in your field. This is not as feasible when you are the only photographer in your department. Need satisfaction enters the picture, because you improve your skills.

Reduction of Tension

Working in a group can sometimes be of benefit to your mental health. The emotional support provided by the group helps you to control tension.[6] It is common practice in work groups for members to share problems (both personal and job related) with each other. When faced with a major problem, having a sympathetic listener often reduces tension. The advice offered by a co-worker might lead to a solution to your problem, further reducing your tension. One woman was becoming increasingly tense about funding her child's education. A co-worker suggested that she apply for a long-term tuition loan offered by a local bank. The troubled woman was able to secure such a loan and her tension level was reduced.

Increased Job Satisfaction

Considerable evidence exists that you are likely to experience a higher level of job satisfaction if you work with a group rather than by yourself. When the opportunity for interaction with other workers decreases, job satisfaction suffers. Many people seem to experience their peak moments of job-related pleasure when in conference with others or in coffee breaks. A counselor from an employment agency made the following comment about secretarial help's preference for working in groups:

> The most difficult slot for us to fill is a secretary–receptionist for a one-person office. Some women think that they would like to work alone by themselves, but they usually find that it doesn't work. One lawyer who was in practice for himself had three women quit in one year. He spent most of his time out of the office. His secretary would be by herself with very little to do. We finally found that lawyer the right person. She is an older woman who basically doesn't like people.

PROBLEMS THAT GROUPS SOMETIMES CREATE FOR YOU

Work groups sometimes create problems for management. The demands that they make for wages and benefits may be more than management can afford. A work group that is hostile toward management may sometimes make a deliberate effort to hold back production. Groups can similarly create problems for the individual who is more concerned with long-range success than acceptance by the group. If you are aware of these potential disadvantages, you may be able to circumvent them. Four potential problems of group membership will be dealt with here: pressures toward conformity, pressures toward mediocre performance, shirking of individual responsibility, and the breeding of conflict. Other problems associated with group effort will be described later in reference to group decision making.

Pressures toward Conformity

A major problem that you face as a group member is that pressure will be placed on you to act in the same manner as the other members of your group. Harmless types of conformity include such things as adhering to a dress code or joining the other members of your work group for an after-work drink on Friday. In some situations, conformity can be detrimental. For instance, one design engineer in a group of five may believe that a car-braking mechanism is unsafe. After learning that his co-workers think that the braking mechanism is safe, he may say to himself, "If the other members of the group disagree with me, I'm probably wrong. Why be an odd ball? I'll call the mechanism safe."

These comments should not be interpreted to mean that conformity is either harmless or detrimental. In many situations, conformity can be beneficial to the group and its members. When all the fork-lift operators in a factory agree to drive no faster than five miles per hour, the net result is a safer work atmosphere. When patients, visitors, and staff members conform to the No Smoking signs surrounding oxygen tents, explosions are avoided.

Another type of conformity that does create problems for you, concerns group pressure to lower your job performance.

Pressures toward
Mediocre Performance

A potential hazard of being well accepted by your work group and identifying with its members is that your performance (and therefore your career) may be held back in the process. To the extent that you try to remain "one of the gang," you will not be able to distinguish yourself from others in a favorable manner. Your allegiance to the group may make it difficult for you to advance into management or to perform your job in a superior manner. Groups sometimes foster mediocre performance, as Nancy's case history illustrates:

> Nancy took the best job she could find for the summer, a chambermaid position at a resort hotel. As she perceived the situation, the pay was good, the hours

OKAY, THAT'S IT FOR TODAY . . . AT LEAST WE FINALLY AGREED ON THE SHAPE OF THE TABLE.

Groups can sometimes foster mediocre performance.

delightful, and the beach superb. However, Nancy was subject to some uncomfortable group pressures. She explains what happened: "I felt some kind of obligation to do my best for the hotel owners. They were treating me fine and I wanted to reciprocate. I charged into my jobs, literally singing as I went about my chores. Within a week I found that the other chambermaids were almost forcing me to take a coffee or cigarette break with them. They told me I was cleaning too many rooms an hour. They wanted me to slow down so they wouldn't look bad. My decision was to tell them to do what they wanted and I would do what I wanted. My decision was the right one. I was invited back the next year as a supervising chambermaid.

Shirking of Individual Responsibility

If you are not strongly work oriented, group assignments can be an invitation to shirk responsibility. Unless assignments are given out carefully to each member of the group, an undermotivated person can often squeeze by without contributing his or her fair share. The responsibility shirker risks being ostracized by the group, but may be willing to pay the price rather than work hard. Shirking the individual responsibility is commonly found in groups such as committees and project teams. For example, when the committee head asks for volunteers to serve on a subcommittee, some people turn their head or look down at the conference table.

Breeding of Conflict

At their worst, groups foster conflict on the job. People within the work group often bicker with each other about matters such as doing a fair share of the undesirable tasks within the department. They also argue about who is dominating the boss's time. Your co-workers may accuse you of playing politics when you go out of your way to please the boss.

Conflict often takes place between groups as well as within the work group. Such intergroup conflict occurs when group members develop the attitude that their work group is more important than the organization as a whole. Rivalries develop, and "beating the opposition" becomes more important than trying to reach goals important to the organization. It is folly to try to outwit the opposition, rather than solving bigger problems. This observation is illustrated by the comments of a manager of an in-plant printing department to one of his supervisors:

> We're being taken advantage of by management. The next time somebody busts into our department demanding a rush job, give him the runaround. Tell him we've got too many rush orders or that we're experiencing machine failure. If that doesn't work, tell him he has to go through me to order printing. If we don't shake them up a little bit, they're going to continue to treat us like servants.

GROUP DECISION MAKING AND PROBLEM SOLVING

Most big decisions in organizations are made by groups rather than individuals. Even if a group of people does not sit together to thrash out a decision, several people provide their input to any major decision. In general, decision making by groups has proved superior to individual decision making.[7] Yet this generalization is not overwhelmingly true. Many talented and imaginative individuals do not require group discussion to make an effective decision.

Group decision making should proceed through the same stages as individual decision making (as described in Chapter 7). In sequence, the group (1) clarifies the problem, (2) searches for creative alternatives, (3) weighs the alternatives, (4) chooses an alternative and implements it, and (5) evaluates the outcome of the decision.

Different Types of Group Decision Making. The term "group decision making" refers to the fact that the group plays a role in making the decision. The opposite would be individual decision making in which the group leader makes a decision without consulting anybody. Group decision making itself takes place in different degrees. One extreme is **consultative** in which the group leader consults with members before making a decision. The other extreme is **democratic** decision making in which the problem at hand is turned over to the group, and they are delegated the authority to arrive at a decision themselves. Midway between the two is **consensus** decision making in which the manager shares the problem with the subordinates as a group. Together they generate and evaluate alternatives and attempt to reach agreement on a solution.[8]

Advantages of Group Decision Making

Groups often fare better than individuals in decision making for several logical reasons.[9] First, a greater variety of alternatives and solutions is considered. "Too many cooks may spoil the broth," but making a broth is a small decision. Assume that the company that you work for is forced to relocate because your present building is to be demolished. You would want to examine a wide variety of possibilities. If several knowledgeable people were brought into the decision-making process, you would uncover a number of worthwhile possibilities.

Second, group decision making is helpful in gaining acceptance and commitment. If you and your friends were planning a vacation together, you would probably have less bickering after the decision were made if it were a joint decision. If one person arbitrarily chose a lakeside cottage, the other members of the group would probably complain heatedly about the mosquitoes. If you all agreed to the lakeside, the mosquitoes would probably be less bothersome. People tend to accept a decision when they have contributed to its making.

Potential Problems
with Group Decisions

Group decisions are often superior to individual decisions. However, they also take much longer and sometimes lead to a compromise decision that is of little value. In deciding where to relocate an office, one faction might endorse a move to an industrial park in the suburbs. Another faction might urge that the company stay downtown. A compromise decision might be to stay on the edge of town, which would be a poor decision in terms of attracting clerical personnel. Two major problems with group decision making are individual dominance and groupthink.[10]

OBVIOUSLY ANOTHER INSPIRED DECISION, MR. BULLSEY.

The "big boss" often dominates the group because people are hesitant to criticize him or her.

Individual dominance means simply that one individual dominates the group, thus negating the potential benefits of input from all the members. Dominance by one member tends to take place more frequently when people in the group are of unequal rank. The "big boss" often dominates the group because people are hesitant to criticize him or her. David Hampton suggests that if you are the head of a group, or a high-status participant, you should do four things to circumvent the problem of individual dominance.[11]

- Refrain from announcing your preferred solution while the group is working through the problem.
- Listen carefully to suggestions from every group member.
- Encourage every group member to participate.
- Demonstrate concern for achieving a high-quality solution.

Groupthink takes place when members of the group try too hard to stick together (be cohesive). It is an extreme form of consensus. The group thinks as a unit rather than as a collection of individuals. They become so clubby that they lose their individual powers of critical analysis. A group of executives deciding to let a product known to have serious defects out to the public is an example of groupthink. So is a group of workers deciding to sabotage an assembly line.

Groupthink was first formally observed in government by Irving Janis, who was studying group decision making in the John F. Kennedy cabinet.[12] In more recent history, the stealing of Jimmy Carter's campaign papers by a small group working for Ronald Reagan appears to have been a product of groupthink. One dissenting voice from any of these staff members and they would not have proceeded to steal documents from their Democratic opponent.

If you are a group leader you should take the following steps to guard against the potential dangers of groupthink:[13]

- Encourage all members of the group to express doubts and criticisms of proposed solutions to the problem.
- Show by example that you are willing to accept criticism.
- Divide the group into subgroups to develop ideas. Then have the subgroups confront one another to examine why they differ.
- Periodically invite qualified outsiders to meet with the group and provide suggestions.
- If groupthink seems to be emerging, bring it to the attention of the group. For instance, you might say, "I get the impression we are too eager to think as one. What is your reaction to this problem?"

GROUP BRAINSTORMING

One of the best methods of understanding how a group can contribute to problem solving is to observe group brainstorming. This method has become a standard way of generating multiple alternatives for solving a problem. The term **brainstorm** has become synonymous with a clever idea. It really means to "storm the brain" in order to search for alternatives. Brainstorming is best suited to finding lists of alternatives to problems. Later, the technical details of how to achieve and implement these alternatives can be worked out. Brainstorming was developed for use in creating advertising campaigns.[14] It is now put to such diverse uses as thinking of new products, making recommendations for new employee benefits, finding ways of raising money for a cause, and searching for new ways to lay out the work groups in a government agency. Brainstorming is not well suited to arriving at complex solutions to problems or working out the details of a plan (for example, how to arrange the equipment in an office). To conduct an effective brainstorming session, keep in mind these straightforward rules:

1. Group size should be about five to seven people. Too few people and not enough suggestions are generated. If too many people participate, the session becomes uncontrolled.
2. No criticism allowed. All suggestions should be welcome, and it is particularly important not to use derisive laughter. As the old saying goes, "They laughed at Thomas Edison."

3. Freewheeling is encouraged. "The more outlandish the idea the better. It's always easier to tame down an idea than to think it up."[15]

4. Quantity and variety are very important. The greater the number of ideas put forth, the greater the likelihood of a breakthrough idea.

5. Combinations and improvements are encouraged. Building on the ideas of others, including combining them, is very productive. "Hitchhiking" is an essential part of brainstorming.

6. Notes must be taken during the sessions either manually or with an electronic recording device. One person serves as a "recording secretary."

7. The alternatives generated during the first part of the session should later be edited for duplication and refinement. At some point the best ideas can be set aside for possible implementation.

8. Do not overstructure by following any of the preceding seven rules too rigidly. Brainstorming is a spontaneous small-group process.

Many people will have the opportunity to use brainstorming either on the job or in personal life. Our attention turns next to a small-group activity that virtually every reader of this book will experience.

HOW TO CONDUCT YOURSELF IN A MEETING

A substantial portion of work life takes place in meetings, particularly if you are a manager. Nonmanagers, too, are frequently asked to attend many meetings, including staff meetings, committee meetings, quality circles, and project teams. It is fashionable to put down meetings with such statements as "Ugh, not another meeting!" or "I wish I didn't have to attend today's meeting. I'd much prefer to work." Along the same lines, the effectiveness of committees is often questioned with comments such as "The main purpose of a committee is to avoid action," or "If committees were popular in Abraham Lincoln's time, the Gettysburg Address would never have been written."

Despite these criticisms, collective effort would be very difficult without formal meetings. A constructive viewpoint about meetings is not to try to avoid them, but to learn how to be an effective contributor to them. The task at hand could possibly serve some worthwhile purpose. Also of significance, meetings represent an exceptional opportunity to be observed by important people in your firm. If you observe the guidelines presented in the following paragraphs, you will most likely perform well in meetings.

Be qualified to serve. People perform the best in meetings when they have the necessary background of knowledge and interest to do a good job. If you know the topic of the meeting in advance, do your homework. Carefully read some relevant information about the topic and/or speak to some knowledgeable people. In this way you will be prepared to make intelligent comments and suggestions during the meeting.

Be punctual and stay to the end. Arriving late at a meeting is taboo unless you are a high-ranking executive who has called the meeting. Leaving early creates an equally negative impression. Why irritate the influential people who might be present at the meeting?

Take notes on key points during the meeting. By so doing you will be able to refer back to useful ideas when you want to formulate a suggestion of your own. The notes can also be used when you are studying the problem at a later point in time. Your taking notes will also serve to impress the meeting chairperson.

Do not dominate or contribute too little. An effective attendee at a meeting participates neither too much nor too little. The dominator quickly irritates others and tends to subvert a major purpose of the meeting—gathering ideas from several people. The person who contributes too little may be perceived as uninterested in the meeting or as too shy to become a leader.

Stick with the agenda. Other people present at the meeting, including the leader, will become annoyed if you digress to irrelevant topics. If somebody else is going off on a tangent, perhaps you can salvage the situation by asking "Excuse me, but how do your comments relate to the agenda?"

Ask intelligent questions. If you do not have relevant ideas to contribute to the meeting, you can at least ask intelligent questions. The ability to ask intelligent questions is characteristic of competent people in all fields. An example of a multipurpose "intelligent question" to ask at most meeting is, "If we follow your suggestion, what would be the impact on other departments in our organization?"

Focus your attention on surmountable problems. Many problem-solving groups make the mistake of spending time discussing "who is to blame for the problem" or "what should have been done to avoid the problem."[16] Rather than try to change the past—an impossible task—it is better for you to focus on how things can be improved in the future.

Avoid getting emotional about the first alternative proposed. Recent experiments suggest that the expression of feeling and emotion about problems should be delayed until after alternatives to the problem have been generated.[17] If group members get too excited about the first alternative that arises, it may shut out serious consideration of later alternatives. So avoid displaying too much enthusiasm or disdain until the problem at hand has been fully explored.

Display good company manners. Your manners, good, bad, or mediocre, are always on display in a meeting. It is therefore important to display good manners, such as being polite and encouraging others. Bad manners frequently displayed in meetings include dozing, blowing cigarette smoke, and eating food during the meeting when it is not formally sanctioned.

Follow through to see if your recommendations are taken seriously. Meetings represent a good opportunity to see how well your ideas are seen as valuable by the organization. One way to see if your ideas are useful is to check back with the meeting chairperson at a later date. In a nonconfrontational manner, you might ask a question of this type, "By the way, what was the upshot of our meeting? I recall suggesting that we bolt down the personal computers for security purposes. Did management find that to be a feasible idea?" Through such follow up, you can develop a sensitivity to the type of solutions the organization will accept.

SUMMARY OF KEY POINTS

☐ A group is a collection of people who interact with each other, are aware of each other, are working toward some common purpose, and perceive themselves to be a group. Groups are the building blocks of the larger organization. A formal group is one deliberately formed by the organization to accomplish specific tasks and achieve objectives. An informal group is one that evolves naturally in an organization to take care of people's desires for friendship and companionship.

☐ Benefits to the individual from belonging to a group include (1) assistance in solving problems, (2) economic power, (3) a feeling of safety, (4) satisfaction of psychological needs, (5) reduction of tension, and (6) increased job satisfaction.

☐ A group can hinder your work performance and/or career in several ways. You might (1) become a conformist in thought and action, (2) be pressured into mediocre performance, (3) shirk your responsibilities, and (4) become heavily involved in conflict.

☐ Group decision making should follow the process recommended for making major individual decisions. Group input into decisions varies from merely being consulted to having full authority for making the decision. Group decision making has two important advantages: (1) a greater variety of alternative solutions are considered, and (2) the chances are improved that the decision will be accepted and that people will feel committed to it. One potential problem with group decisions is that one person within the group, such as a high-ranking individual, may dominate the process. Another problem is that groupthink, an extreme form of consensus, may take place.

☐ Group brainstorming is an easy-to-follow method by which a group arrives at a wide range of potential solutions to a problem. Each group member basically contributes as many ideas as his or her imagination will allow. After awhile the ideas are sorted out and refined.

☐ If you advance in your career, it is almost inevitable that you will be required to attend meetings. A number of suggestions for performing well in them are offered in this chapter. Among the major suggestions are these: (1) be qualified to serve; (2) do not dominate or contribute too little; (3) stick with the agenda; (4) ask intelligent questions; and (5) display good company manners.

GUIDELINES FOR PERSONAL EFFECTIVENESS

1. From the standpoint of your long-term career growth, be willing to loosen your ties with your present or future work group. Identifying too closely with a work group narrows your perspective and may lead to overconformity on your part.
2. Group decision making is an important contribution to improving the quality of decisions. However, it is time consuming and is best reserved for major decisions.
3. When faced with an important problem for which an out-of-the-ordinary solution is required, it could be to your advantage to utilize group brainstorming. As with other skills, brainstorming requires practice to perfect.
4. An important skill for advancing your career is to handle yourself well in meetings. They are a good vehicle for making suggestions to the organization. In addition, many judgments are made about you on the basis of your actions in meetings. To improve your skills as a participant in a meeting, follow the suggestions presented in the chapter.

DISCUSSION QUESTIONS

1. Is a family a group? Why or why not?
2. What behaviors (actions or activities) might you engage in in a group that you would not do acting alone?
3. What informal groups have you observed in a school setting? What are their purposes?
4. Is the class for which you are reading this book a formal or an informal group? Explain.

5. What benefits do people seem to derive from belonging to a church, temple, or mosque?

6. To what extent do the law-making bodies in the United States and Canada rely on group decision making?

7. In what way is groupthink a waste of money and time when it is practiced by employees?

8. Have you ever belonged to a committee that produced a worthwhile result? What did it do right?

9. Have you ever belonged to a committee that produced poor results? What did it do wrong?

10. If you were getting restless and bored at a meeting, would you get up and stretch? Why or why not?

A Business Psychology Problem
THE UNSTOPPABLE COFFEE GANG[18]

Jim Lyons, the newly appointed manager of operations at Gulf Coast Insurance Company, confided to Wendy McPherson, his executive secretary, "We're going to see a lot of changes around here. Last year the company just about broke even. I don't see any need to lay off people, but I do see a need for us to become more efficient."

"What irks me the most is the time being wasted in the office while people sit around in coffee klatches. Around ten in the morning, the place is deserted. About 90 percent of the staff is down in the cafeteria whiling away time, drinking coffee. We could get by on less staff if we could cut down on those coffee breaks. We could lose about 5 percent of our office staff due to attrition and not have to replace them if we could stop the time leak created by the coffee break."

Jim's first management action to curtail the coffee break was to prepare an edict that from now on no coffee breaks would be allowed in the cafeteria. Instead, coffee- and tea-vending machines would be installed at two key locations in the office building. Any employee who wanted coffee or tea could purchase a beverage in the machine and take it back to his or her work station.

One month later the vending machines were installed and the cafeteria was declared off limits to employees except during their lunch break. Shortly thereafter, Jim received a phone call from Mickey, the head of maintenance.

"Mr. Lyons," said Mickey excitedly, "I think we have a major fire hazard on our hands. Since you ended the cafeteria coffee break and installed the vending machines, the employees have found a new way to serve coffee. All of a sudden we have a collection of hot water heaters, Silexes, and those new coffee makers around the office. I first got on to it when one of them shorted and blew a fuse. I understand that the vending machine is losing money. That's what the route man told me."

"Mickey, I appreciate your having brought this problem to my attention," replied Jim, "I'll get on it right away."

The next day Jim Lyons had a memo affixed to every bulletin board and sent to every supervisor. It read in part, "From now on, no unauthorized coffee- or tea-making equipment will be brought into this office. Any employee caught using unauthorized coffee-making equipment will be subject to suspension."

Two weeks later, Jim asked Mickey to make a secretive night inspection of the office. His task was to discover if any coffee pots were still being used in the office. Mickey's investigation turned up no such evidence. Jim also phoned a few supervisors to see if the edict was receiving full compliance. Again, the report was positive. Jim thought to himself that the coffee klatch problem had finally been resolved. Three weeks late, Jody, the personnel manager, came forth with a disconcerting comment:

"Jim, I thought your edict might have been a little heavy handed. And I told you so. I now have evidence that your removal of the coffee pots has created a new problem."

"What's that? I haven't heard of any problems," said Jim.

"Perhaps, then, you haven't been making recent tours of the office at any time from nine to eleven in the morning. You can find little pockets of people drinking coffee in the strangest of places. We found five women from underwriting sitting on the steps of a fire exit. Three fellows and two gals from the claims department were found gathered around the photocopying machine drinking coffee. Worst of all, five people were sitting under a tree on the front lawn with paper cups in their hands. That's hardly what you had in mind with your no coffee pot edict."

"Jody, let me think about this problem for a while longer," mused Jim. Three days later, he sent out a new memo:

"Because of disappointment with certain aspects of the service, the coffee-vending machine will be removed from the building. Therefore, all employees who so desire are allowed a fifteen-minute break per morning to have coffee or other beverage in the cafeteria. Please make sure that this fifteen-minute limit is not exceeded."

1. Why didn't Jim Lyon's plan to stop the time spent on coffee breaks work?
2. How sound was Jim's decision to reinstate the cafeteria coffee break?
3. What does this case tell us about informal groups?
4. What does this case tell us about Jim's managerial skills?
5. What influence did Jim's action have on office morale?

A Business Psychology Exercise
GROUP BRAINSTORMING

Divide the class into groups of about seven people. Each group will then brainstorm one of the following problems, using the guidelines for brainstorming presented in the chapter. If preferred, the groups can substitute a general problem of their own instead of one of those suggested here. Be careful to choose a generic problem, one that does not require a specific background to handle well.

1. How might we effectively utilize the senior citizens in our community?
2. How can we earn extra money, aside from holding a regular job?
3. How do you find new people to date?
4. What can we do individually to become famous?

REFERENCES

[1] Composite definition from two sources: Edgar H. Schein, *Organizational Psychology*, 3rd ed. (Englewood Cliffs, N.J.: Prentice-Hall, 1980), p. 145; W. Clay Hamner and Dennis W. Organ, *Organizational Behavior: An Applied Psychological Approach* (Plano, Texas: Business Publications, 1978), p. 303.

[2] H. Kent Baker, "Tapping into the Power of Informal Groups," *Supervisory Management* (Feb. 1981), p. 18.

[3] James L. Gibson, John M. Ivancevich, and James H. Donnelly, Jr., *Organizations: Behavior, Structure, Processes*, 4th ed. (Plano, Texas: Business Publications, 1982), p. 184.

[4] Ibid., p. 183.

[5] Karen Beadling, "The Office Gang," *Upstate*, Rochester *Democrat and Chronicle* (Dec. 11, 1983), pp. 34–35.

[6] A classic study documenting this observation is Stanley E. Seashore, *Group Cohesiveness in the Industrial Work Group* (Ann Arbor, Mich.: Survey Research Center, University of Michigan, 1954).

[7] Stephen P. Robbins, *Organizational Behavior: Concepts, Controversies, and Applications*, 2nd ed. (Englewood Cliffs, N.J.: Prentice-Hall, 1983), p. 242.

[8] A description of the various styles of group decision making is found in Victor H. Vroom, "A New Look in Managerial Decision Making," *Organizational Dynamics* (Spring 1973), pp. 66–80. For a technical review of the phases of group problem solving, see John A. Seeger, "No Innate Phases in Group Problem Solving," *Academy of Management Review* (Oct. 1983), pp. 683–689.

[9] William F. Glueck, *Management* (Hinsdale, Ill.: Dryden Press, 1977), p. 397.

[10] David R. Hampton, *Contemporary Management* (New York: McGraw-Hill, 1977), p. 397.

[11]Ibid., p. 104.

[12]Irving L. Janis, *Victims of Groupthink* (Boston: Houghton Mifflin, 1972).

[13]Hampton, *Contemporary Management*, pp. 184–185.

[14]Osburn's ideas were first published in 1941. The key reference on the topic is Alex F. Osburn, *Applied Imagination* (New York: Scribner's, 1963).

[15]Jack Halloran, *Applied Human Relations: An Organizational Approach* (Englewood Cliffs, N.J.: Prentice-Hall, 1978), p. 214.

[16]Gary Dessler, *Human Behavior: Improving Performance at Work* (Reston, Va.: Reston Publishing, 1980), p. 277.

[17]Richard A. Guzzo and James A. Waters, "The Expression of Affect and the Performance of Decision-Making Groups," *Journal of Applied Psychology* (Feb. 1982), pp. 67–74.

[18]Reprinted from Andrew J. DuBrin, *Human Relations: A Job Oriented Approach*, 3rd ed. (Reston, Va.: Reston Publishing, 1984), pp. 214–215.

SUGGESTED READING

BRADFORD, LELAND. *Making Meetings Work: A Guide for Leaders and Group Members.* La Jolla, Calif.: University Associates, 1981.

HARE, PAUL A. *Creativity in Small Groups.* Beverly Hills, Calif.: Sage Publications, 1982.

JEWELL, LINDA N., and H. JOSEPH REITZ. *Group Effectiveness in Organizations.* Glenview, Ill.: Scott Foresman, 1981.

KERZNER, HAROLD, and HAS THAMKAIN. *Project Management for Small and Medium Sized Businesses.* New York: Van Nostrand Reinhold, 1983.

NICHOLS, MARY LIPPETT, and VICTORIA E. DAY. "A Comparison of Moral Reasoning of Groups and Individuals on the 'Defining Issues Test.' " *Academy of Management Journal* (March 1982), pp. 201–208.

PALMER, BARBARA C., and KENNETH PALMER. *The Successful Meeting Master Guide for Business and Professional People.* Englewood Cliffs, N. J.: Prentice-Hall, 1982.

PAULUS, PAUL B. ed. *Basic Group Processes.* New York: Springer-Verlag, 1983.

SENGER, JOHN. *Individuals, Groups, and the Organization.* Cambridge, Mass.: Winthrop Publishers, 1980.

SHAW, MARVIN E. *Group Dynamics: The Psychology of Small Group Behavior*, 3rd ed. New York: McGraw-Hill, 1981.

THOMPSON, PHILIP C. *Quality Circles: How to Make Them Work in America.* New York: AMACOM, 1982.

ZANDER, ALVIN. *Making Groups Effective.* San Francisco: Jossey-Bass, 1982.

14

LEADING AND INFLUENCING OTHERS

LEARNING OBJECTIVES

After reading and studying this chapter and doing the exercises, you should be able to

1. Understand the meaning of leadership and power.
2. Be aware of some of the potential satisfactions and frustrations in being a leader.
3. Identify about six characteristics and behaviors of effective leaders.
4. Describe three key leadership styles and explain how the situation influences which style is best.
5. Outline a tentative plan for developing your leadership potential.

WHAT IS LEADERSHIP?

Leadership involves influencing other people to achieve certain objectives. The key word in understanding the concept of leadership is influence. If influence is not exerted, leadership, strictly speaking, has not been performed. A night manager of a hotel might work her designated five nights per week and perform her tasks in a highly satisfactory manner. Guests, employees, and the hotel owner are all kept happy. Her boss checks with her from time to time to see how things are going, but he has very little contact with her.

She performs well without the benefit of a person who influences her performance. She therefore does not require leadership.

Since influencing others is such a complex art (as described in Chapter 12), leadership is a broad topic. Our study of leadership will concentrate on such important considerations as the nature of leadership and leadership positions, the use of power to influence people, different styles of leadership, and developing your leadership potential.

Leadership, Management, and Supervision

Unfortunately for the student of business psychology, and similar subjects, these key terms have different connotations and meanings. Not every manager or scholar has the same thought in mind when he or she is talking about the concepts of leadership, management, and supervision. For the purpose of this book, the following distinctions are drawn:

Leadership is the process of influencing the activities of an individual or a group in efforts toward reaching a goal in a given situation.[1] However, unduly coercive influence tactics such as gun threats are not part of leadership. You can exert leadership whether or not you have the official job title of "manager" or "supervisor."

Management is working with and through individuals and groups to accomplish organizational goals. It involves the coordination of human and material resources toward objective accomplishment. **Supervision** is essentially first-level management. It involves overseeing the work of others with a particular emphasis on leadership.

The concepts of leadership, management, and supervision are thus not identical. Management or supervision involves a wide variety of activities, such as planning, controlling, organizing, scheduling, and directing (synonymous with leading). Many people are effective with the administrative aspects of a supervisory or managerial job, but few people are effective leaders.

Formal versus Informal Leadership

A useful distinction in understanding leadership is that between a formal and informal leader. Assume that you and a few of your friends enjoy flying kites. Because of your expertise in kite flying, good sense of organizing activities, and outgoing personality, your friends come to regard you as the leader of the group. You would then be functioning as an informal leader. Finally, you organize a formal group called the Kite Flying Club. Your friends then appoint you as the club president. Automatically, you have become a formal leader.

In your situation you have both the informal, or personal, qualifications and the formal authority to be the kite club president. The most effective leaders are those who have both strong personal qualifications for the job and sufficient authority delegated by the organization. In some instances a person is given the formal title of leader (such as vice-president of finance), yet few people are influenced by that person. The reason: he or she lacks the personal talents to carry out the responsibilities of the position.

Later in the chapter we will discuss how the various subtypes of formal and informal power are used to influence others.

IS A LEADERSHIP POSITION FOR YOU?

The term leader has a positive connotation to most people. To be called a leader is generally better than to be called a follower. Yet being a formal leader (such as a supervisor, manager, or director) does not always bring personal satisfaction to the individual. Some leadership jobs are more fun than others. The captain of a first-place team has more fun than the captain of a winless team. The owner of a large, successful restaurant has more fun than the owner of a frankfurter stand that is losing money.

You may not know at this stage of your life whether you want to become (or remain) a formal leader. However, it should prove worthwhile for you to examine some of the potential satisfactions and frustrations many people find in being a leader within an organization.

Satisfactions of Leaders

The type of satisfactions that you might receive from being a formal leader depend on your particular leadership position. Factors such as the amount of money that you are paid and the type of people in your group influence your satisfaction. Following are seven sources of satisfaction that many leaders often experience.

A feeling of power and prestige. Being a leader automatically grants you some power. Prestige is forthcoming because many (not all) people think highly of people who are leaders. As an extreme example, some people will address you as formally as Mister or Miss as soon as they learn that you are a manager or supervisor.

A chance to help others. A leader works directly with people, often teaching them job skills and listening to their personal problems. Part of a supervisor's job is to help other people become supervisors. A leader often feels as much of a "people helper" as does a human resources manager or a social worker.

Being a leader automatically grants you some power.

High income. Leaders, in general, get paid more than their subordinates. Thus, if money is important to you, being a leader has built-in satisfaction. The difference in income between leaders and nonleaders is sometimes quite small, a possible source of frustration. Leaders, however, have good potential for higher income. Some top-level business executives earn more money than leading professional athletes or movie stars. In 1985, the average income of company presidents, all size companies included, was approximately $110,000 per year.

Respect and status. Quite similar to prestige, a leader often receives respect from followers. He or she also enjoys a higher status than people who are not in a leadership role. There is a certain status in being elected an official in your club or selected as the supervisor of your work group. When you have the personal qualifications to match your position, your status will be even higher.

Good opportunities for advancement. Once you become a leader, your opportunities for advancement increase. If you are interested in moving up the ladder, obtaining a leadership position is a vital first step. One young man became an assistant manager of a Radio Shack retail store at age 20. By age 25, he was a regional manager earning a higher income than many department heads in large companies.

A feeling of "being in" on things. A side benefit of being a leader is that you receive more inside information than does a follower. For instance, as a first-line supervisor you are eligible to attend supervisory meetings. In those meetings you might be given information that is not to be passed along to nonsupervisory employees. One such tidbit might be plans for expansion of the company or agency.

A chance to control money. A leader is often in the position of helping to prepare a department budget. Even though you cannot spend this money personally, it does provide some satisfaction in knowing that your judgment is being trusted about financial matters. A first-line supervisor sometimes controls an annual budget of over $1,000,000.

Frustrations of Leaders

About one in ten people in the work force is classified as a supervisor or manager. Not every manager or supervisor is a true leader. Yet the problems experienced by these people often stem from the leadership portions of their job. Many people refuse to accept a leadership role because of the many frustrations that they have seen leaders endure. The frustrations experienced by a wide range of people in leadership roles center around the following problems.

Too much casual overtime. People in leadership jobs are quite often expected to spend more hours working than other employees. Since these are unpaid hours, they are referred to as casual overtime. If you own your own business, it would not be unusual for you to work 60, 70, or 80 hours per week. People often give up their own business because of its time demands.

Too many "headaches." It would take several pages to list all the potential problems you face as a leader. Being a leader is one good way to discover the validity of Murphy's law: "If anything can go wrong, it will." A leader is subject to a batch of problems involving people and things. In short, many people find a leadership role to be a source of stress; and many managers experience burnout.

Not enough authority to carry out your responsibility. People in managerial positions repeatedly complain that they are held responsible for things over which they have little control. As a leader you will often be expected to work with a subordinate who you think should be fired, but you lack the power to carry out such an action. Or you will be expected to produce top-quality goods with an antiquated machine. Yet you lack the authority to replace that machine.

Loneliness. The higher you rise as a leader, the more lonely you will be in a certain sense. Leadership limits the number of people that you can confide in. It is awkward to confide in a subordinate the fact that you think your employer is ineffective. It is equally awkward to complain about one subordinate to another. Some leaders feel lonely because they miss being "one of the gang."

Too many personnel problems. A major frustration facing a leader is the number of personnel problems requiring action. The lower your leadership position, the more such problems you face. For instance, the office supervisor spends more time dealing with problem employees than does the vice-president of information systems.

Too much paper work. As work organizations have become more automated and more formal, an abundance of forms has been generated. A common complaint of managers at all levels is that paper work takes up too much of their time. Government regulations over matters such as employee health and safety are another source of substantial paper work for supervisors and other managers.

Too much politics. People at all levels of an organization, from the office messenger to the president, must be aware of office politics. Yet if you dislike politics, it is easier to avoid as an individual worker than as a leader. As a leader you have to engage in politics from three directions: below, sideways, and upward.

HOW LEADERS USE POWER TO INFLUENCE OTHERS

Leaders influence others to do things through the use of *power*—the ability to get others to do things and to influence decisions.[2] When power stems from the formal position you occupy, it is referred to as **position power**. When it stems from your personal characteristics and skills, it is referred to as **personal power**. Here we will examine subtypes of power in detail and point out some guidelines for their proper use. The message for your career is that, if you want to be an effective leader, you must be able to use power in an intelligent and sensitive manner.

Position Power

Position power has three subtypes: legitimate power, reward power, and coercive power.[3]

Legitimate power is the legitimate right of the leader to make certain types of requests. It is the easiest type to understand and accept. People at higher levels in an organization have more power than people below them. However, the culture of an organization helps decide the limits to anybody's power. The supervisor in a Lansing, Michigan, auto assembly plant who tells one of her workers not to purchase a Japanese car may find her orders ignored. Gary Yukl and Tom Taber advise us that, although employees generally accept their boss's right to make requests, they do not like to be given orders in a way that implies they are not as good as the leader. Effective leaders therefore exercise authority by making polite requests rather than arrogant demands.[4]

Reward power refers to the leader's control over rewards valued by the subordinate. For example, if a sales manager can directly reward his or her sales representatives with cash bonuses for good performance, that manager will exert considerable power. Effective leaders do not use rewards as bribes for getting employees to do what they want. Instead, rewards are used to reinforce desirable behavior after it has already taken place.

Coercive power refers to the leader's control over punishments. It is based on fear and thus may create anxiety and defensiveness (as described in Chapter 5). Yukl and Taber note that effective leaders generally avoid the use of coercive power except when absolutely necessary because coercion is likely to create resentment and undermine their personal power. Yet if skillfully used, coercion can get some people to comply with rules, regulations, and orders. One important consideration in using punishment is to find out whether the subordinate is really at fault. If the punishment is justified, it should be imposed promptly and consistently without showing favoritism. For all but the most serious of infractions (such as stealing or fighting), warnings should be given before punishments are actually used. Finally, if punishment must be used, "the magnitude of the punishment should fit the seriousness of the infraction."[5]

Despite the potential value of coercive power, the balance of evidence indicates that rewards are more effective than punishment in influencing employees.[6]

Personal Power

Personal power has two subtypes: expert power and referent power (also referred to as *charisma* or personal charm).

Expert power is the leader's knowledge relevant to the job at hand, as perceived by subordinates. You can also exercise expert power when you do not have a formal leadership position. A relevant example is the engineering technician who is talented at getting industrial robots to work properly. The company becomes dependent on that individual, giving him or her some power with respect to receiving special privileges. To accumulate expert power, a leader should cultivate an image of experience and competence. Credibility must be preserved by avoiding careless statements and rash decisions. It is also important to remain cool. As observed by Yukl and Taber, a leader who appears confused, vacillates, or is obviously panicked will quickly lose expert power.[7]

Referent power refers to loyalty to the leader and the subordinates' desire to please that person. *Charisma* enters the picture because some of the loyalty to the leader is based on an identification with the leader's personality traits and personal characteristics. Two public leaders *perceived* as charismatic by many people were John F. Kennedy and Martin Luther King, Jr. We use the term perceived, because charisma is based on a subjective reaction to the leader's personal characteristics. Despite their general popularity, one could find many people who disliked either Kennedy or King (or both leaders).

Referent power, like expert power, will vary with the amount of favorable interactions between you and your subordinates. Referent power can be increased by being considerate to subordinates, treating them fairly, and defending their interests to higher management. On the other hand a leader can lose referent power quickly if he or she expresses hostility, distrust, and suspicion, rejects employees, or is indifferent toward them. Not defending subordinates' interest to outsiders also erodes referent power. A recommended way of using referent power is to make a personal appeal that evokes subordinate feelings of loyalty, such as "It is very important to me that we raise the productivity of our department."

Although both position power and personal power are important, effective leaders tend to rely more heavily on personal power to influence others.

CHARACTERISTICS AND BEHAVIORS OF EFFECTIVE LEADERS

An important part of understanding leadership is to study the situation in which the leadership takes place. The majority of current studies about leadership pay more attention to the situation than to the leader. True, a man who is an effective supervisor in a potash mine in Saskatchewan might not be an effective school master in a preparatory school in Massachusetts. Despite vast differences in leadership situations, some generalizations can be made about the characteristics and behaviors that help a leader to be effective in a variety of situations. Studying the leader gains increased importance when it is recognized that your ability to size up the situation (a characteristic) is a major contributor to your ability to lead others. We will return to this aspect of leadership later.

What Is Effectiveness?. An effective leader is one who accomplishes results desired by the organization he or she serves. Simultaneously, he or she accomplishes these results without negative consequences to job satisfaction or morale. The next two sections of this chapter deal with aspects of leaders themselves that contribute to their effectiveness.

Is Leadership Unisexual?. An increasing number of women have become leaders in work organizations of all kinds. Thus it is pertinent to ask whether or not the traits and characteristics that make for effective leadership are about the same for men and women. The answer based on both experienced opinion and recent research is "Yes": there is very little difference in the traits and characteristics of men and women who become organizational leaders. A long-term study was conducted at AT&T to compare the personal profiles of men and women who advanced relatively rapidly into managerial positions. Eleven hundred women were compared to 123 men in terms of the characteristics and behaviors that were positively associated with progress in managerial work. A strong similarity was found between the characteristics and behaviors that were associated with good progress into leadership positions for both sexes. The following dimensions of behavior showed virtually the same importance for both men and women managers:[8]

> Oral communication skills
> Leadership attributes
> Energy
> Resistance to stress
> Tolerance of uncertainty
> Need for advancement
> Wide range of interests
> Organizing and planning ability

Similar results were found in another investigation. A continuing study by the Johnson O'Connor Research Foundation shows that women equal men in 13 of 19 skills associated with good management, including creativity, reasoning ability, foresight, and memory for details. Women managers excelled at objectivity, observation, vocabulary, and ability to visualize ideas. Men surpassed women managerial leaders in handshake grip and visualizing a finished product.[9] (Since so many people *perceive* a firm handshake to be a leadership quality, it behooves both men and women to develop a firm and dry, handshake.)

Twelve Key Characteristics and Behaviors

The preceding discussion of male and female leaders points to some relevant leadership traits and characteristics. If you want to become an effective leader, it is important to have more information about the inner qualities and outward behaviors of leaders. Following is a list of twelve key leadership characteristics and behaviors, several of which were mentioned in the male versus female comparisons.

1. Sound human relations skills. Working effectively with people does not necessarily mean that a leader is particularly easygoing with them. It means that a leader relates to people in such a way that he or she captures their trust and cooperation. It also means getting things accomplished through people in a constructive, helpful manner.

2. Technical competence. The closer a manager is to working with the technical aspects of an organization, the more technically competent he or she must be. Supervisors and middle managers who are not technically competent—those who do not understand the actual work performed by a department—run the risk of not establishing rapport with their subordinates. To be effective, the manager of the copy center department should know something about large volume copying and duplicating.

3. Self-confidence. An effective leader is usually a self-confident individual. Research has shown this to be true in a wide variety of leadership situations, from high school athletics, to the shop floor, to the head of a SWAT (strategic weapons and tactics) team. However, effective leaders are not so self-confident that they do not listen to suggestions from others or to constructive criticism.

4. Strong work motivation and high energy. Leadership positions tend to be demanding, both physically and mentally. A successful incumbent must be willing to work hard and long in order to achieve success. Jay Hall's study of managers revealed that effective leaders are driven by a need for self-fulfillment.[10] There is another reason that strong work motivation is required for effectiveness: a person has to be willing to accept the heavy responsibility that being a leader often entails. As one department manager said, "Whoever thought being a manager would mean that I would have to fire a woman with three children to feed?"

5. Good problem-solving ability. Leaders in most situations do not have to be brilliant, but they should be somewhat brighter than most of their subordinates. Too high problem-solving ability can be a detriment in some managerial jobs in business. People are often selected for leadership positions because of their high performance on intelligence tests (as well as factors such as their experience and personality). The reason is that people with extraordinary problem-solving ability prefer abstract mental games to dealing with everyday problems.

6. Sensitivity to people. Being sensitive to the feelings and needs of people has long been recognized as an important leadership behavior. (It is really a subset of good human relations skills). Recent research documents the fact that insensitivity to others prevents many up-and-coming managers from realizing their full potential. In a study of executive leadership, psychologists compared "derailed" executives with those who had progressed to senior management positions. The leading category of fatal flaws was insensitivity to others, characterized by an abrasive, intimidating, bullying style.[11] You will recall that abrasiveness can also damage your reputation with co-workers. The loss-prevention manager described in the case on page 296 is a good example of manager who lacks sensitivity to people.

7. *Need for achievement.* Business leaders, in particular, have a strong need to get things accomplished for accomplishment's sake (defined as the **achievement need**). Part of the achievement need is enjoying building things from the ground up, taking sensible risks, and desiring frequent feedback on how well you are doing.[12] Entrepreneurial leaders (those who own and operate businesses) are the best known category of people with high achievement need. How could you tell at this stage in your life whether or not you have a strong achievement need?

8. *Need for power.* Since leaders influence others primarily through the use of power, it makes sense that effective leaders have at least moderately strong needs for power. The need for power in this context refers to wanting to control others. A distinction can be drawn between leaders who crave power so they can perform a social good, versus those who crave power to serve their own ends. Most people would argue that Martin Luther King, Jr., craved socialized power, and that a mob leader craves self-serving power.

9. *Stability of performance.* An affective leader is able to perform in a stable manner despite heavy job pressures, including uncertainty.[13] One reason many technically minded people find being a leader so frustrating is that the job is uncertain and inexact. When asked how he liked his job as a bookkeeping supervisor, an accounting student replied, "It's a little rough. All the accounting problems I get at school come out even. In dealing with people, nothing does."

10. *Holding others to high standards of performance.* Another complex leadership behavior of note is to hold others to high standards of performance. If you as a leader expect others to succeed, they are likely to live up to your expectations. Management professor Burt K. Scanlon puts it this way, "Low expectations breed low performance and apathy, while high expectations lead to high performance and a more demanding performance tone."[14] As described in our discussion of self-motivation, this phenomenon has been called the Pygmalion effect in leadership.

11. *Good work habits.* A disorganized, unplanful, impulsive leader is an ineffective leader. With the increasing paper-work requirements of most leadership positions, he or she has to be all the more organized, planful, and attentive to details. Personal efficiencies or good work habits are so important for success that an entire chapter is devoted to them in the part of this book that deals with realizing your potential (see Chapter 16). Good work habits also contribute directly to productivity.

12. *Ability to size up people and situations.* A leader with good insights is able to make better work assignments and do a better job of training and developing subordinates. An insightful leader also avoids blunders that can lead to an erosion of his or her support from the group. An example of insensitivity would be to demote an employee three months before his or her

retirement. Why humiliate somebody on the way out after many years of good service? He or she probably would not perform effectively in the new short-range assignment. An exception would be demoting a near-retirement individual who was creating actual harm to the organization. This ability to size up people and situations has been identified as the most important inner quality possessed by an effective leader. Having such insight allows one to size up the situation before asserting oneself as a leader. Two leadership researchers speculate that this type of insight is not a traditional personality trait. Instead, it is a complex behavior that involves the ability to perceive the needs and goals of a group and to adjust one's approach to action accordingly.[15] In short, an effective leader has good intuition into people and situations.

Later in this chapter we will go into more detail about adapting one's leadership approach to the situation. But first it is important to study several different approaches to or styles of leadership.

THREE KEY LEADERSHIP STYLES

One way of understanding how leaders operate in practice is to draw some stereotypes of their behavior, called leadership styles. A style is a leader's characteristic way of behaving in most situations. Most leadership theories include a system of classifying leaders into such styles. About six approaches to describing leadership styles are in current use.[16] Most of them include some variation on the basic scheme of classifying leaders as autocratic, participative, or free rein. Each leadership style is based on the amount of authority or control the leader is willing to give to subordinates.

Autocratic Leadership (Boss-Centered)

Autocratic leaders attempt to retain most of the authority. They characteristically make a decision and then announce it. An authoritarian leader (another synonym for an autocratic leader) makes a decision in a confident manner and assumes that subordinates will gladly comply. He or she often gives little consideration to what subordinates are likely to think about the decision. An autocratic leader is sometimes seen as rigid and demanding by subordinates. Autocratic leaders are sometimes referred to as task oriented, because they seem to focus more on the task to be accomplished than on the needs and feelings of their subordinates.

Some autocratic leaders are highly effective. Former U.S. President Lyndon B. Johnson was known to be highly autocratic in his dealings with subordinates. A benevolent autocrat is a strongly task oriented leader whose efforts benefit people in the long run. They are able to accomplish things in a heavy-handed way without offending too many people. Many founders of successful companies manage in the style of a benevolent autocrat. The McDonald restaurant chain is run on an autocratic approach to management.[17] Each restaurant in the chain must rigidly follow a policy of Q, S, and C, or quality, service, and cleanliness. You lose your franchise if you stray too far from company policy.

Participative Leadership (Consultative and Democratic Styles)

A participative leader is one who shares decision making with members of the group. He or she is also described as Theory Y in approach, people oriented, or relations oriented. Participative leaders rarely make a decision without consulting others. Instead, they would engage in behavior such as (1) present the idea and invite questions; (2) present a tentative decision subject to change; (3) present the problem, get suggestions, and make the decision.[18]

There are basically two types of participative leaders, democratic and consultative. Democratic leaders confer final authority on the group. They are essentially collectors of group opinion. Democratic leaders help the group to accomplish what it wants to accomplish and abide by the group decision. Consultative leaders require a high degree of involvement from subordinates. But they make it clear that they alone have the authority to make final decisions.

Japanese Managers Use a Consultative Style. Participative management is gaining widespread acceptance in North America, owing to the popularity of Japanese-style management. Many executives and scholars believe that part of the productivity gains achieved by Japanese firms can be attributed to the participative (or consultative) style of their managers. Quality circles are but one example of participative management. Management decision making in a Japanese firm usually proceeds in this manner. A proposal is initiated by a middle manager, most often under the order from top management. The middle manager then engages in informal discussion and consultation with co-workers and supervisors. When all concerned are familiar with the proposal, a request for a decision is made formally. Since there has already been considerable discussion over the issue, the decision is inevitably ratified, often in a ceremonial group meeting. An important point is that ratification of the decision does not indicate unanimous approval, but it does imply a willingness to implement the decision.[19]

Evaluation of Participative Leadership. The participative leadership style is well suited to working with competent and well-motivated people. Such people want to get involved in making decisions and giving feedback to the boss.

Participative leadership is time consuming and at times ill-suited to the occasion. Two prominent leadership researchers contend that leadership situations that do not call for problem solving are ill-suited to participative management. In such situations, where problems are structured and solutions available, they argue that techniques of participative management are not only ineffective and wasteful but are also a misrepresentation of the subordinate's role, in which the subordinate is led to believe that he or she is helping to solve a problem that has, in fact, already been solved from the organization's point of view.[20]

Free-Rein Leadership (the Subordinate-Centered Style)

The free-rein leadership style is also referred to as *laissez-faire* ("allow them to do"). Free-rein leaders are the most casual of all. They issue general goals and guidelines to the group and then do not get involved again unless requested. The only limits directly imposed on the group are those specified by the leader's boss. "So long as it doesn't violate company policy, do what you want." Such extreme degree of group freedom is rarely encountered in a work organization. One exception might be a research group in which scientists, engineers, and technicians are granted the freedom to solve problems as they see fit.

A real problem with free-rein leadership in practice is that it frustrates many subordinates. Most people feel a leader is paid to give direction and advice. People often characterize a free-rein leader as weak and ineffective. In one business school an instructor ran a seminar using the free-rein style of teaching. Student evaluations of the course emphasized the fact that the instructor was "undynamic," "lazy," or, worse, "did nothing to prepare for the course."

ADAPTING TO THE SITUATION: THE KEY TO EFFECTIVE LEADERSHIP

Jennie, the office manager of a small company that produced insulating materials from recycled cellulose products, noticed a morale problem. Her staff had been overworked for three months owing to a surge in demand for insulating materials. To help relieve some of the tension, and as a show of appreciation, Jennie scheduled a Roast Beef and Rap for her workers. The company served a cold roast beef banquet one Friday afternoon. While dining, people were encouraged to talk about the problems that they were facing. The session was a huge success from the standpoint of management and the employees. People appreciated management's show of concern and appreciation.

Jennie displayed effective leadership in this particular situation because she adapted to the demands of the moment. She saw what action needed to be taken to deal with a tense climate among her employees, and she took appropriate action. Most of leadership theory and research in the last several decades suggests that the key to effective leadership is adapting to the demands of the situation. To be an adaptive leader, you have to be able to recognize the key elements in a given situation. Two such major factors are (1) the characteristics of your subordinates and (2) environmental demands and pressures.

Personal Characteristics of Subordinates

The type of people that you are leading heavily influences which leadership style works best. In general, competent people—those who are well trained, intelligent, and well motivated—need a minimum of guidance or emotional support from a superior. The leader in such a situation is best advised to "get out of the way" of subordinates. In other words, a loose approach to leading the group would work the best.

Another characteristic of subordinates that influences the most effective leadership style is their degree of authoritarianism.[21] Authoritarian (strict and unyielding) people have a tendency to prefer directive or authoritarian leaders. Also, they tend to dislike or even distrust a permissive or democratic style of leadership. Authoritarian people prefer to have things spelled out for them in precise detail.

The optimum leadership style can be influenced by how well the subordinates think that they can perform the assigned task. In simple terms, if you are confident in what you are doing, you might even resent a boss telling you how to perform your job.

Job Pressures and Demands[22]

Factors related to the job itself and the conditions surrounding the job also influence which leadership style is best. An effective leader takes these into account in adapting to the leadership situation.

Under conditions of heavy stress, threat, or pressure, most people want a leader to take forceful charge of the situation. In crisis situations, people are pleased to have the leader give specific orders and directives. A troubled business corporation elected a new president with a firm belief in financial controls. Although he made many enemies in the process, the company was successful in averting disaster. A middle manager in the company commented:

> At first we all hated the guy. He was almost ruthless about laying off long-term employees. He cut the corporate staff in half. He increased our workload and decreased our staff. In the end though we realized that he saved the company from bankruptcy. Without his take-charge attitude, we would all be out of jobs.

Under conditions of heavy stress, threat, or pressure, most people want a leader to take forceful charge of the situation.

Ambiguous assignments also influence which leadership style is best. When a person cannot tolerate ambiguity (such as unclear assignments) very well, he or she would prefer to have a leader provide such guidelines. The result for the person would be less tension. But those who like ambiguity (so they can provide their own guidelines) prefer a leader who does not meddle in their work. A research associate was asked by her superior if she wanted clarification on a vague assignment. She answered, "No, the fun is in figuring out what you're supposed to be doing."

As the size of the work group increases, subordinates may prefer that the leader play a more active role in coordinating activities. In addition to lowering the frustration of subordinates, clarifying and coordinating activities may improve performance. When work groups are smaller (about six to nine members), the group members themselves can divide up responsibilities without much help from their leader.

The *type of technology* is another influence that helps determine which leadership style is best. One extreme in technology would be the supervision of a craftlike operation where the workers are highly skilled and self-sufficient. They would need a minimum of guidance and structure, particularly about technological matters. A leader in such a situation should therefore emphasize giving the workers autonomy (freedom to make their own decisions).

The other technological extreme is a mass-production operation where the contribution of one department is tied into the contribution of other departments. An automobile assembly plant would be one such operation. Deviations from standard cannot be tolerated, so the managers involved have to ensure that policies and procedures are rigidly enforced.

Can Leader Traits and Characteristics Be Ignored?

In discussing factors that influence which leadership style is best, the conclusion should not be reached that leadership traits and characteristics are unimportant. A case in point: no matter what the situation, adequate problem-solving ability on the part of the leader is required. Sensitivity to people is also required to some extent in every situation. As one supervisor who works in a newspaper pressroom said, "I can just look at the expression on the face of one of my people and tell if he's going to need some extra attention from me that day."

DEVELOPING YOUR LEADERSHIP POTENTIAL

Almost anything you do to improve your individual effectiveness will have some impact on your ability to lead others. If you take a memory improvement course, attend a Dale Carnegie program, study this book carefully, apply the research findings in *Stogdill's Handbook of Leadership* to your own situation, or improve your physical fitness to help manage stress, you stand some chance of enhancing your leadership potential. Four major strategies should be kept in mind if you are seeking to improve your leadership potential.

Education, Training, and Leadership Development Programs

Almost any program of business training or education can be considered a program of leadership development. Courses in human relations, humanistic psychology, management, or business psychology are of obvious relevance to someone currently occupying or aspiring toward a leadership position. Many of today's leaders in profit and nonprofit organizations hold formal degrees in business. Specific training programs are also quite helpful in improving your leadership potential. Among them might be skill development programs in interviewing, employee selection, listening, assertiveness training, transactional analysis, budgeting, planning, work habit improvement, resolving conflict, and communication skills.

A more focused way of improving your leadership potential is to attend development programs designed specifically to improve your ability to lead others. Such programs are frequently offered through college counseling centers, the various "Y" organizations, and human resource departments in private firms and governmental agencies. Leadership programs of this nature have two important features in common. First, you are given feedback from other people and from questionnaires about your current leadership style (or leadership tendencies if you are now a leader). The feedback from others takes place in the context of a group experience much like the personal growth groups described in Chapter 4. For instance, another participant in the program might say to you, "If you want to become a good leader, you must learn to be more tolerant of people." Second, you also attend lecture and discussion groups about leadership concepts and principles.

Leadership Experience

No program of leadership improvement can be a substitute for leadership experience. Because leadership effectiveness depends somewhat on the situation, a sound approach is to attempt to gain leadership experience in different settings. A person who wants to become an executive is well advised to gain supervisory experience in at least two different organizational functions (such as marketing and manufacturing).

First-level supervisory jobs are an invaluable starting point for developing your leadership potential. It takes considerable skill to effectively manage a Wendy's restaurant or direct a public playground during a summer. A first-line supervisor frequently faces a situation where subordinates are poorly trained, poorly paid, and not well motivated to achieve company objectives.

Modeling Effective Leaders

Want to improve your leadership effectiveness? Carefully observe a capable leader in action and incorporate some of his or her approaches into your own behavior. You may not be able to or want to become that person's clone, but you can model what that person does. For instance, most inexperienced leaders have a difficult time confronting others with bad news. Watch a good confronter handle the situation, and try that person's approach the next time you have some unfavorable news to deliver to another person.

Increasing Your Self-Confidence

Since self-confidence is a universal characteristic of effective leaders, those who want to become effective leaders should elevate their self-confidence to an appropriate degree. People interested in elevating their self-confidence have tried various do-it-yourself, professional, and commercial approaches. Many a person who does not feel confident enough to meet daily challenges has undergone psychotherapy or counseling, often with good results. To achieve the same ends, many others have engaged in weight lifting, taken Karate lessons, joined Toastmasters, or had cosmetic plastic surgery. Perhaps one of the real reasons people enter any kind of personal improvement program is to achieve a boost in self-confidence.

A general approach to boosting your self-confidence is to experience success (accomplish your goals) in a variety of situations. (Refer back to Chapter 4 for more details about elevating your self-confidence.) A confident scuba diver may not be generally self-confident unless that same person also achieves success in activities such as taking exams in accounting, attracting people to date, parallel parking a car, operating a computer, and balancing a checkbook. First you establish some goals, achieve them, set some more difficult goals, achieve them, and continue the process.

If your self-confidence is presently on the low side, we recommend that you first obtain a few easy victories. Start with small tasks that you know you can achieve. For instance, a person trying to learn how to use computers might start with the simplest computer use of all—withdrawing money from an automatic teller machine. You can then proceed to word processing and numerical computations. To develop your self-confidence to a higher degree, you will ultimately have to achieve something that stretches your capability. In the example at hand, if you write a computer program that works, you will probably become confident about using computers.

SUMMARY OF KEY POINTS

☐ Leadership is the process of influencing other people to achieve certain objectives without the use of undue force or coercion. Unless influence has been exerted, leadership has not taken place. Formal leadership is that bestowed on you by the organization, such as the title of department head. Informal leadership refers to your personal power to influence others, irrespective of the authority granted you by the organization. A leadership position is often a source of satisfaction to its holder stemming from factors such as power, prestige, and high income. At other times, being a leader carries with it a number of frustrations such as dealing with personnel problems and paper work.

☐ Leaders influence people through the use of power. The three subtypes of position power are legitimate power (formal authority), reward power (the ability to control rewards), and coercive power (the ability to control punishments). The two types of personal power are expert power and referent power (loyalty stemming from an identification with the leader).

☐ Some traits, characteristics, and behaviors are related to being an effective leader in a wide variety of situations for both men and women. The 12 described here are (1) human relations skills, (2) technical competence, (3) self-confidence, (4) motivation and energy, (5) problem-solving ability, (6) sensitivity to people, (7) need for achievement, (8) need for power, (9) stability of performance, (10) high expectations for subordinates, (11) good work habits, and (12) ability to size up people and situations.

☐ A leadership style is basically a stereotype of how a leader behaves, particularly in relation to how much control the leader shares with the group. An autocratic leader retains almost all control. Participative-style leaders are divided into two types: (1) consultative leaders, who consult with subordinates and (2) democratic leaders, who turn over problems to the group. A free-rein leader turns over virtually all control to the group. The Japanese style of management is generally consultative.

☐ An effective leader adapts to the situation. Two major influences on the situation are (1) the personal characteristics of subordinates (such as their competence) and (2) pressures and demands. The latter is composed of such factors as the amount of pressure faced by the work group, the clarity of assignments, the size of the group, and the type of technology.

☐ Four general strategies for improving your leadership potential or your leadership ability are (1) receive education and training in leadership-related topics and attend leadership development programs, (2) obtain actual leadership experience, (3) model effective leaders, and (4) increase your self-confidence through such means as building up a series of successes.

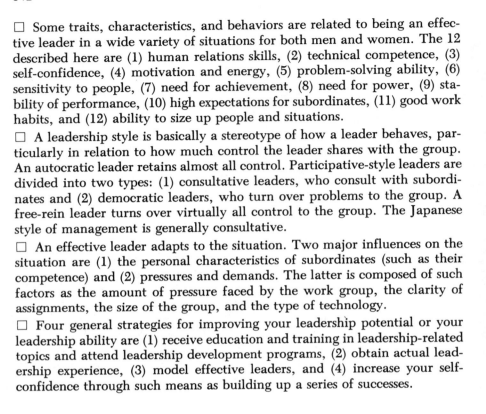

GUIDELINES FOR PERSONAL EFFECTIVENESS

1. Most of the traits, characteristics, and behaviors associated with effective leadership can be improved upon with education, training, or experience. Thus, you do not have to be a "born leader" to improve your leadership potential or skill. For instance, you may be a disorganized person, but work habits can be improved by practicing the right things (see Chapter 16).

2. Although leadership is situational, this does not mean that there are only one or two situations in which you could function effectively as a leader. There is usually a group of related situations in which each person (who has leadership ability) can function effectively. For instance, if you are a competent office supervisor, you could probably also manage a retail store or a post office branch.

3. Almost all leadership experience is helpful in developing your long-range leadership potential. A difficult leadership assignment can prove to be valuable experience because it requires more leadership skill to lead poorly motivated than highly motivated people.

DISCUSSION QUESTIONS

1. Would you want to hold a leadership position in a work organization? Why or why not?
2. Can leading television talk-show personalities or newscasters be considered leaders? Explain.
3. Describe a leader you know or have heard of who has considerable legitimate power but very little personal power. What effect has this had on his or her subordinates?
4. Explain whether or not the job of a college professor is that of a leader.
5. Assume that you were assigned to select a person to be the chief of an oil-drilling rig in the North Sea. What characteristics would you look for, and how would you measure them?
6. Which of the traits, characteristics, and behaviors of effective leaders do you think would be the most difficult to develop? Why?
7. Suppose that you were supervising a group of older women working on the line in a button factory. All these women are experienced in button making. Explain which style of leadership you think would be best suited to leading them.
8. Explain which style of leadership would be best suited to leading a small group of astronauts.
9. How would you describe the leadership style of (1) the president of the United States or (2) the prime minister of Canada?
10. Why is a knowledge of human motivation considered to be essential for effective leadership?

A Business Psychology Problem
"I THOUGHT A BOSS WAS SUPPOSED TO MAKE DECISIONS"

Gerry, a junior construction estimator, has been on his job three months with Tunney Construction Corporation. You have been working at Tunney for several years. Quite satisfied with your work at the company, it was you who recommended that Gerry apply for a job at Tunney. One day Gerry comes to you for advice:

"Please don't think I'm ungrateful, but I have a strange problem in working with my boss, Rolf. He seems to be a nice guy. I think he knows a lot about construction estimating. Also, he seems pretty good at paper work."

"What's your problem, then?"

"Rolf simply won't give me any advice or make any decisions for me. Just the other day I was handed a tough estimating job to carry out. It involves making an estimate on insulating the basement of an old factory. I hardly know where to begin with the job.

"I asked Rolf for his advice. He answers my questions with a question: 'What do you think is the best procedure?' I then tell him I don't have the background yet to recommend a good procedure."

"How did Rolf respond to that comment?"

"He gave me a blank stare and said, 'You feel you don't have the right background to make such a decision.'

"I guess you could say my frustration is that I thought a boss was supposed to make decisions. If you can't go to your boss for help, what's the use of having a boss?"

1. What advice can you offer your friend, Gerry?
2. What leadership style does Gerry's boss seem to be using?
3. How do you think Rolf would defend his leadership style?

A Business Psychology Role Play
CONTRASTING LEADERSHIP STYLES

In each of the three following role-plays, a subordinate is given the assignment of estimating the cost of insulating a basement of an old factory. The subordinate later informs the supervisor that he or she doesn't have enough experience to make the right estimate. One person plays the role of the subordinate asking for help from the boss in making the estimate. Three pairs of people are thus required. In situation A, the subordinate makes the request to an authoritarian boss. In situation B, the request is made to a participative boss; in situation C, the request is made to a free-rein boss. If you are playing the role of the boss, think through how each style of leader would react to the request.

REFERENCES

[1]Paul Hersey and Kenneth H. Blanchard, *Management of Organizational Behavior: Utilizing Human Resources*, 3rd ed. (Englewood Cliffs, N.J.: Prentice-Hall, 1977), p. 68.

[2]Stephen P. Robbins, *Management: Concepts and Practices* (Englewood Cliffs, N.J.: Prentice-Hall, 1984), p. 220.

[3]This well-accepted categorization of power is from John R. P. French, Jr., and Bertram Raven, "The Bases of Social Power," in Dorwin Cartwright and Alvin F. Zander, eds., *Group Dynamics: Research and Theory* (New York: Harper & Row, 1960), pp. 607–623.

[4]The suggestions for using each of the five types of power are based on Gary Yukl and Tom Taber, "The Effective Use of Managerial Power," *Personnel* (March–April 1983), pp. 37–44.

[5]Ibid., p. 42.

[6]Philip M. Podsakoff, William D. Todor, and Richard Skov, "Effects of Leader Contingent and Noncontingent Reward and Punishment Behaviors on Subordinate Performance and Satisfaction," *Academy of Management Journal* (Dec. 1982), pp. 810–821.

[7]Yukl and Taber, "Effective Use," p. 42.

[8]Richard J. Ritchie and Joseph L. Moses, "Assessment Center Correlates of Women's Advancement into Middle Management: A 7-Year Longitudinal Study," *Journal of Applied Psychology* (May 1983), p. 229.

[9]Norma Peterson, "Male, Female Managers: More Similar Than Different," Gannett News Service Story printed in Rochester *Democrat and Chronicle* (March 22, 1983), p. 10D.

[10]Jay Hall, "What Makes a Manager Good, Bad, or Average?" *Psychology Today* (Aug. 1976), p. 53.

[11]Morgan W. McCall, Jr., and Michael M. Lombardo, "What Makes a Top Executive?" *Psychology Today* (Feb. 1983), p. 28.

[12]David C. McClelland, "Achievement Motivation Can Be Developed," *Harvard Business Review* (Jan.–Feb. 1965), p. 10.

[13]"Committee Seeks 'Value Added' Exam for Students, Added Value for B Schools," American Assembly of Collegiate Schools of Business *Newline* (Oct. 1982), p. 1.

[14]Burt K. Scanlon, "Managerial Leadership in Perspective: Getting Back to Basics," *Personnel Journal* (March 1979), p. 169.

[15]David A. Kenny and Stephen J. Zaccaro, "An Estimate of Variance Due to Traits in Leadership," *Journal of Applied Psychology* (Nov. 1983), p. 678.

[16]A summary of these style classifications is found in Andrew J. DuBrin, *Foundations of Organizational Behavior: An Applied Perspective* (Englewood Cliffs, N.J.: Prentice-Hall, 1984), Chapter 12. See also Hersey and Blanchard, *Management of Organizational Behavior.*

[17]"The Hamburger That Conquered the Country," *Time* (Sept. 17, 1973).

[18]The classic article about these three basic leadership styles is Robert Tannenbaum and Warren H. Schmidt, "How to Choose a Leadership Pattern," *Harvard Business Review* (March–April 1958), pp. 95–101.

[19]Nina Hatvany and Vladimir Pucik, "An Integrated Management System: Lessons from the Japanese Experience," *Academy of Management Review* (July 1981), p. 473.

[20]Martin M. Chemers and Fred E. Fiedler, "The Effectiveness of Leadership Training: A Reply to Argyris," *American Psychologist* (April 1978), p. 392.

[21]Alan C. Filley, Robert J. House, and Steven Kerr, *Managerial Process and Organizational Behavior*, 2nd ed. (Glenview, Ill.: Scott, Foresman, 1976), p. 255.

[22]Our discussion of environmental pressures and demands is based on information in Elmer Burack, *Organization Analysis: Theory and Application* (Hinsdale, Ill.: Dryden Press, 1975), pp. 315–318.

SUGGESTED READING

ALSTON, JON P. "Three Principles of Japanese Management," *Personnel Journal* (Oct. 1983), pp. 758–763.

BASS, BERNARD M. *Stogdill's Handbook of Leadership: A Survey of Results*, Revised and Expanded Edition. New York: Free Press, 1981.

CRITTENDEN, VICKY L., and WILLIAM F. CRITTENDEN. "Male and Female Students' Perceptions of Women in Management," *Collegiate News & Views* (Spring 1983), pp. 27–31.

EDEN, DOV, and ABRAHAM B. SHANI. "Pygmalion Goes to Boot Camp: Expectancy, Leadership, and Trainee Performance," *Journal of Applied Psychology* (April 1982), pp. 194–199.

HALL, JAY. *The Competence Process: Managing for Commitment and Creativity.* The Woodlands, Texas: Teleometrics International, 1982.

MACCOBY, MICHAEL. *The Leader: A New Face for American Management.* New York: Simon & Schuster, 1981.

MCCLELLAND, DAVID C. "Leadership Motive Pattern and Long-Term Success in Management," *Journal of Applied Psychology* (Dec. 1982), pp. 737–743.

"The New Entrepreneurs." *BusinessWeek*, April 18, 1983, pp. 78–82.

NUWER, HANK. "Joe Paterno: Team Builder," *Success* (Oct. 1983), pp. 22–26.

YUKL, GARY. *Leadership in Organizations.* Englewood Cliffs, N.J.: Prentice-Hall, 1981.

15

COMMUNICATING WITH PEOPLE

LEARNING OBJECTIVES

After reading and studying this chapter and doing the exercises, you should be able to

1. Understand how effective communication relates to your career success.
2. Become a more effective communicator.
3. Understand the role of nonverbal communication in the workplace.
4. Develop a strategy for overcoming common barriers to communication.
5. Recognize that you can develop your communication skills in several different modes.
6. Gain insight into the application of transactional analysis to improve interpersonal communication.

Communicating with people is an inescapable requirement of all but the most routine, low-level jobs. Even people whose work does not primarily involve contact with people (such as an engineering technician) must communicate with people to ask questions or explain their work. Communication is also the basic process by which managers and staff specialists accomplish their work. A manager can coordinate the work of others only if he or she receives information from some people and transmits it to others. And an occupational safety and health specialist can only keep employees out of physical danger if he or she gets relevant information across to them.

The purpose of communication is to gather, process, and disseminate information, which makes it a vital activity in any place of work.[1] Despite its importance in getting work accomplished, communication remains a major problem facing most individuals and most organizations. Work organizations typically suffer from communication snags, and many people are held back in their career because they are poor communicators.

The information presented in this chapter is aimed toward reducing communication problems between people. To accomplish this purpose, we will explain the nature of various facets of communication and also provide a number of suggestions for improving one's communication effectiveness.

STEPS IN THE COMMUNICATION PROCESS

A convenient starting point in understanding how people communicate is to examine the steps involved in the transmission of a message. The process involves the following sequence of events: ideation, encoding, transmission over a medium, receiving, decoding, understanding, and, finally, taking action. The clouds above and below the diagram in Figure 15–1 symbolize barriers

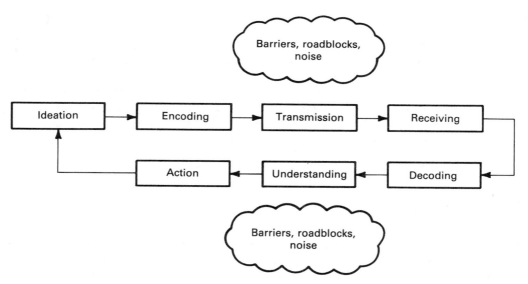

FIGURE 15–1
Steps in the communication process.

to communication (or noise, roadblocks, and so forth) that can take place at any stage in communication. Later in the chapter we will deal with the challenge of overcoming major barriers to communication.

The communication process is cyclical. Upon decoding a message, understanding it, and then taking action, the receiver sends out his or her own message, and the cycle is repeated at least once. Assume that a man named Conrad wishes to communicate to his boss, Barbara, that he wants a salary increase.

Step one is *ideation* by Conrad. He organizes thoughts about this sensitive problem. This stage is both the origin and the framing of the idea or message in the sender's mind. Conrad says to himself, "I think I'll ask for a raise."

Step two is *encoding*. Here the ideas are organized into a series of symbols (words, hand gestures, body movements, drawings) designed to communicate to the intended receiver. Conrad says, "Barbara, there is something I would like to talk to you about if you have the time. . . . "

Step three is *transmission* of the message orally or in writing. In this situation the sender chose the oral mode.

Step four is *receiving* of the message by the other party. Barbara can only receive the message if she is attentive to Conrad.

Step five is *decoding* the symbols sent by the sender to the receiver. In this case, decoding is not complete until Barbara hears the whole message. The opening comment, "Barbara, there is something I would like to talk about . . . " is the type of statement often used by employees to broach a sensitive topic, such as discussing a resignation or salary increase. Barbara therefore listens attentively for more information.

Step six, *understanding*, follows the decoding process. Barbara has no trouble understanding that Conrad wants a salary increase. When communication barriers exist (as described later in this chapter), understanding may be limited.

Step seven is *action*. Barbara understands Conrad's request, but does not agree. She acts by telling Conrad that he will have to wait three more months until his salary will be reviewed. Action is also a form of feedback, because it results in a message being sent back to the original sender from the receiver.

Communication Directions. The conversation between Conrad and Barbara illustrated two directions of communication: upward (from subordinate to superior) and downward (from superior to subordinate). The third common form of communication is sideways (one co-worker to another). A less frequent form of communication is diagonal. This would happen if a manager from one department communicated with a lower-ranking employee in another department. To complete the picture, can you visualize communication in a zigzag direction?

People who are adept at sending messages in one direction are not necessarily adept at communicating in other directions. For example, some people are comfortable in communicating with co-workers, but they are too shy to communicate effectively with superiors. And some bosses are good at sending messages down the organization, but they are not good at listening to messages sent to them from employees.

FORMAL AND INFORMAL COMMUNICATION PATHWAYS

In addition to traveling in more than one direction, messages are sent over more than one pathway. Organizational communication takes place over both formal and informal channels or pathways.

Formal Communication Pathways

Formal communication pathways are easy for most employees to understand. They represent the official, sanctioned path over which messages are supposed to travel. Suppose Jack is working as an admitting clerk in a hospital. He formulates an idea that he thinks would improve the productivity of his department—purchasing a computer to store and retrieve intake information about patients. The formal pathway for his suggestion would be something of this nature: admitting clerk → admitting office supervisor → manager of administrative services → chief hospital administrator → hospital board of directors. In other words, Jack's message would have to follow the formal chain of command (or organization structure).

Work flow is another important factor that shapes the formal path for sending and receiving messages. If you are a quality specialist in a manufacturing plant, you might be expected to communicate your observations about a product defect directly to a manufacturing supervisor. Or a sales representative might initiate work for a credit analyst. The "rep" makes a tentative sale on a big piece of equipment. Before the customer is approved for receiving the equipment prior to paying for it in full, the credit analyst must approve the customer's credit rating.

Informal Communication Pathways

The paths by which messages travel from person to person are more numerous than those designated by the organization chart or those prompted by the work flow. *Informal pathways* account for some of the most baffling communication problems. A good way of gaining insight into these pathways is to study the grapevine, rumors, and gossip (everybody's favorite topic).

The Grapevine. The term grapevine traces back to the Civil War when intelligence telegraph wires were strung from tree to tree in a way that resembled a grapevine. The messages transmitted by these lines were typically garbled and unclear, much like the grapevine in an office.[2] Yet there are times when information transmitted along the grapevine is accurate. Accurate or inaccurate, good or bad, the grapevine is the major informal communication network in an organization. Keith Davis offers this helpful description of the office grapevine:

> Being flexible and personal, it spreads information faster than most management communication systems operate. With the rapidity of a burning powder train, it filters out of the woodwork, past the manager's door and the janitor's closet, through steel walls or construction glass partitions and along the corridors.[3]

The grapevine is sometimes used deliberately by management to transmit information that it may not wish to transmit formally. One example would be to feed the grapevine with the news that salary increases will be very small this year. When increases turn out to be average, most employees will be satisfied. A related use of the grapevine is to measure the reaction of employees to an announcement before it is transmitted through formal channels.[4] If the reaction is too bad, management can sometimes modify its plans, such as not going ahead with a program of shortening vacations.

Rumors. A rumor is a message transmitted over the grapevine, although not based on official word. The message can be true or false. An important problem with rumors is that they are capable of disrupting work and lowering morale. A dress company in Brooklyn found itself the victim of an untrue rumor that created morale problems during its peak season. A disgruntled employee started the rumor that the company had formalized plans to subcontract its dressmaking to a company in Pakistan. Consequently, most of the work force would be laid off after this season. When the owner learned of the problem, he held a company-wide meeting to dispel the rumor.

Preventive measures are the most effective strategy for managing rumors, according to Walter St. John. He advises management to be alert to situations that promote rumors. Among them are when employees are confused about what is happening and information is unclear, incomplete, or lacking, and when there is excessive anxiety and conflict present in the workplace.[5] Despite these preventive measures, there may be times when management or an individual has to combat a potentially harmful rumor. Here are several things that can be done:

- First, try to wait it out. The rumor may run its course before doing too much damage.

- If the rumor persists, make it news. If you talk about the rumor and then deny it, nobody has an exclusive.
- To cut the rumor short, communicate the information that people want. Do so promptly, clearly, accurately, and factually. At the same time, keep open formal channels of communication and encourage employees to use them. ("Call my secretary for an appointment any time you want to see me, about anything you think is important.")[6]

Gossip. A special form of rumor is gossip, the idle talk or tidbits of information about people that are passed along informal communication channels. We all know that gossip can hurt peoples' reputation and wastes time (it is often the raw material for schmoozing). Yet, gossip also serves a number of useful purposes on the job. Among them are the fact that gossip can be a morale booster, a socializing force, and a guidebook to group norms.

Gossip can improve morale by adding spice and variety to the job. It may even make some highly repetitive jobs bearable. Robert Wieder notes that in an increasingly technological and depersonalized workplace, gossip may be an important humanizing factor. At the same time it is a deep-well source of employee team spirit.[7]

Gossip serves as a socializing force because it is a mode of intimate relationship for many employees. People get close to each other through the vehicle of gossip. It also serves as the lifeblood of personal relationships on the job. Gossip acts as a guidebook because it informs employees of the *real* customs, values, and ethics of the work environment. For instance, a company might state formally that no employee can accept a gift of over ten dollars from a supplier. Gossip may reveal, however, that some employees are receiving expensive gifts from suppliers. Furthermore, the company makes no serious attempt to stop the practice.

NONVERBAL COMMUNICATION ON THE JOB

Most of our discussion about communication so far has emphasized the use of words, or verbal communication. However, about 60 percent of communication between people occurs at the nonverbal level. **Nonverbal communication** refers to the transmission of messages through means other than words. The general purpose of nonverbal communication (NVC) is to communicate the feeling behind your message. For instance, you can say "no" with a clenched fist or with a smile to communicate the firmness of your position. The terms **body language** and **silent message** mean about the same thing as NVC.

Nonverbal communication is as broad a topic as the study of language itself. Here we will concentrate on four aspects of NVC that are particularly useful on the job: gestures, facial expressions, posture, and interpersonal distance. We will also mention *neurolinguistic programming*, because it is an interesting development in NVC that has gained recent attention both on and off the job.

Gestures. Your hand movements convey specific information to others. Positive attitudes toward another person are shown by frequent gesturing. In contrast, dislike or disinterest usually produces few gestures. An important exception here is that some people wave their hands while in an argument, sometimes to the point of making threatening gestures. The type of gesture displayed also communicates a specific message:

> Random fidgeting, such as drumming the fingers or twiddling the thumbs, is a set of gestural activities which convey extremely negative attitudes. Similarly, aggressive gestures with clenched fists and menacing postures convey hostile feelings, while infrequent use of relaxed, open-palm gestures toward the other person typically conveys positive attitudes.[8]

Gestures are also said to provide clues to our levels of dominance and submission. Anthropologist David Givens and psychiatrist Albert Scheflen conducted painstaking research on the meaning of gestures. Their findings pointed out that the gestures of dominant people are typically directed outward toward the other person. (As just noted, this could also mean a positive attitude.) Examples include the steady, unwavering gaze and the touching of one's partner. Submissive gestures are usually protective, such as touching oneself or shrugging one's shoulder.[9]

Facial Expressions. Using your head, face, and eyes in combination provides the clearest indications of interpersonal attitudes. Looking at the ceiling—without tilting your head—combined with a serious expression almost always communicates the message, "I doubt what your saying is true." As is well known, maintaining eye contact with another person improves communication with that person. To maintain eye contact, it is usually necessary to correspondingly move your head and face. Moving your head, face, and eyes away from another individual is often interpreted as defensiveness or a lack of self-confidence.

The astute salesperson learns to know how well his or her sales presentation is going by watching the customer's facial expressions. If the potential customer is frowning or looking "bored," it is a signal to modify the presentation. Similarly, if the potential customer looks enthused, it may be the signal to take the order!

Posture. Your posture communicates a variety of gestures. If you stand erect, it usually conveys the message that you are self-confident and experiencing positive emotion. If you slump, you will appear to be either lacking in self-confidence or down in the dumps. The preceding statements point to a disturbing aspect of NVC. One person may slump as a consequence of having grown up with people who slump. Thus, that person may slump even on very happy days. Yet others will interpret slumping as a sign of low self-confidence and a negative mood.

Another interpersonal meaning of posture involves the direction of leaning. Leaning toward another individual suggests that you are favorably disposed toward his or her message; leaning backward communicates the opposite message. Openness of the arms or legs serves as an indicator of liking or caring. In general, people establish closed postures (arms folded and legs crossed) when speaking to people they dislike.

Can you think of an aspect of your posture that conveys a specific message?

Interpersonal Distance. The placement of one's body relative to somebody else is another way of communicating a message. One study showed that people located in relatively close proximity are seen as warmer, friendlier, and more understanding than people located farther away.[10] The implication is that if you want to convey positive attitudes to another person (of either sex) get close to him or her. As common sense suggests, putting your arm around somebody else or touching that person is interpreted as a friendly act. A popular book about how to motivate people recommends that managers should touch employees when they give out praise. Touching is believed to convey sincerity.[11]

Cultural differences should be kept in mind in interpreting the meaning of interpersonal distance and any other nonverbal cues. For example, a French male is likely to stand closer to you than an English male, even if they have equally positive attitudes toward you.

Neurolinguistic Programming. At several places in this text we describe self-improvement programs that are modeled after techniques of psychotherapy. One example is assertiveness training. A more recent development is neurolinguistic programming, a method of communication that combines features of hypnosis, linguistics, and nonverbal behavior. "Neuro" refers to the way the human nervous system processes communication. "Linguistic" refers to the way that words, tone, timing, gestures, and inflection can be used in communication. "Programming" refers to using a systematic technique to communicate with others.[12]

The use of neurolinguistic programming (NLP) on the job centers around the assistance it may provide you in understanding others and establishing rapport with them. You first have to get on another person's wavelength. NLP points out that everybody perceives the world primarily through one dominant sense: seeing, hearing, or feeling. Another person's conversation will provide some clues as to the dominant sense ("I see what you're saying," "I look at things this way," "What you say feels good to me"). You, like the NLP therapist, build rapport by matching the sense imagery of the person you are dealing with. You fall into the style of their conversation, even adopting their posture and breathing pattern—nonverbal behaviors.[13]

The serious student of NLP would have to become highly observant of many silent cues provided by others, such as their breathing rate or the twitching of their eyebrows. According to Eric Marcus, one of the most effective ways of establishing rapport is to subtly imitate the other person. And the most successful NLP technique is to mirror another person's breathing pattern. Marcus uses this example:

> A manager is confronted by an angry union shop steward concerning disciplinary action taken against a member. In the normal course of events, the breathing rate of both people will fluctuate in keeping with the process of the discussion. In this case, rapid, shallow breathing, a subconscious signal of anger, will only elicit anger in response. But if the manager instead deliberately paces his own breathing rate to match that of his antagonist, and gradually decreases his breathing rate, tension will be dispelled and rapport established.[14]

A minor form of hypnosis enters the picture because the "mirroring" produces a suggestible state in the other person. He or she thus begins to comply with your demands. Another possible explanation of why NLP works is that it is a form of empathy (understanding the other person's point of view). And empathy typically leads to improved communication between people. Whatever the explanation, neurolinguistic programming could prove to be a practical method of making good use of nonverbal communication.

OVERCOMING BARRIERS TO COMMUNICATION

Communication rarely proceeds as smoothly as we would like. Some interference usually takes place between idea and action, as suggested by the "clouds" in Figure 15–1. So many potential barriers exist that it would be extremely difficult for you to manage all of them. The most general strategy for reducing barriers to communication is to be sensitive to the fact that such barriers do exist. Another general strategy for overcoming barriers to communication is for you to become a more effective communicator. Specific methods of improving your communication skills are discussed later in this chapter. Here we will describe eight methods of increasing the odds that your

Communication rarely proceeds as smoothly as we would like.

message will produce the desired results. It is important to remember that the purpose of communication is usually to produce some kind of action.

Understand the Receiver

Understanding the person who you are trying to reach is a fundamental principle of overcoming communication barriers. The more you know about your receivers, the better able you are to deliver your message in an effective manner. Three important aspects of understanding the receiver are (1) developing empathy, (2) recognizing that person's motivational state, and (3) understanding the other person's frame of reference.

To develop **empathy,** you are required to figuratively place yourself in the receiver's shoes. To accomplish this, you have to imagine yourself in the other person's role and assume the viewpoints and emotions of that individual.[15] Assume a 25-year-old office systems specialist has the responsibility of helping an older group of clerks learn how to make better use of office automation (OA). The systems specialist should ask himself or herself, "If I had been using manual and electric equipment for 20 years, how keen would I be to shift to electronic equipment? What would be my fears? My hang-ups?" Answering these questions might help the specialist communicate in a compassionate and tolerant manner to the older clerks.

The receiver's **motivational state** could include any active needs and interest at the time. People tend to listen attentively to those messages that show promise of satisfying an active need. The hungry person who ordinarily does not hear low tones readily hears a whispered message, "How would you like to eat dinner?" And management usually listens attentively to a suggestion that is framed in terms of cost savings or increased profits.

People perceive words and concepts differently because their vantage points and perspectives differ. Such differences in **frames of reference** create barriers to communication. To reduce this barrier, you have to understand where the receiver "is coming from." An amusing example of different frames of reference creating a communication barrier took place in a financial services agency.

Jeb, a second-year agent, showed his sales figures for the month to his boss, Gary. Proud of his good results, Jeb said, "Well, what do you think of this kind of production for a man of my age?" Gary replied, "That's fine if you want to make $35,000 a year for the rest of your life." Jeb responded, "Sounds fine to me."

Gary looked at him quizzically and said, "You mean you'd be happy making $35,000 a year for the rest of your life? I made that comment to shake you up a bit." Jeb answered, "No disrespect Gary, but where I come from $35,000 is one big lump of money. My parents never came close to that."

Engage in Two-Way Communication

Effective face-to-face communication proceeds in two directions.[16] An exchange of information or a transaction takes place between people. Person A may send messages to person B to initiate communication, but B must react to A to complete the communication loop. One reason written messages frequently fail to achieve their purpose is that the sender of the message cannot be sure what meanings are attached to its content. Face-to-face transactions help clarify meanings because they communicate feelings as well as facts. Electronic bulletin boards create a similar communication barrier. Instead of interacting directly with another person in the office, a message is sent to the other person's display terminal. In the process, the human touch (specifically, the feeling behind the message) is often lost.[17] The antidote is to communicate in person those messages that are likely to have an emotional meaning (usually any message of major importance).

One-way communication sometimes takes place even when the second party responds to the first party. In such instances, the second party is not responding to what the other person is really saying. Two-way communication usually requires that the parties respond to each others feelings. Another way of looking at the same issue is to examine the difference between a monologue and a dialogue. In a dialogue, the parties understand what each other is *really* saying. Personal life is filled with examples of the difference between one- and two-way communication or monologues and dialogues. A comparison of the difference between a monologue and a dialogue is shown in Exhibit 15–1.

Exhibit 15–1

A COMPARISON BETWEEN A MONOLOGUE AND A DIALOGUE

Is It Our Money or Your Money?
A. *Monologue between wife and husband*

"Bill, I thought of something when I signed the joint income tax form the other day. Although all our assets are shared by state law, our three banking accounts are in your name. Why is that? Don't you trust my judgment about financial matters?"

"Why are you complaining about a technical detail like that? It's the husband's job to protect his wife from having to worry about things like bank accounts. What's for dinner?"

"The whole thing doesn't sound quite right to me. I feel left out of things."

"You find the pickiest things to complain about."

B. *Dialogue between wife and husband*

"Bill, I thought of something when I signed the joint income tax form the other day. Although our assets are shared by...."

"It sounds like you're discontented about the way I have arranged things financially. Maybe you feel you should have more power in these matters."

"Exactly. Your having total control over the bank accounts makes me feel like a second-class citizen in our marriage."

"My intent was not to make you feel like a second-class citizen. It's just been a long-held belief of mine that only one person in a marriage should be in charge of the bank accounts. How would having separate accounts appeal to you?"

"Maybe that would be a good compromise. I appreciate your not being pigheaded about the whole topic."

Use Multiple Channels

Repetition usually enhances learning. Repetition also enhances communication, particularly when different channels are used to convey the same message.[18] Effective communicators at many job levels follow up verbal (spoken) agreements with written documentation. Since most communication is subject to at least some distortion, the chances of a message being received as intended increase when two or more channels are used.

It has become standard practice in many large companies for managers to use a multiple-channel approach to communicating the results of a performance appraisal. The subordinate receives a verbal explanation from his or her superior of the results of the review. He or she is also required to read the form and indicate by signature that he or she has read and understands the meaning of the review.

Communicate Honestly

A major reason that many communicators (including people in public office and business executives) do not get their messages across is that they have lied or communicated half-truths in the past. To the extent that people lie, a communication barrier is erected for the transmission of future messages. A concrete way of demonstrating that you are an honest communicator is to back up your spoken or written messages with action.[19] Keep your promises and you will eliminate one more barrier to communication.

Use Verbal and Nonverbal Feedback

To be able to conclude that your message has been received as intended, it is helpful to ask for feedback. A frequent managerial practice is to conclude a conference with a question such as, "Okay, what have we agreed on today?" Unless feedback of this nature is obtained, you will not know if your message has been received until the receiver later carries out (or fails to carry out) your request. After speaking to a group that you are trying to influence, it would be helpful to ask them to state what message they thought you were trying to convey. Nonverbal cues are sometimes more revealing than verbal cues. Here are three examples of nonverbal behavior (or body language) that could help you to interpret whether or not your comments were being accepted:

- You are making a sales pitch about encyclopedias to a family. Both the husband and the wife move forward in their chairs toward you, while the two adolescent children lean back on their chairs. You probably have the parents about sold on the proposition, but you need to work more with the children.

- You ask a person of the opposite sex to go on an overnight camping trip with you. He or she firmly squeezes your hand while saying, "Let me think about it for a few moments." His or her answer will probably be "yes."
- You ask your boss when you will be eligible for a promotion and he looks out the window, cups his mouth to cover a yawn, and says, "Probably not too far away. I would say your chances aren't too bad." Keep trying. He is not yet sold on the idea of promoting you in the near future.

Decrease Physical Barriers

Do you ever try to communicate with somebody while standing in the doorway of their office or room? Do you ever try to communicate with somebody with a huge desk separating the two of you? In both situations your communications effectiveness would probably increase if you reduced the barriers. In the first instance, it would be helpful to enter the room and stand closer to the person. In the second situation, it would be preferable to move around the table to a point where you are both seated at two adjacent corners of the desk.

In a conference setting, a major way of increasing and improving person-to-person communication is to seat people in a circle without a table separating them. (Student chairs with an arm big enough for notetaking are particularly useful in this regard.) Communication is also enhanced when people are seated on the floor in a circle. Such an approach is often used in personal growth groups, but rarely in business conferences.

Increase the Opportunity for Informal Interaction

Another effective way of decreasing physical barriers is to provide employees with ample opportunity to chat with each other about work-related topics. Informal interaction of this type is particularly important for employees involved in creative or complex work. "Batting around" ideas with a co-worker can help clarify your thinking on a challenging problem. Support for this conclusion was found in a study about research and development (R&D) professionals. Diffusion of important technical information increased considerably under these conditions:

1. Short distances were created between the work areas of the professionals. Those whose offices were located only 17 yards from important information sources (key people) communicated much more than those employees whose offices were 27 yards away from the sources.

2. Informal meetings were enhanced through clustered offices of professional people together and establishing common lounge areas and eating places.[20]

The same two approaches can facilitate gossiping and schmoozing. With work-oriented professionals, however, this does not appear to be a serious risk.

Use Appropriately Difficult Language

"From this point forward you folks are going to have to interface with a CAD/CAM, robotics configuration in our operations environment," said the production engineering manager to the production workers. Seeing mostly blank stares on the faces of his intended receivers, the manager rephrased his message, "In the future, a lot of our production work is going to be computerized." At first the manager was falling prey to a common communications barrier, speaking at too high a level of complexity for the intended receiver. The manager recovered by rephrasing his message in a form that was (1) simpler and (2) less filled with jargon.

It is not always advisable to avoid complexity and jargon. People may feel patronized when you send messages that are too easy to understand. Jargon may also play an important psychological role because it communicates the message that the sender believes the receiver is part of his or her in-group. In an effort to reduce complexity, some people create communication barriers. One way to alienate your intended receivers, for example, is to say, "I'm going to explain this to you in such a way that even a lay person can understand it."

Avoid Communication Overload

A major communication barrier facing today's managers and specialists is communication overload. So much information comes across one's desk that it is often difficult to figure out which information should receive one's attention and which should be discarded. If all office communications were attended to, the actual work of the firm would go virtually unattended.[21] Photocopying machines and computer printers have been a major contributor to communication (or information) overload. A flood of information reaching a person acts as a communication barrier because people have a tendency to block out new information when their capacity to absorb information becomes taxed. Literally, their "circuits become overloaded," and they no longer respond to messages.

To help overcome this problem, it is advisable for firms to be selective in the amount of information they send to employees. Toward this end, it is now becoming common practice for managers to be sent only summaries of general information, while critical information is sent in fuller form. Also, some executives subscribe to executive abstract services. Their function is to provide executives with brief summaries of business and general news.

You can decrease the chances of suffering from information overload by such measures as carefully organizing and sorting through information before plunging ahead with its reading. Speed reading may also help, provided you stop to read carefully the most relevant information.

IMPROVING YOUR LISTENING SKILLS

Convinced that most people don't listen well, a Los Angeles woman decided to test her opinion by engaging in small talk at the office. "By the way, I've just been fired," she said cheerfully. "Oh really?" came the reply. "How very nice for you."

One point illustrated by this incident is that most people would be better communicators if they listened more attentively. This is true because listening is a basic part of the communication process. Unless you receive messages as they are intended, you cannot properly perform your job or be a good companion. Listening has even been described as our primary communication activity. Studies demonstrate that we spend about 80 percent of our waking hours communicating. And 45 percent of that time is spent in listening.[22] Listening is a particularly important skill for anybody whose job involves troubleshooting, since one needs to gather information in order to solve problems.

Another reason that improving the listening skills of employees is important is that insufficient listening is extraordinarily costly. Listening mistakes lead to retyping of letters, rescheduling of appointments, reshipping of orders, and recalling of defective products. Also of note, ideas get distorted by up to 80 percent as they travel up the organization in a large firm.[23]

A major step forward in improving one's listening skills would be to improve concentration. If you concentrate intently on the sender of the message, you will receive much more information than if you pay superficial attention. Furthermore, much forgetting is due to never having received a message correctly in the first place. The suggestions presented next will help you to improve your listening skill if they are practiced regularly.[24] We are referring to listening in both face-to-face situations and when one is listening to a speaker.

1. Control your emotion. Learn not to get too excited about a speaker's point, pro or con, until you are sure you understand it. Do not make up your mind immediately as to whether the person sending the message is "good" or "bad."

2. Listen for key ideas. Facts serve as documentation for ideas of broader significance. If your boss tells you that your desk is messy, he or she may also be telling you that you are disorganized in a number of ways. Simply cleaning up your desk will not cure the problem.

3. *Think along with the speaker.* Rephrase in your own words the essential ideas of the speaker. In this way the facts the other person is transmitting to you will develop meaning. Since meanings are better remembered than raw facts, you will acquire more information.

4. *Listen for total meaning.* Look closely to discover the feeling behind the facts. Nonverbal cues will often be a tip-off as to how the sender really feels about his or her message. At times it will be necessary to ask for clarification to obtain the true meaning. Suppose that your boss says to you, "I wonder if we're putting you under too much pressure." Asking, "What do you mean by that?" could reveal at least two different meanings. Your boss could mean that you look like you're faltering under the pressure. Or he or she could mean that you have been carrying an unfair burden.

5. *Capitalize on the fact that thought is faster than speech.* The average rate of speech is 125 words a minute for English. We think, and therefore listen, at almost four times that speed. A poor listener tends to daydream when encountering all but the most rapid speaker. A better approach is to challenge, anticipate, mentally summarize, weigh the evidence, and listen for the tone of voice to gauge feeling.

6. *Resist internal and external distractions.* When listening, try to leave your problems and concerns behind (for example, did I leave the lights on in my car?). External distractions also have to be resisted. While listening to the speaker, try to ignore that hard-falling rain outside or that physically attractive person adjacent to you. As one listening expert states, "A good listener intuitively fights distractions."[25]

7. *Judge content not delivery.* Poor speakers as well as good speakers may have something important to say. One of the most noted scientists in his field is considered to be one of the poorest teachers at his university. Therefore, be careful not to tune out a speaker whose delivery is poor. Judge the content and be less concerned about errors in delivery.

8. *Work at listening.* Listening is hard work, as most psychotherapists will tell you. The bad listener shows no energy output, but instead fakes attention. In contrast, the good listener works hard at receiving messages and exhibits an active body state.

IMPROVING YOUR FACE-TO-FACE SPEAKING SKILLS

Most people could use improvement in public speaking, but only high-level executive positions require that the incumbent give speeches. What most people do need is improved ability to express their ideas in face-to-face encounters, such as conferences and two-way discussions. Any course in conference leadership would help you to achieve this end. Four experience-based suggestions (if carried out) should help the reader to improve his or her face-to-face speaking skills.

1. Take the opportunity to speak in a meeting whenever it arises. Volunteer comments in class and committee meetings, and capitalize on any chance to be a spokesperson for a group.

2. Obtain feedback by listening to tape recordings or dictating equipment renditions of your voice. Attempt to eliminate vocalized pauses and repetitious phrases (such as "OK" or "you know") that detract from your communication effectiveness. Ask a knowledgeable friend for his or her opinion on your voice and speech.

3. Use appropriate models to help you to develop your speech. A television talk show host or commercial announcer may have the type of voice and speech behavior that fits your personality. The goal is not to imitate that person, but to use him or her as an approximate guide to generally acceptable speech.

4. Practice interviewing and being interviewed. Take turns with a friend conducting a simulated job interview. Interview each other about a controversial current topic or each other's hobby.

5. Learn to relax just prior to speaking. Seasoned professional speakers have learned early in their careers to exhale or consciously relax their muscles a few seconds before beginning their presentation. This relaxation technique is all the more important when the stakes are high, such as bringing a controversial problem to your boss's attention.

IMPROVING YOUR NONVERBAL
COMMUNICATION SKILLS

Body language and other forms of nonverbal communication can also be improved. Published information about this type of self-improvement is difficult to find. Here are four suggestions to tentatively consider.

1. Obtain feedback on your body language by asking others to comment on the gestures and facial expressions that you use in conversations. Have a video tape prepared of you conferring with another individual. After studying your body language, attempt to eliminate those mannerisms and gestures that you think detract from your effectiveness (such as moving your knee from side to side when being interviewed).

2. As mentioned for face-to-face speaking, learn to relax when communicating with others. Take a deep breath and consciously allow your body muscles to loosen. The tension-reducing techniques discussed in Chapter 8

should be helpful here. A relaxed person makes it easier for other people to relax. Thus, you are likely to elicit more useful information from other people when you are relaxed.

3. Use facial, hand, and body gestures to supplement your speech. (But do not overdo it.) A good starting point is to use hand gestures to express enthusiasm. You can increase the potency of enthusiastic comments by shaking the other person's hand, nodding approval, smiling, or patting him or her on the shoulder.

4. Avoid using the same nonverbal gesture indiscriminately. To illustrate, if you want to use nodding to convey approval, do not nod with approval even when you dislike what somebody else is saying. Also, do not pat everybody on the back. Nonverbal gestures used indiscriminately lose their communications effectiveness.

5. Try to maintain the proper physical distance from people when conversing with them. The better you know someone, the safer you are in standing close to him or her. Most people consider it an invasion of their *territorial space* if you move within six inches of them while speaking. Cultural differences exist about acceptable closeness. French males, for example, stand closer together when speaking than do American males. If your purpose is strictly business, allow about one and a half feet between the two of you when you are communicating.

IMPROVING YOUR WRITING SKILLS

Every reader of this book has probably already taken one or two courses designed to improve writing skills, and many other courses have a writing component. Nevertheless, since written communication skills are so important in business, five brief suggestions are in order. They may serve as a refresher and perhaps give you at least one new insight. In addition, you are invited to use Exhibit 15–2 to diagnose your own writing skill.

Exhibit 15–2

COMMUNICATIONS IQ TEST

Take this "IQ" test to find out how effective your writing is and how well you are communicating with your audience. Answer each question honestly, based on your personal writing habits. Specifically, when you set out to write a letter, memo, report, speech, or other communication, do you:

	YES	NO	UNCERTAIN
1. "Size up" your reader, his interests, needs, goals, and personality?	☐	☐	☐
2. Set your objective first, write to it, and then rate your effectiveness in reaching it?	☐	☐	☐
3. Assess the amount of information required to reach your objective?	☐	☐	☐
4. Use your opening remarks to interest and intrigue your reader?	☐	☐	☐
5. Mentally outline the facts for presentation?	☐	☐	☐
6. Select a particular language to meet the needs of both the situation and the reader?	☐	☐	☐
7. Make your writing say and do what you want it to, unbound by convention?	☐	☐	☐
8. Consider the graphic layout and visual effects of what you put on paper?	☐	☐	☐
9. Vary sentence length and paragraph structure, as well as inject vivid language where appropriate?	☐	☐	☐
10. Produce a "breather" or change of pace to encourage action?	☐	☐	☐
11. Create the correct tone, mood, attitude, or impression for the reaction you want?	☐	☐	☐
12. Give your reader a definite course to follow—or action to take—at the end of your presentation?	☐	☐	☐

TEST SCORING: If you have marked less than ten boxes in the "yes" column, your "IQ" is dangerously low and your written communications are not bringing you the results they should. If this is true, you should seek "professional help" immediately to cure your communications problems.

(SOURCE: Robert R. Max, "What's Your Communications "IQ"? *Supervisory Management*, April 1977, p. 13.)

1. Read a book about effective business report writing and attempt to implement the suggestions it offers.[26]

2. Read material regularly that is written in the style and format that would be useful to you in your career. The *Wall Street Journal* and *BusinessWeek* are useful models for most forms of job-related writing. Managerial and staff jobs require you to be able to write brief, readily understandable memos and reports. If your goal is to become a good technical report writer, continuously read technical reports in your field or specialty.

3. Practice writing at every opportunity. As a starting point, you might want to write letters to friends and relatives or memos to the field. Successful writers constantly practice writing. Many people who become an overnight success with a first book have already published a large number of articles.

4. Get feedback on your writing. Ask a co-worker to critique a rough draft of your reports and memos. Offer to reciprocate; editing other people's writing is a valuable way of improving your own. Feedback from a person with more writing experience and knowledge than you is particularly valuable. For instance, comments made by an instructor about a submitted paper would be highly valued.

5. Learn to use a word processor. Writing will always be a tedious process unless you mechanize the process. Typing in place of writing by hand is one moderate step forward; learning to use a word processor is a giant step forward. People often think of word processing (the combination of a typewriter with a computer) as a method of increasing the speed of one's writing. My observation is that the true payoff may be in writing quality, rather than speed—although the gains in speed may also be impressive. Writing quality improves because it is so easy to correct mistakes and edit your writing as you go along. You can also rearrange your paragraphs. And when it comes time to do a second draft of your paper, you simply recall the original document from the computer memory and re-edit. My one caution to the reader, however, is that word processors are much more temperamental than typewriters or writing pads. After every several pages of written input, command the computer to print. At this stage of their development, many word processors sometimes refuse to store or retrieve input. Or the disks used in small computers sometimes fail.

TRANSACTIONAL ANALYSIS: A WAY OF IMPROVING YOUR COMMUNICATION WITH PEOPLE

Transactional analysis (TA) was at one time a form of psychotherapy used to help people with severe emotional conflicts straighten out their lives. It has evolved into a complicated set of procedures for improving the way people relate to each other in both work and personal life. Transactional analysis is included in this chapter because, at an overall level, it can be considered a way of improving communication among people. A general goal of TA training is to help people relate to each other in a mature, adult manner, thus easing tension and getting important things accomplished.

Here we will describe several keystone ideas in TA. You are cautioned that what we say here is not 100 percent consistent with all other discussions of TA. The problem is that TA specialists often differ with each other on their explanation of key concepts of transactional analysis. After presenting the basic concepts, we will explain how TA might be used to improve interpersonal communication.

Ego States

When you are dealing with another person, you are really dealing with a set of three major personality segments (according to TA). You are also operating from a set of personality segments. Each of these personality segments is called an **ego state.** The latter term refers to a consistent combination of thought, feelings, and related behavior. When an ego state is operating, our insides and outsides tend to be synchronized.[27] Each ego state has its own set of beliefs and behaviors, and each relates to other people in a different manner.[28]

Children have six ego states. But in adult life, only three ego states are consistently effective in getting people what they need and want. The three main ego states (to be described next) are the Child, the Adult, and the Parent. For those interested in technical detail, the effective need-fulfilling ego states are called the Natural Child, the Adult, and the Nuturing Parent. The ineffective, need-blocking ego states are called the Critical Parent, Rebellious Child, and Compliant Child.

The Parent. The parent ego state dictates that we act as our parents once did. When you are in the Parent state, you are being your mother, father, or other important people who influenced you in your early childhood. The parent ego state can be considered a body of recordings in the brain that reflects the unquestioned events perceived by people during their childhood. The parent is highly judgmental and moralistic. A person acting in the Parent state will display such characteristics as being overprotective, distant, dogmatic, indispensable, and self-righteous. Certain physical and verbal clues tell you that someone is acting as a Parent. These include the wagging finger to show displeasure, reference to laws and rules, and reliance on ways that were successful in the past.[29]

The Adult. When people are acting and thinking rationally, when they are gathering facts and making judgments based on these facts, they are in the

Adult ego state. The adult is an information seeker and processor who basically follows the decision-making process described in Chapter 7. You can tell a person is in the Adult ego state when he or she concentrates and engages in factual discussion. A major goal in TA is to put your Adult in charge of your Child and Parent. This is referred to as "keeping the Adult in executive position." Emotionally mature, healthy individuals thus have the Adult ego state running their personalities.[30]

The Child. People are born with the segment of personality called the Child ego state. It reflects needs, wants, and feelings. When people feel and act as they did in childhood, they are in their Child ego state. It is the data that are recorded in the brain as a result of experiences taking place through ages one to five. Characteristics of the child include creativity, conformity, depression, anxiety, dependence, fear, and hate. Because childhood experiences are so varied, people show varied behavior when in their child state. Despite this variation, a clue that a person is being a child is when he or she is nonlogical and demands immediate gratification of impulses. Other clues are temper tantrums, giggling, coyness, attention seeking, and stoney-faced silence.

Analysis of Transactions. To apply TA to relationships between people, it is necessary to identify the transactions taking place between the different ego states. Much of what takes place in a TA workshop involves the analysis of transactions. Recognizing the ego states of the two people involved in the transaction can help a person communicate and interact more effectively. Transactions are classified into complementary and crossed (noncomplementary). When transactions between people are complementary (positive strokes), effective interaction is the result. When transactions are crossed (when one person gives negative strokes to the other), we have ineffective interaction.

Complementary transactions are shown in Figure 15–2. All are effective transactions because both people receive the positive stroking that they want.

In cell I, a boss acting in an adult state might say to a subordinate, "When will I get my report?" The subordinate replies, "It will be ready tomorrow at three o'clock."

In cell II, the boss, in a parent state, says "Be here early tomorrow; it's an important day." To which the subordinate replies, "Don't worry. I'll be here."

In cell III, the child-acting boss says, "Let's have a few drinks at lunch." The subordinate replies, "Maybe we can even drink right up to quitting time."

In cell IV, the child-acting boss says, "We're so overwhelmed with work in this department, I don't think we'll ever catch up." In a parent-like fashion, the subordinate responds, "I'll get things under control."

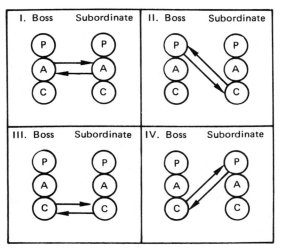

P is parent; A is adult; C is child

FIGURE 15-2
Complementary transactions.

Crossed transactions, shown in Figure 15-3, result in negative strokes and ineffective transactions between people.

In cell I, the boss, in a child state, says, "I desperately need your cooperation," hoping for a parent reponse. Instead, the boss hears, "I'm doing all I can right now. What more do you expect?"

In cell II, the parent boss, hoping for a child response from his subordinates, says, "Your work is sloppy and needs immediate correction." Instead, a parentlike subordinate says, "I'll be the judge of the neatness of my work."

In cell III, an adult boss, hoping for an adult response, says, "Have you ever thought of attending a personal growth group?" Acting as a parent, the subordinate says, "That, sir, constitutes an invasion of privacy."

In cell IV, a parent-acting boss says, "You are totally without self-discipline." Instead of acting as a whipped or obedient child, the subordinate responds in an adult manner, "In what way am I lacking in self-discipline?"

Life Scripts and Life Positions

Another key concept in TA is that the individual develops a life script—a plan or drama acted out during a person's life. It is as if people have a compulsion to live a preprogrammed life. Some people are forever manipulating others; some are losers; some are winners; some are chronic procrastinators. If a manager understands the script being followed by a subordinate, co-worker, or superior, it might make it easier to deal with that person. For

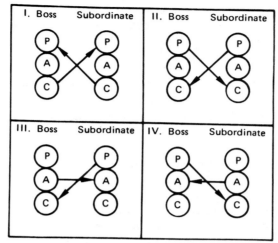

P is parent; A is adult; C is child

FIGURE 15-3
Crossed transactions.

example, if Michelle is a "winner," all things being equal her boss will send her out on a difficult mission.

In early childhood, the person develops a life script by being submerged in a culture, interacting with the family unit, viewing television, and being exposed to printed information. Part of developing a life script is finding answers to questions such as: Who am I? What am I doing here? Who are these people around me? What are these people doing here?

A script leads to the development of a life position. Once these life positions have been established, they become a set of expectations that the individual uses to guide his or her behavior. The four life positions, to be described next, may also be considered sets of assumptions about one's self in relation to others.[31]

I'm Not OK—You're OK. In this life position, the Child predominates because the child frequently feels inadequate in comparison to the more confident and powerful adult. A person who follows this script is subject to frequent depression. An employee who assumes "I'm not OK—You're OK" may need reassurance and affection from the boss.

I'm OK—You're Not OK. This is the life position of the parent ego state—experienced, all-knowing, guiding, correcting, and controlling. In extreme, this life position leads to paranoidlike (very suspicious) thinking. Employees whose scripts have lead to this life position frequently blame others when things go wrong on the job.

I'm Not OK—You're Not OK. This is a pathological life position, usually stemming from prolonged mental illness. Few people maintaining this position prosper on the job. When they are able to stay employed, their jobs are unskilled, involving minimum contact with people.

I'm OK—You're OK. This is the ideal life position on which authentic, game-free relations are based. The mature adult ("healthy, well-rounded employee") has developed a script that leads him or her to believe "I'm OK—You're OK."

Using TA to Get Through to People

Transactional analysis is supposed to be of major benefit to its followers. Yet there is a big gap between reading about TA or attending TA training and applying it to your own life. The description of TA in this chapter and Chapter 12 (in relation to game playing) only points you toward an understanding of several of its major concepts. The examples presented next will help you understand how TA might improve your communications, and therefore your relationships, with people.

Removing Communication Blocks. A direct application of TA is to overcome communication blocks between you and another person. The key here is to decide which ego state the other person is using: parent, adult, or child. Referring to the arrows in Figure 15–2, you strive for a complementary transaction. If someone is acting as an adult, the best way to "get through" to that person is to act as an adult yourself. Child-to-child, parent-to-child, and child-to-parent transactions all help you to communicate better with another individual. The interchanges between people presented earlier to explain Figure 15–2 are all examples of using TA to remove communication blocks.

Improving Your Managerial Style. Transactional analysis has much to say about leadership styles. If you want to be an authoritarian boss, it is usually necessary to maintain parent-to-child transactions with people. In some situations, this helps you to overcome communication barriers. However, in the long run it is more beneficial to the organization to have more people relating to one another in an adult-to-adult manner. Such transactions require a participative style of management. Using this approach, the leader is able to achieve a climate of mutual trust and respect for each other's competence. A follower of TA will thus strive to be a participative leader in most situations.

The free-rein management style is sometimes a child-to-child relationship. A leader of this type leaves subordinates to their own devices and provides no leadership. In the long range, the organization suffers and the individuals are left with a feeling of frustration because they have not accomplished much.[32]

You can enhance your relationship with others by dispensing positive reinforcement.

Giving Positive Strokes to Folks. An important message of TA is quite similar to that derived from reinforcement theory (PR): you can enhance your relationships with others by dispensing positive reinforcement. Transactional analysis has a set of "cute" terms of its own for the same approach to handling people. Perhaps you have met a person who attended a weekend workshop in TA or read a book on the subject. Often he or she will make statements such as "Wow, that was a warm fuzzy," or "I guess you need some stroking." If TA makes you more sensitive to the importance of positive reinforcement in daily relationships, that alone is an important contribution.

Follow TA Rules of Communication

Abe Wagner has gathered together a number of suggestions for improving your communication with people, based on TA. He suggests that changing your words can change your personality, and it also invites others to change their personalities. His rules relate directly to the idea of owning your own feelings, thoughts, and behavior, and no one else's. Several of his tips are as follows:

1. Use the word I. Speak in the first person when you want to express your own point of view and feelings, instead of using "one," "people," "they," or so forth. The word "I" personalizes your comments and indicates that you take responsibility for your own ideas.

2. Say "I won't" instead of "I can't." To say "I can't" implies that you have no control over your actions and this is rarely the case. To say "I won't" implies that it is your decision not to do something.

3. Avoid saying "I don't know" when you do know. Save "I don't know" for occasions when you are asked for information you really do not have. If you do know something but are not willing to share your answer, "I'd rather not say" is an OK response.

4. Avoid hedging. When you have a definite point of view, avoid words like "perhaps," "probably," and "maybe," or "I'm not sure." Definite points of view encourage others to be open with you in return.

5. Don't try, do. You communicate much stronger conviction to another person when you say you will do something, rather than you will try to do something. Which sounds more effective, "I will try to be to Tuesday's meeting on time" or "I will be at Tuesday's meeting on time"?

6. Use eye contact. Eye contact is an important aspect of nonverbal communication, and it is a good indicator of which of your ego states is operating. The Child breaks eye contact; the Parent looks down from above; the Adult uses a comfortable, level gaze.[33]

SUMMARY OF KEY POINTS

☐ Communication is the transmission of a message from a sender to a receiver. Its purpose is to gather, process, and disseminate information, making it a vital work activity. The seven steps in the communication process are ideation, encoding, transmission, receiving, decoding, understanding, and action. Interference, or barriers to communication, can take place at any of these steps.

☐ Organizational communication takes place in several different directions and over both formal and informal pathways. Formal pathways are the official, sanctioned path over which messages are supposed to travel. The formal chain of command and the actual flow of work both help shape formal communication channels. Informal pathways are more numerous than formal pathways. The grapevine is the major informal communication network in an organization.

☐ A rumor is a message transmitted over the grapevine, although not based on official word. Rumors are capable of disrupting work and lowering morale. Providing people with timely and accurate information is a good way of both preventing and stopping rumors. Gossip is a special form of rumor that does waste time, but also serves a few useful purposes. Gossip can be a morale booster, a socializing force, and a guidebook to group norms.

☐ Nonverbal communication refers to the transmission of messages through means other than words. It is used to communicate the feeling behind your message. Four common forms of NVC are gestures, facial expressions, posture, and interpersonal distance. Neurolinguistic programming is a self-improvement program designed to help you understand others and establish rapport with them. To use NLP, you have to attend carefully to the nonverbal behavior of the other person and then mirror that behavior. The mirroring leads to rapport with, and sometimes control of, the other person.

☐ The first step in overcoming communication barriers is to recognize that they exist. Specific methods of overcoming these barriers include (1) understand the receiver, (2) engage in two-way communication, (3) use multiple channels, (4) communicate honestly, (5) use verbal and nonverbal feedback, (6) decrease physical barriers, (7) increase the opportunity for informal interaction, (8) use appropriately difficult language, and (9) avoid communication overload.

☐ Another general strategy for overcoming communication barriers is to improve your communication skills. Four modes of communication should receive attention: listening, speaking, nonverbal, and writing. Since improving your communication skills is covered in other courses, only a brief set of suggestions for such improvement is described in this chapter.

☐ Transactional analysis is a way of improving your communication and the quality of your relationships with others. A general goal of TA training is to help people relate to each other in a mature, adult manner. Applying TA to your job or personal life requires that you learn its jargon and be able to analyze the transactions that take place between yourself and others.

☐ One major concept of TA holds that the human personality is divided into three segments, called ego states—the Parent, Adult, and Child. To apply TA to relationships between people, it is necessary to identify the transactions that take place between the different ego states. Complementary transactions result in positive strokes and effective interaction. Crossed transactions result in negative strokes and ineffective transactions. Another major TA concept is that life scripts lead to life positions—sets of assumptions about one's self in relation to others. The mature, healthy adult maintains the life position "I'm OK—You're OK."

GUIDELINES FOR PERSONAL EFFECTIVENESS

1. Practice two-way rather than one-way communication if you are concerned about getting your message across. While delivering your message, ask for verbal feedback and be sensitive to nonverbal cues about how your message is getting across.
2. Effective speaking, writing, listening, and nonverbal skills are a valuable asset to anybody whose job involves dealing with people. Improving your communication skills is therefore a success factor in your career.
3. Strive for adult-to-adult relationships with others. To get started, act and think rationally when the people you are communicating with are also acting in an adult manner. When others are acting in a parent or child manner, you will have to use the appropriate ego state to improve communications. Refer to Figure 15–2 as a guide.

DISCUSSION QUESTIONS

1. Prospective employers say repeatedly that one of the most important attributes they look for in a new hire from business school is good communication skills. Why so much emphasis on communication skills?

2. From the manager's standpoint, what are some disadvantages of engaging in dialogues, rather than monologues, with subordinates?

3. Describe two specific steps an employee might take to convince others that he or she is an honest communicator?

4. Think of the last time you shopped for an automobile or other major purchase. What kind of nonverbal communication did the salesperson use to help influence you to make a purchase?

5. What physical barriers to communication exist in a classroom? In what way do instructors sometimes decrease these barriers?

6. How would you rate the communications IQ of your local newspaper? (See Exhibit 15–2.)

7. Why do you think it is much less tension provoking to listen than to write or think?

8. How would you react if a co-worker of the same sex stands about six inches from you when the two of you are engaged in work-related conversation? What about a co-worker of the opposite sex?

9. What kinds of nonverbal communication have you observed deaf people use?

10. An acquaintance of yours spills a cup of hot coffee on your desk, drenching some important papers. Some coffee also spills on your clothing. How would you respond to your acquaintance, using each of the three ego states: Parent, Adult, and Child?

11. What is the most important message you get from TA?

A Business Psychology Problem
THE ELECTRONIC MAIL RESISTORS

Deborah Winslow, chief administrator at Tucson Group Health, was proud of her accomplishment. After 13 months of negotiating with other executives, including the board of directors, her health maintenance organization (HMO) converted to an electronic mail system. She realized that no other HMO in Arizona had made such a complete attempt to decrease paper work in favor of electronic mail. In Deborah's evaluation, employees of Tucson Group Health were wasting too much time sending printed letters to each other. Now any employee with one hour of training could learn to communicate to other employees via electronic mail. Deborah was looking toward an annual cost savings of $25,000.

Four months after the start-up, Dr. Aaron Goldfarb, Deborah's boss, asked her how well the new electronic mail system was performing. Cupping her chin in her right hand, Deborah replied, "I have to give you a dual answer. From a technological standpoint, we have bought a beautiful piece of office automation. We have not had one serious malfunction with the equipment. It is also very user friendly. No employee has said he or she cannot understand how to use the equipment."

"What's the other standpoint?" asked Aaron.

"We have bombed out from a human use standpoint. Despite the electronic mail system, our employees are still dropping by each others' offices and work stations to chat. And anytime they have an important message, they bypass electronic mail. To be candid, we are using the new system to pass along trivial messages to each other. So far it has not become a real time saver nor a method of really improving communications. I'm getting some vibes that HMO employees think the electronic mail is too impersonal. They prefer the human touch."

Dr. Goldfarb replied, "I'm no expert on office communications. However, that's a pretty expensive toy you have installed. If you can't get our employees to use it in a meaningful way, I'd say remove the system."

1. What strategy do you recommend for Deborah if she wants to keep her system?

2. What communication barriers is the electronic mail system encountering?

REFERENCES

[1]Michael L. Peters, "How Important Is Interpersonal Communication?" *Personnel Journal* (July 1983), p. 554.

[2]Donald A. Laird, Eleanor C. Laird, and Rosemary T. Freuhling, *Psychology: Human Relations and Work Adjustment*, 6th ed. (New York: McGraw-Hill, 1983), p. 270.

[3]This composite definition is derived from Davis's statements in Keith Davis, *Human Relations in Business* (New York: McGraw-Hill, 1957), p. 244, and "Tending the Grapevine," *Time* (June 18, 1973), p. 67.

[4]Walter St. John, "In-House Communication Guidelines," *Personnel Journal* (Nov. 1981), p. 877.

[5]Ibid.

[6]The first three suggestions are credited to Frederick Koenig as quoted in Jane See White, "Biggest Companies: Target of Biggest Rumors," Rochester *Democrat and Chronicle* (April 7, 1980), p. 1C. The fourth suggestion is from St. John, "In-House Communication," p. 877.

[7]Robert S. Wieder, "Psst! Here's the Latest on Office Gossip," *Success* (Jan. 1984), pp. 22–25.

[8]John Baird, Jr., and Gretchen Wieting, "Nonverbal Communication Can Be a Motivational Tool," *Personnel Journal* (Sept. 1979), p. 609. Much of our discussion of nonverbal communication is based on the Baird and Wieting article, pp. 607–610.

[9]Salvatore Didato, "Our Body Movements Reveal Whether We're Dominant or Submissive," Rochester *Democrat and Chronicle* (Dec. 20, 1983), p. 1C.

[10]M. Patterson, "Spatial Factors in Social Interaction," *Human Factors* (no. 3, 1968), pp. 351–361.

[11]Kenneth Blanchard and Spencer Johnson, *The One Minute Manager* (New York: Berkley Books, 1983), p. 44.

[12]Eric H. Marcus, "Neurolinguistic Programming," *Personnel Journal* (Dec. 1983), p. 972.

[13]"Reprogramming the Patient," *Time* (Dec. 1983), p. 79.

[14]Marcus, "Neurolinguistic Programming," p. 795.

[15]James L. Gibson, John M. Ivancevich, and James H. Donnelly, Jr., *Organizations: Behavior, Structure, Processes*, 4th ed. (Plano, Texas: Business Publications, 1982), p. 406.

[16]An enlightening discussion of this topic is found in Harold J. Leavitt, *Managerial Psychology*, 4th ed. (Chicago: University of Chicago Press, 1978), p. 117–126.

[17]Daniel Goleman, "The Electronic Rorschach," *Psychology Today* (Feb. 1983), p. 42.

[18]Gibson, Ivancevich, and Donnelly, *Organizations*, p. 406.

[19]Ibid., p. 407.

[20]Robert T. Keller and Winford E. Holland, "Communicators and Innovators in Research and Development Organizations," *Academy of Management Journal* (Dec. 1983), p. 748.

[21]Charles A. O'Reilly, III, "Individuals and Information Overload in Organizations: Is More Necessarily Better?" *Academy of Management Journal* (Dec. 1980), p. 684–696. See also "How Brokers Avoid Drowning in Data," *BusinessWeek* (Nov. 15, 1982), pp. 135, 138.

[22]John W. Richter, "Listening: An Art Essential to Success," *Success* (Sept. 1980), p. 26.

[23]Ibid.

[24]This list is based on several sources: Ralph G. Nichols, "Listening Is a 10-Part Skill," in *Managing Yourself,* presented by the editors of *Nation's Business,* not dated; Richter, "Listening," p. 26: and the Xerox Effective Listening Program.

[25]Richter, "Listening," p. 26.

[26]Among the many good texts on this topic is Raymond V. Lesikar, *Basic Business Communication,* rev. ed. (Homewood, Ill.: Irwin, 1983). See also the Suggested Reading section at the end of this chapter.

[27]Dudley Bennett, *TA and the Manager* (New York: AMACOM, 1976), p. 1.

[28]Abe Wagner, *The Transactional Manager: How to Solve People Problems with Transactional Analysis* (Englewood Cliffs, N.J.: Prentice-Hall, 1981), p. 7.

[29]Muriel James, *The OK Boss* (Reading, Mass.: Addison-Wesley, 1975), p. 32.

[30]Wagner, *Transactional Manager,* p. 18.

[31]Our discussion of life scripts and life positions is based somewhat on Laird W. Mealiea, "The TA Approach to Employee Development," *Supervisory Management* (Aug. 1977), p. 12.

[32]Donald D. Bowen and Raghu Nath, "Transactions in Management," *California Management Review* (Winter 1975), pp. 81–83.

[33]The italicized statements are quoted from Wagner, *Transactional Manager,* pp. 85–98.

SUGGESTED READING

"A Personal Achievement Guide to Communication," *Success* (July 1982), pp. 27–34.

BARNARD, JANET C. "The Principal Players in Your Communication Network," *Supervisory Management* (June 1983), pp. 20–24.

BROWN, LELAND. *Communicating Facts and Ideas in Business,* 3rd ed. Englewood Cliffs, N.J.: Prentice-Hall, 1982.

D'APRIX, ROGER. *Communicating for Productivity.* New York: Harper & Row, 1982.

KLAUSS, RUDI, and BERNARD M. BASS. *Interpersonal Communication in Organizations.* New York: Academic Press, 1982.

MAHONEY, FRANCIS X. "Team Development, Part 3: Communication Meetings," *Personnel* (Jan.–Feb. 1982), pp. 49–58.

RADER, MARTHA H. "Dealing with Information Overload," *Personnel Journal* (May 1981), pp. 373–375.

REPP, WILLIAM. *Complete Handbook of Business English*. Englewood Cliffs, N.J.: Prentice-Hall, 1983.

ROGERS, CARL R. "Barriers and Gateways to Communication," *Harvard Business Review* (July–Aug. 1951), pp. 46–52.

ST. JOHN, WALTER D. "Successful Communication between Supervisors and Employees," *Personnel Journal* (Jan. 1983), pp. 71–77.

PART FIVE

REALIZING YOUR POTENTIAL

16 Improving Your Personal Productivity
17 Achieving a Satisfying and Rewarding Career

In this final part of the book, we present a substantial amount of information and describe a number of skills aimed specifically at helping you gain career thrust. The previous parts of the book are also aimed at self-development, but the following two chapters focus on specific career development skills. Chapter 16 is based on the premise that the key to personal productivity is good work habits and time management (assuming you already have good skills and motivation). Chapter 17 is about specific career-building strategies, such as finding the right field, finding a suitable job, and then moving ahead in your career.

16

IMPROVING YOUR
PERSONAL PRODUCTIVITY

LEARNING OBJECTIVES

After reading and studying this chapter and doing the exercises, you should be able to

1. Become a more productive individual.
2. Deal more effectively with any tendencies you might have toward procrastination.
3. Understand how your attitudes and values influence your work habits and management of time.
4. Be familiar with skills and practices that could improve your personal productivity.

Assume that the instructor for this course announced that a term project will be due December 31, 1999, the absolute latest. Close to that date a handful of people would ask for an extension into the year 2000. Among the excuses offered would be, "I just didn't have time to do the paper with all those celebrations going on." "I would have been ready, but my word processor broke down December 30th." "Just my luck. My brother-in-law is getting married the same day that the project is due."

Work Habits, Time Management, and Personal Productivity. One reason for improving your work habits and time management is to avoid the trap faced by people who are always late with projects, even if the lead time is 20 years!

Two other reasons are also of major significance. People who use good work habits and who manage time well tend to be more successful in their careers than poorly organized people. Another reason for having good work habits is that you will then have more time to spend on personal life. You will also enjoy your personal life more if you are not preoccupied with unfinished tasks. Good work habits and time management thus lead to improved productivity both in work and personal life.

Personal productivity refers to your level of efficiency and effectiveness. Efficiency means that you accomplish tasks with a minimum of wasted time, material, and fanfare. If you are a collection agent and it costs you $900 to collect $950 in past due accounts, you are not being very efficient. Effectiveness refers to accomplishing important results, while at the same time maintaining high quality. Efficiency and effectiveness are related. Being efficient often clears the way for being effective. If you are on top of your job, it gives you the time to work on important tasks and to strive for quality.

We have organized information about becoming more productive into three categories that show some overlap. One is overcoming procrastination, a problem that plagues everybody to some extent. The second is developing the attitudes and values that foster efficiency and effectiveness. The third category is the lengthiest: developing the proper skills and techniques that lead to personal productivity.

DEALING WITH PROCRASTINATION

Procrastination is the major time waster for most employees and students. Unproductive people are the biggest procrastinators, but even highly productive people have some problems with procrastination. A reporter for *People* magazine had this to say about procrastinators: "Some of the most talented writers in the country are practically starving. Magazine editors respect their talents, but they know that if these writers are given an assignment, it will not be completed on time. The writers I'm talking about just can't get it together to meet deadlines."[1]

Why People Procrastinate

People procrastinate for many different reasons. One is that they perceive the task to be done as unpleasant, such as asking a friend to return the $50 that he or she borrowed from you. Another reason we procrastinate is that we find the job facing us to be overwhelming, such as unpacking after a move.[2] Psychiatrist Henry Everett believes that the major cause of procrastination is an inner fear of the consequences of your actions.[3]

We agree with Everett's analysis, especially when it is recognized that these consequences can take several forms. One possible negative consequence is a negative evaluation of your work. For example, if you delay preparing a report for your boss or instructor, that person cannot criticize its quality. Bad news is another uncomfortable consequence of action that procrastination can sometimes delay. If you think you have an impacted wisdom tooth, by delaying making an appointment with the dentist, you will not receive the diagnosis: "You have an impacted wisdom tooth. You will need oral surgery. The total fee should be less than $800."

Techniques for Reducing Procrastination

A general method of coping with procrastination is to raise your level of awareness about the problem. When you are not accomplishing enough to meet your school work, job, or personal goals, ask yourself if the problem could be one of procrastination. Then through self-discipline, try to overcome that incident of inaction. You might also consider trying one or more of the four techniques described next.

Calculate the Price of Procrastination. Time-management consultant Alan Lakein believes that you can reduce procrastination by calculating its price.[4] One example is that you might lose out on obtaining a high-paying job you really want by not having your résumé and cover letter ready on time. Your cost of procrastination would include the difference in salary between the job you do find and the one you really wanted. Another cost would be the loss of potential job satisfaction.

Create Some Momentum to Get You Moving. One way to get momentum going on an unpleasant or overwhelming task is to set aside a specific time to work on it. If you have to write a report on a subject you dislike, you might set aside Sunday from 1 P.M. to 3 P.M. as your first attack on the project. Another way to create some momentum is to find a leading task to perform. (A leading task is an easy, warm-up activity.)[5] If you were procrastinating about painting your apartment, you might purchase the brush and paint as a way of getting started.

Apply Behavior Modification to Yourself. Give yourself a pleasant reward soon after you accomplish an unpleasant chore, rather than procrastinating. You might, for example, go jogging in a light mist after having completed a tough take-home exam. The second part of the strategy is to punish yourself with something you despise immediately after you procrastinate.[6] How about cleaning out a refrigerator-freezer as a punishment for mailing out bills late?

Make a Commitment to Other People. Try to make it imperative that you get something done on time by making it a commitment to one or more other people. You might announce to co-workers that you are going to get something accomplished by a certain date. If you fail to meet this date, you are likely to feel embarrassed. One court reporter told a judge, "You will have the complete transcript of this trial within 30 days. If I don't get it done, please don't let me in your courtroom again for six months." (Typing out a court transcript after a trial is an arduous task that lends itself to procrastination.)

DEVELOPING THE PROPER ATTITUDES AND VALUES

Developing good work habits and time-management practices is often a matter of developing the right attitudes toward your work and toward time. If, for example, you think that your school work or job is important and that time is a precious resource, you will be on your way toward developing good work habits. In this section we describe a group of attitudes, values, and beliefs that can help a person become more productive through better use of time and improved work habits.

Become a Goal-Oriented Person

As described in Chapter 6, setting goals can lead to direct improvements in performance. One reason goal setting helps in this way is that being committed to a goal propels you toward good use of time. Imagine how efficient most employees would be if they were told, "Here is five days of work facing you. If you get it finished in less than five days, you can have all that saved time to yourself." One negative side effect, however, is that the employees might sacrifice quality for speed.

Having goals, and thus becoming a goal-oriented person, is perhaps the first step in any serious program of improving personal productivity.

Try to Discover What Is Blocking You

Some forms of poor work habits and time-management practices are caused by personal problems. If you can figure out what this problem is, you might be able to overcome problems like forgetting to do important assignments. One potential block is the fear of success. People who fear success believe that success will bring with it some uncomfortable effect, such as isolation or abandonment.[7] Or some people may simply prefer to avoid the responsibility that success will bring. And a quick way to avoid success is to hold onto inefficient work habits and to squander time.

It would take a shrewd bit of self-analysis to determine if you feared success. A recommended approach would be to supplement self-analysis by discussing the topic with a trusted friend and/or professional counselor.

Unresolved personal problems can also block your productivity. This is especially true because effective time utilization requires good concentration. When you are preoccupied with a personal or business problem, it is difficult to give your full efforts to the task at hand. The solution is to do something constructive about whatever problem is sapping your ability to concentrate (as discussed in the chapter about stress and burnout). Sometimes a relatively minor problem, such as driving with an expired operator's license, can impair your work concentration. At other times, a major problem, such as how to best take care of a parent who has suffered a stroke, interferes with work. In either situation, your concentration will suffer until you take appropriate action.

Value Good Attendance and Punctuality

Good attendance and punctuality are expected of both experienced and inexperienced employees. Also, you cannot be productive if you are not physically present in your work area. An important exception is if an employee works at home. Such arrangements should be clarified in advance with one's immediate superior. Keep in mind, too, that being late for or absent from meetings sends out the silent message to most people that you do not regard the meeting as important.

Avoid Perfectionism

Thoroughness is a virtue on most jobs, until it reaches the point of diminishing returns. If every typographical error were removed from a newspaper, the price of the paper would have to be increased. Even worse, the paper would usually be late. Striving for excellence is certainly worthwhile. Striving for perfection is often self-defeating. Edwin Bliss provides a telling anecdote about the place of perfectionism in business:[8]

> Sir Simon Marks, who was chairman of the consistently profitable Marks & Spencer retailing chain in Great Britain, maintained that those who make a fetish of perfection are wasting time and money that could be allocated elsewhere. Hence his system of "sensible approximation" in inventory procedures. His motto: "The price of perfection is prohibitive."

Learn to Say No

"Of all the time-saving techniques ever developed, perhaps the most effective is the frequent use of the word *no*," points out Edwin Bliss.[9] You cannot take care of your own priorities unless you learn to tactfully decline requests from other people that interfere with your work.

If it is important to you to complete studying for an exam, you must resist the request of your neighbor to spend two hours throwing a frisbee around the front lawn. Your boss, of course, is more difficult to turn down than a neighborhood frisbee player. Bliss suggests that if your boss interrupts your work with an added assignment, "Point out to your boss how the new task will conflict with higher-priority ones and suggest alternatives." When your boss recognizes that you are motivated to get your major tasks accomplished, and not to avoid work, you'll have a good chance of avoiding unproductive tasks.

A word of caution. Do not turn down your boss too frequently. Much discretion and tact is needed in using this approach to work efficiency.

Strive for Both Quantity and Quality

Most employers want a great deal of work accomplished, but they also need high quality; in other words, they demand true productivity. Thus a commitment to both quality and quantity leads to effective work habits. As a first principle, work as rapidly as you can just before the point at which you are committing an unacceptable number of errors. Striving for perfection is not worth the price, but achieving high-quality goods and services is highly valued in most firms today.

Ask, "What is the Best Use of My Time Right Now?"

A major tool for improving your efficiency and effectiveness is to ask Lakein's question: "What is the best use of my time right now?"[10] This question helps you to justify your every action. Lakein notes that a particularly good time to ask his question is when you have been interrupted by a visitor or phone call. When its over, he advises to check whether you should go back to what you were doing or on to something new.

Your answer to Lakein's question may be different when asked about what seems to be a comparable situation. One day you are waiting for an elevator in your office building. You ask "What is the best possible use of my time right now?" Your answer is, "Certainly not waiting for an elevator. I'll jog up the stairs and get some needed exercise."

One week later you are again waiting for the elevator. You ask the same question. This time your answer is, "Waiting for the elevator is a good use of my time right now. It's about time I touched base with a few employees from different departments in the company."

Recognize the Importance of Rest and Relaxation

A valid attitude to maintain is that overwork can be counterproductive, leading to negative stress and burnout. Proper physical rest contributes to mental alertness. Workaholics, people who are obsessed with work, often approach their jobs in a mechanical, unimaginative manner. (A small number of workaholics, however, are creative people at the top of their fields. But to these people, work is truly relaxing.)

Constant attention to work or study is often inefficient. It is a normal human requirement to take enough rest breaks to allow oneself to approach work or study with a fresh perspective. Each person has to establish for himself or herself the right balance between work and leisure, within the bounds of freedom granted by the situation. A young middle manager painted this picture of working conditions at his company, "Sure, I believe in leading a balanced life. But at my company you can't if you want to climb the ladder. Management expects us to work about 60 hours per week. You dare not be caught entering the building after 8 in the morning or leaving before 6:30 at night."

Develop a Strong Work Ethic

The most comprehensive value of all that will lead to improved productivity is to develop a strong work ethic—a firm belief in the dignity and value of work. It is related to being goal-oriented, but is even more comprehensive. For example, one could set the goal of earning a high income. It would lead to some good work habits, but not necessarily a high commitment to quality. A person with a strong work ethic believes in quality, is highly motivated, and minimizes time-wasting activities, including too much schmoozing.

If you have a weak work ethic, developing a strong one is difficult. One approach is to work in, or prepare for, a field that you find exciting (see Chapter 17).

DEVELOPING THE PROPER SKILLS AND TECHNIQUES

So far we have discussed two important general strategies for improving your personal productivity. One is to minimize procrastination, while the other is to develop the appropriate attitudes, values, and beliefs. You also need the right skills and techniques to become efficient and effective. Most books, articles, and workshops dealing with the topic of work habits and time management cover similar ground. Next we summarize most of the skills and techniques mentioned in these sources, along with a few new ones.

Prepare a List and Set Priorities

At the heart of every time-management system is list making. We described this technique briefly in relation to setting daily goals (refer to Figure 6–2). Almost every successful person in any field composes a list of important and less-important tasks that need to be done. Some executives and professional people delegate their list making and errand running to a subordinate. Before you can compose a useful list, you need to set aside a few minutes a day to sort out the tasks at hand. Such activity is the most basic aspect of planning.

As implied in Figure 6–2, many people find it helpful to set up "do" lists for both work and personal life.

Where Do You Put Your Lists? Some people dislike having small do lists stuck in different places. One reason is that these lists are readily lost among other papers. A time-management consultant recommends instead that you use a notebook, either looseleaf or spiral-bound, that is small enough to carry around with you. The notebook becomes your master list to keep track of errands, things to do or buy, and general notes to yourself about anything requiring action.[11]

Setting Priorities. Everything on a person's do list is not of equal importance; therefore, priorities should be attached to each item on the list. A typical system is to use A to signify critical or essential items, B to signify important items, and C for the least important ones. Although an item might be regarded as a C (for example, refilling the cellophane-tape dispenser), it still has a contribution to make to your management of time and sense of well-being. Many people report that they obtain a sense of satisfaction from crossing off an item on their list, however trivial. Second, if you are at all conscientious, small, undone items will come back to interfere with your concentration.

Use a Computerized Calendar. Software is available that can turn your personal computer into an electronic calendar to help you keep track of appointments and lists of chores.[12] The first step, of course, would be to enter into your computer's memory your appointments, tasks, and errands. For instance, a person might enter the following:

3/1	Meet with Ms. Godwin to discuss term project.
3/6	Get inventory audit started.
3/7	Lunch with Liz to discuss St. Patrick's Day party.
6/10	Start shopping for gift for parents' Silver Anniversary.

From this point forward, the computer's information-processing capabilities could be tapped. Suppose you couldn't remember the date of your upcoming luncheon date with Liz. You would command the computer to "Find lunch date with Liz." Or, if you were an extremely busy person, you might have reason to ask the computer to tell you when you had the next opening for lunch. Another use of this type of software is to command the computer to flag key appointments and chores. One computer sales representative boasted that her computer has become her personal secretary since she began using the calendar program.

Concentrate on One Task at a Time

Effective executives have a well-developed capacity to concentrate on the problem or person facing them, however surrounded they are with other obligations. The best results from concentration are achieved when you are so absorbed in your work that you achieve the *flow* experience (see Chapter 5). Intense concentration leads to crisper judgment and analysis and also minimizes major errors. Another useful by-product of concentration is that it helps reduce absentmindedness. If you really concentrate on what you are doing, the chances diminish that you will forget what you intended to do. Author Walter Olesky aptly describes how concentration is tied in with personal productivity:

> Most of the really successful people, in whatever field, subordinate everything to the main purposes of their lives. When they are at work, they display extraordinary powers of concentration. These men and women often bewilder their fellow workers, because they never seem to work hard, or for any period of time. Their secret lies in their power to concentrate, and thus to obtain maximum results with a minimum of apparent effort.[13]

Concentrate on High-Output Tasks

To become more effective on the job or in school, you have to concentrate on tasks in which superior performance could have a large payoff. No matter how quickly a restaurant manager pays the utility bill, this effort will not make the restaurant a success. However, looking for a new special that customers will appreciate is an example of a "high-output" item. Looking for high-output items for your effort is akin to looking for a good return-on-investment for your money.[14]

In following the A-B-C system, you should devote ample time to the essential tasks. You should not pay more attention than absolutely necessary to the C (least important) items. However, if you find that working on C items is tension reducing, then do so, but recognize that you must return to A items as soon as you feel relaxed. When the suggestion of working on high-output items is offered, many people respond, "I don't think concentrating on important tasks applies to me. My job is so filled with routine, I have no chance to work on breakthrough ideas." True, most jobs are filled with routine requirements. What a person can do is spend some time, perhaps just one hour per week, concentrating on tasks that may prove to have high output.

Stay in Control of Paper Work

Although it is fashionable to decry the necessity of having to do paper work in responsible jobs, the effective career person does not neglect paper work. Paper work essentially involves taking care of minor administrative details such as correspondence, personnel reports, and inventory forms. Unless paper work is efficiently attended to, a person's job may get out of control. Once a job is out of control, it may lead to a stress reaction for the job holder.

Ideally, a small amount of time should be invested in paper work every day. Nonprime time (when you are at less than your peak of efficiency, but not overfatigued) is the best time to take care of paper work.

Work at a Steady Pace

In most jobs, and in most programs of study, working at a steady pace pays dividends in efficiency. The spurt worker creates many problems for management, while the spurt student is in turmoil at exam time or when papers are due. Some employees take pride in working rapidly, even when the result is a high error rate. An important advantage of the steady-pace approach is that you accomplish much more than someone who puts out extra effort just once in a while.

The completely steady worker would accomplish just as much the day before a holiday as on a given Monday. That extra hour or so of productivity adds up substantially by the end of the year. Despite the advantages of maintaining a steady pace, some peaks and valleys in your work may be inevitable. The seasonal demands placed on public accountants and related workers is a prime example.

Schedule Similar Tasks Together

An efficient method of accomplishing small tasks is to group them together and perform them in one block of time. To illustrate, you might make most of your telephone calls in relation to your job from 11 to 11:30 A.M. each workday morning. Or you might reserve the last hour of every workday for correspondence. When you go downtown, think of all the errands that you have that can best be done downtown. Over a period of time you save a number of wasted trips.

By using this method you develop the necessary pace and mental set to knock off chores in short order. In contrast, when you flit from one type of task to another, your efficiency may suffer.

Make Use of Bits of Time

A truly productive person makes good use of miscellaneous bits of time, both on and off the job. While waiting in line at a bank or post office, you might update your "do" list; while waiting for an elevator, you might be able to read a 100-word report; and if you have finished your day's work ten minutes before quitting time, you can use that ten minutes to clean out a drawer in your desk. By the end of the year your productivity will have increased much more than if you had squandered these bits of time.[15] A young man from

Nebraska, who was transferred to New York City, explains how this strategy helped his personal life:

> When I lived in Nebraska, I could never find a good time to get my reading done. I'm talking about both the daily newspaper and office correspondence. When I did this type of reading at home, it seemed to interfere with my relationship with my wife and child. After I was transferred to the Big Apple, I became a subway commuter. Despite being jostled by the crowd, I could get all my reading done on workdays. The result was more relaxed time with my family.

Break Down the Task into Manageable Units

Every once and awhile you may be faced with such a large, complex job to accomplish that you feel overwhelmed and become immobilized. You will recall that this feeling of being overwhelmed can lead to procrastination. The problem is all the more acute when more than one of these "elephants" is facing you. A well-accepted principle in this situation is to "eat the elephant one bite at a time." Break down the project into small chunks and begin with a few simple, almost trivial parts of the project. For example, when an office is relocated to a new building, the unpacking project that faces employees seems almost hopeless. Begin by unpacking one or two small boxes, and at least you have made a start.

A similar approach is also referred to as the "swiss cheese method." Since the job is so large, you simply attack it one bite at a time, leaving little holes of accomplishment. The swiss cheese method is based on the dual assumption that the task is huge and that you cannot spend much time on it each day. When you use the tactic of breaking down the task into small units, it is assumed the big task does not have to be accomplished in short order.

Remember Where You Put Things

Learning to concentrate can help you combat absentmindedness. Remembering where you put things is a related technique. People waste a good deal of time looking for items such as files, keys, or the auditron for the office copying machine. If you can remember where you put items of this nature, you can save a lot of wasted time and motion. Peter Turla and Kathleen Hawkins offer two practical suggestions for remembering where you put things. First, have a parking place for everything. This would include putting your keys back in the same place on entering your living quarters.[16]

Second, make visual associations. To have something register in your mind at the moment you are doing it, make up a visual association about the act. Suppose that you have delivered an important file to Joanne Shippe, an administrative assistant in your office. To remember that Ms. Shippe did receive the file, visualize that file floating away on a "ship."

Set a Time Limit for Certain Tasks

As a person becomes experienced with certain projects, he or she is able to make accurate estimates of how long a project will take to complete. A paralegal assistant might say, for example, "Getting this will drawn up for the lawyer's approval should take two hours." A good work habit to develop is to estimate how long a job should take and then proceed with a strong determination to get that job completed within the estimated period of time.

A productive variation of this technique is to decide that some low- and medium-priority items are only worth so much of your time. Invest that much time in the project, but no more. Preparing a file on advertisements that cross your desk is one example.

Capitalize on Your Natural Energy Cycles

The old saws, "I'm a morning person" or "I'm a night person," have scientific substantiation. According to the advocates of biorhythms, people vary somewhat as to their hours of peak efficiency. A week of charting should help you to determine the hours at which your mental and physical energy is apt to be highest or lowest.

After you have determined your strong and weak energy periods, you should be able to arrange your work schedule accordingly. Tackle your intellectually most demanding assignments during your energy peaks. Avoid creative work or making major decisions when fatigue has set in. It may be all right for a 25-year-old intern to patch a wound in his or her 23rd consecutive hour of work, but for most of us, crucial tasks demand a fresh outlook.

Keep an Orderly Desk

A controversial point about work habits is whether or not a clean and orderly desk actually improves one's productivity. Some people contend, "What differences does the appearance of my desk make? What really counts is whether or not I can find the things I need." Furthermore, some time-management specialists contend that an orderly desk is not linked directly to productivity.[17]

A partial resolution of the controversy is to recognize that a tidy desk is more important in some types of work than in others. Executives tend to prefer a well-organized desk, whereas artists, writers, scientists, and professors tend to prefer a cluttered desk. If you work in a bureaucracy, an orderly

Tackle your intellectually most demanding assignment during your energy peaks.

desk is impressive. A disorderly desk gives you a negative image. Keep in mind, also, that a clean and orderly desk will almost never be perceived negatively by an employer.

An orderly desk has two striking advantages. First, it helps you concentrate on one piece of paper at a time—an important habit for improving personal productivity. Second, it decreases substantially the amount of time you devote to searching for notes, forms, and other work-related material. Another good reason exists for keeping an orderly desk in the modern office or factory. So much of your desk space may be consumed by a display terminal that you are compelled to tightly organize the space you have left for other things.

Clean Up Every Six Months

An orderly desk, file cabinet, or attaché case does not inevitably indicate an orderly mind, but it does help most people become more productive. Less time is wasted, and less energy is expended if you do not have to hunt for information that you thought you had on hand. Knowing where information is and what information you have available is a way of being in control of your job. When your job gets out of control, you are probably working at less than peak efficiency.

Even the most orderly career person should clean out his or her work area every six months. Two hours devoted to office housekeeping may give you some hints as to whether or not you are taking care of all the things that you should on your job. You might be surprised as to what has filtered down to the bottom of your in-basket.

Ben and his two brothers ran a small contracting business that they inherited from their father. When Ben came up with an idea for expanding the business, he would jot it down on a sheet of paper, in his wallet, or on his desk blotter. Learning about the "Clean up every six months" suggestion in a management course for small business persons, Ben decided to give this simple idea a try. He describes what happened:

> That little housecleaning escapade must have resulted in $25,000 worth of new business for our firm. And they were all my ideas that I had never done anything about. I came up with about eight ideas for new services that I had forgotten I had dreamed of.
>
> One of the ideas was to contract out on cleaning up pigeon droppings off statues and awnings. The work wasn't glamorous but our reputation for that kind of work spread. Another approach was to go from house to house in old neighborhoods and clean attics of rubbish. Another profitable item was a house exterior cleaning service.
>
> As an offshoot of my in-basket cleanup, I've developed an orderly new file for business ideas. Now I won't have to hunt the office to retrieve ideas that I jotted down in miscellaneous places. I'll know where my good ideas are filed.

Try to Minimize Interruptions

Many managerial, professional, and technical jobs are fraught with interruptions, such as unanticipated phone calls, unscheduled visitors, sudden meetings, and job emergencies. One could argue, of course, that all these are part of the job and should therefore not be regarded as interruptions. Legitimate or illegitimate, these unanticipated breaks in your work often make it difficult to keep momentum going on a major task.

One solution to the problem of interruptions is for you to schedule a period of time during the day in which you have uninterrupted work time.[18] You give co-workers a definite time during which you want to be disturbed with emergencies only. It is also helpful to inform co-workers of the nature of the important work you ordinarily conduct during your quiet period. You might say, for example, "I have to tally the sales figures every Friday afternoon."

In trying to ward off interruptions, you must make the distinction between a schmoozer and somebody with a legitimate reason for communicating with you. Team effort requires frequent interaction among co-workers about work-related topics.

Be Decisive

An often overlooked way of improving your personal productivity is to be decisive. Move quickly, but not impulsively, through the problem-solving and decision-making steps outlined in Chapter 7 when you are faced with a nonroutine decision. Once you have evaluated the alternatives to the problem, choose and implement one of them.

Superintelligent and highly educated people are sometimes poor decision makers because they keep on collecting facts. The result is that they procrastinate instead of acting. Some people of more modest intelligence waste time when faced with a decision, not because they want more facts, but because they are fearful of committing themselves. In short, if you agonize too long over too many decisions, your personal productivity will suffer.

Use Time and Motion Principles

Efficiency experts have developed rules or guidelines for simplifying routine and repetitive work. Although most of these principles were developed many years ago to improve the productivity of people performing manual work, some apply to office work. Duane Schultz has summarized the major findings of time and motion analysis.[19] They are presented here for possible application in higher-level jobs.

1. Minimize the distance workers must reach to obtain tools, equipment, supplies, or operate machines. Reaching motions should be as short as possible. (Keep this in mind in laying out your office automation equipment.)

2. Both hands should begin and end their movement at the same time. Movements of both hands should be symmetrical and simultaneous. (For instance, reach for pencils with your left hand and typing paper with your right hand.)

3. The hands should always be in motion, except during official rest breaks. (True enough, if you are performing manual work. But if you are paid to think, this idea is counterproductive.)

4. The hands should never be given tasks that could be performed more appropriately by other parts of the body, particularly the legs and feet. (If you have to push around office furniture, try to use your legs as much as possible to avoid back strain.)

5. If possible, work materials should be held by a mechanical device such as a vise, instead of being held by the hand. (A typist or input clerk can save a lot of time by inserting source material in a suitable holder. This

saves time otherwise lost to moving the document around the type-writer keyboard or input device.)

6. Circular movements of the hands between two points are more efficient than straight-line movements. This is especially true if the movement is made repeatedly and quickly. (You might use this principle if you have to stock or restock some shelves, such as when an office is being relocated.)

7. The work area should be arranged to permit workers to sit or stand alternately to perform the job. (Many executives today use stand-up desks to supplement their sit-down desks. Alternating positions relieves fatigue and helps prevent strain on the spinal cord.)

8. Wherever possible, tools should be combined to eliminate the wasteful motions of putting one tool down and picking up another one. (The information-processing systems that use the same machine as an electronic typewriter, input device, and printer capitalize on this principle. It can save you time from moving back and forth from the information processor to the typewriter.)

9. Movements should always occur in the direction in which the force of gravity will assist the movement. (Pulling an office machine down is preferable to pushing it up—but then somebody will have to reverse the process!)

10. Picking up and handling objects should be accomplished in such a way as to require the least amount of small, precise movements. (Keep small items such as paper clips and ball pens in large containers so you will not have to fumble round trying to pick them up. Also, use large-sized hand calculators rather than the credit-card-size ones.)

GETTING STARTED IMPROVING YOUR PERSONAL PRODUCTIVITY

Assume you were able to implement every suggestion in this chapter and you also followed carefully the decision-making steps outlined in Chapter 7. You would now be on the road toward being one of the most productive and well-organized people in your field. The flaw in this logic is that no one is equipped to implement immediately every suggestion. One limiting factor is that you might not be able to identify (or do much about) the underlying problems blocking your efficiency and effectiveness.

The recommended way to improving your personal productivity is to start small. Select one or two strategies that seem focused in on a major work-habit or time-management problem facing you. Try out the strategy. Monitor your progress and move on to another strategy. In addition to this advice, consult this chapter's Guidelines for Personal Effectiveness.

Personal Characteristics and Work Habits. An important note of caution is in order about the ease with which people can improve their personal productivity. It has already been mentioned that a person needs the right talent and motivation to make much improvement feasible. Another important consideration is that certain personality characteristics are also related to work habits and time management. At the top of the list is **compulsiveness,** or a tendency to pay careful attention to detail and to be meticulous. An individual with a compulsive personality takes naturally to being well organized and neat. If you are less concerned about detail and meticulousness by nature, it will be more difficult for you to develop exceptional work habits.

People who are highly spontaneous and emotional also tend to be naturally inclined toward casual work habits. Being overly compulsive can also be a detriment to personal productivity. The compulsive person may have a difficult time concentrating on important tasks. Instead they tend to get hung up on details and become the unproductive type of workaholic. The truly productive person finds an optimum balance between concern for detail and time, on the one hand, and being able to look at the "big picture" on the other.

SUMMARY OF KEY POINTS

☐ By improving your work habits and time management, you can improve both your job productivity and enhance your personal life. Personal productivity refers to your level of efficiency and effectiveness, and thus includes the idea of performing quality work.

☐ Procrastination is the major time waster for most employees and students. People procrastinate for many reasons, including their perception that the task is either unpleasant or overwhelming, and an inner fear of the consequences of their action. The feared consequences can be positive or negative. Awareness of the procrastination problem may lead to its control. Four other techniques recommended for reducing procrastination are (1) calculate the price of procrastination; (2) create some momentum to get you moving; (3) apply behavior modification to yourself; (4) make a commitment to other people about getting something done.

☐ Developing good work habits and time-management practices is often a matter of developing the right attitudes toward your work and toward time. Nine such attitudes, values, and beliefs are as follows:

1. Become a goal-oriented person.
2. Try to discover what is blocking you.
3. Value good attendance and punctuality.
4. Avoid perfectionism.

5. Learn to say no.
6. Strive for both quantity and quality.
7. Ask, "What is the best use of my time right now?"
8. Recognize the importance of rest and relaxation.
9. Develop a strong work ethic.

☐ Sixteen skills and techniques to help you become more efficient and effective (and therefore more productive) are as follows:

1. Prepare a list and set priorities.
2. Concentrate on one task at a time.
3. Concentrate on high-output tasks.
4. Stay in control of paper work.
5. Work at a steady pace.
6. Schedule similar tasks together.
7. Make use of bits of time.
8. Break down the task into manageable units.
9. Remember where you put things.
10. Set time limits for certain tasks.
11. Capitalize on your natural energy cycles.
12. Keep an orderly desk.
13. Clean up every six months.
14. Try to minimize interruptions.
15. Be decisive.
16. Use time and motion principles.

☐ The best way to begin improving your personal productivity is to start small. Select one or two attitudes, beliefs, or techniques that appear particularly relevant to your circumstances and give them a try. Monitor your progress and then move on to another strategy.

GUIDELINES FOR PERSONAL EFFECTIVENESS

Reading about these methods of improving your work habits alone will not lead to permanent changes in behavior. You must select one or two areas in which you are particularly weak and then begin to implement a remedial plan of action.[20]

Suppose that you recognize that your day is filled with time leaks because you rarely accomplish what you set out to. Try these steps.

1. Identify the two most obvious time leaks. Perhaps (a) time wasted in gathering your friends for lunch and (b) stopping work 15 minutes before quitting time.
2. For the next five workdays force yourself to plug these time leaks. You might have to say to your friends, "I'm only taking 30 minutes for lunch today. I want to avoid bringing home work tonight. So I'll meet you in the cafeteria at 11:45 sharp."
3. If this approach works, move on to subtle and difficult leaks such as a tendency to daydream when work pressures lessen.
4. Now try another time-management method of improving your work habits that you think applies to one of your areas for needed improvement.

DISCUSSION QUESTIONS

1. It has been argued that well-organized people are rigid and that they lack spontaneity (thus they irritate other people). What is your opinion on this issue?
2. Benjamin Franklin said, "To love life is to love time, since time is the stuff that life is made of." What is your reaction to this statement?
3. To what extent are your work habits influenced by your basic personality traits?
4. How might several of the techniques for improving your effectiveness and efficiency be applied directly to improving your social life?
5. When you meet a stranger, how can you tell if he or she is well organized?
6. What use do you make of bits of time?
7. In what way does competing in athletics help a person become more conscious of making good use of time?
8. Give an example from your own life in which striving for perfection was not worth the effort.
9. What is your reaction to the statement, "A clear and orderly desk reflects a clear and orderly mind"?
10. What is the best use of your time right now?

A Business Psychology Problem
THE OVERWHELMED ADMINISTRATIVE ASSISTANT

Mary looked into the storeroom mirror and thought to herself, "You're looking bad, kid. Somehow you've got to get your life straightened out. You're on a treadmill, and you don't know how to get off. But it's a bad time to be thinking about myself right now. It's time to meet with my boss, Beatrice. I wonder what she wants?"

Beatrice Reynolds began the meeting with Mary in her usual open manner: "Mary, I'm concerned about you. For a long time you were one of the best administrative assistants in our firm. You received compliments from me and the other department heads who had contact with your department. Now you're hardly making it. You've become so irritable, so lacking in enthusiasm. And a lot of your work contains glaring errors and is also late. The reason I'm bringing the subject up again is that things have gotten worse. What's your problem?"

"I wish it were only one problem, Beatrice. I feel like the world is caving in on me. I work here about 40 hours a week. I'm trying to upgrade myself in life. As you know I'm taking two courses in a business administration program. If I can keep up the pace, I'll have an associate's degree by next spring. But it's getting to be a grind."

"How are things at home, Mary?"

"Much worse than they are here. My husband works, too, and he's getting fed up with never seeing me when he comes home. It seems that when he's home, I'm either working late at the office, in class, or studying at the library. Thursday is the one weekday night I'm home for sure. And that's Tony's bowling night."

"Our son, Steve isn't too happy either. He's only five but the other day he asked me if Daddy and I were getting divorced. Steve doesn't see us together much. When he does see us, he can feel the tension between us."

"So, you're under pressure at the office and at home," said Beatrice.

"Add school to that list. I'm having a devil of a time getting through my business statistics course. If I flunk, my chances of getting a degree are set back considerably."

"Do the best you can, Mary. I'm sympathetic, but I need better performance from you."

As Mary left Beatrice Reynold's office she said, "Thanks for being candid with me. My problem is that my boss, my husband, my child, and my professors all want better performance from me. I wish I knew how to give it."

1. What suggestions can you offer Mary for working her way out of her problems?
2. Why is this case included in a chapter about improving your personal productivity?
3. How well do you think Beatrice Reynolds handled the interview?

A Business Psychology Exercise
IMPROVING YOUR PERSONAL PRODUCTIVITY

Studying this chapter will rarely lead to improvements in efficiency and effectiveness. You need to back up studying these ideas with a specific plan of action for improvement as described in the chapter sections Getting Started Improving Your Personal Productivity and Guidelines for Personal Effectiveness. A useful mechanical aid toward achieving this end is to study the checklist presented next, which covers the techniques mentioned in this chapter. Pick out the five or six items on the checklist in which you need the most help. For each item you select, write a one- or two-sentence action plan. Suppose you checked the item "Be Decisive." Your action plan might take this form:

- Next time I'm faced with an important decision, I'll make up my mind within two days, instead of the usual entire week.
- I'll make note of the date on which the problem faced me and the date on which I finally made up my mind.

THE PERSONAL
PRODUCTIVITY CHECKLIST

Attitude, Value, Belief, Skill, or Technique

1. Be aware of procrastination problem. _____
2. Calculate the price of procrastination. _____
3. Create some momentum to get you moving. _____
4. Apply behavior modification to yourself. _____
5. Make a commitment to other people. _____
6. Become a goal-oriented person. _____
7. Try to discover what is blocking you. _____
8. Value good attendance and punctuality. _____
9. Avoid perfectionism. _____
10. Learn to say no. _____
11. Strive for both quantity and quality. _____
12. Ask, "What is the best use of my time right now?" _____
13. Recognize the importance of rest and relaxation. _____
14. Develop a strong work ethic. _____
15. Prepare a list and set priorities. _____
16. Concentrate on one task at a time.

17. Concentrate on high-output tasks.   _____
18. Stay in control of paper work.   _____
19. Work at a steady pace.   _____
20. Schedule similar tasks together.   _____
21. Make use of bits of time.   _____
22. Break the task down into manageable units.   _____
23. Remember where you put things.   _____
24. Set time limits for certain tasks.   _____
25. Capitalize on your natural energy cycles.   _____
26. Keep an orderly desk.   _____
27. Try to minimize interruptions.   _____
28. Be decisive.   _____
29. Use time and motion principles.   _____
30. Manage time leaks (see Guidelines).   _____

REFERENCES

[1]Personal communication with Cable Neuhaus, January 1983.

[2]Michael LeBoeuf quoted in Priscilla Petty, "Saying No to Unproductive Jobs Frees Time for High-Priority Goals," Rochester *Democrat and Chronicle* (June 21, 1983), p. 10D.

[3]Henry C. Everett, M.D., "Conquering Procrastination," *Success* (June 1981), p. 26.

[4]Alan Lakein, *How to Gain Control of Your Time and Your Life* (New York: Wyden Books, 1973), pp. 141–151.

[5]LeBoeuf, in "Saying No to Unproductive Jobs."

[6]Albert Ellis and William J. Knaus, *Overcoming Procrastination* (New York: New American Library, 1979), p. 111.

[7]Bryce Nelson, "Do You Fear Success?" *New York Times* story reprinted in Rochester *Democrat and Chronicle* (Feb. 16, 1983), p. 1A.

[8]Edwin C. Bliss, *Getting Things Done: The ABC's of Time Management* (New York: Scribner's, 1976), p. 55.

[9]Ibid., p. 75.

[10]Lakein, *How to Gain Control*, p. 99.

[11]Stephanie Winston, *Getting Organized* (New York: Warner Books, 1979), p. 28.

[12]William Brohaugh, "Computerizing Your Calendar," *Success* (Nov. 1983), pp. 14–16.

[13]Walter Olesky, "Concentration," *Success* (Oct. 1983), pp. 28, 30.

[14]Andrew Grove, *High Output Management* (New York: Random House, 1983).

[15]Warren Keith Schilit, "A Manager's Guide to Efficient Time Management," *Personnel Journal* (Sept. 1983), p. 740; Winston, p. 43.

[16]Peter A. Turla and Kathleen L. Hawkins, "Remembering to Remember," *Success* (May 1983), p. 60.

[17]See, for example, Dru Scott, *How to Put More Time in Your Life* (New York: New American Library, 1980), p. 172.

[18]Peter A. Turla and Kathleen L. Hawkins, "A Personal Achievement Guide to Time Management," *Success* (Nov. 1982), p. A6.

[19]Adapted from Duane P. Schultz, *Psychology and Industry Today*, 2nd ed. (New York: Macmillan, 1978), pp. 364–365.

[20]These guidelines are developed in part from Ed Roseman, "How to Gain Control of Your Time," *Product Management* (July 1975), pp. 23–27.

SUGGESTED READING

DAVIDSON, JAMES. *Effective Time Management: A Practical Workbook.* New York: Human Sciences Press, 1978.

DOUGHTERY, GREG. "Protecting Your Privacy," *Success* (April 1982), pp. 10–12.

DOUGLASS, MERRILL E., and DONNA N. DOUGLASS. *Manage Your Time, Manage Your Work, Manage Yourself.* New York: AMACOM, 1980.

JANUZ, LAUREN R., and SUSAN K. JONES. *Time Management for Executives.* New York: Scribner's, 1981.

MORANO, RICHARD A. "Executive Time Management I: Organizational Support for Better Time Management," *Advanced Management Journal* (Winter 1978), pp. 36–40.

SCHULER, RANDALL S. "Managing Stress Means Managing Time," *Personnel Journal* (Dec. 1979), pp. 851–854.

TURLA, PETER A., and KATHLEEN L. HAWKINS. *Time Management Made Easy.* New York: Dutton, 1984.

WEBBER, ROSS A. *Time Is Money: The Key to Managerial Success.* New York: Free Press, 1980.

17

ACHIEVING A SATISFYING AND REWARDING CAREER

LEARNING OBJECTIVES

After reading and studying this chapter and doing the exercises, you should be able to

1. Appreciate the fact that you must take responsibility for managing your own career.
2. Recognize those aspects of a job that will most probably contribute to your satisfaction.
3. Understand how people select fields and occupations for themselves.
4. Conduct an effective job campaign for yourself.
5. Describe at least ten career-advancement strategies.
6. Understand how and why people switch careers.

TAKING RESPONSIBILITY FOR YOUR OWN CAREER

"I'm pleased to be assigned to your department," said a young inventory control specialist to his new boss. "But could you tell me where this job will lead? I'm very interested in properly planning my career." His boss replied, "Just do your job, and the company will take care of planning your career."

However well intended this boss, the inventory control specialist should not leave the management of his career to somebody else. Although most large firms today have formal programs of career development for employees, you must still assume the major responsibility for managing your own career. One fundamental reason is that in our mobile society you might change employers voluntarily or involuntarily. A new analysis of this problem contends:

> Effective career management should no longer be viewed as the responsibility of the personnel department; rather, individuals now must assume authority and responsibility for their own careers as they chart out career paths on an inter-organizational basis. What complicates this problem further is that only a few individuals are both technically prepared and willing to handle this new assignment.[1]

The major purpose of this chapter is to present information that will help you manage (or develop) your own career. The information is organized according to the logical flow of events a person faces in building a career:

1. Understanding what makes for career satisfaction.
2. Finding a suitable field and an occupation within that field.
3. Finding a job.
4. Selecting relevant career-advancement tactics and strategies.
5. Switching careers if the need arises.

CONTRIBUTORS TO CAREER SATISFACTION

Not everybody achieves job (and therefore career) satisfaction for the same reasons. Yet hundreds of studies about the topic suggest that, when certain key conditions are met, most people experience satisfaction.[2] Above all, job satisfaction results from attaining conditions or values that are compatible with one's needs. To the extent that people experience these eight conditions or values, they rate their job as satisfying. A satisfying career is one filled with jobs that allow these conditions to be met.

Mentally challenging work. Some people like to daydream on the job and not be bothered with mental challenge. Most people, however, crave some intellectual stimulation during their working day. The amount of challenge should be just enough so that the individual can meet it successfully.

Personal interest in the work itself. Job satisfaction is usually the result when you are interested in what you are doing. Many people, for example, enjoy jobs that enable them to tinker around with problems.

Work that is not too physically challenging. Work that stretches the physical limits of an individual tends to become unsatisfying. Many garbage men find their jobs too physically demanding. Some executives are dissatisfied with the heavy travel demands of their job. Some professional football players find that the physical abuse that they take on the job outweighs its high status and pay.

Rewards for performance that are fair, informative, and in line with the individual's goals. These conditions are closely related to the conditions for making effective use of money as a motivator (see Chapter 5). An *informative* reward is one that tells you how well you have performed, such as receiving a bonus for error-free work.

Working conditions that are compatible with your physical needs and that help make reaching work goals possible. If you were a 55-year-old typist with arthritis, it would contribute to your job satisfaction if you had an easy-to-manipulate electronic typewriter. Your satisfaction would stem from both the prevention of pain and the fact that your machine would help you achieve your goal of typing accurately and rapidly.

High self-esteem on the part of the individual. All things being equal, people derive more satisfaction from high- than low-status occupations. A job that is seen by others as valuable contributes to our self-esteem. Feelings of self-esteem also stem from doing work that the individual feels is worthwhile. One man owned a gambling parlor that generated enough profits to provide luxuriously for himself, his present and former wives, and his seven children. Yet at age 28 he entered school to earn a degree in business. Asked why he bothered enrolling in school, the gambling entrepreneur replied, "I want to go to law school someday. I don't want my kids to tell people their dad is a hustler."

People in the workplace who help the employee to attain job values such as interesting work, pay, and promotions, whose basic values are similar to the employee's, and who minimize conflict and confusion. Part of job satisfaction stems from having competent managers and staff people who are sensitive to the needs of people.

Work that is consistent with specific job values. Major job values include autonomy, creativity, helping others, security, and performing technical work (as touched on at several places in the text).[3] To the extent your job allows you to perform work that meets these specific values, your job satisfaction will increase. For example, some first-level supervisors have high job satisfaction because they can both help people (the service value) and stay close to technical work at the same time.

How Do You Find Such Satisfying Jobs? The eight conditions just described are for most people an ideal toward which to strive. Identifying such jobs requires a good deal of questioning and observation. People to question include experienced job holders and personnel specialists. After jobs such as these have been identified, you have to use sensible career-advancement strategies to help you land one. In general, jobs of higher rank provide a better opportunity for meeting these conditions or values.

Another important consideration is that, as you are given more responsibility, you also have more latitude to create a satisfying job. For instance, if you are a supervisor, manager, or staff specialist, you can sometimes ask to take on an additional assignment that you think would fit your personal interests. One supervisor asked to be part of a team that was investigating a new office location. She did so because she had an intense interest in real estate.

FINDING A FIELD AND AN OCCUPATION

A starting point in establishing a satisfying and rewarding career (and therefore a successful one) is to find a field compatible with your interests. Many readers of this book may have already identified a general field they wish to enter or are already working in that field. But many other readers are probably still in the process of identifying a field of work and an occupation within that field that will contribute to their life satisfaction. The process of choosing a career is a complex subject. First, we will identify six of the conventional ways in which people find a field and occupation to pursue.

1. *Influence of parent, relative, or friend:* "My uncle owned a pharmacy, so I became interested in pharmacy at an early age."

2. *Reading and study:* "While in high school I read about astronomy, and decided that I wanted to be an astronomer."

3. *Natural opportunity:* "I was born into the business. Who would give up a chance to be a vice-president by the time I was 25? Our family has always been in the retail business."

4. *Forced opportunity:* "I had never heard about electronics until I joined the army. They told me I had aptitude for the field. I enjoyed working as an electronics technician. After the army I applied for a job with IBM as a field service engineer. It has worked out well."

5. *Discovery through counseling and/or testing:* "I took an interest test in high school. My guidance counselor told me that I had interests similar to those of a social worker. Not knowing what else to do, I decided to become a social worker." (This is the most systematic of the six methods mentioned here.)

6. *Matching yourself with a compatible person:* A novel way of finding a field and occupation within that field is first to locate a person with

whom you have similar interests. You then choose that person's field of work for yourself, using this reasoning, "I seem to like what that person likes in most things. All things being equal, I would probably like the kind of work that person does."

Making Use of Occupational Information

In addition to the conventional methods just listed, it is important to search for valid information about career fields so you can find a good fit between yourself and existing opportunities. Few people take advantage of the voluminous information available about careers and career planning. Yet most libraries and bookstores are well supplied with this type of information. In this section we will describe three different ways of obtaining occupational information. Later we will return to the subject again in reference to finding growth opportunities for yourself.

Reference Books about Career Information. The most comprehensive source of occupational information is the *Occupational Outlook Handbook*, published every two years by the U.S. Department of Labor. Each occupation listed is described in terms of (1) the nature of the work, (2) places of employment, (3) training, (4) other qualifications for advancement, and (5) employment outlook. Using the *Handbook*, one can find answers to such questions as, "What do correction officers do and how much do they earn?" A similar source is the *Encyclopedia of Careers and Vocational Guidance*.

Computer-assisted Career Guidance. Several career guidance information systems have been developed for access by computer. They go one step beyond printed information because you can ask questions (interact with) the computer. A widely used system of this type is the *System of Interactive Guidance* (SIGI).[4] It is based on the *Handbook* just mentioned and information from employed people in the field. The purpose of SIGI is to help individuals learn three things: (1) which values are important to them, (2) factual information about various occupations, and (3) how to make better career decisions. SIGI has five subsystems, each contributing to learning about occupations.

You begin with the *Values* subsystem, which rates how much you like each value, such as independence and leadership. The second subsystem is *Locate*, which shows you the occupations listed in SIGI that match your values. The third subsystem, *Compare*, gives the user a chance to ask up to 28 questions about the listed occupations. One such question would be, "What is the income potential?" *Planning* is the fourth subsystem. It provides information about the type of education and the special skills and abilities required for the occupation. *Planning* takes into account both interest in a particular field and an individual's willingness to prepare for the occupation, in terms of education and training.

Strategy is the fifth subsystem. It helps you evaluate the advantages or disadvantages of an occupation for you in terms of rewards, risks, and values. Ideally, *Strategy* helps you combine reward and risk to make a sound occupational choice.

Career Information in Newspapers and Speaking to People. The general topic of careers is so popular today that it is regularly covered in newspaper and magazine articles. Career columns and feature stories about job opportunities are found from time to time in the business sections of many newspapers. These articles are usually based on current industry surveys, recent government statistics, and interviews with successful people in the field under scrutiny. Job descriptions contained in classified ads can also provide valid information.

By speaking directly to key people yourself, you can generate some of your own first-hand information about occupations. Many people have identified a field to pursue precisely in this manner. Seek out a person gainfully employed in any field or occupation in which you might be remotely interested. Most people welcome the opportunity to talk about themselves and the type of work they do. If you do not know anyone engaged in the career field that interests you, do some digging. A few inquiries will usually lead to a person you can contact. It is preferable to interview that person in his or her actual work setting in order to obtain a sense of the working conditions people face in that field.

Speaking to people at different stages and levels of responsibility can be illuminating. If you ask a neophyte teller about the banking field, you will receive a very different answer from that of a 40-year-old vice-president of commercial loans.

A note of caution. As you seek occupational information, many people will probably say that, although they are happy in their work, there are better ways to make a living. For example, if you ask a lawyer about his or her field, you will most likely be told something to the effect, "Don't believe all those stories about lawyers being wealthy. We work long and hard for our money. And then there's always the problem of people not paying their bills. I think you're better off in another field."

CONDUCTING THE JOB CAMPAIGN

Some people who have identified a career field never have to look for a job. Some of them enter into family businesses. Others are in such high-demand occupations that employers come looking for them (two current examples are electronic engineers and medical secretaries). And some people capitalize on chance opportunity, with small effort on their part (such as being offered a job by a neighbor). Most other people have to conduct a job campaign to find employment at various times in their career. Included in the job campaign are job-hunting tactics and preparing a job résumé and cover letter.

Job-Hunting Tactics

Most people already have some knowledge about how to find a job. Some of the ideas discussed next will therefore be familiar to you, yet some will be unfamiliar. We recommend using this list of tactics and methods as a checklist to ensure that you have not neglected something important. It is easy to overlook the obvious when job hunting because your emotions may cloud your sense of logic. This list should be supplemented with the advice offered by placement offices and job-finding books and manuals.[5]

Identify Your Job Objective(s). A proper job search begins with a clear perception of what kind of job or jobs you want. Most people can more readily identify the jobs that they don't want than those that they do want. Your chances for finding employment are directly proportional to the number of positions that will satisfy your job objective. One woman with a background in writing might be willing to accept only a job as a newspaper reporter (always a difficult position to find). Another woman with the same background is seeking a job as (1) a newspaper reporter, (2) a magazine staff writer, (3) a copywriter in an advertising agency, (4) communications specialist in a company, or (5) copywriter in a public relations firm. The second woman has a better chance than the first of finding a job.

Identify Your Potential Contribution. A man responded by phone to a want ad with this initial comment: "Hello, this is Tom Crawford. I've just got to have a job. I've been laid off and I have a family to support. I need something right away." Poor Tom probably did need the job, but the company he was calling was more interested in *receiving* than in *giving* help. If Tom had used the following approach, he might have increased his chances for being granted an interview (and hopefully getting hired): "Hello, this is Tom Crawford. I see you need somebody to help ship packages; I know how to ship packages in a fast and economical way. When could I talk to you about it in person?"

Use Multiple Approaches. A standard method of job finding is to exhaust all possible approaches. Many an individual has claimed, "I've tried everything," when they have only pursued a few job-finding channels. Among the possible approaches are college placement offices, private employment agencies, state employment services, classified ads in local and national newspapers, trade journals and magazines, employment booths at trade associations and conventions, inquiries through friends and relatives, and cold-canvassing. Another standard approach is to place a situation-wanted ad in local and national newspapers. An ad similar to the following helped one business school graduate find a job:

> Pro-establishment problem solver wants in on your management-training program. Try me, I'll give you a big return on your investment.

Use the Insider System. Only one in five job openings is likely to be advertised or listed with employment agencies. Employers tend to use external sources of job candidates primarily when they have jobs that are hard to fill. An exception is that for many jobs affirmative action programs (a method of achieving equal employment opportunity) dictate that all vacancies be posted. Employers traditionally fill the four out of five jobs that are not publicized in this manner:

1. Friends fill the job or they are filled with people recommended by these friends.
2. Friends and relatives of employees are given the first chance at job openings.
3. The jobs go to people who have applied directly to the firm without knowing that any opening existed. Many experienced job hunters mail letters of inquiry to hundreds of companies.[6]

A job seeker thus might canvass friends and relatives to learn of openings for which they are qualified. Another approach is to directly cold-canvass virtually any prospective employer using an unsolicited letter of inquiry. (See the section later about attention-getting letters.)

Be Specific with Your Friends about the Job You Are Seeking. If you plan to tap into the insider system through friends, tell them exactly the job you are seeking. An example is that instead of saying, "I'm looking for something in the health-care field," say, "I want to be the office manager in a large group medical practice." The justification for being so specific is that people make better connections with specific rather than general information.[7] Unfortunately, there is one risk in being too specific: you may be excluded from some possible job opportunities that your friends think are not in your line of interest.

Keep Your Number of Business Contacts Growing. The more contacts you make, the better your chances are of being recommended for a job opening. Some people carry this tactic to the extreme by striking up conversations with strangers in airports and social gatherings for the purpose of making a job contact for potential use in the future. Referred to as **networking,** this tactic is also recommended for career advancement in general.

Be Persistent. Career consultant Marilyn Moats Kennedy observes that, even in a recession, about 10 percent of the people who take a job fail after three months. Sometimes they are fired at the end of the probationary period, or they leave because of low interest or inability to perform on the job. Therefore, check back with the firms who said you were their second choice.[8] Another reason for being persistent is that it keeps pressure on yourself. Without this self-pressure, some people become too lethargic about conducting a job campaign. It is important to remember that finding a job is frequently one of the most challenging "jobs" in a person's career.

Be Willing to Handle Some Rejection. Finding a job can result in considerable rejection. It is not uncommon for a recent graduate or an experienced career person to send out 150 letters of inquiry to find one job. When your job search is confined to places that are trying to fill a position that matches your speciality, you still may have to be interviewed many times in order to land a suitable job. Often you will be rejected when it appears to you that your qualifications match perfectly those required for the job opening. The hiring manager may have interviewed another applicant that he or she thinks is even better qualified than you. Or the same person may have felt a stronger "chemistry" between himself or herself and another candidate. In short, do not take rejection personally. It is an inevitable part of job hunting.

The Job Résumé and Cover Letter

No matter what method of job hunting you choose, inevitably somebody will ask you for a résumé. The author is aware that many job-hunting books are adamant about not handing out a résumé, but instead insisting on a personal interview. The reality is that virtually every company requires a résumé before seriously considering a job candidate from the outside. Sometimes you will be asked to complete a job-application form instead of, or in addition to, a résumé. Résumés are also important for job-hunting within your own firm. You may need one to be considered for a transfer within a large firm.

Résumé Purpose. Remember that the purpose of a résumé is to help you obtain a job interview, not a job. Very few people are hired without a personal interview, although it can happen if the demand for your skills is strong enough. Your résumé must therefore attract enough attention for an employer to invite you for an interview (or, in rare circumstances, offer you a job sight unseen). Effective résumés are straightforward, factual presentations of a person's experiences and accomplishments. They are neither overdetailed nor too sketchy.

Résumé Length and Format. Considerable debate and subjective opinion exist about the desirable length for a résumé. For a recent graduate with limited work experience, a one-page résumé may be acceptable. For more experienced people, it would seem too short. And less than a one-page résumé would seem superficial for almost anybody. A four-page or longer résumé may irritate an impatient employment specialist. Two or three pages is therefore recommended for most purposes.

To attract attention, some job seekers print résumés on tinted paper, in a menulike folder, or on an unusual-sized paper. Still others do not print them. Instead, they dictate the résumé onto a tape cassette. (Can you think of any swifter method of irritating a prospective employer?) If done in a way to attract positive attention to yourself, the nonconventional résumé formats have merit. The menulike folder has worked well for a number of job seekers. It should therefore be given consideration if it is not being overused in your community. But do not (as one joker did) label your job objective "the appetizer," your work experience "the entree," and your education "the dessert."

Different Types of Résumés. The three major types of job résumé are the chronological, functional, and accomplishment.[9] The résumé presented in Figure 17–1 combines some features of all three types and is therefore a good compromise to suit the tastes of many different prospective employers.

The chronological résumé. This traditional form of résumé begins with your most recent experience and works back to your earliest relevant work experience. Most prospective employers want the kind of information found on the chronological résumé. Career counselor Ted Jackson says to use the chronological résumé if the job you are seeking is a natural progression from your former job or school. If you have had a good work history or experience reflecting occupational growth, a chronological résumé will highlight these achievements.

The functional résumé. Using this format, you organize your information in the résumé according to the functions (or activities) performed. Each paragraph contains information related to your experience in that category and does not mention dates. Typical headings would be Supervisory Experience, Sales Experience, and Technical Work. The functional section of the résumé supplements, but does not replace, the chronological section.

The accomplishment résumé. Another approach to preparing a résumé is to summarize and highlight your job accomplishments. You target your accomplishments to the requirements of a particular position. For example, in Figure 17–1 the résumé writer emphasizes his sales accomplishments. If he were applying for a position as a customer-service specialist, he would emphasize an accomplishment such as "Saved company $46,000 in lost production time by doubleshooting problem on numeric control machine." A résumé that listed only accomplishments would be unacceptable to most hir-

JOB RÉSUMÉ

Scott Wayland
170 Glenview Drive
Dallas, Texas   75243

August 8, 1960
Single, no dependents
(312)   385-3986

JOB OBJECTIVE	Industrial sales, handling large, complex machinery. Willing to work largely on commission basis.
CAPABILITIES	Professional sales representative. Able to size up customer manufacturing problem and make recommendation for appropriate machinery. Precise in preparing call reports and expense accounts.
MAJOR ACCOMPLISHMENT	In one year sold at a profit $250,000 worth of excess machine inventory. Received letter of commendation from company president.

WORK HISTORY

1982–present	Industrial account representative, Bainbridge Corporation, Dallas. Sell line of tool and die equipment to companies in Southwest. Duties include servicing established accounts and canvassing new ones.
1980–1982	Inside sales representative, Bainbridge Corporation. Answered customer inquiries. Filled orders for replacement parts. Trained for outside sales position.
1976–1980	Tool and die maker apprentice, Texas Metals, Inc., Dallas. Assisted senior tool and die makers during four-year training program. Worked on milling machines, jigs, punch presses, numeric control devices.

FORMAL EDUCATION

1976–1980	Madagascar College, Dallas, Texas. Associate Degree in Business Administration; graduated with 3.16 grade point average. Courses in marketing, sales techniques, consumer behavior, accounting, and statistics. President of Commuter's Club.
1972–1976	Big Horn High, Dallas. Honors student; academic major with vocational elective. Played varsity football and basketball. Earned part of living expenses by selling magazine subscriptions.

PERSONAL INTERESTS AND HOBBIES	Personal computer enthusiast (write programs for own computer), scuba diving, recreational golf player, read trade and business magazines.

References on request.

FIGURE 17–1
General-purpose job résumé.

ing managers and personnel specialists. They would still want to know the basic facts about you contained in the chronological résumé.

Common Mistakes Found in Résumés. Abundant useful information is available about résumé preparation. Nevertheless, many job seekers continue to prepare résumés that virtually disqualify them from further consideration in the eyes of employers. Do your best to avoid most of the following errors by editing your own résumé and asking at least two other people to do the same.[10]

- Too lengthy, containing much useless information. Or written in narrative, rather than short, punchy statements.
- Disorganized, including the same type of information presented under different headings.
- Poorly typed or word processed, including narrow margins and writing in the margins, or using a faded ribbon.
- Skimpy or insufficient information (only dates, titles, and incomplete addresses).
- Excessive information, including general information (such as a listing of the product line of an employer like IBM).
- No listing of accomplishments or skills.
- Misspellings, typographical errors, typographical errors corrected by pen, poor grammar, and frequent abbreviations.
- Starting sentences with phrases such as "I did," "I was," "I am," instead of verbs like initiated, created, supervised, and so on.
- Overly elaborate résumé, such as calligraphy, fancy typesetting, or plastic binder.
- So much emphasis on nontraditional résumé that basic facts are missing (for example, work experience and addresses of schools attended). Since the company official cannot verify facts or assess qualifications, he or she places résumé in circular file.

The Cover Letter. A résumé should be accompanied by a cover letter explaining who you are and why you are applying for this particular job. The cover letter customizes your approach to a particular employer, while the résumé is a more general approach. Most job applicants use the conventional (and somewhat ineffective) approach of writing a letter attempting to impress the prospective employer with their background. A sounder approach is to capture the reader's attention with a punchy statement of what you might be able to do for them. Later in the letter you might present a one-paragraph summary of your education and the highlights of your job and educational experience. Here are two examples of opening lines geared to two different types of jobs:

1. Person seeking employment as customer service manager in a large automobile dealership: "Do you want your old customers to return to your dealership when it's time to purchase a new car? Then give me the chance to help you operate a smooth-running, 'service with a smile' customer-service department."

Capture the letter reader's attention with a punchy statement of what you might be able to do for them.

2. Person looking for position as administrative assistant in hospital where vacancy may or may not exist: "Is your hospital drowning in paper work? Let me jump in with both feet and clear up some of the confusion. Then you can go back to taking care of sick people."

Note that the second opening line may come across as a little brash to suit some tastes. It is important to use an opening line therefore that suits your personality. John Hitchcock has prepared a worksheet for writing a cover letter (see Figure 17–2) that can be adapted to any job. The attention-grabbing opening line would be used as the start of paragraph 1.

Handling Yourself in a Job Interview

After a prospective employer has reacted favorably to your cover letter and résumé, the next step is to invite you for a job interview. The most important general strategy for performing well in a job interview is to present a positive, but accurate picture of yourself. Your chances of performing well in a job increase if you are suited for the job. "Tricking" a prospective employer into hiring you when you are not qualified is therefore a self-defeating tactic in

---

Worksheet for Cover Letter

Your address
Town, street, zip code
Date

Name of person, Title (e.g., Personnel Manager)
Name of firm
Address
Town, street, zip code

Dear Mr., Mrs., or Ms. Smith:
   Paragraph 1: State the type of job that you want.
   Paragraph 2: Summarize your qualifications.
   Paragraph 3: Ask for interview. State your availability.
   Paragraph 4: Do not forget "Thank you."

Yours truly,
Signature
Name typed out
Alternative address
location

FIGURE 17–2
Cover letter format developed by John F. Hitchcock.

terms of your career. Outright deception, such as falsifying one's educational or employment record, is widely practiced. However, if the person is hired and the deception is discovered later, that employee is subject to dismissal. Here we will describe a number of important tactics and strategies to keep in mind when being interviewed for a job you would like to obtain.

Establish a Link between You and the Employer. A good rapport builder between you and the prospective employer is to mention some plausible link between you and that firm. Organizations that serve the public such as retail stores, supermarkets, and hospitals provide natural opportunities for links between you and them. To illustrate, if being interviewed for a position at a Gold Circle Department Store, one might say, "It's fun to visit the office part of Gold Circle. Our family has been buying its housewares and garden supplies here for years."

Plausible links can also be drawn between the job candidate and public-sector organizations. A woman used this rapport builder in applying for a job as a tax investigator for New York State: "As part of my tax accounting course, we analyzed a case about how a small business owner feared his upcoming tax audit. The conclusion to the case was that, since he was an honest businessman, he had nothing to fear." (She got the job.)

Ask Perceptive Questions. While being interviewed for a job, it is important to ask some questions yourself. The best questions are those that reflect an interest in the content of the job. A rule of thumb is to ask only questions of real interest to you. An experienced employment interviewer is usually adept at detecting questions asked simply to impress him or her. Following are eight questions of the type that will usually meet with good reception in an employment interview.

1. If hired, what would I actually be doing?
2. What kind of advancement opportunities are there in your firm for outstanding performers?
3. Whom would I be working with aside from people in my own department?
4. What is the company's attitude toward people who make constructive suggestions?
5. Can you tell me what kind of person you would ideally like to hire for this positon?
6. How are new hires trained and developed in your company?
7. What would you consider to be outstanding performance in this job?
8. Is there anything I've said so far that requires more elaboration or further explanation?[11]

Inevitably, the job applicant will want to ask about salary and benefits. In general, it is helpful to wait for the interviewer to take the initiative on this topic. If you are forced to take the initiative, ask about salary after you have talked about yourself and the job has been discussed. The reason for asking about salary at this point is that, if the company is sold on you, they may be willing to offer you a starting salary toward the top of the range.

Most jobs have fairly narrow salary ranges surrounding them, so you cannot negotiate over too wide a range. The less job experience and specialized training you have, the weaker your bargaining position. It is helpful to point out that the starting salary is of some concern to you, but that you are more concerned about the long-range earning potential for good performers.

Prepare in Advance. In addition to having good questions to ask during the job interview, it is necessary to prepare in advance in other ways. Be familiar with pertinent details about your background, including your social security number and names and addresses of references. Do your homework regarding your potential employer. It is important to know some basic facts about the firm in which you are seeking employment. Annual reports, brochures about the company, and sometimes newspaper and magazine articles should provide valuable information. *BusinessWeek*, for example, runs stories about most of the major business corporations.

Typically, you have to spend some time in a company waiting room before the job interview. Invest this time in reading company brochures left for visitors in the waiting room. A brief conversation with one or two current employees might provide some basic knowledge about the firm. Speaking to people who use the products or services of the firm can also provide valuable insights.

Be Ready to Discuss Your Strengths and Weaknesses. Many interviewers will ask you to discuss your strengths and weaknesses. It is therefore useful to prepare in advance for such questioning. (Some other frequently asked questions are shown in Figure 17–3.) Everyone has weaknesses or at least needs to improve in certain areas. To deny them is to appear uninsightful or defensive. However, you may not want to reveal weaknesses that are unrelated to the job (such as a fear of drowning). A mildly evasive approach is to describe weaknesses that could be interpreted as strengths. A case in point: "I am so opposed to making mistakes, that I have been criticized for spending too much time with details." Do you think this approach is unethical?

Show How You Can Help the Employer. Remember the example of Tom Crawford presented on page 413? During a telephone inquiry about a job opening, he explained what he could do for the company, rather than what they could do for him. A similar tactic was recommended in preparing a cover letter. Use the "here is how I can help you" strategy at every stage of the job-finding process throughout your career.

Encourage the Interviewer. Frequently, the person interviewing you for a position would welcome the opportunity to talk about the company or himself or herself. At the right moment, ask the interviewer's opinion about the working conditions in the company, the future of the company, or what kind of work he or she does. As the interviewer says something that makes sense to you, subtly respond in this way: "You have a point there," or "It seems like you have given careful thought to this topic," or even "That's very informative."

Your interviewer is then likely to describe you as "insightful," "intelligent," "clear-thinking," or a "good listener." These are all desirable qualities for an employee.

Write a Follow-up Letter. Your responsibilities in the job-hunting process do not end with the employment interview. The vital next step is to mail a

An important way of preparing for job interviews is to rehearse answers to the types of questions you will most likely be asked by the interviewer. The following questions are some of the same type found in most employment interviews. Rehearse answers to them prior to going out on job interviews. One good rehearsal method is to role-play the employment interview with a friend who asks these typical questions.

1. Why did you apply for this job?
2. What are your career goals?
3. What do you expect to be doing five years from now?
4. What salary are you worth?
5. How much money do you expect to be earning ten years from now?
6. What are your strengths (or good points)?
7. What are your weaknesses (or areas of needed improvement)?
8. Why did you prepare for the career you did?
9. How would you describe yourself?
10. How would other people describe you?
11. Why should we hire you instead of other candidates for the same job?
12. How well do you work under pressure?
13. What makes you think you will be successful in business?
14. What do you know about our firm?

FIGURE 17-3
Questions frequently asked of job candidates.

courteous follow-up letter several days after the interview, particularly if you want the job. You should state your attitudes toward the position and the company and summarize any conclusions reached about your discussion.[12] A follow-up letter is a tip-off that you are truly interested in the position. Some employers remove from consideration those candidates who do not submit follow-up letters.

CAREER-ADVANCEMENT STRATEGIES AND TACTICS

The approaches to improving your personal relationships on the job described in Part Three of this book can be regarded as ways of advancing your career. People who cultivate higher-ups and co-workers are in essence making plans for career advancement. The procedures for career goal setting described in Chapter 6 should also be regarded as an important strategy for advancing one's career. Here we will examine a number of other tactics and strategies for getting ahead in your career. However, indiscriminate use of any one of these tactics may backfire. For example, if you overdo the strategy of finding the right organization, you may never find a company good enough for you.

It is also important to choose methods of getting ahead that fit your circumstance and personal style. A case in point is the advice given later about taking risks. An adventuresome person without dependents would find this tactic to be ideal. A cautious, conservative person with dependents might find this tactic to be anxiety provoking.

Make an Accurate Self-Appraisal. The most important ingredient in mature career planning is to have an accurate picture of your strengths, areas for improvement, and preferences. Completing the Self-Knowledge Questionnaire presented in Chapter 4 would be a helpful starting point. All the methods of learning about the self described in Chapter 4 would be relevant to career planning. In review, feedback about the self can be obtained professionally through career counselors, through performance appraisal review sessions, or by obtaining peer evaluations. The latter type of information can be obtained in personal growth groups or more informally through asking significant people their opinion of you.

One sales representative constructed a brief form asking questions about himself, such as "What have I done that displeased you this year?" He gave this form to customers, his boss, and the clerical staff in his office. The information he received helped him become more effective with others. In this regard, he learned that he was standing too close to people (violating their *personal space*) when he talked to them.

Stick with What You Do Best. Any serious study of getting ahead in your career leads to the conclusion that the true path to career success is to identify your best talents and build a career around them. Becoming wealthy and achieving recognition are by-products of making effective use of your talents. Newspaper columnist and college lecturer Sydney Harris claims that he has only one piece of advice for young people who come to him for career counseling. It consists of ten, one-syllable words: "Find out what you do best and stick with it."[13]

Identify Growth Fields and Growth Companies. A sound strategy for career advancement is to seek jobs where possibilities for growth exist. Generally, this means seeking out growth industries, but it can also mean seeking out growth firms or areas of the country with plentiful job opportunities. Information about growth opportunities may be found in government publications (such as the *Occupational Outlook Handbook*), books on the topic, and the newspapers. Local banks and the chamber of commerce can be a valid source of information about growth firms in your area. A summary of good job opportunities for the twenty-first century (and also for the closer future) is presented in Table 17-1.

TABLE 17-1

A sample of emerging careers for the twenty-first century

PROFESSIONAL

Cable TV auditor	Energy auditor	Information research scientist	Security engineer
Career counselor	Engineering geologist	Lead system analyst	Selenologist
Career change counselor	Environmental engineer	Licensed therapeutic recreation	Sex therapist
Certified alcohol counselor	Ethicist	specialist	Software writer
Certified financial planner	Family mediator	Marine geologist	Solar architect
Child advocate	Forecaster	Mineral economist	Solar designer
Communications specialist	Forensic scientist	Molecular biologist	Solar energy consultant
Computer designer	Fusion engineer	Neutrino astronomer	Space colonist
Computer scientist	Gene splicing worker	Ombudsman	Space botanist
Computer security specialist	Geneticist	Oncology nutritionist	Sports psychologist
Computer systems analyst	Genetic counselor	Phobia therapist	Strategic planner
Data base designer	Geriatric nurse	Planetary engineer	Thanatologist
Data base engineer	Health physicist	Planetary scientist	Theoretical chemist
Divorce mediator	Hibernation specialist	Professional ethnicist	Underwater archeologist
Documentation specialist	Human services expert	Public affairs psychologist	Volcanologist
Ecologist	Image consultant	Robot engineer	Wind prospector
EDP auditor	Information broker	Robotic scientist	

PARAPROFESSIONAL

Exercise technician	Hotline counselor	Licensed psychiatric technician	Social work aide
Family and planning midwives	Lawyer's aide	Medical aide	Teacher's aide
Home health aide	Library aide	Sex counselor	Veterinary aide

MANAGERIAL AND SUPERVISORY

Complaints manager	Employee relocation services	International sales and	Technical services manager
Data base administrator	director	marketing manager	Telecommunications marketing
Data base manager	Executive VIP for international	International systems director	director
Director of human resources	product planning	New product manager	Transplant coordinator
Director of software	Halfway house manager	Site selector specialist	Underwater hotel, pavilion
developments	Information coordinator	Space launch director	or observatory director
EDP audit systems manager	Information manager	Systems analysis manager	

SALES

Cable TV salesperson	Distributor of new business	Salesperson for talking	Telecommunication salesperson
Computer salesperson	equipment	encyclopedias	Telephone salesperson
Digital radiography sales	Phonovision salesperson	Sales trainer	
representative	Robot salesperson	Software salesperson	

SMALL BUSINESS

Aquaculture	Financial consultant	Music store	Specialized food services
Artist (graphic)	Financial planner	New health foods	Telephone answering service
Book club sales	Fish farmer	Orthotist	Training services
Catering and fast food	Freelance writer	Picture framer	Truffle nursery
Child daycare service	Home correspondence courses	Plant and pet service	Tutor
Computer games developer	Information salesperson	Publishing	Videodating services
Consultant	Inventor	Self-employment	
Electric car service station	Manufacturer of talking signs	Shrimp and trout fish farming	

SKILLED

Asteroid miner	Computer programmer	Holographic inspection specialist	Nuclear fuel technician
Bioconversion technologist	Computer service technician	House husband and house wife	Nuclear reactor technician
Biomedical technician	Cryogenic technician	Industrial robot technician	Positron emission tomograph (PET)
Bionic medical technician	Cyborg technician	Laser technician	technician
Computer assisted design	Diagnostic medical sonographer	Lunar miner	Rehabilitation housing technician
(CAD) technician	Dialysis technician	Materials utilization technician	Space mechanic
Computer assisted manufac-	Exotic welder	Mechanic for hydrogen powered	Solar engineering technician
turing (CAM) specialist	Fiber optic technician	automobiles	Telecommunications technician
Computer axial tomagrapher	Hazardous waste technician	Medicine aid technician	Underwater culture technician
(CAT) technologist	Hibernation technician	Microbiological mining	
		technician	

SEMI-SKILLED   UNSKILLED

Battery technician	Paramedics		Home companion
Bio-gas technician	Courier		House pet and plant sitter
Computer graphics assistant			TV monitor (guard)

SOURCE: S. Norman Fiengold, "Tracking New Career Categories Will Become a Preoccupation for Job Seekers and Managers," *Personnel Administrator* (Dec. 1983), p. 90.

Find the Right Organization for You. Ideally, you should work for an organization where there is a good fit between your style and its style. For example, if you are adventuresome and aggressive, you would most likely prosper in a firm that itself is aggressive and adventuresome (like Apple Computers). Although finding a fit between your personality and the personality of the organization may sound difficult to achieve, it may prove vital to getting ahead in your career.

Information about a potential employer can be found through such means as reading annual reports (if it is a business corporation) and asking the opinion of a broker, customer, or supplier. Best of all, seek the opinion of several current or past employees. Choosing the wrong organization can be hazardous to your career. An organization that is "wrong" for you can be "right" for another person, and vice versa. You may not be able to tolerate an organization that expects its higher-level employees to work a 55-hour week under intense pressure. Another person might thrive in such an atmosphere.

Perform Well in Your Present Job. Common sense and research evidence support the idea that you have to be effective where you are before you can think about moving ahead.[14] Good job performance is the foundation on which you build your career. Job competence and talent are still the major success ingredients in all but the most political firms (those where favoritism outweighs merit). Before anybody is promoted in virtually every organization, the prospective new boss asks, "How well did this person perform for you?"

Obtain Broad Experience. A widely accepted strategy for getting ahead in your career is to strengthen your credentials by broadening your experience. Broadening can come about by performing a variety of jobs or sometimes by performing essentially the same job for different firms. At one time it was believed that **job-hopping** (moving from firm to firm) led to more rapid advancement than being loyal to one employer. Evidence collected during the last decade, however, points to the value of staying with one firm in order to advance your career. Managers who stay with the same firm tend to make more money and have bigger jobs than those who move from firm to firm.[15]

One practical way of obtaining broad experience is to become part of a management trainee program, where you rotate from department to department, after which you are permanently assigned to one department. Another way is to be assigned to or volunteer for committees and special projects.

Take Sensible Risks. People who make it big in their careers usually take several sensible risks on their journey to success. Among these risks would be to work for a fledgling company that offers big promises but a modest starting salary or to take an overseas assignment with no promise of a good job when you return. Industrial relations manager Michael Oliver offers this advice:

> If you want to achieve something really creative, thus enhancing your profession, then try a little risk taking. That doesn't mean you should pick up a lance and seek out a windmill. Balance your risk taking with good sense so you will be able to reach a new comfort level somewhere between the role of a bureaucratic follower and leaper of tall buildings. The goal should be to develop credibility without perpetrating a maverick reputation.[16]

Swim against the Tide. A special case of taking sensible risks is to swim against the tide (take an unconventional path to career success). It involves placing yourself in a job setting where the competition might not be so overwhelming. Suppose that a man from Quebec City who is fluent in English and French is seeking a position in international marketing. He might be best advised to seek employment in a company not overloaded with people who can converse fluently in both English and French. Instead of seeking employment in Montreal, he might look for a job in Toronto or New York City. His background would then be at a premium. He would have the edge in competition for jobs dealing with French companies.

As with any other career-planning strategy, swimming against the tide requires good judgment to implement. The same company that has few French-speaking employees might have an informal policy against promoting a native of Quebec into a key job!

Find a Sponsor. A well-proved path to career advancement is to find somebody at a high place in the company who is impressed with your capabilities. A sponsor of this type can even be a blood relative or one by marriage. One reason that special assignments are so helpful to career progress is that they provide you with the opportunity to be seen by a variety of key people in your organization. Many an employee who has performed well in an activity such as the United Way has found a bigger job in the process. In general, any tactic that brings favorable attention to yourself can help you find a sponsor. Some of the suggestions made in Chapter 10 for impressing superiors fall into this category.

Find a Mentor. Mentors are bosses who take subordinates under their wings and guide, teach, and coach them. Mentorship is an important development process in many occupations: master–apprentice, physician–intern, teacher–student, and executive–junior executive.[17] Most corporate presidents have had mentors who were an instrumental part of their success. An emotional tie exists between the less-experienced person (protégé) and the mentor. The mentor therefore serves as a positive model. A relationship with a sponsor involves much less teaching, coaching, and formation of emotional ties. It is possible to have more than one mentor at a given point in one's career.

Take an unconventional
path to career success . . .

Mentoring is now used as a form of management development. For example, at IBM mentoring has taken the form of a network of administrative assistants to senior executives. The company identifies high-potential managers early in their careers and gives them 1-year to 1½-year assignment with top executives. The system has a twofold purpose: The assistant relieves the executive of many administrative details, while the executive gets to watch the assistant in action and help teach him or her management skills.[18] The type of advice mentors offer is shown in Exhibit 17–1.

An executive placement specialist points out the danger of being a mentoree: "There is a real risk in allowing yourself to be identified as someone's prodigy, and I've seen as many people get damaged by it as helped by it. If your mentor falls out of favor, the likelihood is that you will too."[19]

Exhibit 17–1

CAREER ADVICE TO YOUNG MEN AND WOMEN

As part of a study, Robert Pearse asked experienced managers to give some career advice to young men and women. The sampling of the managers' advice presented represents the kind of advice mentors give to mentorees. You will observe that much of the advice follows concepts of business psychology.

"Expect to live with frustration and also to learn from it. Above all, believe in yourself."

"Learn all you can about jobs and about your organization while you are on the way up. Be aggressive and show initiative. Also, use that precious quality 'common sense' in making your key decisions."

"Get varied job experience. Move from job to job as quickly as possible. Assume as much responsibility as you can comfortably handle at each stage of your career."

"Learn early on in your career what realistic, achievable goals are. Then set realistic goals for both your personal advancement and your company contributions. Establish as quickly as possible what is the right balance between your personal and your business life."

"It might sound trite, but work hard, be patient, broaden your interests within the company and industry. Make sacrifices if you have to to earn career advancement. Give that little extra something when needed."

"Be as objective as you can in evaluating your own strengths and weaknesses. Plan and implement a program to reduce or eliminate your weaknesses. Seek out opportunities to demonstrate your abilities."

"First, try to take a broad spectrum of college courses in both management and human behavior. Second, set goals for your career. They shouldn't be inflexible, but they will give you the perspectives that will help you with both your timing and patience if you have to wait at some level."

"Look for work you love to do, work that seems like play, work that makes you excited to be alive. Exercise absolute fairness and integrity. Money alone is not a fair exchange for 40 years of happiness and contentment on the job. I actually look forward to my next 25 years in business."

Source: Robert F. Pearse, *Manager to Manager II: What Managers Think of their Managerial Careers* (New York: AMACOM, 1978), pp. 58–63.

Document Your Accomplishments. Keeping an accurate record of what you have accomplished in your career can be valuable when being considered for promotion. An astute career person can point specifically to what he or she has accomplished in each position. Here are two examples from different types of jobs:

1. As ski shop store manager, increased sales to deaf skiers by 338 percent in one year by hiring a deaf interpreter to work in our shop on Saturday mornings.
2. As industrial engineer, saved my company $72,000 in one year by switching from steel to nylon ball bearings in our line of bicycles and baby carriages.

Develop a Network of Contacts. An important career-advancement strategy is to develop a large number of contacts who may be able to help you. These forms of help include recommending you for a job inside or outside your firm, helping you with sticky job problems, providing you with emotional support, and buying your goods and services. Networking is of obvious importance in sales, but it is also helpful in many occupations. John Molloy studied hundreds of successful people in a variety of occupations. One of the conclusions he reached was, "The overwhelming majority of successful men and women we spoke to had a large network of friends."[20] **Networking** is also referred to as the "good old boy" or "good old girl" system.

Consider Your Spouse. Working couples or **dual-career families** are commonplace today. A dual-career family is a type of working couple in which both are serious about their careers, rather than simply holding jobs to meet expenses.[21] When one of the working partners is transferred or promoted, the impact on the other partner has to be carefully considered. In the past, a husband's career carried the most weight. Today both a woman's occupation and/or her community involvement carry more weight than they did in the past. An increasing number of men are refusing transfers to another city because of its potential adverse impact on their wives or children.

Considering your spouse helps advance one's career because it removes a potential source of friction—spouse discontentment and resentment. In turn, the considerate spouse can concentrate more on work.

Capitalize on Luck. Few people do well in their careers without a good break along the way. Lucky events include your company suddenly expanding and therefore needing to promote people into key jobs; your boss quitting on short notice and you being asked to take over his or her job; or the industry in which you are working suddenly experiencing a boom, like home video recorders in the 1980s.

A good strategy is not to simply wait for luck to come your way. Instead, manage luck to some extent by recognizing opportunities and taking advantage of them. A case in point is the man who became the national service manager in charge of service centers for small computers. He told a case writer:

> Several years ago a job opened up as national manager in charge of machine-repair centers for our company. Most of the hot-shots saw this as a dead-end job. They figured that repair work had no glamour. But I could see unlimited possibilities. If people wanted to keep their home computer equipment running, they would need reliable service. Sure enough, our repair business expanded like mad. And my job became a true executive position.

Look Successful. A basic career-advancement tactic is to project a successful image. Your clothing, your desk and work space, and your speech should project the image of a successful but not necessarily a flamboyant person. The suggestions made about dress and appearance in Chapter 11 thus apply both to adjusting to the organization and getting ahead.

Appearing physically fit is also part of a success image. Man or woman, a person with a well-rested, trim, and muscular appearance has a slight edge over the competition, all things being equal. Discrimination against overweight people is widely practiced in business. The reason offered is that overweight people are high health risks. Being underweight can also detract from your success look, although it may not have as great a negative impact on your career as being overweight.

Hitch Your Wagon to Yourself. The ultimate strategy for developing career thrust is to have faith in what you are doing and to persist in doing it well. If you hitch your wagon to yourself, you will not be bothered by your critics. Eventually, your contributions will be recognized because what you are doing is worthwhile and of value to your employer or employers. Hitching your wagon to yourself is your career foundation. Other strategies for getting ahead are designed to supplement this basic strategy. If you lack technical, interpersonal, or administrative skills and ideas of your own, you are lacking the basis for a successful career.

CAREER SWITCHING

The New American Dream could very well be finding a satisfying second career (or even third or fourth career) when the present career has gone stale. Every month hundreds of corporate employees leave their jobs to try self-employment in such activities as running a franchise restaurant or starting a new business from scratch.[22] A dramatic example is that of a middle-aged couple who both quit their jobs to start a dating service that eventually earned them a living. Younger people, too, may find the need to switch careers. Even switching majors can be considered an early form of career switching.

Switching careers usually requires long-range planning. The economy can only absorb so many proprietors of small stores or franchise restaurant owners. Another consideration is that some of these franchise fast-food restaurants have a start-up fee of $300,000. Sometimes a long-term avocation can be converted into an occupation, providing a high level of skill has been developed. A representative example is an admissions director at a college who had been selling real estate quite successfully on a part-time basis for many years. When admissions work lost its excitment for her, the admissions director became a full-time real estate agent. Within six months of working at real estate sales full time, she was earning more money than her previous combined income from admissions work and real estate.

To switch careers effectively, you should follow the suggestions for finding a field or first career. In addition, the potential career switcher is well advised to follow the advice offered in a current guide to finding another career. To avoid making what might turn out to be a costly and time-consuming error, you should:

1. narrow your interests to a few specific areas or job titles,
2. try part-time work in your desired area,
3. get into an apprenticeship program (this usually requires completion of some specialized education),
4. do volunteer work in your field of interest,
5. take a course or two in the potential new field, or
6. determine if you should return to college full-time or part-time.[23]

SUMMARY OF KEY POINTS

☐ You must accept the major responsibility for developing your career despite whatever help is offered by your employer. One reason is that you are likely to change employers either voluntarily or involuntarily.

☐ Job and career satisfaction tends to be achieved under the following conditions: (1) mentally challenging work, (2) personal interest in the work itself, (3) work that is not too physically demanding, (4) performance rewards that are fair, informative, and meet a person's goals, (5) working conditions that meet your physical needs and help you to get your work done, (6) work that leads to high self-esteem, (7) people in the workplace who help you satisfy your needs and values, and (8) work that is consistent with specific job values.

☐ Finding a field for yourself is often done in a happenstance manner, using conventional methods. Another approach is to make systematic use of occupational information. This would include reading reference books about careers, computer-assisted career guidance, reading career information in newspapers, and speaking to employed people.

☐ Recommended job-hunting tactics include (1) identify your objectives, (2) identify your potential contribution, (3) use multiple approaches, (4) use the insider system, (5) be specific with your friends about your job interests, (6) keep your number of business contacts growing, (7) be persistent, and (8) be willing to handle some rejection.

☐ Effective job résumés are straightforward, factual presentations of a person's experiences and accomplishments. Three types of résumés are the chronological, functional, and accomplishment. A recommended résumé format is presented in Figure 17–1. Do your best to avoid mistakes commonly made in résumés. A résumé should almost always be accompanied by a cover letter explaining who you are and why you are applying for this particular job.

☐ Keep the following tactics and strategies in mind when being interviewed for a job: (1) establish a link between you and the employer, (2) ask perceptive questions, (3) prepare in advance, (4) be ready to discuss your strengths and weaknesses, (5) show how you can help the employer, (6) encourage the interviewer, and (7) write a follow-up letter.

☐ Building good personal relationships on the job, and setting goals are important career advancement strategies. In addition, consider the following:

1. Make an accurate self-appraisal.
2. Stick with what you do best.
3. Identify growth fields and growth companies.
4. Find the right organization for you.
5. Perform well in your present job.
6. Obtain broad experience.
7. Take sensible risks.
8. Swim against the tide.
9. Find a sponsor.
10. Find a mentor.
11. Document your accomplishments.
12. Develop a network of contacts.
13. Consider your spouse.
14. Capitalize on luck.

15. Look successful.

16. Hitch your wagon to yourself.

□ Switching careers requires long-range planning and also involves many of the same approaches as finding an initial field. It is helpful to phase into a new career by trying it out part-time and preparing for it educationally.

GUIDELINES FOR PERSONAL EFFECTIVENESS

1. Some people achieve career success (including both rewards and satisfaction) without a deliberate, planned effort. For the vast majority of people, attaining these ends requires careful planning. Planning is particularly helpful when you are getting started in your career and during its early stages. Planning includes choosing a field, finding a job, and using career-advancement tactics and strategies.
2. Should you be confronted with the task of finding a job, do not be overly apprehensive. Much useful information has been collected to aid you in the job-finding process. Following this information carefully will increase your chances of finding suitable employment.
3. Any of the strategies and tactics described in this chapter must be used with selectivity. A helpful approach is to select those suggestions that seem to fit your personality and preferences. Avoid those tactics and strategies that you think are in conflict with your values.

DISCUSSION QUESTIONS

1. In your opinion, do most people have satisfying and rewarding careers? What evidence do you have to support your opinion?

2. In what occupations do people seem the most satisfied? What seems to contribute to their satisfaction?

3. If you have already found a field and occupation for yourself, what method did you use to find that field and occupation?

4. What steps have you taken to manage your career? In other words, what career planning have you already done?

5. "Winging it" is the alternative to career planning. If some very successful people are "wingers" rather than "planners," why should you plan your career?

6. Which do you think are the two most useful career-advancement tactics and strategies described in this chapter? Why are they useful to you?

7. An 18-year-old high school senior comes to you for advice. She states, "I'm looking for a career that will bring me the greatest possible self-fulfillment." What advice can you offer her?

8. What do you think are the advantages and disadvantages of job-hopping as a career-advancement strategy?

9. A person with low self-confidence said at a career-development workshop, "I'm afraid the method called Hitch Your Wagon to Yourself won't work in my case. I'm not talented enough for it to apply to my situation." What advice can you offer this man?

10. What forces in our society do you think have contributed to the popularity of career switching?

A Business Psychology Problem
THE PROPERTY MANAGER IN TURMOIL

Bonnie Fraser decided to cash in on her business school training and experience as an administrative assistant. She responded to this ad in a Pittsburgh newspaper for a job in Florida.

PROPERTY MANAGER

For 300+ apartment complex in Fort Lauderdale, Florida. Experience in all facets of multihousing, resident retention, marketing, rent collections, accounting, budget control, and sales ability. Self-motivated, take-charge person. Must be able to live on property. Excellent salary and fringe benefits.

Through pluck, luck, and an impassioned plea that she was a fast learner, Bonnie did get the job. She relocated to Florida and soon found she loved everything about Florida but her job. When her parents came down to visit her six months after her relocation, Bonnie gave them this tale of woe:

"Folks, I'm facing an early career crisis. Florida is more fun than I could have dreamed. Springtime in Ft. Lauderdale alone is worth a million bucks to me. I've made more good friends in six months here than I made in my last five years in Pittsburgh. When I'm not working, its nonstop fun and sun. But the job is the pits. It's too many headaches. I'm forever hustling for new reliable tenants and trying to collect rent from the existing tenants. Every problem on the property falls in my lap."

When her parents asked Bonnie why she didn't look for a new and less stressful job in the area, Bonnie answered:

"You don't understand my new lifestyle. I have a new car and an apartment full of furniture bought on time. This jobs pays much better than anything else around. And besides I live rent free. It seems like there is no turning back."

1. What career advice can you offer Bonnie?
2. To what extent do you think Bonnie has done a poor job of setting priorities for her values?
3. What concepts and methods of business psychology described in previous chapters would be relevant in helping Bonnie?

A Business Psychology Role-Play
THE JOB INTERVIEW

As described in Figure 17–2, a good way to prepare for a job interview is to rehearse answers to frequently asked questions. In this role-play, one student will be the interviewer and one the interviewee. The job in question is that of property manager for a large apartment complex in Florida. (See the brief job description given previously.) Assume the interviewee really wants the job (just as Bonnie did). The interviewer, having taken a course in business psychology, will ask many of the questions shown in Figure 17–2. The interviewer, however, will also have other specific questions such as "Why do you want to work in Florida?"

Before proceeding ahead with the role play, both people should review the information in this chapter about the job interview and in Chapter 15 about listening.

REFERENCES

[1]Andrew F. Sikula and John F. McKenna, "Individuals Must Take Charge of Career Development," *Personnel Administrator* (Oct. 1983), p. 90.

[2]Edwin A. Locke, "The Nature and Causes of Job Satisfaction," in Marvin D. Dunnette, ed. *Handbook of Industrial and Organizational Psychology* (New York: Wiley, 1983), p. 1328. This book is a reprint of the 1976 edition published by Rand McNally.

[3]Thomas J. DeLong, "Reexamining the Career Anchor Model," *Personnel* (May–June 1982), p. 53.

[4]*System of Interactive Guidance and Information* (SIGI), Educational Testing Service, Princeton, New Jersey.

[5]Two such books are Richard N. Bolles, *What Color Is Your Parachute? A Practical Guide for Job Hunters and Career Changers* (Berkeley, Calif.: Ten Speed Press, revised about every year); and Thomas J. Moffatt, *Land That Job!* (New York: Harper & Row, 1982).

[6]Richard Lathrup, *Who's Hiring Who*, rev. ed. (Berkeley, Calif.: Ten Speed Press, 1979).

[7]Marilyn Moats Kennedy, "How to Job Hunt," *Success* (Oct. 1982), p. 30.

[8]Ibid.

[9]Tom Jackson, "Writing the Targeted Resume," *BusinessWeek's Guide to Careers* (Spring 1983), pp. 26–27.

[10]Most of this information is adapted from ibid., and John W. Zehring, "18 Rules for Resume Writers," in Bill Repp, *Why Give It Away When You Can Sell It?* (Rochester, N.Y.: Creative Communications, 1982), pp. 121–124.

[11]Questions 5, 6, and 7 on this list are from Marcia R. Fox, "How to Clinch the Off-Campus Interview," *BusinessWeek's Guide to Careers* (Spring 1983), p. 24.

[12]Clarke G. Carney, Cinda Field Wells, and Don Streufert, *Career Planning: Skills to Build Your Future* (New York: Van Nostrand Reinhold, 1981), p. 148.

[13]Sydney J. Harris, "Career Advice: Stick with What You Do Best," syndicated column printed in Rochester *Democrat and Chronicle* (Sept. 16, 1982), p. 3C.

[14]Susan L. Colantuono, *Build Your Career: A Workbook for Advancing in an Organization* (Amherst, Mass.: Human Resources Development Press, 1982), Chapter 1; Joseph A. Raelin, "First-job Effects on Career Development," *Personnel Administrator* (Aug. 1983), pp. 71–76.

[15]Malcom N. Carter, "Job Hop," *Money Magazine,* reprinted in Rochester *Democrat and Chronicle* (Oct. 25, 1981), p. 1F.

[16]Michael L. Oliver, "Taking Risks Will Get Your Career Moving," *Personnel Journal* (April 1983), p. 319.

[17]David Marshall Hunt and Carol Michael, "Mentorship: A Career Training and Development Tool," *Academy of Management Review* (July 1983), p. 475.

[18]Claudia H. Deutsch, "Guidance Counselors," *TWA Ambassador* (Sept. 1983), p. 14.

[19]Ibid.

[20]John T. Molloy, *Molloy's Live For Success* (New York: Bantam Books, 1982), p. 187.

[21]Richard E. Kopelman, Lyn Rosensweig, and Laura H. Lally, "Dual-Career Couples: The Organizational Response," *Personnel Administrator* (Sept. 1982), pp. 73–81.

[22]A popular book with dozens of case histories about career switchers is Gail Sheehy, *Pathfinders* (New York: Morrow, 1981).

[23]Quoted from Linda Kline and Lloyd L. Feinstein, "Creative Thinking for Switching Careers," *Success* (March 1983), p. A2.

SUGGESTED READING

BOLLES, RICHARD N. *The Three Boxes of Life and How to Get out of Them.* Berkeley, Calif.: Ten Speed Press, revised regularly.

BusinessWeek's Guide to Careers, published semi-annually by McGraw-Hill, New York.

CONNELL, JOHN J. "The Future Office: New Technologies, New Career Paths," *Personnel* (July–Aug. 1983), pp. 23–32.

Encyclopedia of Careers and Vocational Guidance. New York: J. G. Ferguson, distributed by Doubleday & Company. See current edition.

HASTINGS, ROBERT E. "No-fault Career Counseling Can Boost Middle- and Upper-Middle Management," *Personnel Administrator* (Jan. 1982), pp. 22–27.

HICKERSON, KARL A., and RICHARD C. ANDERSON. "Career Development: Whose Responsibility?" *Personnel Administrator* (June 1982), pp. 41–49.

JOBIN, JUDITH. "Career Counseling: Inspiration or Rip-Off?" *Woman's Day* (Nov. 15, 1983), pp. 88, 90, 92.

LOUGHARY, JOHN W., and THERESA M. RIPLEY. *Career and Life Planning Guide.* Chicago: Follett Publishing, 1982.

OSIPOW, SAMUEL H. *Theories of Career Development,* 3rd ed. Englewood Cliffs, N.J.: Prentice-Hall, 1983.

POWELL, GARY N. "Career Development and the Woman Manager—A Social Perspective," *Personnel* (May–June 1980), pp. 22–32.

GLOSSARY

Action plan   A description of what needs to be done to achieve an objective or bring performance back to an acceptable standard.

Anxiety   Generalized feelings of fear and apprehension that usually result from a perceived threat. Feelings of uneasiness and tension usually accompany anxiety.

Assertiveness training (AT)   A self-improvement training program based on behavior therapy that teaches people to express their feelings, and act with an appropriate degree of openness and assertiveness.

Authority   The right to control the actions of others; control that is sanctioned by the organization or society.

Autocratic leadership   A leadership style in which the leader attempts to retain most of the authority. The autocratic leader typically makes a decision and then announces it to the subordinates.

Behavior modification   A system of motivation that intends to change the behavior of people by manipulating incentives (thus changing the person's environment). Desired responses are rewarded, whereas undesired responses are ignored or punished.

Behavior pattern   Essentially, the typical way an individual acts or behaves in a similar situation. Your behavior pattern, for example, may be to perform your best under pressure.

Behavior shaping   See *shaping of behavior*.

Behavioral science   Any science concerned with the systematic study of human behavior. The primary behavioral sciences are psychology, sociology, and anthropology.

Behaviorism   A school of thought in psychology based on the assumption that psychologists should study overt behavior rather than mental states or other unobservable aspects of living things.

Brainstorming   A conference technique of solving specific problems, amassing information, and stimulating creative thinking. The basic technique is to encourage unrestrained and spontaneous participation by group members. Also called *group brainstorming*, but it can be practiced alone.

Bureaucracy   A rational, systematic, and precise form of organization in which rules, regulations, and techniques of control are precisely defined. A typical bureaucracy has many layers of management and many specialists.

Business psychology   The application of systematic knowledge about human behavior to improve personal and organizational effectiveness in work settings.

Career-advancement strategy   Any systematic plan, ethical or unethical, aimed at improving your chances for success at work over the long range. Swim Against the Tide is one such strategy.

Career counselor   An individual whose professional role is to provide counseling and guidance to individuals about their careers. Career counselors often work in an educational setting, but others offer their services to the public for a fee.

Career goals   Specific positions, types of work, or income levels that a student or employed person aspires to reach.

Career switching   Changing from one career to another at any point during one's working life, involving much more commitment than merely changing jobs.

Classical conditioning   A basic form of learning in which a stimulus that usually brings forth a given response is repeatedly paired with a neutral stimulus (one that does not typically evoke the response). Eventually, the neutral stimulus will bring forth the response when presented by itself (such as feeling hunger pangs when the factory lunch whistle blows).

Cognitive   Referring to the intellectual, rather than the emotional, aspects of human behavior. A cognitive process is the means by which an individual becomes aware of objects and situations. It includes learning, reasoning, and problem solving.

Cognitive psychology   A movement within, or branch of, psychology that attempts to explain the behavior of human beings in terms of their intellectual, rational selves.

Common sense   Sound, practical judgment that is independent of specialized knowledge, training, or the like. Also natural wisdom not based on formal knowledge.

Communication   The passage of information between or among people (or animals) by the use of words, letters, symbols, or body language.

Communication overload   A condition in which the individual is confronted with so much information to process that he or she becomes overwhelmed and therefore does a poor job of processing information. Also referred to as *information overload*, the condition often serves as a stressor.

Computer shock (or stress)   A strong negative reaction to being forced to spend many more hours working at a computer than one desires. In addition to typical stress symptoms, the condition includes a glassy-eyed detached look, aching neck muscles, and a growing dislike for high technology.

Conflict   Simultaneous arousal of two or more incompatible motives. Often accompanied by tension, anxiety, or frustration.

Confrontation Bringing forth a controversial topic or contradictory material in which the other party is personally involved. To say, "Your actions irritate me," is a confrontation.

Coping To contend with something or somebody on even terms or with success, such as coping with tension or irrational people.

Counterproductive person One whose actions lead him or her away from achieving work goals, often because of a personality quirk.

Creative climate An organizational climate or atmosphere that actually encourages people to seek and bring forth creative solutions to problems.

Creativity The ability to process information in such a way that the result is new, original, and meaningful.

Crucial subordinate An individual who performs well in a crucial assignment upon which the superior's performance is dependent.

Decision The passing of judgment upon an issue under consideration. Arriving at a choice among alternatives.

Delegation The process by which authority and work assignments are distributed downward in an organization.

Dialogue A conversation between two or more people in which the individuals react to each other's statements and thoughts. It is the opposite of a monologue.

Disarm the opposition A technique of conflict resolution in which you disarm the other person by agreeing with his or her criticism of you.

Drive level The amount of effort a person puts forth toward reaching a goal.

Effectiveness The extent to which an individual, organization, or machine achieves worthwhile or important results.

Ego involvement A situation that exists when you feel you are personally involved in and committed to the outcome of an activity or event. Your self-concept becomes involved; therefore, you care about the outcome.

Ego state According to transactional analysis, the human personality is divided into three parts, called ego states (parent, adult, and child). Technically defined, an ego state is a system of feelings and experiences related to the pattern of behavior that a person develops in the stages of growing up.

Emotion Any strong agitation of the feelings triggered by experiencing love, hate, fear, joy, and the like.

Encounter group A small therapy or training group that focuses on expressing feelings openly and honestly. Encounter groups are now frequently referred to as personal growth groups.

Ergonomics A field related to business psychology that attempts to design machinery, equipment, and the work environment to fit human characteristics, both physical and psychological. Also referred to as *human engineering* or *engineering psychology*.

Eustress An amount of stress that makes you come alive; a positive force in the lives of people.

Expectancy In the psychological sense, a hunch a person has that a particular behavior will satisfy a particular need. You might have the expectation that receiving a suggestion from your employer will satisfy your need for recognition.

Expectancy theory A theory of human motivation that centers around the idea that people will expend effort if they believe the effort will lead to a desired outcome. Also considered is whether or not that outcome (for example, getting the job done) will lead to a reward (such as a large salary increase).

Feedback Information that tells you how well or poorly you have performed. Also, knowledge of results about one's behavior that helps you to judge the appropriateness of your responses and make corrections where indicated.

Feelings Any emotional state or disposition, such as the feeling of happiness or sadness. Feelings are closely related to attitudes.

Flexitime (flextime, flexible working hours) A method of organizing the hours of work so that employees have flexibility in choosing their own hours. People on flexitime are required to work certain core hours, such as 11 A.M. to 3 P.M., but they have flexibility in which hours they work for the rest of the day.

Flow experience A feeling of total absorption in the task at hand, often leading to a reduction in tension. People can experience flow in both creative and noncreative work.

Fogging A way of responding to manipulative criticism by openly accepting the criticism. Such as "Yes, it's true I was one hour late for work today."

Followership Behavior related to following the directions or orders of a leader: the opposite of leadership.

Formal group A group that forms in response to the demands and processes of the formal organization. An officially sanctioned group.

Formal organization The organization as it is supposed to be or as it is written on paper. It is the official, sanctioned way of doing things.

Framework A basic system or design for understanding something. A framework serves as a basic outline or model.

Free-rein leadership A style of leadership in which the leader issues general goals and guidelines to the group and then does not get involved again unless requested. Also called *laissez-faire* leadership.

Frustration Thwarting or blocking of a need, wish, or desire.

Frustration tolerance The amount of frustration a given individual can handle without suffering adverse consequences. When a person is fatigued, his or her frustration tolerance decreases.

Game A repeated series of exchanges between people that appears different on the surface than its true underlying motive.

Gentle confrontation A method of conflict resolution in which the person with a gripe openly, but tactfully, brings the problem to the attention of the person with whom he or she disagrees.

Goal An event, circumstance, object, or condition for which a person or animal strives.

Goal-setting theory A systematic explanation of how goal setting increases productivity. The theory emphasizes the value of both difficult and specific goals.

Grapevine The major informal communication network or pathway in an organization. Used in the transmission of both rumors and official information.

Group   A collection of individuals who regularly interact with each other, who are psychologically aware of each other, and who perceive themselves to be a group.

Group cohesiveness   The attractiveness of the group to its members that leads to a feeling of unity and "stick-togetherness."

Group norms   The unwritten set of expectations or standards of conduct telling group members what each person should do within the group.

Groupthink   An extreme form of consensus or agreement that may take place when the group tries too hard to stick together.

Halo effect   An error in perception in which the favorableness or unfavorableness of our prime impression of another tends to make us see that person as all good or bad.

Herzberg's two-factor theory of motivation   The view advanced by Herzberg that factors leading to satisfaction and motivation are not the same as those leading to dissatisfaction and nonmotivation. Factors that give you a chance to satisfy high-level needs are satisfiers and motivators.

High-output tasks   Those tasks in which superior performance could have a large payoff (thus doing those tasks leads to high output).

Human behavior   Actions or activities engaged in by people, including both external (such as movement) and internal activities (such as thinking and feeling).

Human relations   The art and practice of using systematic knowledge about human behavior to achieve organizational and/or personal objectives. Similar to organizational behavior and business psychology.

Human relations movement   Basically, the growth of human relations in organizations. It took the form of a concentrated effort by some managers and their advisors to become more sensitive to the needs of employees or to treat them in a more humanistic manner.

Humanistic psychology   An approach to psychology that emphasizes the dignity and worth of people along with their many other positive but intangible or "soft" attributes.

I'm OK—You're OK   A key concept of transactional analysis (TA) that signifies the life position of the mature, healthy adult.

Individual differences   The basic concept of psychology that human beings show variation on almost every trait and characteristic. For instance, people show individual differences in height, intelligence, hearing ability, and aggressiveness.

Industrial and organizational psychology   Basically, the field of business psychology; the field of psychology that studies human behavior in a work environment. Overlaps considerably with the field called organizational behavior.

Industrial humanism   The application of a humanistic philosophy to managing workers. It includes a willingness to satisfy many higher-level needs of workers on the job.

Informal group   A natural grouping of people in a work situation that evolves to take care of people's desires for friendship and companionship.

Informal organization   A pattern of work relationships that develops to both satisfy people's social needs and to get work accomplished. The informal organization is not written down on paper and includes informal groups.

Insider system   A job-hunting technique in which a person searches for nonadvertised jobs that are usually offered to company insiders, friends and relatives of insiders, or applicants who write unsolicited letters to the firm.

Intellectual style   The unique and characteristic way in which an individual solves problems. For example, he or she may be impulsive or reflective.

Intelligence   The capacity to acquire and apply knowledge, including solving problems. Technically, intelligence refers to the capacity to learn, the ability to deal with abstractions, the ability to manipulate symbols, and the ability to handle new situations.

Intervening variable   A factor that influences a process even though it is not an intentional input into the process. For example, a person's mood at the time may influence his or her decision making.

Intuition   Direct perception of truth or fact that seems to be independent of any reasoning process. A keen and quick insight that can be helpful in solving complex problems.

Inversion of means and ends   A situation in which following orders or performing your specialized activity becomes more important than the overall goal that you are trying to accomplish. If a factory supervisor becomes so safety conscious that all production is shut down, an inversion of means and ends has taken place.

Job burnout   The general discomfort, fatigue, cynicism, helplessness and hopelessness, and apathy stemming from not receiving the rewards you anticipated from work.

Job campaign   All the activities involved in finding a job, including preparing a list of prospective organizations, writing a résumé and cover letter, getting in touch with friends who can help you, and so forth.

Job design   The basic way in which a job is set up or designed. Job design can be an influential factor in employee motivation and satisfaction.

Job enlargement   Increasing the scope of a job, usually with the intention of increasing both satisfaction and performance.

Job enrichment   A system of job design that attempts to increase worker motivation by making the nature of the job more exciting, rewarding, challenging, creative, or responsible.

Job performance   The output of a job activity; how well a person does in meeting the demands of his or her job.

Job satisfaction   The amount of pleasure or contentment associated with a job. In contrast, job *motivation* refers to the effort directed toward achieving job goals.

Job sharing   A situation in which two people share the same job, both usually working half-time. Job sharing is sometimes used as a solution to the problem of two people whose family situations only allow for half-time work.

Leadership   The process of influencing other people to achieve certain objectives.

Leadership potential   A person's basic capacity or aptitude for carrying out a leadership role. It stems from both inborn and acquired traits and characteristics.

Leadership style   The characteristic manner or typical approach a particular person uses in leading people. Many different leadership styles are possible including participative, autocratic, and free rein.

Life position   A basic concept of transactional analysis (TA) that relates to how people feel about themselves and others. The most famous life position is I'm OK–You're OK.

Line responsibility or authority   The activities of departments or other units of the organization that contribute directly to the organization's production of goods or services.

Locus of control   A personality characteristic that determines people's perception of how their lives are controlled. *Internalizers* perceive control of their lives as coming from inside themselves, while *externalizers* believe that their lives are controlled by external factors.

Management by objectives (MBO)   A system of management in which people are held accountable for reaching objectives that they usually set jointly with their superiors. Objectives at lower levels within the organization contribute to the attainment of goals set at the top of the organization.

Managerial expectations   A general term for how managers feel about the capabilities and performance potential of subordinates. Such expectations tend to influence performance.

Maslow's need hierarchy   A widely quoted and accepted theory of human motivation developed by Abraham Maslow, emphasizing that people strive to fulfill needs. These needs are arranged in a hierarchy of importance—physiological, safety, belongingness, esteem, and self-actualization. People tend to strive for satisfaction of needs at one level only after satisfaction has been achieved at the previous level.

Mentor   A boss who takes a subordinate under his or her wing and guides, teaches, and coaches that person, forming an emotional tie between the two.

Middle manager   Manager or supervisor whose place in the organization lies between first-level management and top-level management (board of directors, president, vice-presidents). The middle manager's job involves considerable coordination of the work of others.

Modeling   A form of learning in which a person learns a complex skill by watching another person or group of persons perform that skill. Also called learning by imitation.

Motivation   An inner state of arousal directed toward a goal. Work motivation is essentially motivation directed toward the attainment of organizational goals.

Motivator   Job elements or incentives that energize you to action, that is, exert a motivational impact upon you.

Motive   A need or desire coupled with the intention to attain an appropriate goal. Your motive in attending school might be to secure a better job for yourself.

Muscle monitoring   A method of stress reduction in which a person becomes aware that his or her muscles have tightened and then consciously relaxes them.

Need ladder   A synonym for the need hierarchy in which needs are arranged in a ranking of importance: physiological, safety, belongingness, esteem, and self-actualization.

Negative reinforcement   Similar to positive reinforcement, negative reinforcement attempts to reinforce the desired behavior. Instead of providing a positive reward, the person is allowed to avoid something negative (such as a penalty) when he or she makes the desired response.

Neuroticism   A broad personality trait that refers to a person's level of emotionality. The more neurotic the individual, the less the emotional control. The term emotionality has now replaced neuroticism.

Objective   A specific end state or condition aimed for that contributes to a larger goal. Your objective might be to perform well this week in order to help reach your goal of having a successful career. The terms goal and objective are now used interchangeably.

Office politics   Any method of gaining an advantage for yourself that is not strictly related to merit in a job environment. For example, laughing at your boss's jokes or finding a sponsor.

Operant conditioning   A form of conditioning in which certain of the person's spontaneous actions or responses are rewarded, ignored, or punished, resulting in a strengthening or weakening of that response. Also known as behavior modification or positive reinforcement.

Organizational psychology   That branch of business psychology that studies the interplay between people and organizations, emphasizing small groups and larger organizational units. Similar to other subfields of business psychology, the boundaries of this field are loose.

Participative leadership   An approach to leading others in which subordinates share decision making with the leader. Emphasized by the human relations or behavioral school of management thought.

Perceptual defense   A general tendency in perception to see things in such a way that our view of the world remains consistent. Perceptual defense is also used to deny events that we consider unpleasant for whatever reason.

Perfectionism   A propensity for setting extremely high standards along with a displeasure at achieving anything less. A perfectionistic person is often obsessed with details.

Performance appraisal   A formal system of measuring, evaluating, and reviewing performance.

Personal growth group   Small training or development groups similar in design and intent to encounter groups. People usually attend personal growth groups to learn more about themselves and "get in touch with their feelings."

Personality   Persistent and enduring behavior patterns of the individual that tend to be expressed in a wide variety of situations.

Person–role conflict   A situation that occurs when the role(s) that your organization expects you to occupy is in conflict with your basic values. Your company may ask you to fire substandard performers, but this could be in conflict with your humanistic values.

Positive reinforcement   Receiving a reward for making a desired response, such as getting approval from a boss for being prompt.

Power   The ability to control resources, to influence important decisions, and to get other people to do things.

Problem-solving ability   Essentially, mental ability or intelligence used for the purpose of solving problems.

Productivity   The amount of work produced by employees whether the "product" is goods or services. Productivity also takes into account how efficiently the output is attained and its quality.

Psychoanalysis   A type of long-term psychotherapy in which patients are encouraged to explore early memories and their unconscious. Also a theory of personality that focuses on unconscious motivation.

Punishment   The presentation of an undesirable or aversive consequence for a specific behavior, or removing something desirable because of a certain response.

Pygmalion effect   The phenomenon that people perform according to your expectations of them, particularly with respect to superior–subordinate relationships.

Realistic goal   A goal that a person finds challenging, but not so difficult that it usually results in failure and frustration.

Receiver   The person who is sent the message in an instance of communication.

Reciprocity   A form of work motivation in which the superior and subordinate exchange favors. If the subordinate shows good work motivation, the superior grants him or her a favor in exchange.

Reinforcer   A reward that is used to strengthen or reinforce a response in operant conditioning.

Role   Behavior, or a sequence of behaviors, expected of an individual occupying a given position within a group.

Role ambiguity   A condition that exists when you are uncertain of your true responsibilities. Often accompanied by a feeling of uneasiness.

Schmoozing   The act or process of engaging in social interaction with other individuals during normal working hours. It includes such activities as "chitchatting" and making telephone calls for social purposes.

Scientific problem solving   A systematic way of solving problems involving six steps: observe; detect and measure; speculate and specify; collect and measure; analyze and interpret; and change.

Selective perception   An unconscious process by which only selected aspects of a given stimulus are received and processed by the individual. A tendency to perceive what we want to perceive.

Self   The total being of the individual or the person. Also one's own interests, welfare, or advantage. It is important to understand yourself in order to understand others.

Self-acceptance   An attitude that what you do and what you are is favorable. Similar to self-liking or tolerance for both your strengths and weaknesses.

Self-actualization   Making maximum use of the potential in oneself. Similar to self-fulfillment.

Self-concept   The way in which a person views himself or herself. Also your knowledge and understanding about yourself or your identity.

Self-confidence   A basic belief in your ability to achieve the outcome you want in many situations or in a specific situation.

Self-discipline   Disciplining or training oneself, usually for purpose of self-improvement. For example, some people are able to overcome nervous habits through self-discipline.

Self-disclosure   The process of revealing how you are reacting to the present situation. Also, telling others something of significance about yourself.

Self-esteem   Similar to self-respect; a favorable impression or evaluation of oneself.

Sender   The person who attempts to transmit a message in an instance of communication.

Sensory information   Information that is received by any of the senses, such as sight, hearing, smell, touch, or the muscle sense.

Serendipity   The gift of unintentionally finding valuable things while you are looking for something else.

Sexual harassment   Any unwanted sexual advancement toward another individual, including spoken comments, touching, or demands for sexual favors.

Shaping of behavior   Inducing somebody to achieve the desired response by first rewarding any action in the right direction and then rewarding only the closest approximations. Using this approach, the desired response is finally attained.

Sport psychology   An application of psychology to enhancing the performance of athletes through such methods as improving concentration, reducing stress, and overcoming mental blocks.

Staff   Employees who advise line management but who do not have the formal authority to implement their recommendations. One example would be a public relations specialist.

Stimulus   Physical energy that arouses an individual and produces an effect on that person.

Stress   The nonspecific response of the body to any demand placed on it. Job stress is a condition wherein job-related factors interact with the worker to change his or her inner state so that the person is forced to deviate from normal functioning.

Stressor   A source of stress acting on the individual or group.

Structuralism   An older school of thought in psychology that analyzed the structure of the mind by analyzing conscious sensory experience and reducing it to its basic elements. *Introspection* was used to investigate the contents of the mind.

Synergy   The action of two or more people to achieve an effect that none of the people could achieve individually. The whole is greater than the sum of the parts.

Task force   A small group of individuals called together to solve a problem or explore and develop a new idea for an organization. Members are usually picked on the basis of their potential contribution or knowledge rather than on the basis of rank.

Tension   Mental or emotional strain; a feeling of internal uneasiness that is usually associated with stress or an unsatisfied need.

T-group   A popular form of encounter group that is particularly unstructured. T-groups (as part of sensitivity training) were originally developed for training managers to be more open and honest with people, but are now widely used in nonwork settings.

Theory X Douglas McGregor's famous statement of the traditional management view that considers people as usually lazy and needing to be prodded by external rewards. A rigid and task-oriented approach to management.

Theory Y Douglas McGregor's famous statement of an alternative to traditional management thinking. It emphasizes that people seek to fulfill higher-level needs on the job, and that management must be flexible and human relations oriented.

Transactional analysis (TA) A technique for improving interpersonal relationships that looks upon every human relationship as a transaction between the ego states (parent, adult, child) of people.

Transcendental meditation (TM) A system of almost total relaxation involving the achievement of a physiological state of deep rest.

Value The importance a person attaches to something such as education, religion, or sports.

Workaholic (work addict) A person addicted to work to the extent that it has adverse consequences for family and personal life. The condition may also interfere with job effectiveness, as the person often loses perspective and objectivity.

Work habits A person's characteristic approach to work, including such things as organization, handling of paper work, and the setting of priorities.

INDEX

SUBJECT INDEX